Advances in Pattern Recognition

Springer

London
Berlin
Heidelberg
New York
Barcelona
Hong Kong
Milan
Paris
Singapore
Tokyo

D1331365

Advances in Pattern Recognition is a series of books which brings together current developments in all areas of this multi-disciplinary topic. It covers both theoretical and applied aspects of pattern recognition, and provides texts for students and senior researchers.

Springer also publishes a related journal, **Pattern Analysis and Applications**. For more details see: http://link.springer.de

The book series and journal are both edited by Professor Sameer Singh of Exeter University, UK.

Also in this series:

Statistical and Neural Classifiers: An Integrated Approach to Design
Šarūnas Raudys
1-85233-297-2

Advanced Algorithmic Approaches to Medical Image Segmentation
Jasjit Suri, Kamaledin Setarehdan and Sameer Singh (Eds)
1-85233-389-8

Principles of Visual Information Retrieval
Michael S. Lew (Ed.)
1-85233-309-X

Ian T. Nabney

NETLAB

Algorithms for Pattern Recognition

With 76 Figures

 Springer

Ian T. Nabney, BA, PhD
Cardionetics Institute of Bioinformatics, Aston University, Aston Triangle,
Birmingham, B4 7ET

Series editor
Professor Sameer Singh, PhD
Department of Computer Science, University of Exeter, Exeter, EX4 4PT, UK

British Library Cataloguing in Publication Data
Nabney, Ian
   NETLAB : algorithms for pattern recognition. - (Advances in
   pattern recognition)
   1.Pattern recognition systems 2.Computer algorithms
   I.Title
   006.4
   ISBN 1852334401

Library of Congress Cataloging-in-Publication Data
Nabney, Ian, 1963-
   NETLAB : algorithms for pattern recognition / Ian Nabney.
     p. cm. -- (Advances in pattern recognition)
   Includes bibliographical references and index.
   ISBN 1-85233-440-1 (alk. paper)
     1. Image processing--Digital techniques. 2. Pattern recognition systems. 3. Computer
   algorithms. I. Title. II. Series.
   TA1637 .N33 2001
   006.4--dc21   2001020313

ISBN 1-85233-440-1 Springer-Verlag London Berlin Heidelberg
Springer-Verlag is part of Springer Science+Business Media GmbH
springeronline.com

© Ian T. Nabney 2002
Printed in Great Britain
2nd printing, with corrections 2003
3rd printing with corrections 2004
4th printing 2004

Typesetting: Camera-ready by author
Printed and bound at the Athenæum Press Ltd., Gateshead, Tyne & Wear
34/3830-543 Printed on acid-free paper SPIN 113675898

Preface

Introduction

Many current applications in neural computing are not successful because they are carried out in an *ad hoc* fashion. The chief reasons for this are that most introductory texts do not approach the subject within a pattern recognition framework and that computer software does not support a principled development approach. The aim of this book and the accompanying software is to provide students and practitioners with the knowledge and tools to get the most out of neural networks and related models.

This book is based around the NETLAB software toolbox and it

- supplies both algorithm knowledge and practical tools for a principled approach to application development,
- brings together relevant theory with details of how to implement models efficiently and flexibly,
- makes some of the leading edge research in the pattern recognition field accessible in a highly usable form,
- provides researchers with a tool kit as a basis for developing new ideas, and
- contains many worked examples and demonstration programs to illustrate the theory and help the reader understand the algorithms and how to use them.

The NETLAB toolbox is designed to provide the central tools necessary for the simulation of theoretically well founded neural network and related pattern analysis algorithms. It includes software implementations of a number of algorithms which are not widely available, and which are rarely if ever included in standard neural network simulation packages. These include:

- Probabilistic Principal Component Analysis (PPCA) and mixtures of PPCA;
- Generative Topographic Mapping;
- Neuroscale neural network based Sammon mapping;
- evidence framework for Bayesian inference;
- hybrid Monte Carlo for Bayesian inference;
- Gaussian processes;

- Gaussian mixture-based error function for multi-layer perceptron (Mixture Density Networks).

However, the principles behind the toolbox are more important than simply compiling lists of algorithms. Data analysis and modelling methods should not be used in isolation; all parts of the toolbox interact in a coherent way, and implementations of standard pattern recognition techniques (such as linear regression and K-nearest-neighbour classifiers) are provided so that they can be used as benchmarks against which more complex algorithms can be evaluated. This interaction allows researchers to develop new techniques by building on and reusing existing software, thus reducing the effort required and increasing the robustness and usability of the new tools.

The NETLAB toolbox has been implemented in the MATLAB™ environment. MATLAB was chosen since it supports a high level mathematical programming style that allows the algorithms to be coded in a simple fashion, it has extensive visualisation facilities, it is widely used in both industry and academia, and runs on all three main computing platforms (Unix™, Windows™ and Macintosh™).

Use as a Course Text

This book is intended to complement Bishop (1995); while all the algorithms in NETLAB are described here, for the complete motivation and background the reader should refer to it for the relevant material. Other texts, for example Ripley (1995) and Webb (1999), can also be used to support this book. The opportunity has been taken to extend the scope to include some more recent developments in the field of neural networks, and to expand on some of the topics covered in Bishop (1995). In such cases more of the relevant theoretical background is included. There is not sufficient space here to discuss all the practical issues involved in application development: Tarassenko (1998) goes into more detail.

Each chapter covers a group of related pattern recognition techniques and includes examples of how the techniques can be used on practical problems based on demonstration programs in NETLAB, worked examples of how NETLAB can be extended to related models, and exercises. Many of the graphs have had to be adapted because colour could not be used in the book. The exercises are designed to provide problems with a range of difficulty (from easy (*) to difficult (* * *)) that will test the student's understanding of pattern recognition techniques and the issues (both from numerical analysis and software engineering) involved in their implementation. In a few cases, a problem may require some knowledge of material later in the book.

Pre-requisites

In a book of this size it is not possible to explain all the details of the theoretical background of every model as well as their implementation in software. Thus techniques that are now considered 'standard' (such as multi-layer perceptrons and radial basis function networks) are defined briefly on the assumption that the reader can obtain more details from other texts (such as those mentioned in the previous section), while algorithms that haven't appeared before in book form are described more fully. Nevertheless, the book is self-contained in the sense that every equation that is needed for an algorithm is described, even if the motivation for it is not always given.

The mathematical pre-requisites have been kept to a minimum, but it is necessary to have a good working knowledge of vector and matrix algebra, differential and integral calculus for several variables, and elementary probability theory. The level of prior knowledge is equivalent to that taught in 2nd year undergraduate engineering courses in the UK. Two appendices cover more advanced linear algebra and basic numerical error analysis.

Overview

The first chapter provides an introduction to the software tools used in the book. A brief tour of MATLAB is included, with a particular focus on efficient and robust programming methods. The chapter also includes an overview of the NETLAB toolbox and describes the introductory demonstrations. A selection of generic NETLAB functions are used to illustrate some key principles of MATLAB programming. The worked examples show how data pre-processing techniques can be integrated with NETLAB models.

Chapter 2 covers multivariate optimisation algorithms. These are implemented as general purpose routines that can be used for a wide variety of applications. Some simple algorithms, based on gradient descent, are also included to show their limitations and motivate the use of more complex, and much faster, techniques. The way in which these general optimisation functions can be applied to the problem of optimising parameters in a NETLAB model is also discussed, and the structural and functional requirements for any new user-defined model to interact correctly are made clear. The worked example is a simple technique for constrained optimisation.

Modelling the probability density of data is a very important tool for application developers as well as forming a building block for many other models. In Chapter 3 there is a detailed treatment of one of the most important methods for doing this, namely Gaussian mixture models. The Expectation Maximisation training algorithm, variants of which are used for other models, is defined, and the implementation and practical use of it are also discussed. Simpler models, K-means clustering and K-nearest-neighbour classifiers, are also included; these act as useful benchmarks for more complex techniques. The worked example shows how multiple Gaussian mixture models, one trained on each class, can be combined to form a classifier.

In Chapter 4 we introduce the simplest form of predictive data model, where there is a single layer of adaptive weights. These are Generalised Linear Models (GLMs), which play an important role in application development by providing a useful benchmark since they are fast to train. The key point introduced in this chapter is the connection between output activation functions, the cost function used in training, the data representation, and the type of problem. The worked example shows how advanced techniques from linear algebra can be used to reduce the sensitivity of training to noise and regularise the network by constraining the magnitude of the weight vector.

The multi-layer perceptron (MLP) is the most commonly used neural network in applications, and is given a comprehensive treatment in Chapter 5. The theory and implementation of forward propagation, error functions, and computation of the error gradient, Hessian matrix and other derivatives are all covered. Mixture Density Networks (MDNs), an extension of MLPs to model arbitrary conditional distributions and multi-branched functions, are also described in detail. The special implementation required to make their training computationally efficient is a particular focus. The worked example in this chapter shows how the basic two-layer MLP model can be extended easily to include direct connections from the input to the output layer.

The second most commonly used neural network, particularly useful where fast training is a requirement, is the radial basis function network (RBF), which is treated in Chapter 6. This shows how both general optimisation algorithms and specific training routines can be used to determine the network parameters. The worked example illustrates the use of smoothing matrices to determine the optimal number of hidden units.

Chapter 7 covers a particular strength of NETLAB; its repertoire of visualisation methods. Moving on from classical techniques, such as Principal Component Analysis and Sammon maps, there has been a lot of recent research activity in both latent variable models (such as the Generative Topographic Mapping) and topographic methods (such as Neuroscale). In both these techniques, RBF networks are used to provide an efficient yet general method for implementing the required non-linear mapping. The worked example implements the linear visualisation method of canonical variates, which is a linear technique suitable for labelled data.

The last three chapters are all concerned with the Bayesian perspective on data modelling and inference. Chapter 8 describes a variety of sampling algorithms, both simple and complex. These are important techniques to make it feasible to compute numerically the high-dimensional integrals used in Bayesian inference. Of particular importance are the Markov Chain sampling methods (Metropolis–Hastings and hybrid Monte Carlo) which make these integrals a practical proposition for neural network models with large numbers of weights. The worked example implements diagnostic routines to decide when a Markov Chain sample has converged to the correct distribution.

The Bayesian approach to neural networks is described in Chapter 9. NETLAB implements two approaches: the evidence procedure, in which distributions are approximated so that integrals can be computed analytically, and sampling, in which numerical integration is carried out for the true distribution. These methods can be applied to all three of the main prediction models (GLM, MLP and RBF). The chapter also shows how error bars on predictions can be given and the importance of input variables assessed. The worked example shows how the approximate Bayesian approach can be made more accurate for classification problems.

Gaussian processes have been used in spatial statistics for a long time, but their application to other data analysis problems is much more recent. The attraction of this model, which is discussed in Chapter 10, is that the first level of Bayesian inference can be carried out exactly, and that the prior distribution is defined directly in function space, making it easier for the user to understand the effect of hyperparameters on the model. This chapter develops the theory of Gaussian processes from scratch, starting from Bayesian RBF networks used for regression. The worked example shows how to extend Gaussian processes to classification tasks.

Accessing the Software

The NETLAB toolbox is available from the Neural Computing Research Group website at

http://www.ncrg.aston.ac.uk/netlab

This free software is covered by a very open license based on that used for BSD. It requires MATLAB™ version 5.0 or later. The programs require just under 5Mb of disk space and the help text (in HTML format) is about 2.6Mb. Installation instructions are included on the web page. A complete set of software for the worked examples in this book is also available from the web site.

Although most of the NETLAB demonstration programs and examples in this book use synthetic (the polite term for 'toy') datasets to illustrate the way in which algorithms work, the real purpose of NETLAB is to allow users to develop robust and principled solutions to real applications on real-world data, which does not usually come from simple distributions with well-understood noise models. There are some good electronic sources of data which can be used to augment the datasets supplied with NETLAB and to provide a more realistic test of the software.

- UCI Machine Learning Repository:

- CTI Statistics data sources:

  http://www.stats.gla.ac.uk/cti/links_stats/data.html

- Handwritten digit datasets:

  http://www.research/att.com/~yann/exdb/mnist/index.html

- DELVE archive:

  http://www.cs.toronto.edu/~delve

- NIST datasets:

  http://www.nist.gov/public_affairs/database.htm

- Ripley's archive:

  http://markov.stats.ox.ac.uk/pub/PRNN

Notation

To make reading the book easier I have adopted a number of notational conventions, similar to those used in Bishop (1995). Matrices are denoted by upper case bold letters, such as A, vectors, which are taken to be column vectors, are denoted by lower case bold letters, such as v, while scalar values are (usually) lower case in italics, such as x. Entries in matrices and vectors are denoted by subscripts, so the ijth element of A is written A_{ij}. The length of a vector is denoted by $\|v\|$ and the determinant of A is $|A|$. The symbol δ_{ij} denotes the Kronecker delta, so

$$\delta_{ij} = \begin{cases} 1 & \text{if } i = j \\ 0 & \text{otherwise} \end{cases} \qquad (0.1)$$

An upper case P is used to denote a probability value or a probability mass function (for a discrete random variable), while a lower case p is used to denote a probability density function. By the usual abuse of notation, $p(x)$ and $p(y)$ denote distributions of distinct random variables X and Y, even though the same symbol p is used in both cases. We shall use the notation $N(\mu, \Sigma)$ to denote a multivariate Gaussian distribution with mean μ and covariance matrix Σ. Both log and ln are used for the *natural* logarithm (i.e. to base e). The symbol $\mathcal{L}$ is used to denote the *log likelihood* $\sum_n \log p(x_n)$ of a dataset.

Acknowledgements

It is only through writing this book that I have come to realise why other authors' acknowledgements are so long. I have benefitted greatly from the assistance of many people in bringing this project to fruition, and it is a pleasure to have this opportunity to thank them.

Neither the NETLAB software nor this book would have ever have come about without Chris Bishop's invitation to join him in the project. Much of the basic structure of the toolbox was thrashed out by us during the course of the early prototypes. I am very grateful to David Barber, David Evans, Markus Svensén, Mike Tipping, and Chris Williams for allowing me to base some NETLAB functions on their software. I would also like to thank Mehdi Azouzzi, Lars Hjorth, David Lowe, Cazhaow Qazaz, Iain Strachan, Peter Tiño and other members of the Neural Computing Research Group for their comments on earlier versions of the toolbox and help with some of the figures. Users of NETLAB have also been generous in making suggestions for its improvement, and Ahi Vehtari has been particularly helpful in this regard.

It is customary in academic texts to finish the acknowledgements with a rather desperate apology to the author's family for having neglected them while the book was written. Fortunate in many ways, I am particularly blessed with a clear-sighted wife and two strong-minded daughters who would never allow me to neglect my duties, so instead of apologising, I can thank them for all the pleasure they gave me during the writing of this book.

Birmingham, August 2001   *Ian Nabney*

Contents

1. Introduction

The neural network software toolbox NETLAB described in this book has been written using the programming language provided by the MATLAB package produced by The MathWorks Inc. The purpose of this chapter is to provide sufficient background information about the software environment to allow the reader to understand the NETLAB programs. There are two aspects of this: first we introduce the basic functionality of the MATLAB package, focusing particularly on matrix manipulation, graphing and programming; then we give an overview of the NETLAB toolbox and its philosophy. To illustrate these ideas, we also describe some of the general purpose NETLAB functions. The worked example shows how simple data normalisation can be implemented efficiently in MATLAB using vectorised operations.

Table 1.1. Functions in this chapter.

Generic Routines	
datread	Read data from ASCII file
datwrite	Write data to ASCII file
consist	Check that arguments to a NETLAB function are consistent
conffig	Display confusion matrix
confmat	Compute confusion matrix
hinton	Plot Hinton diagram for weight matrix
hintmat	Compute patches for Hinton diagram
mlphint	Plot Hinton diagram for MLP network
Demonstration Programs	
demhint	Demonstrate Hinton diagrams for MLP
demnlab	GUI-based access to NETLAB demonstrations
demtrain	Demonstration of network training

1.1 Introduction to MATLAB

MATLAB is an interpreted language for numeric computation and visualisation. It offers high level facilities for dealing directly with mathematical constructs. The particular benefits that it offers for pattern recognition are:

1. Support for linear algebra and matrix operations. The basic type in MATLAB is a double precision matrix. The software was originally developed as a linear algebra package (MATLAB stands for MATrix LABoratory) and has efficient and numerically stable algorithms for matrix inversion, eigenvalues etc.
2. Visualisation facilities. The built-in graphing and plotting functions are easy to use for both two-dimensional and three-dimensional plots.
3. High productivity. The high-level operations and interpreted environment make it easy to prototype and refine ideas quickly.
4. Ease of extension. Functions and scripts can be written in the MATLAB language (in 'M-files') and these can then be called in exactly the same way as the core functionality of MATLAB. In fact, the toolboxes that extend the functionality of MATLAB to more specialist areas are written in this way. NETLAB itself consists of a set of M-files.
5. Portability. Software written in the MATLAB language is portable to any platform that runs MATLAB, including Unix machines, PCs and Macintoshes. This means that NETLAB can be used to train networks on high performance machines and then run on lower performance machines.

This section is not intended to replace the MATLAB manuals or detailed textbooks on MATLAB; it covers the main features needed to understand and use NETLAB.

- Basics: matrices, operators, help facilities.
- Plotting: two-dimensional and three-dimensional graphs.
- Programming in MATLAB: M-files, data structures, debugging.

This section discusses MATLAB version 5, which is the minimum level required for NETLAB. Although NETLAB is compatible with later versions of MATLAB, it does not make use of any additional features introduced after version 5.

1.1.1 MATLAB Basics

The main user interface to MATLAB is a command line interpreter. The user controls MATLAB dynamically by creating variables and calling functions. The objects that MATLAB works with are *matrices*: 2-d rectangular arrays of double precision (or complex) numbers. Operations and commands in MATLAB are intended to work with matrices just as they would be written down on paper. In NETLAB, datasets are represented as matrices where each row is a single pattern and the columns represent the variables.

Matrices

To enter a matrix, you should follow these conventions:

- Separate entries with white space or commas.
- Use a semi-colon ; to denote the end of each row.
- Surround the entries with square brackets [and].

The statement

```
>> A = [8 1 6; 3 5 7; 4 9 2]
```

results in the output

```
A =

     8     1     6
     3     5     7
     4     9     2
```

In this section we shall use the MATLAB prompt >> to distinguish lines typed by the user from the system response. This will be dropped in later sections. By default, MATLAB will output the result of every command. To suppress this, you should terminate your command with a semi-colon ;. Thus, typing

```
>> A = [8 1 6; 3 5 7; 4 9 2];
```

still sets A to be the same matrix, but there is no output. The vast majority of NETLAB commands end in a semi-colon. Without this, the user would be overwhelmed with the results of all the intermediate calculations, and the programs would run extremely slowly since they would be spending most of their time printing results on the screen.

To access the value of the i, jth element of A, type A(i, j). For example, typing

```
>> b = A(1, 2)
```

results in the following output

```
b =

     1
```

Note that matrix indices start from 1. The colon operator : gives access to 'slices' of a matrix. To obtain the second row of the matrix, type

```
>> c = A(2, :)
```

which gives the following output:

```
c =

     3     5     7
```

To obtain the third column, type

```
>> d = A(:, 3)
```

which gives the following output:

```
d =

     6
     7
     2
```

NETLAB uses these row and column operators very frequently.

Vectors are matrices with a single row or column. A particularly useful way of forming row sequence vectors is using the colon operator :. The line

```
>> x = 0:0.1:1;
```

generates a row vector x of length 11 containing the values from 0 to 1 with increments of 0.1. This construction is often used to generate the x-axis points in graphs. With just two values, e.g. x = 0:4, the increment is taken to be 1.

Most MATLAB functions can be applied to an entire matrix in a single call. So the command

```
>> y = sin(2 * pi * x);
```

generates regularly spaced values from a sine curve.

Matrix Operations

In principle, most matrix operations can be written in MATLAB just as they are on the page. So to add two matrices A and B (which must have the same dimensions), just type:

```
A + B;
```

Similarly, if A is an $m \times n$ matrix and B is a $p \times q$ matrix, then if $n = p$, A*B is their product, an $m \times q$ matrix. The transpose of A is given by A'.

Matrix division is slightly more subtle and intricate. MATLAB provides two division operators: \ and /.

- Left division. If A is a non-singular square matrix, then A\B is equivalent to inv(A)*B. More precisely, X=A\B is a solution to the equation $A * X = B$ with the minimum number of non-zero elements. This operation is defined whenever B has as many rows as A.
- Right division. If A is a non-singular square matrix, then B/A is equivalent to B*inv(A). More precisely, X=B/A is a solution to the equation $X * A = B$. This operation is defined whenever B has as many columns as A.

MATLAB also supplies *array* operations that work on an element by element basis. They are written with the same symbols as the usual operations with an extra 'dot' to distinguish them.

If x and y have the same dimension, then

$$x.*y = [x_{ij}*y_{ij}],$$

$$x./y = [x_{ij}/y_{ij}],$$

$$x.\wedge y = [x_{ij}^{y_{ij}}].$$

For example, consider the following MATLAB fragment:

```
1  >> a = [1 0; 3 5];
2  >> b = [2 9; 4 6];
3  >> c = a.*b
4
5  c =
6      2    0
7     12   30
```

Logical Operators

The usual set of relational operations are available. Equality is denoted by == and inequality is denoted by ~=. The result of a relational operation is a matrix of ones and zeros, where each true entry has the value 1 and each false entry has the value 0.

The MATLAB function **find** returns the indices of those elements in a matrix that satisfy some logical condition; this can be used to pick out and modify data elements that satisfy some relational condition. The following code fragment first of all picks out all elements of Y that are greater than 3, and then replaces them with the value 10.

```
>> i = find(Y > 3.0);
>> Y(i) = 10 * ones(size(i));
```

Note how we deal with matrices as a whole in preference to manipulating individual elements.

Another example of matrix level logical operations comes from the NETLAB function rbffwd. Here we want to compute $N \log(N)$ for a non-negative matrix N. When $(N)_i = 0$ this is undefined, but $\lim_{n\to 0} n \log n = 0$, so we use the following MATLAB code:

```
z = n2.*log(n2+(n2==0));
```

The matrix n2==0 has entries that are zero except where $(n_2)_i = 0$, where it is one. Hence   a = n2+(n2==0) has entries

$$(a)_i = \begin{cases} (N)_i & \text{if } (N)_i \neq 0 \\ 1 & \text{if } (N)_i = 0. \end{cases} \tag{1.1}$$

This implies that log(a) is the same log(n2) except for the zero entries of n2, where it has the value zero. Multiplying each element of this by the corresponding element of n2 gives the required result.

Help Facilities

MATLAB is a very powerful tool with hundreds of built-in functions. Even the most hardened MATLAB veteran may occasionally forget the name of a function or the order of its arguments. Fortunately, there is an on-line help facility that provides information on most topics. You can get help on NETLAB with the same mechanism.

To get help on a specific function, you need only type help followed by the function name. So, to find out about the function mean, you should type:

```
>> help mean
```

A more general information search is provided by lookfor. This enables you to find out what functions MATLAB provides for certain operations. For example, to find out which MATLAB functions are related to calculating covariances, type:

```
>> lookfor covariance
```

This will return a list of the functions with a one line description of each.

You can find out what variables you currently have by typing:

```
who
```

The related function whos lists the variables together with their size.

The command helpwin brings up a small window which provides a hypertext like interface to the on-line help material. The command helpdesk provides access through an HTML browser to a really comprehensive set of reference material, with much more material than is available in the standard on-line help.

1.1.2 MATLAB Plotting

MATLAB has an extensive set of plotting and graphical facilities, and we can only scratch the surface of what is available here.

As an example, let us create and plot a toy dataset: the noisy sine wave. The simplest form of the plot function takes the x vector as its first argument, and the y vector as its second argument. Different line styles (or scatter plots) can be defined with a third argument. (For more detail, just type help plot.)

```
x = 0:0.05:1;
plot(x, sin(2*pi*x) + 0.1*randn(size(x)), 'k+')
```

which gives a scatter plot of the data with a black plus sign for each point (see Fig. 1.1). The function randn generates samples from a standard normal distribution (i.e. a Gaussian with zero mean and unit variance). The function rand generates samples from a uniform distribution on the interval $(0, 1)$. Note that the axes automatically scale so that all the plot is visible. To gain more control over the scaling, the axis function should be used.

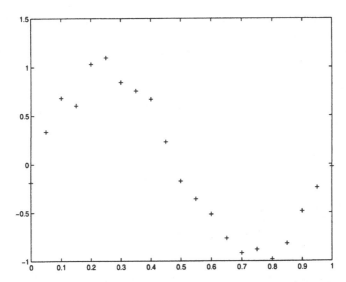

Fig. 1.1. Plotting demonstration. Noisy sine wave data (*plus signs*).

Each time a `plot` command is issued, the figure is cleared of all previous information. You can use the command `hold on` to add further information (such as legends and axis labels) or additional plots to the figure.

To obtain hard copy of your graph, use the `print` function. It is nearly always best to save the figure into an intermediate PostScript file. To do this, type:

`print foo -deps`

which will save the figure in the file `foo.eps`. You can also save figures as M-files (by omitting the `-deps` qualifier), which means that they can be manipulated in MATLAB later (for example, to add further plots).

Other useful two-dimensional plot types include:

- `semilogy`, which uses a log scale on the y-axis and a linear scale on the x-axis;
- `semilogx`, which uses a log scale on the x-axis and a linear scale on the y-axis;
- `loglog`, which uses a log scale on both axes;
- `imagesc`, which displays a matrix as a colour image;
- `hist`, which displays a histogram of a dataset.

We also use some three-dimensional plots for displaying a function of two variables $z = f(x, y)$. To do this, we construct a matrix Z whose i, jth element represents the value of the function over a grid with x- and y-coordinates stored in the matrices X and Y respectively. The plotting functions used in NETLAB are:

- surf and mesh, which display a function of two variables as a surface or wire-frame plot respectively;
- contour, which displays lines of constant z-value in a two-dimensional view.

In order to construct the matrices X, Y and Z, it is convenient to use an additional MATLAB function meshgrid. The following code fragment, which is from the NETLAB function demglm1, is typical:

```
1   x = -4.0:0.2:5.0;
2   y = -4.0:0.2:5.0;
3   [X, Y] = meshgrid(x,y);
4   X = X(:);
5   Y = Y(:);
6   grid = [X Y];
7   Z = glmfwd(net, grid);
8   Z = reshape(Z, length(x), length(y));
9   v = [0.1 0.5 0.9];
10  [c, h] = contour(x, y, Z, v);
```

The purpose of this fragment is to produce a contour plot of the output of a Generalised Linear Model (contained in the variable net) over the region $[-4, 5] \times [-4, 5]$. The result is shown in Fig. 1.2. Lines 1–2 compute a regular

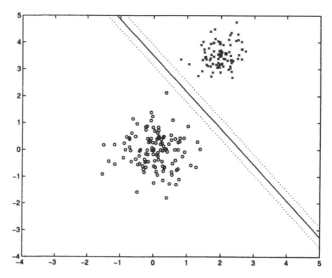

Fig. 1.2. Contour plot of GLM output. Decision boundary (*solid line*) and 0.1 and 0.9 output levels (*dotted line*) are shown with training data from class 1 (*crosses*) and class 2 (*circles*).

mesh of values in x- and y-directions. This is turned into a complete rectangular grid with all combinations of the values in x and y; the x-coordinates are in the matrix X and the y-coordinates are in the matrix Y (line 3). The pair of values X(i, j) and Y(i, j) represent the coordinates of the point [x(i) y(j)].

However, the function glmfwd, that generates the output from the Generalised Linear Model, takes its input data in the form of a matrix with dimension n x d, where n is the number of data points and d is the dimension of the input space (which is 2 here). Therefore it is necessary to reshape the data. Lines 4–5 convert X and Y into column vectors and line 6 puts these column vectors side by side in a matrix grid. The network predictions are then made (line 7) in the matrix Z, which has dimension n x 1 (since the model has a single output variable).

The contour function expects its data to be represented in grid form, so in line 8, the matrix Z is reshaped to grid form. Line 9 specifies the levels for the contour lines, and line 10 generates the contour plot.

1.1.3 Programming in MATLAB

One of the most powerful features of MATLAB is the ease with which the functionality of the core tool can be extended. New functions can be written as text files and can then be called immediately at the command line without any need for compilation or other processing. This is one reason why MATLAB is such a productive environment to work with; small adjustments to programs can be made and tested very quickly.

Functions and Scripts

Extensions to MATLAB are written as text files (called M-files, because they have .m extension) that contain MATLAB commands. M-files are invoked at the MATLAB prompt by typing their name (without the extension). MATLAB searches for a file with that name in the current working directory followed by the directories in the search path. There are two types of M-file:

- *Scripts* automate a fixed sequence of instructions. The variables in scripts are still available at the command line once a script terminates. Scripts are most useful for running experiments. Most of the NETLAB demonstration programs are written as scripts (see, for example, demmlp1).
- *Functions* are more flexible than scripts, in that they can take arguments and return values, which allows the user to abstract away from fixed variables. Because of this, functions are more reusable than scripts. For example, the NETLAB function mlp, which creates a multi-layer perceptron data structure, is called 15 times in NETLAB functions and scripts, but no NETLAB script is called by any other NETLAB M-file.

The NETLAB toolbox is a set of functions contained in M-files that call both core MATLAB functions and other NETLAB functions.

As an example, here is the complete listing of the NETLAB function rosen, which computes the function

$$y = 100 * (x_2 - x_1^2)^2 + (1 - x_1)^2. \tag{1.2}$$

The file rosen.m contains the following text:

```
1    function y = rosen(x)
2    %ROSEN   Calculate Rosenbrock's function.
3    %
4    %       Description
5    %       Y = ROSEN(X) computes the value of Rosenbrock's function
6    %       at each row of X, which should have two columns.
7    %
8    %       See also
9    %       DEMOPT1, ROSEGRAD
10   %
11   y = 100 * ((x(:,2) - x(:,1).^2).^2) + (1.0 - x(:,1)).^2;
```

Line 1 defines this M-file to be a function that takes a single argument x and returns a single variable y. Multiple arguments are separated by commas, and multiple return values are contained in square brackets. In the following NETLAB example, the function pca takes two input arguments data and N and returns two variables PCcoeff and PCvec.

```
function [PCcoeff, PCvec] = pca(data, N)
```

The % symbol indicates that the rest of the line is a comment and is ignored by the MATLAB interpreter. The first contiguous comment block (lines 2–10 in this example) is printed when the user types help rosen. The very first comment line (called the H1 line) is searched for keywords by the lookfor command.

In this way, the function is automatically integrated with the MATLAB help system, though it doesn't become part of the searchable HTML data accessed by helpdesk.

1.1.4 Programming Facilities

As well as the commands that we have seen already, the MATLAB language offers additional facilities to make it possible to carry out more complex programming tasks. These include control flow (such as branches and loops) and a range of data types (including structures and strings). MATLAB also supports a limited form of object orientation; however, the complexity that this introduces outweighs the benefits that it brings for code reuse and hence it is not used in NETLAB.

Control Flow

MATLAB has two types of branch statement; if and switch. The switch statement should be used when different actions are needed for a small number of distinct cases. The following example is taken from mlpfwd, which propagates values forward through an MLP. The final output depends on the activation function used in the outputs given by net.outfn.

```
1   switch net.outfn
2     case 'linear'    % Linear outputs
3       y = a;
4     case 'logistic'  % Logistic outputs
5       y = 1./(1 + exp(-a));
6     case 'softmax'   % Softmax outputs
7       temp = exp(a);
8       nout = size(a,2);
9       y = temp./(sum(temp,1)*ones(1,nout));
10    otherwise
11      error(['Unknown output function ', net.outfn]);
12  end
```

Note that, unlike a C switch statement, different cases do not 'fall through'. In the example, if net.outfn is the string 'linear' then only line 3 is executed. The otherwise case (equivalent to default in C) is executed if none of the other cases matches (line 11). It is good practice always to include an otherwise statement in a switch to detect error conditions. Here, no other activation function for MLPs is supported, and it is better to raise an error rather than quietly continue with erroneous results.

The if statement can be used, in conjunction with elseif, to perform complex decisions involving arithmetic and logical operations. An end statement is used to complete an if statement. In the following fragment from mlpprior, there are three different cases:

```
1   if size(aw1) == [1,1]
2       indx = [ones(1, nin*nhidden), zeros(1, nextra)]';
3   elseif size(aw1) == [1, nin]
4       indx = kron(ones(nhidden, 1), eye(nin));
5       indx = [indx; zeros(nextra, nin)];
6   else
7       error('Parameter aw1 of invalid dimensions');
8   end
```

The MATLAB size function returns a vector of length two containing the number of rows and the number of columns. This fragment performs different actions if aw1 is a scalar (1×1 matrix), line 2, a row vector, lines 4–5, or any other size, line 7.

The MATLAB language allows iteration over a sequence of instructions using a for loop. The syntax has the form

```
for n = v
  % loop body
end
```

where v is a vector containing the values that n should take at each iteration. The most common form of v is a sequence vector:

```
1   g = zeros(ndata, net.nwts, net.nout);
2   for k = 1 : net.nout
```

```
3     delta = zeros(1, net.nout);
4     delta(1, k) = 1;
5     for n = 1 : ndata
6       g(n, :, k) = rbfbkp(net, x(n, :), z(n, :), n2(n, :),...
7         delta);
8     end
9   end
```

In this fragment, taken from the NETLAB function rbfderiv there are two nested loops: k runs from 1 to net.out in integer steps (line 2), and for each value of k, n runs from 1 to ndata (line 5).

Loops are typically much less efficient than matrix operations. For example, the following two fragments of code calculate the sine of all the entries in a vector. First the vectorised form:

```
% Vectorised form
t = 0:0.01:10;
y = sin(t);
```

Now the loop form:

```
% For loop form
i = 0;
for t = 0:0.01:10
  i = i + 1;
  y(i) = sin(t);
end
```

The first version runs approximately 25 times faster than the second. This is for two reasons.

1. The function sin is called 1001 times in the second fragment, and just once in the first. There is a significant overhead in MATLAB when calling a function.
2. The vector y used to hold the result is extended by one element on each iteration of the loop. This involves many calls to the MATLAB memory allocation functions.

If you must use a loop version of the code, pre-allocate the vector so that it doesn't have to be resized on each execution of the loop.

```
y = zeros(1, 1001);
i = 0;
for t = 0:0.01:10
  i = i + 1;
  y(i) = sin(t);
end
```

This version is still slower than the vectorised form, but is considerably faster than the original loop form.

It is possible to write several MATLAB functions in a single text file. Only one of these functions can be seen from outside the file, which makes this facility of limited use. For example, it is not possible to write a single module to manipulate a data structure in an object-based way. However, it does help to modularise the code, and is used in NETLAB to enable certain random number generators to initialise and restore their state (for example, the Metropolis sampler metrop) and to isolate conceptually distinct functionality (for example, the sub-function rearrange_hess in glmhess).

One final useful programming tool is the ability to call functions with a variable number of arguments or return values. This can be used to write functions that compute only those return values that are needed. For example, consider the NETLAB function pca that is used for principal component analysis (PCA).

```
1    function [PCcoeff, PCvec] = pca(data, N)
2
3    if nargin == 1
4      N = size(data, 2);
5    end
6
7    if nargout == 1
8      evals_only = logical(1);
9    else
10     evals_only = logical(0);
11   end
12
13   % Find the sorted eigenvalues of the data covariance matrix
14   if evals_only
15     PCcoeff = eigdec(cov(data), N);
16   else
17     [PCcoeff, PCvec] = eigdec(cov(data), N);
18   end
```

pca can be used to compute both principal values PCcoeff and principal components PCvec: these are the eigenvalues and eigenvectors respectively of the data covariance matrix. However, the eigenvectors are much more computationally costly to compute (about $O(13N^3/3)$ additional operations compared with about $O(30N^2 + (2N^3/3))$ for eigenvalues alone, where N is the number of columns in the data). This function tests the number of output arguments it has been invoked with (lines 7–11) using the MATLAB variable nargout and only computes the eigenvectors if required.

Similarly, if the data has a large number of columns it can be more efficient to compute just the first few principal components. This number can be specified as the second argument N. If only one argument is used in the function call (which is determined by testing the MATLAB variable nargin), then N has the default value of the number of columns in the data matrix (lines 3–5). Another example of the use of nargin is the NETLAB function consist.

Data Types

MATLAB is not strongly typed, unlike many programming languages, but it does support data types other than matrices and strings. The most important of these are:

- structures;
- multi-dimensional arrays;
- cell arrays;
- functions.

Structures Structures are variables that have named fields which can contain any sort of data. The data is accessed via the field name. Structures are normally created simply by adding fields to a variable which has not previously been initialised to a matrix value. The following fragment comes from the NETLAB function gmm which creates a Gaussian mixture model:

```
1   mix.type = 'gmm';
2   mix.nin = dim;
3   mix.ncentres = ncentres;
```

The first line creates a variable mix and makes it a structure with a single field type. Lines 2–3 then add new fields to the structure.

Multi-dimensional Arrays Matrices are not restricted to two dimensions. Many built-in MATLAB functions have been extended to accept arrays with more than two dimensions as arguments. To create a 3-by-4-by-5 array of ones, for example, use

```
A = ones(3, 4, 5);
```

In NETLAB Gaussian mixture models with full covariance matrices use three-dimensional arrays to store the (two-dimensional) covariance matrices, one for each kernel.

In general, multi-dimensional arrays are more useful for storing information than for processing it. This is because there are no arithmetic operators defined for general arrays, so computing useful mathematical functions normally has to be done by iterating over one of the dimensions, which is inefficient. Thus while data may be stored in a multi-dimensional array for clarity, it may be converted into a (more opaque) matrix for computational efficiency.

Cell Arrays Standard MATLAB matrices and strings must contain just one type of data (numeric/logical and characters respectively). A cell array can contain different types of data (including data structures) in each element. A cell array can be multi-dimensional, and its elements are accessed with curly braces rather than round brackets.

Like multi-dimensional arrays, cell arrays are more useful for storing information than processing it efficiently. There are two main areas in NETLAB where cell arrays are used:

- Arrays of data structures. Some data models, for example the Mixture Density Network (MDN), generate an output that is a data model for each input pattern, a Gaussian mixture model in the case of the MDN. Thus when a matrix of input patterns is presented to an MDN, it generates an array of mixture models, and this is represented as a cell array. (For details see Section 5.7.3.)
- Arrays of strings. Ordinary string arrays in MATLAB consist of a two-dimensional matrix containing characters. They are restricted to the case where each row contains the same number of elements, which makes manipulating text rather complicated. In a cell array, each line of text is stored in a separate cell and can be of arbitrary length.

Function Variables It is often useful to be able to define functions that operate on other functions. The NETLAB toolbox contains several general purpose optimisation functions that can be used to find the minimum value of an arbitrary function. At a higher level, the NETLAB function `netopt` trains a network model using a user-specified optimisation function. Such *generic* functions are passed the function that they work with as a string variable:

```
x = scg('rosen', x, options, 'rosegrad');
```

Here the scaled conjugate gradient optimisation routine `scg` is used to optimise the function `rosen.m` using its gradient function `rosegrad.m`. The declaration of `scg` (slightly simplified for clarity) is

```
function x = scg(f, x, options, gradf)
```

so that the variables `f` and `gradf` represent the function and its gradient respectively. To call those functions inside `scg`, we use the MATLAB function `feval`:

```
fold = feval(f, x);
```

Debugging

MATLAB provides tools to help with the debugging process. Syntax errors in M-files are found when the code is loaded and compiled to the internal MATLAB representation. Scripts do not create a local workspace, and so the variables they use can be inspected when the script evaluation is completed (even if an error occurs) and MATLAB returns to the base workspace. However, the same is not true for local variables inside functions.

The MATLAB symbolic debugger offers sophisticated control over the debugging process. It works only on functions and not on scripts, though it is easy enough to temporarily change a script to a function by simply including the keyword `function` and a function name at the head of a script. Breakpoints can be set and cleared; they are also cleared automatically if the function is edited. The facilities offered are similar to those in Unix symbolic debuggers such as **dbx** and **gdb**. Breakpoints are set using the command **dbstop**:

```
dbstop at 23 in foo
```

where **at** and the line number are optional. Once the program has stopped, the commands **dbstep** and **dbstep in** advance execution by one step (moving into function calls in the latter case). The command **dbcont** executes all code until the next breakpoint. Any MATLAB command can be issued at the interpreter prompt when execution stops, which allows the user to inspect variables.

Profiling

The aim of profiling is to determine which parts of a program are taking the longest to execute so that the effort put into speeding up the program can be directed in the most effective way.

The simplest form and most machine-independent form of profiling is to count the number of basic floating point operations (flops) used by a program. The MATLAB function **flops** provides an approximate count.

```
1  flops(0)
2  x = scg('rosen', x, options, 'rosegrad');
3  opt_flops = flops;
```

In this fragment, taken from the NETLAB program **demopt1**, the flop counter is reset to zero in line 1, and the number of operations consumed by line 2 is measured in line 3. Note that **flops** is not supported in MATLAB v. 6.0 since the underlying numerical algebra engine has been changed.

The **flops** measure has the advantage of being independent both of the machine and the load from other programs and so gives portable results. However, the number of operations is not the only determinant of the speed of a program. We have seen that vectorised code can be up to 25 times faster than code based on a loop, but the operation count for both versions is the same. It is therefore useful to be able to time programs as well; this can be done using the MATLAB functions **tic**, which resets a timer, and **toc**, which returns the time elapsed since the last call to **tic**. The fragment above can be changed to *time* the call to **scg**:

```
1  tic;
2  x = scg('rosen', x, options, 'rosegrad');
3  opt_time = toc;
```

This timer works at a resolution of 1 second (it is finer resolution in MATLABv. 6.0), so for reliable results it may be necessary to run the code of interest many times inside a loop.

To provide finer grained timing information, both in terms of timing precision and apportioning time to different parts of code, MATLAB provides a **profile** function. This will provide a profiling report for a single M-file.

Using the information in this report the profiler can then be run recursively on the most computationally demanding functions at the next level down in the hierarchy recursively until the bottlenecks are determined.

Once the slowest parts of a program have been identified there are two possible ways to speed them up. Where possible, it is best to improve the efficiency of the algorithm used or its MATLAB implementation (for example, by vectorising a loop). If this is not possible, the bottlenecks can be rewritten in another programming language (usually C) and then interfaced to the MATLAB program using the MEX file mechanism (see MATLAB manuals for more information).

Programming Tips

When writing your own MATLAB functions and scripts or extending the NETLAB toolbox there are several important points to bear in mind to arrive at robust and efficient programs.

1. For efficiency, loops with large numbers of iterations should be avoided where possible and replaced by vectorised code, even if this increases the number of flops. Where loops must be used, it is worth arranging the calculation to reduce the number of iterations.

2. Always write help text for your functions. At some point in the not too distant future you won't remember their calling syntax or how they work.

3. Comments are useful to make code clearer. However, bear in mind that they do add a small overhead to the execution time of a function, so be sparing with the number of comment lines in short heavily-used functions.

4. MATLAB searches for functions based on the name of the M-file, not on the function name defined in the M-file. This means that if the name of the M-file does not match the name of the function contained in the file, the results may be confusing!

5. Don't use built-in MATLAB function names for variable or function names as then the MATLAB functions will not be accessible. This is why the NETLAB Rosenbrock function is called `rosen` and not `rose`: there is a MATLAB plotting routine called `rose`. For similar reasons, be careful about using variables named i and j since MATLAB uses these to represent the square root of -1. NETLAB does not need complex numbers, so it does use variables named i and j quite frequently (though it is arguable that it would be better not to).

6. To find out where a particular function, say `foo`, is located, type

   ```
   which foo
   ```

   at the MATLAB interpreter prompt. This is useful when there are several functions with the same name in different parts of the search path. It can also be used to check whether there is a built-in function with a given name to avoid the problems described in Item 5.

7. A frequent requirement in NETLAB is to create a matrix by repeating a vector. For example, we may need to create the 3×2 matrix

$$A = \begin{bmatrix} 2 & 3 \\ 2 & 3 \\ 2 & 3 \end{bmatrix} \tag{1.3}$$

from the row vector $b = (2\ 3)$. This can be done in one of two ways:

- Matrix multiplication by a suitable vector of ones. Remembering the formula for the size of a matrix product, we see that the results of pre-multiplying the 1×2 vector b by a matrix of size 3×1 (i.e. a column vector with three rows) is a 3×2 matrix. This leads to the formula

$$A = \begin{bmatrix} 1 \\ 1 \\ 1 \end{bmatrix} b \tag{1.4}$$

and the MATLAB code
```
A = ones(3, 1)*b;
```
- Using the MATLAB function repmat. This creates a new matrix by replicating (or 'tiling') an existing matrix. In its simplest form, it is passed two arguments to specify the number of rows and columns in the tiling. For our example, the required code is
```
A = repmat(b, 3, 1);
```

8. Use simple mechanisms for making your code more robust. In switch statements, otherwise cases prevent a silent failure when unexpected values are met. The consist function (see Section 1.2.2) is used by NETLAB to check the consistency of arguments; it is equally valid for functions that extend NETLAB.

1.2 The NETLAB Toolbox

The NETLAB toolbox is designed to provide the central tools necessary for the simulation of theoretically well-founded neural network algorithms for use in teaching, research and applications development. In this section we give an overview of the facilities provided by NETLAB and a gentle introduction to the way it works through a more detailed analysis of some of the generic functions it provides.

1.2.1 Overview of NETLAB

Here we explain the basic principles of NETLAB, show how to write a simple program using NETLAB, and describe the key introductory demonstration programs.

Basics NETLAB consists of a library of more than 150 MATLAB functions and scripts. All the functions come with on-line help, and further explanation is available via HTML files.

Every model of any complexity is stored as a MATLAB data structure. These data structures simplify the syntax of functions, reduce the probability of coding errors, ensure that all the relevant information is kept together, and guard against users from passing the wrong model to a function. There is a 'constructor' function for each type of model that builds and initialises the relevant data structure. Each model has a short prefix that is used for all of its associated functions. For example, the Gaussian mixture model has the prefix gmm. A call to the constructor function

```
net = gmm(1, 2, 'spherical')
```

generates the following data structure

```
       type: 'gmm'
        nin: 1
   ncentres: 2
    nparams: 6
 covar_type: 'spherical'
     priors: [0.5000 0.5000]
    centres: [2x1 double]
     covars: [1 1]
```

The models have been designed to have compatible data structures to maximise their reuse. For example, the Gaussian mixture model is used when training RBF networks, in Mixture Density Networks, and in the Generative Topographic Mapping.

To make the models as generic as possible, model conventions are used for certain common functions. For example, the function to forward propagate inputs through a model is always named <type>fwd, where <type> denotes the type of the model. Thus the forward propagation for a multi-layer perceptron is called mlpfwd. This makes it easier to write generic functions to manipulate models. For example the following code can be used to forward propagate a vector x through any NETLAB model net:

```
fn_string = [net.type, 'fwd'];
y = feval(fn_string, net, x);
```

By following these conventions when extending NETLAB you can ensure that the new models you develop will be compatible with all the existing models. There are particularly important conventions for optimisation (Section 2.8.1) and Bayesian learning (Section 9.3).

As well as the usual MATLAB data file formats, NETLAB provides two utility functions datread and datwrite to read and write data files respectively. The data file is stored in plain text format with a short header followed by the data itself. The header has the form

```
nin 2
nout 1
ndata 12
```

where nin specifies the number of input variables, nout the number of output variables, and ndata the number of data points, set to 2, 1 and 12 respectively in this example. Each subsequent line corresponds to a single pattern, with the first nin values for the input variables, and the remaining nout values for the output variables, all separated by white space. For unsupervised learning problems, nout can be zero.

Getting Started

The equivalent of the Computer Science "Hello world" program in NETLAB is a script that generates some data, trains an MLP, and plots its predictions.

```
1   % Generate the matrix of inputs x and targets t.
2   x = [0:1/19:1]';
3   t = sin(2*pi*x) + 0.2*randn(ndata, 1);
4
5   % Set up network parameters.
6   net = mlp(1, 3, 1, 'linear');
7
8   % Set up vector of options for the optimiser.
9   options = foptions;
10  options(1) = 1;      % This provides display of error values.
11  options(14) = 100;   % Number of training cycles.
12
13  % Train using scaled conjugate gradients.
14  [net, options] = netopt(net, options, x, t, 'scg');
15
16  % Plot the trained network predictions.
17  plotvals = [0:0.01:1]';
18  y = mlpfwd(net, plotvals);
19  plot(plotvals, y, 'ob')
```

This script illustrates the main steps in developing any model in NETLAB: loading or generating data (lines 2–3); creating and initialising a model (line 6); training the model (lines 9–14); making predictions (line 18). It is discussed in more detail in Section 5.6.1.

Demonstration Programs

Often the fastest way to develop a model for a new application is to adapt an existing script. NETLAB has more than 30 demonstration programs which illustrate every model in the toolbox. These demonstration programs contain a lot of informative material output to the screen; on removing all the clc, disp and pause commands, the skeleton is revealed. The underlying set of commmands can then be adapted its new context.

The program demnlab has been provided to give an overview of the facilities in NETLAB. It provides a simple graphical interface to all of the demonstration programs grouped in thematic menus.

- Regression: multi-layer perceptron (MLP); radial basis function (RBF) network; Mixture Density Network (MDN).
- Classification: Generalised Linear Model (GLM), MLP, K-nearest-neighbour (KNN).
- Density Modelling and Clustering: Gaussian mixture model (GMM); Neuroscale; Generative Topographic Mapping (GTM); K-means clustering.
- Bayesian Methods: sampling priors; evidence procedure for MLP; automatic relevance determination (ARD); Gaussian process (GP).
- Optimisation and Model Visualisation: algorithm comparison; Hinton diagrams.
- Sampling: Markov chain Monte Carlo (MCMC) sampler; hybrid Monte Carlo (HMC) for MLP.

A good way to understand the properties of particular models and algorithms is to use the demonstration programs as the basis of experimenting with different properties, for example, by changing the amount of training data, the noise levels, numbers of hidden units etc. Of course, it is safest to edit a copy of the scripts in your own workspace.

If you don't even want to write a script as simple as the "Hello World" program, then the demonstration program demtrain can be used to train and evaluate an MLP network on NETLAB format datasets. It has a GUI which allows the user to set the number of hidden units, output activation function, and number of training epochs. Once the network has been trained, it is saved in a MATLAB format file mlptrain.net. This can be read in using the MATLAB function load.

1.2.2 Generic Functions

In this section we shall discuss three function groups that can be used with a wide range of NETLAB models and that illustrate some of the principles of MATLAB programming discussed earlier in this chapter: argument checking, distance calculation, confusion matrices, and Hinton weight diagrams.

Argument Checking

Most of the functions in NETLAB operate on a data structure representing the current state of a model and matrices representing datasets. If a NETLAB user makes a mistake, and passes the wrong model or data to a function, then it is very likely that this will be detected by MATLAB, but that the error message generated will not help the user work out what has gone wrong. To make life easier for the user, the NETLAB function consist checks that the model and data are as expected. This function is called in most of the NETLAB functions (62 at the current count), and has been omitted from the description of NETLAB functions in subsequent chapters precisely because it is so common.

The consist function is a good example of the treatment of variable numbers of input arguments. This is because, depending on the function calling consist, it may be possible to check some or all of: the type of the model, the dimensions of the data inputs, and the dimensions of the data outputs.

For this function to work correctly, certain assumptions are made about the data structure model:

- There is a field model.type that contains a string representing the type of model (e.g. 'mlp'). This should match the prefix used in all the functions that manipulate the model (e.g. 'mlpfwd').
- There is a field model.nin that contains the number of inputs to the model.
- There is a field model.nout that contains the number of outputs from the model. If there are no outputs, then this field should be omitted.

When creating any new models within the NETLAB framework, you should adhere to these assumptions so as to be able to use the consist function.

```
1   function errstring = consist(model, type, inputs, outputs)
2
3   % Assume that all is OK as default
4   errstring = '';
5
6   % If type string is not empty
7   if ~isempty(type)
8     % First check that model has type field
9     if ~isfield(model, 'type')
10      errstring = 'Data structure does not contain type field';
11      return
12    end
13    % Check that model has the correct type
14    s = model.type;
15    if ~strcmp(s, type)
16      errstring = ['Model type ''', s, ...
17        ''' does not match expected type ''', type, ''''];
18      return
19    end
20  end
21
22  % If inputs are present, check that they have correct dimension
23  if nargin > 2
24    if ~isfield(model, 'nin')
25      errstring = 'Data structure does not contain nin field';
26      return
27    end
28
29    data_nin = size(inputs, 2);
30    if model.nin ~= data_nin
31      errstring = ['Dimension of inputs ', num2str(data_nin), ...
32      ' does not match number of model inputs ', num2str(model.nin)];
33      return
34    end
```

```
35   end
36
37   % If outputs are present, check that they have correct dimension
38   if nargin > 3
39     if ~isfield(model, 'nout')
40       errstring = 'Data structure does not contain nout field';
41       return
42     end
43     data_nout = size(outputs, 2);
44     if model.nout ~= data_nout
45       errstring = ['Dimension of outputs ', num2str(data_nout), ...
46           ' does not match number of model outputs ', ...
47           num2str(model.nout)];
48       return
49     end
50   % Check that inputs and outputs have same number of points
51     num_in = size(inputs, 1);
52     num_out = size(outputs, 1);
53     if num_in ~= num_out
54       errstring = ['Number of input patterns ', num2str(num_in), ...
55       ' does not match number of output patterns ', num2str(num_out)];
56       return
57     end
58   end
```

The first check (lines 7–20) that is made is whether the expected type (given by the second argument) matches the type of the model (line 15). The second check (lines 23–35) tests whether the number of variables in the dataset inputs (given by the number of columns in the matrix) matches the number of model inputs (line 30). The third check (lines 38–49) tests whether the number of outputs in the dataset outputs (given by the number of columns) matches the number of model outputs (line 44). The fourth check (lines 51–58) tests the consistency of the datasets: the number of patterns (rows of the matrices) should be the same (line 53).

If all the tests are passed successfully, then an empty string is returned (line 4); otherwise the string contains an error message appropriate to the first test that fails (each failed test immediately returns: see, for example, line 18). A typical call to consist can be found in mlperr, the function that calculates the error for a multi-layer perceptron on a dataset with inputs x and targets t:

```
1   function [e, edata, eprior] = mlperr(net, x, t)
2
3   errstring = consist(net, 'mlp', x, t);
4   if ~isempty(errstring);
5     error(errstring);
6   end
```

If all the tests in consist are passed, then the return value errstring is empty, and the test in line 4 will be passed. Otherwise the error function will be called: this halts execution and returns the user to the interpreter prompt with an error message detailing which function failed and printing errstring. The reason that error is not called directly inside consist is that it is more useful to know which function calling consist was in error, as then it is easier to track down the programming error.

If a NETLAB function does not require a target dataset, then consist can be called with just three arguments. This example is extracted from mlpfwd, the function to propagate patterns forward through a multi-layer perceptron:

```
1  function [y, z, a] = mlpfwd(net, x)
2
3  errstring = consist(net, 'mlp', x);
4  if ~isempty(errstring);
5    error(errstring);
6  end
```

Distance Calculation

There are many places in NETLAB where it is necessary to calculate the squared Euclidean distance between two sets of data points, represented by the matrices x and c. The resulting matrix N has entries N_{ij} representing the squared distance between the ith row of X and the jth row of C. The NETLAB function dist2 uses the identity

$$\|x - c\|^2 = \|x\|^2 - 2x^T c + \|c\|^2 \tag{1.5}$$

to vectorise the calculation (lines 9–10). The drawback of this method of calculation is that it can increase the rounding errors, so any negative results (which can only be the result of rounding error) are set to zero in line 13.

```
1  function n2 = dist2(x, c)
2
3  [ndata, dimx] = size(x);
4  [ncentres, dimc] = size(c);
5  if dimx ~= dimc
6    error('Data dimension does not match dimension of centres')
7  end
8
9  n2 = (ones(ncentres, 1) * sum((x.^2)', 1))' + ...
10     ones(ndata, 1) * sum((c.^2)',1) - 2.*(x*(c'));
11
12 if any(any(n2<0))
13    n2(n2<0) = 0;
14 end
```

Confusion Matrices

Confusion matrices are a useful way of presenting the results of a classification model on a dataset. They provide detailed information on the performance of the model on each class. In a confusion matrix C, the rows represent the true classes and the columns represent the predicted classes; the entry C_{ij} is the number of examples from class i that were classified as class j. From this it is easy to see that the ideal matrix is one whose off-diagonal entries are all zero.

The NETLAB function confmat computes a confusion matrix and also the overall classification accuracy. It is a simple example of the use of logical and arithmetic operators on matrices to vectorise code.

```
1  function [C,rate] = confmat(Y,T)
2
3  [n c] = size(Y);
4  [n2 c2] = size(T);
5
6  if n~=n2 | c~=c2
7    error('Outputs and targets are different sizes')
8  end
9
10 if c > 1
11   % Find the winning class assuming 1-of-N encoding
12   [maximum Yclass] = max(Y', [], 1);
13   TL=[1:c]*T';
14 else
15   % Assume two classes with 0-1 encoding
16   c = 2;
17   class2 = find(T > 0.5);
18   TL = ones(n, 1);
19   TL(class2) = 2;
20   class2 = find(Y > 0.5);
21   Yclass = ones(n, 1);
22   Yclass(class2) = 2;
23 end
24
25 % Compute classification rate
26 correct = (Yclass==TL);
27 total = sum(sum(correct));
28 rate = [total*100/n total];
29
30 C=zeros(c,c);
31 for i = 1:c
32   for j = 1:c
33     C(i,j) = sum((Yclass==j).*(TL==i));
34   end
35 end
```

The inputs to the function are the true classifications T and the model predictions Y.

- If there are two classes, then it is assumed that the targets are 0 or 1 for the first and second class while the predictions are in the range $[0, 1]$ (for example, probabilities of membership of class 2). This means that both T and Y are column vectors.

- If there are $c > 2$ classes, then it is assumed that the targets use a 1-of-c encoding; there is a vector of c values for each example which are all zero except for the entry corresponding to the class the example belongs to. Thus $t_j^{(n)} = \delta_{ij}$ if the nth example belongs to class $\mathcal{C}_i$. The predictions are also assumed to be a c-dimensional vector, with the predicted class being the largest value.

The matrix TL contains the true label for each example. For more than two classes, this is computed in line 13 since multiplying the vector 1:c by T' picks out the single non-zero entry in each row of T. For two classes, it is assumed that any target value greater than 0.5 belongs to the second class, and all other targets to the first class (lines 17–19). Note how both calculations are performed using matrix operations rather than a loop over each entry.

The matrix Yclass contains the predicted label for each example. For more than two classes, this label is taken to be the class corresponding to the largest prediction (line 12) in a single matrix operation. For two classes, the predicted label is computed in the same way as for the targets (lines 20–22).

Line 26 picks out the correctly classified examples where the predicted and true labels match, creating a matrix with ones only in the entries where the two match and zeros elsewhere. Line 28 puts the correct percentage and number of examples as two entries in the return vector rate.

Lines 30–35 compute the confusion matrix. This is pre-allocated (line 30) for efficiency. A double loop is needed to compute C_{ij}. The matrix Yclass==j is zero except for examples where the predicted class is $\mathcal{C}_j$. So multiplying this matrix element-wise by TL==i gives zero entries except where the predicted class is $\mathcal{C}_j$ and the true class is $\mathcal{C}_i$. Although there is a double loop over the entries of C this is not a serious loss of efficiency since the number of classes is usually small and the inner part of the loop is vectorised. Examples of the use of confmat can be found in Fig. 1.3, demmlp2 and demtrain. The matrix can be displayed as a figure using the NETLAB function conffig.

Hinton Diagrams

A Hinton diagram is a useful method for visualising the weights in a neural network. Each weight is represented by a square whose size is proportional to the magnitude of the weight and whose colour represents the sign (white for positive and black for negative).

The NETLAB function mlphint generates two figure windows, one displaying the first-layer weights and biases, and the other displaying the second-layer weights and biases. For each layer the weights in a row represent those fanning into a given unit and the bias weight is separated from the rest by a red vertical line. The demhint program shows how this function works.

The task of calculating the coordinates and colours of the squares for mlphint is performed by the NETLAB function hintmat.

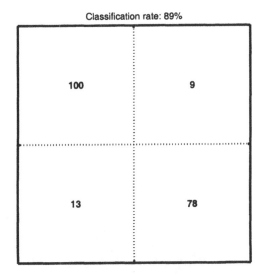

Classification rate: 89%

100   9

13   78

Fig. 1.3. Example of a confusion matrix produced by `conffig`.

```
1  function [xvals, yvals, color] = hintmat(w);
2
3  w = flipud(w);
4  [nrows, ncols] = size(w);
5
6  scale = 0.45*sqrt(abs(w)/max(max(abs(w))));
7  scale = scale(:);
8  color = 0.5*(sign(w(:)) + 3);
9
10 delx = 1;
11 dely = 1;
12 [X, Y] = meshgrid(0.5*delx:delx:(ncols-0.5*delx), ...
13     0.5*dely:dely:(nrows-0.5*dely));
14 xtemp = X(:);
15 ytemp = Y(:);
16
17 xvals = [xtemp-delx*scale, xtemp+delx*scale, ...
18         xtemp+delx*scale, xtemp-delx*scale];
19 yvals = [ytemp-dely*scale, ytemp-dely*scale, ...
20         ytemp+dely*scale, ytemp+dely*scale];
```

The column `color` returned from `hintmat` contains one entry per weight; it is 2 for positive weights and 1 for negative weights. These values are used when displaying the Hinton diagram as indices into a colour map which has two entries: black and white. The matrices `xvals` and `yvals` contain the x- and y-coordinates respectively of each square. These are passed to the MATLAB function `patch` to plot the squares. The coordinates are calculated by `hintmat` so that the squares do not overlap. The `scale` for each square is the distance from the square centre to each edge; this is set to 0.45 times the maximum weight in the matrix m (lines 7–8). The colour map `color` is computed in line 9. The MATLAB function `sign(w(:))` returns a column vector containing +1 corresponding to positive values in w and −1 corresponding to negative values.

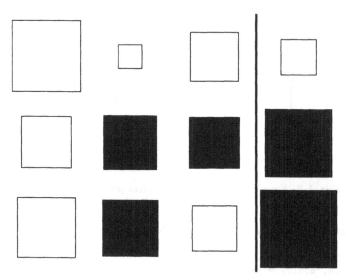

Fig. 1.4. Hinton diagram for output layer of MLP with three hidden and three output units.

The next step is to calculate the positions of the centres of the squares. They are placed in a rectangular grid at unit intervals (lines 10–11) with the bottom left-hand square placed at $(0.5, 0.5)$ (lines 12–13). Lines 17–20 compute the coordinates of the four vertices in four columns. An example taken from `demhint` is shown in Fig. 1.4.

The following fragment comes from the NETLAB function `hinton`.

```
1  [xvals, yvals, color] = hintmat(w);
2  h1 = figure('Color', [0.5 0.5 0.5], ...
3    'NumberTitle', 'off', ...
4    'Colormap', [0 0 0; 1 1 1], ...
5    'Units', 'pixels');
6  set(gca, 'Visible', 'off', 'Position', [0 0 1 1]);
7  hold on
8  patch(xvals', yvals', color', 'Edgecolor', 'none');
```

The background colour is set to mid-gray in line 2 to make the colours of the squares stand out. The patch coordinates xvals and yvals are assumed to be $n \times m$ matrices, where m is the number of vertices of each patch (equal to 4) and n is the number of patches.

1.3 Worked Example: Data Normalisation

In many of the worked examples and exercises in this book you will need to modify NETLAB functions. There are two ways in which this can be done without destroying the original version of NETLAB. For example, suppose that you are editing the function mlpfwd.

1. Change the name of the NETLAB function before editing it, say to mlpnewfwd. The main problem with this is that if other parts of NET-LAB that you are using call mlpfwd, they will call the standard NETLAB version and not mlpnewfwd. Thus many other parts of NETLAB will need to be edited.
2. Copy the NETLAB function to a directory in your local area before editing it, but keep the name the same. This will work provided you are in this directory when running any NETLAB scripts. Because MATLAB always searches the current directory for a function before looking at the rest of the path, the special version of mlpfwd will be used in preference to the NETLAB version no matter which NETLAB function calls it.

It is common practice to scale input variables so that they have similar magnitudes. This means that network weights can all be expected to have similar values if the inputs are equally important, and so can be initialised randomly. Without normalisation, network training often gets stuck in a local optimum because some of the weights are a very long way from their best values.

To normalise the data we treat each input variable independently and, for each variable x_i, we calculate its mean $\bar{x}_i$ and variance σ_i^2 on the training data. The rescaled variables are defined by

$$\tilde{x}_i^n = \frac{x_i^n - \bar{x}_i}{\sigma_i}, \tag{1.6}$$

and have zero mean and unit variance. The following function implements this transformation.

```
1  function y = normal(x)
2  % NORMAL Transforms data to zero mean and unit variance
3  % x is the input data matrix.
4  % y is the returned data where each variable has zero mean and
5  % unit standard deviation.
6
7  n = size(x, 1);
8
9  mu = mean(x);
10 s  = std(x);
11
12 e = ones(n, 1);
13 y = x - e*mu; % Make y have zero mean
14 y = y ./ (e*(s + (s==0)));
```

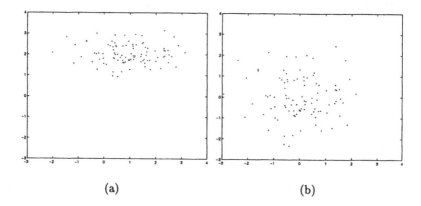

(a)   (b)

Fig. 1.5. Demonstration of data normalisation. (a) Original dataset drawn from a Gaussian with diagonal covariance and non-zero mean. (b) Normalised dataset.

Following the usual MATLAB convention, each row of the input matrix x represents a pattern. The comments in lines 2–5 are the help text for this function. The mean (line 9) and standard deviation (line 10) of each variable are computed using MATLAB matrix functions. To avoid a loop we need to create matrices that are the same size as x so that (1.6) can be computed with array operations. The matrix e*mu is equal to

$$
M = \begin{bmatrix}
\bar{x}_1 & \bar{x}_2 & \cdots & \bar{x}_d \\
\bar{x}_1 & \bar{x}_2 & \cdots & \bar{x}_d \\
\vdots & \vdots & \vdots & \vdots \\
\bar{x}_1 & \bar{x}_2 & \cdots & \bar{x}_d
\end{bmatrix}
\tag{1.7}
$$

where d is the number of columns in x and M has n rows. Hence line 13 computes

$$
y = x_i^n - \bar{x}_i
\tag{1.8}
$$

and line 14 computes (1.6). The matrix s + (s==0) is equal to s except where s(i) equals zero, where it is one. This ensures that there is no division by zero in line 14 (which could happen if a variable was constant within rounding error); any variables with zero variance are left untouched. The effect of normal on a sample of data is shown in Figs. 1.5 and 1.6. Note how the data is translated to the origin. The covariance structure is a circle if the original covariance was diagonal, but if the original variables were correlated, then this structure remains in the normalised data. Data whitening using PCA (see Section 7.1) turns any Gaussian distribution into the unit sphere.

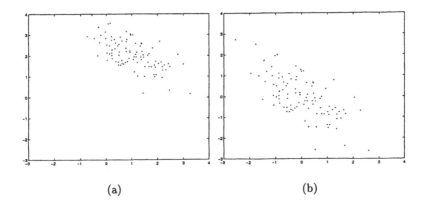

(a)   (b)

Fig. 1.6. Demonstration of data normalisation. (a) Original dataset drawn from a Gaussian with correlation between two variables and non-zero mean. (b) Normalised dataset.

Exercises

1.1 (⋆) Create two datasets of your own using MATLAB. Save the data as text files, and then edit the files to convert them to NETLAB format. Using demtrain, load one dataset, train an MLP, and then test the network on the second dataset.

1.2 (⋆⋆) Extend demtrain to allow RBF networks as well. There will need to be a drop-down menu to choose the hidden unit activation function.

1.3 (⋆) Using the MATLAB functions imagesc and cov, write a function that displays the correlation structure of a dataset as an image.

1.4 (⋆) Apply the MATLAB profiler to demgmm1 to find which function(s) demand the most computational effort. You will need to (temporarily) make demgmm1 a function by adding the line

```
function demgmm1
```

to the head of the file. Once you have found out which lines of demgmm1 use the most time, trace down the function hierarchy to find the NETLAB function that is most expensive.

1.5 (⋆⋆) Rewrite the bottleneck function identified in Exercise 1.4 in C and interface it to the appropriate sub-function of demgmm1 using the MEX compiler. Time the new version and compare the results with the all-MATLAB program.

1.6 (⋆⋆) Write Hinton diagram demonstration programs for the GLM and RBF models using mlphint and hinton as a guide.

1.7 (⋆⋆) Extend the confusion matrix functions so that the user may (optionally) see the effect of a cost matrix on the classification results. The confusion matrix should be calculated using thresholds that lead to minimum cost classifications, and the overall accuracy should be supplemented with the misclassification cost. You should assume that the NETLAB model outputs the conditional class probability $p(C_i|x)$ for each class C_i.

Let L be the loss matrix, where L_{ij} is the cost of assigning an example to class C_j when it really belongs to class C_i. Then an example x should be classified as C_i if

$$\sum_{k=1}^{c} L_{kj} p(C_k|x) < \sum_{k=1}^{c} L_{ki} p(C_k|x). \tag{1.9}$$

1.8 ($\star$) Investigate the effect of normalisation using the `normal` function on data drawn from a mixture of Gaussians.

1.9 ($\star\star$) In classification problems with just two classes, it is possible to evaluate a classifier more thoroughly than with a confusion matrix by computing the Receiver Operator Characteristic (ROC) curve. This plots the true positive rate against the false positive rate of a classifier as the classification threshold varies from 0 to 1.

Let TP, TN, FP, FN denote the number of examples classified as true positive, true negative, false positive and false negative respectively. The *sensitivity*, or true positive rate, is defined as $TP/(TP + FN)$, and the false positive rate is defined as $FP/(TN + FP)$; this is equal to 1 minus the *specificity*, equal to $TN/(TN + FP)$.

The area under the ROC curve can be interpreted as the probability that the classifier predicts the correct ordering of a pair of examples, one drawn from each class. It is known to statisticians as the Wilcoxon statistic, and can be viewed as a measure of the overall quality of a classification model not restricted to a particular choice of decision threshold. Using `confmat` and `conffig` as models, implement two MATLAB functions: one to compute the ROC curve and the area under it, and the other to plot the result.

2. Parameter Optimisation Algorithms

Learning in neural networks and other statistical models is usually formulated in terms of minimising an error function E. This error is a function of the adjustable parameters (or weights) in the network.

The problem of minimising a smooth function of many parameters is one which has been studied for many years, and many algorithms developed for other purposes are directly applicable to the problem of training neural networks. In this chapter we shall discuss several of the most important practical algorithms, while later chapters will discuss other algorithms (such as expectation maximisation (EM) and iterated re-weighted least squares (IRLS)) which are only applicable to certain models with a specific form of error function.

Most of the algorithms which are described in this chapter have shown good performance in training neural networks in a wide range of problems. However, there is no universally optimal algorithm, so it is always useful to have a choice from several. In this chapter we first discuss how to control the optimisation algorithms. The interface is designed to be compatible with the MATLAB optimisation toolbox, although no functions from that toolbox are required. It is worth noting that the interface to the sampling algorithms in NETLAB is similar to that used for optimisation algorithms. We then cover line search, which is a special case of one-dimensional minimisation, adapted for use in multi-dimensional optimisation algorithms. Gradient descent, the simplest optimisation algorithm, is then introduced and its limitations described. Next we review an important class of algorithms which use the technique of *conjugate gradients* including a relatively recent version that has the advantage of not requiring a line minimisation subroutine. We then cover the other major class of optimisation algorithms known as quasi-Newton methods. Following this, we discuss how the general purpose optimisation algorithms can be applied to neural networks in NETLAB. Finally, the worked example shows how the methods described in this chapter can be extended to deal with constrained optimisation problems. All the functions discussed in this chapter are listed in Table 2.1.

Because maximising f is completely equivalent to minimising $-f$, minimisation algorithms can be used to solve any optimisation problem. It is often helpful to consider the problem of optimisation geometrically. The *function*

Table 2.1. Functions in this chapter.

Optimisation Functions	
conjgrad	Conjugate gradients optimisation
demopt1	Demonstration of optimisation algorithms
gradchek	Gradient checking
graddesc	Gradient descent optimisation
linef	Function evaluation on a line
linemin	Line search
minbrack	Minimum bracketing
netopt	Optimisation for neural networks
olgd	On-line gradient descent for neural networks
quasinew	Quasi-Newton optimisation
scg	Scaled conjugate gradients optimisation

surface lies 'above' the *search space*. For neural networks these are the *error surface* and *weight space* respectively. In general, it is not possible to find a solution to the optimisation problem in closed form. Instead, we use algorithms that take steps in the search space of the form

$$x_{j+1} = x_j + \alpha_j d_j \tag{2.1}$$

where j labels the iteration. Algorithms differ in the the choice of the *search direction* d_j and the method used to determine the *step size* α_j.

2.1 Controlling the Algorithms

We shall use the function scg, which implements a scaled conjugate gradients algorithm, to illustrate how to use the NETLAB optimisation functions. All the general purpose optimisation algorithms in NETLAB assume that the user is trying to find a local minimum of a function which has a known gradient. There are two further compulsory arguments to the optimisation functions: the starting point for the optimisation procedure, and an *options* vector which is used to control the algorithm. Thus the code fragment

```
options = foptions;
y = scg('foo', x, options, 'foograd');
```

initialises the options vector to its default values (defined by MATLAB), and then uses scg to find a local minimum of the function defined in the M-file foo.m with gradient defined in foograd.m starting from the vector x. The result of the optimisation procedure is returned in the vector y.

Usually the function and gradient will be defined as the names of functions written as MATLAB M-files, but it is also possible to use MATLAB expressions instead.

```
y = scg('sin(2*pi*x)', y1, options, '2*pi*cos(2*pi*x)');
```

There are 18 elements in the options vector[1]. Only some of these locations are relevant to any particular optimisation algorithm: to find out more details for a specific algorithm, use the MATLAB on-line help. By invoking help for foptions, you can find out the generic uses of each entry, together with the default values assigned by the foptions function.

2.1.1 Information Display

The value of options(1) is used to control the display of information during the execution of the optimisation algorithms. If this field has the value 0, then warning messages only are displayed at the MATLAB prompt. (The most common of these is that the algorithm has gone through all the iterations specified without the termination criteria being met.) If this field has a positive value, then the current value of the function being optimised is displayed at each iteration of the algorithm as well as any warning messages. If this field has a negative value, then no information at all is displayed, not even warning messages.

A very useful feature of the optimisation algorithms when debugging the function to be optimised is the gradient checking procedure. If options(9) is set to one, then a generic function gradchek is called. This function checks that gradf really does compute the gradient of f at the initial search point. It does this by comparing gradf(x) with a finite difference approximation to the same value. The central difference formula

$$\frac{\partial f}{\partial x_i} \approx \frac{f(x_i + \epsilon) - f(x_i - \epsilon)}{2\epsilon} + \mathcal{O}(\epsilon^2) \tag{2.2}$$

is used with a step size ϵ of 10^{-6}. The output is arranged in three columns: the gradient calculated using gradf; the gradient calculated using central differences; and the values of the first method minus the second method. The third column is significantly different from zero if the derivative and function do not match. (It won't be exactly zero due to the approximation error in (2.2) and rounding error in its computation.)

The following example shows the result of using gradchek on the NETLAB functions rosen and its derivative rosegrad (Section 2.1.4) at the point x=[-1 1].

```
>> gradchek(x, 'rosen', 'rosegrad');
Checking gradient ...
```

---

[1] MATLAB version 6 also allows structures to be used to control optimisation functions.

```
analytic    diffs     delta

-4.0000   -4.0000   0.0000
       0         0        0
```

2.1.2 Termination Criteria

The optimisation algorithms terminate in one of two different circumstances:

1. The maximum allowed number of iterations has been reached. This number is given by options(14). If this value is non-positive, it is set to the default of 100.

2. Both termination criteria for the distance moved in search space and the change in the function value are met.

   • The distance moved in search space at iteration τ is given by $\|\Delta x^{(\tau)}\|$. If this is less than options(2), then the termination criterion for the distance moved is met. The default value of options(2) supplied by foptions is 1e-4. Note that all NETLAB optimisation algorithms (*unlike* the MATLAB optimisation toolbox) do *not* make a call foptions(options);

   This is because there are cases where setting options(2) to zero is useful (for example, to ensure that all iterations specified by options(14) are completed), but a call to foptions resets the value to the default value of 1×10^{-4}.

   This termination criterion has the drawback that it is not invariant under rescaling of the inputs. For this reason it is best to ensure that the inputs are measured on similar scales. An alternative criterion is

   $$|x_i^{(\tau+1)} - x_i^{(\tau)}| \leq \epsilon_i. \tag{2.3}$$

   However, this would require a vector of limits ϵ_i and so would be incompatible with the MATLAB toolbox. Fletcher (1987) recommends a termination criterion of this type for conjugate gradient algorithms.

   • The change in the function value at iteration τ is given by

   $$|f^{(\tau+1)} - f^{(\tau)}|. \tag{2.4}$$

   If this value is less than options(3) then the change in function value termination criterion is met. The treatment of this limit by foptions is the same as for options(2). Fletcher (1987) recommends the use of this termination criteria for Newton-like methods.

2.1.3 Extra Arguments and Return Values

The function interface described at the start of this section is the basic way of calling the optimisation algorithms. However, for more complicated circumstances, it is possible to pass additional arguments and return additional values.

As an example, consider the interface to the function `conjgrad`, which implements a conjugate gradient algorithm.

```
[x, options, errlog, pointlog] = conjgrad(f, x, options, gradf, ...
                                  varargin)
```

There are three optional return values in addition to the final search point.

- The `options` vector contains additional information about the optimisation process. In particular, `options(8)` contains the function value computed at the return value `x` where the search terminated.
- The `errlog` vector contains the sequence of function values at the search points moved to during the algorithm. If a search point is rejected by the algorithm (for example, because the function value increases at that step), then the previous function value is repeated.
- The `pointlog` contains the search points moved to during the algorithm. Again, the previous search point is repeated if a step is not taken.

The final optional argument `varargin` to `conjgrad` allows an arbitrary number of additional arguments to be passed to the function `f` and gradient `gradf`. They follow the formal parameter `x` in the function syntax. For example, if `foo` and `foograd` take two arguments,

```
function y = foo(x, t)
```

the first of these, `x`, is the one that is optimised for by `conjgrad` during execution. So the function call

```
x = conjgrad('foo', x, options, 'foograd', t);
```

uses the conjugate gradient algorithm to find

$$\min_{x} foo(x, t) \tag{2.5}$$

where t is fixed. We shall use this feature frequently to train neural networks, because to computing the value of the error function for a neural network requires both the training inputs and targets, and so these datasets must be passed as additional arguments to the optimisation algorithm. The optimisation of neural networks is discussed further in Section 2.8.

2.1.4 Demonstration Program

Although optimisation routines are used throughout NETLAB there is also a dedicated optimisation demonstration program `demopt1`. This program compares the performance of four generic optimisation routines when finding the minimum of Rosenbrock's function

$$y = 100 * (x_2 - x_1^2)^2 + (1 - x_1)^2, \tag{2.6}$$

which has long been used as a simple test problem for non-linear optimisation algorithms. The routines are quasi-Newton (`quasinew`), conjugate gradients (`conjgrad`), scaled conjugate gradients (`scg`), and gradient descent (`graddesc`).

If the function demopt1 is called with no arguments, then optimisation starts from the traditional position $(-1, 1)$. Alternatively, a vector of length 2 may be used to define a different starting position. The following call starts the optimisation algorithms from the point $(-2, 3)$.

```
demopt1([-2, 3])
```

Rosenbrock's function has a number of useful properties that make it suitable for this demonstration:

- The domain is $\mathbb{R}^2$, so it is possible to plot the set of search points and compare the paths taken by different algorithms.
- The global minimum of the function is at a known position: $(1, 1)$.
- It is a quartic function of the input variables, so the assumption of many optimisation algorithms that the function is quadratic near a minimum does not hold exactly.
- The steepest path from the traditional starting position to the minimum follows a curved path in search space. This tests both the choice of search direction, and the line minimisation algorithm used.

The value of Rosenbrock's function is calculated by the NETLAB function rosen (the function rose is built in to MATLAB), while its gradient is calculated by rosegrad.

```
 1  function demopt1(xinit)
 2
 3  if nargin < 1 | size(xinit) ~= [1 2]
 4    xinit = [-1 1];        % Traditional start point
 5  end
 6
 7  options = foptions;      % Standard options
 8  options(1) = -1;         % Turn off printing completely
 9  options(3) = 1e-8;       % Tolerance in value of function
10  options(14) = 100;       % Max. 100 iterations of algorithm
11
12  a = -1.5:.02:1.5;
13  b = -0.5:.02:2.1;
14  [A, B] = meshgrid(a, b);
15  Z = rosen([A(:), B(:)]);
16  Z = reshape(Z, length(b), length(a));
17  l = -1:6;
18  v = 2.^l;
19  fh1 = figure;
20  contour(a, b, Z, v)
21
22  x = xinit;
23  flops(0)
24  [x, options, errlog, pointlog] = ...
25    quasinew('rosen', x, options, 'rosegrad');
26  opt_flops = flops;
27
28  x = xinit;
29  flops(0)
```

```
30  [x, options, errlog2, pointlog2] = ...
31    conjgrad('rosen', x, options, 'rosegrad');
32  opt_flops = flops;
33
34  x = xinit;
35  flops(0)
36  [x, options, errlog3, pointlog3] = ...
37    scg('rosen', x, options, 'rosegrad');
38  opt_flops = flops;
39
40  x = xinit;
41  options(7) = 1; % Line minimisation used
42  flops(0)
43  [x, options, errlog4, pointlog4] = ...
44    graddesc('rosen', x, options, 'rosegrad');
45  opt_flops = flops;
46
47  plot(pointlog4(:,1), pointlog4(:,2), 'bd', 'MarkerSize', 6)
48  plot(pointlog3(:,1), pointlog3(:,2), 'mx', 'MarkerSize', 6)
49  plot(pointlog(:,1), pointlog(:,2), 'k.', 'MarkerSize', 18)
50  plot(pointlog2(:,1), pointlog2(:,2), 'g+', 'MarkerSize', 6)
51  lh = legend('Gradient Descent', 'Scaled Conjugate Gradients', ...
52    'Quasi Newton', 'Conjugate Gradients');
```

After setting the start point xinit (lines 3–5), the function then initialises the options vector that is used for all four algorithms in lines 7–10. The changes made to the standard options vector ensure that each algorithm runs silently (even without warning messages), that the termination criterion for the change in function value between cycles is 1×10^{-8} and the change in input vector is 1×10^{-4}. In addition, each algorithm is run for at most 100 cycles.

The next block of code (lines 12–20) displays a contour plot of Rosenbrock's function with the contours set at levels 2^l for $l = -1, 0, \ldots, 6$. The x and y ranges of the plot are contained in the vectors a and b respectively. Each of the four algorithms is run from the same starting position as in lines 22–26.

There are two principal machine-independent measures that can be used to compare the efficiency of the optimisation algorithms: the number of floating point operations (*flops*) used to find the minimum, and the number of function and gradient evaluations required. On simple optimisation problems, such as this one, the evaluation of the function and its gradient is cheap, and so for two algorithms that take a comparable number of cycles to find the minimum, the number of floating point operations is dominated by the overhead of computing the search direction. However, for training most neural networks and similar models, the computation of the error involves a pass through a dataset that may contain many thousand examples. For such applications, the efficiency will be dominated by this task and the overheads of the optimisation algorithm will be negligible.

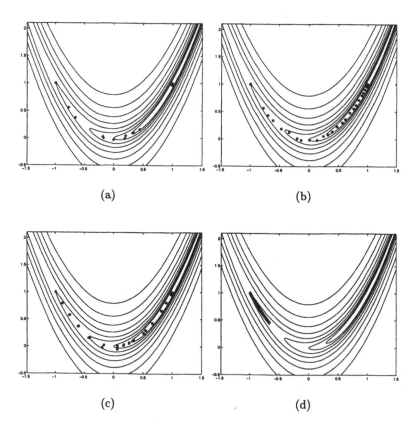

Fig. 2.1. Search paths of optimisation algorithms applied to Rosenbrock's function with a maximum of 100 iterations starting from $(-1, 1)$. Minimum at $(1, 1)$. (a) quasi-Newton (29 iterations); (b) conjugate gradients (15 iterations); (c) scaled conjugate gradients (44 iterations); (d) gradient descent (100 iterations).

The final section of code (lines 47–52) superimposes the search path of each algorithm on the original contour plot. From Fig. 2.1 we can see that the quasi-Newton, conjugate gradient and scaled conjugate gradient algorithms all follow the curved path to the minimum reasonably well, while the gradient descent algorithm descends this path very slowly and has not moved even a quarter of the distance within the full 100 iterations. The reasons for this will be discussed further in Section 2.4.

2.2 Quadratic Approximation at a Minimum

Most non-linear optimisation algorithms make use of a local quadratic approximation to a function near a minimum. The usual second-order multivariate Taylor series expansion around a point x_m gives

$$f(x) \approx f(x_m) + (x - x_m)^T g + \frac{1}{2}(x - x_m)^T H (x - x_m), \qquad (2.7)$$

where g is the gradient of f evaluated at x_m and H is defined to be the Hessian matrix evaluated at x_m

$$(H)_{ij} \equiv \left. \frac{\partial f}{\partial x_i \partial x_j} \right|_{x_m}. \qquad (2.8)$$

If x_m is a minimum of f, then the gradient of f at x_m is zero, and (2.7) reduces to

$$f(x) \approx f(x_m) + \frac{1}{2}(x - x_m) H (x - x_m). \qquad (2.9)$$

Note that H is positive semi-definite at a minimum (i.e. all eigenvalues are non-negative). This is illustrated by Fig. 2.2 for the one-dimensional case.

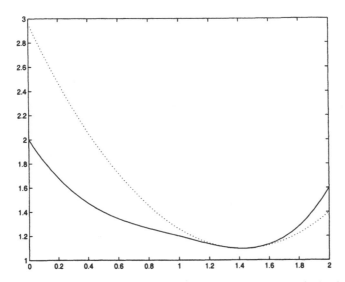

Fig. 2.2. Quadratic approximation near a minimum. Function (*solid line*) with minimum at 1.4 is approximated by a parabola (*dotted line*).

In multi-dimensional search spaces, optimisation methods that do use derivative information explore the geometry of the function more effectively than those which don't. From a given point, there are infinitely many directions to search in: a single dot product $(\nabla f)^T v$ determines whether moving in the direction $v \in \mathbb{R}^n$ is uphill or downhill. This dot product involves just $O(n)$ operations. In one dimension, there are just two directions to move in, so evaluating f at a test point is nearly as good as evaluating f'.

2.3 Line Search

Line search is the process of minimising a function in a given direction d. By writing

$$\tilde{f}(\alpha) = f(x + \alpha d), \tag{2.10}$$

where x is the starting point of the search, we can see that this is equivalent to minimising a one-dimensional function $\tilde{f}(\alpha)$. There are three issues to consider: what precision it is reasonable to try to achieve; how to find the minimum; and how to initialise the algorithm by *bracketing* the minimum. The functions described in this section are rarely called directly by a NETLAB user; instead they form a component of the multivariate optimisation algorithms discussed later in the chapter.

2.3.1 Precision

A *bracketing interval* is a triple $a < b < c$ such that

$$f(b) < f(a) \qquad \text{and} \qquad f(b) < f(c). \tag{2.11}$$

If f is continuous, then it is guaranteed that a minimum lies in the interval $[a, c]$. This is the equivalent of a bracket $[a, b]$ with $f(a)f(b) < 0$ used when finding a zero.

Before trying to find a minimum to high precision, it is worth considering the form of f near to a minimum at a point b. Simplifying (2.9) to the one-dimensional case by using $H = f''(b)$, we obtain

$$f(x) \approx f(b) + \frac{(x-b)^2}{2} f''(b), \tag{2.12}$$

where $f''(b) \geq 0$ at a minimum. If ϵ denotes machine precision, then $f(x) \approx f(b)$ if

$$\frac{(x-b)^2}{2} f''(b) \leq \epsilon |f(b)| \tag{2.13}$$

$$\Longleftrightarrow |x - b| \leq \sqrt{\frac{2\epsilon |f(b)|}{|f''(b)|}} = b\sqrt{\epsilon} \sqrt{\frac{2|f(b)|}{b^2 |f''(b)|}}. \tag{2.14}$$

The term

$$\sqrt{\frac{2|f(b)|}{b^2|f''(b)|}} \tag{2.15}$$

is known as the *curvature scale* of the function f, and is about $O(1)$ for polynomial functions. Hence we conclude that the smallest reasonable fractional width of the bracketing interval is about $\sqrt{\epsilon}$, and that there is little point in trying to locate minima to greater precision than this. For the double precision arithmetic used in MATLAB, $\sqrt{\epsilon}$ is about $1 \cdot 5 \times 10^{-8}$. In fact, depending on the particular multivariate optimisation algorithm used, it may not be necessary to find the line minimum to such a high degree of precision. For some algorithms, more time is spent in line searches than in computing search directions.

2.3.2 Line Minimisation Algorithms

The techniques used for one-dimensional minimisation can be divided into *dissection* methods and *fitted polynomial methods* (e.g. quadratic interpolation).

Dissection methods successively sub-divide the bracket into smaller intervals. Golden section search chooses the new trial point $x \in (a, c)$ so as to ensure that the new bracket is as narrow as possible. If $b - a < c - b$, then x is chosen so that

$$\frac{(x - b)}{(c - b)} = \phi = \frac{3 - \sqrt{5}}{2} \tag{2.16}$$

where ϕ is the so-called *golden ratio*. If $x > b$ then the new bracket is (a, x) if $f(x) > f(b)$ and is (b, c) if $f(x) < f(b)$. A similar choice is made if $x < b$. This algorithm is very robust, since no assumption is made about the function being minimised, other than continuity.

By assuming a little more, we can derive a more efficient algorithm. Near a minimum, (2.12) shows that f is approximately quadratic. Therefore, given a bracketing triplet $\{a, b, c\}$, we can *interpolate* a parabola through the points $(a, f(a))$, $(b, f(b))$ and $(c, f(c))$, and use the minimum of the parabola as the next search point x:

$$x = b - \frac{1}{2} \frac{(b - a)^2 [f(b) - f(c)] - (b - c)^2 [f(b) - f(a)]}{(b - a) [f(b) - f(c)] - (b - c) [f(b) - f(a)]}. \tag{2.17}$$

This algorithm cannot be used as it stands, since there is no guarantee that x lies inside the bracketing triplet. Furthermore, if b is already at or near the minimum of the interpolating parabola, then the new point x is close to b (see Fig. 2.3). This causes slow convergence if b is not close to the local

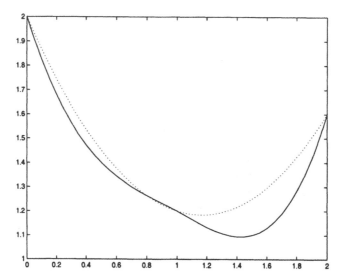

Fig. 2.3. Quadratic interpolation through bracketing triple (0, 1, 2). Parabola (*dotted line*) minimum is at 1 but function (*solid line*) minimum is at 1.4.

minimum of f. By contrast, the rate of convergence of the golden section algorithm is guaranteed over the whole range of x.

This suggests using a *hybrid* algorithm which combines the best features of both methods. The linemin function in NETLAB uses a robust combination of the two approaches in Brent's algorithm (Brent, 1973; Press *et al.*, 1992). This algorithm uses only the function and not its gradient. This means that it does not always converge as quickly as other algorithms available, but it does have a more dependable rate of convergence. The calling syntax is

```
[x, options] = linemin(f, pt, dir, fpt, options, varargin);
```

where f is the function to be minimised, pt is the start point for the search, dir is the direction in which the search is to be carried out, and fpt is the value of f at the start point. (fpt is included, since it is often already computed by the multivariate optimisation algorithms that call linemin and it is therefore more efficient not to recompute it.) Note that linemin assumes that dir is a downhill direction: i.e. that the gradient of f has a negative inner product with the vector dir. The return variable x is the multiple of dir to reach the local line minimum found by linemin (i.e. the value of α at the minimum of (2.10). The local minimum itself is at pt + x.*dir.

```
1   function [x, options] = linemin(f, pt, dir, fpt, options, ...
2           varargin)
3
4   if(options(14))
5     niters = options(14);
6   else
```

```
7    niters = 100;
8  end
9  options(10) = 0; % Initialise count of function evaluations
10 display = options(1);
11
12 f = fcnchk(f, length(varargin));
13
14 phi = 1.6180339887499;
15 cphi = 1 - 1/phi;
16 TOL = sqrt(eps);
17 TINY = 1.0e-10;
18
19 [br_min, br_mid, br_max, num_evals] = feval('minbrack', ...
20   'linef', 0.0, 1.0, fpt, f, pt, dir, varargin{:});
21 options(10) = options(10) + num_evals;
22
23 w = br_mid;      % Where second from minimum is
24 v = br_mid;      % Previous value of w
25 x = v;           % Where current minimum is
26 e = 0.0;         % Distance moved on step before last
27 fx = feval('linef', x, f, pt, dir, varargin{:});
28 options(10) = options(10) + 1;
29 fv = fx; fw = fx;
30
31 for n = 1:niters
32   xm = 0.5.*(br_min+br_max); % Middle of bracket
33   % Make sure that tolerance is big enough
34   tol1 = TOL * (max(abs(x))) + TINY;
35   if (max(abs(x - xm)) <= options(2) & ...
36       br_max-br_min < 4*options(2))
37     options(8) = fx;
38     return;
39   end
40
41   if (max(abs(e)) > tol1)
42     % Construct a trial parabolic fit through x, v and w
43     r = (fx - fw) .* (x - v);
44     q = (fx - fv) .* (x - v);
45     p = (x - v).*q - (x - w).*r;
46     q = 2.0 .* (q - r);
47     if (q > 0.0) p = -p; end
48     q = abs(q);
49     % Test if the parabolic fit is OK
50     if (abs(p) >= abs(0.5*q*e) | p <= q*(br_min-x) | ...
51         p >= q*(br_max-x))
52       if (x >= xm)
53         e = br_min-x;
54       else
55         e = br_max-x;
56       end
57       d = cphi*e;  % Golden section
58     else
59       % Take the parabolic step
```

```
60        e = d; d = p/q; u = x+d;
61        if (u-br_min < 2*tol1 | br_max-u < 2*tol1)
62          d = sign(xm-x)*tol1;
63        end
64      end
65    else
66      % Step before last not big enough, so do golden section step
67      if (x >= xm)
68        e = br_min - x;
69      else
70        e = br_max - x;
71      end
72      d = cphi*e;
73    end
74    % Make sure that step is big enough
75    if (abs(d) >= tol1)
76      u = x+d;
77    else
78      u = x + sign(d)*tol1;
79    end
80    % Evaluate function at u
81    fu = feval('linef', u, f, pt, dir, varargin{:});
82    options(10) = options(10) + 1;
83    % Reorganise bracket
84    if (fu <= fx)
85      if (u >= x)
86        br_min = x;
87      else
88        br_max = x;
89      end
90      v = w; w = x; x = u;
91      fv = fw; fw = fv; fx = fu;
92    else
93      if (u < x)
94        br_min = u;
95      else
96        br_max = u;
97      end
98      if (fu <= fw | w == x)
99        v = w; w = u;
100       fv = fw; fw = fu;
101     elseif (fu <= fv | v == x | v == w)
102       v = u;
103       fv = fu;
104     end
105   end
106   if (display == 1)
107     fprintf(1, 'Cycle %4d  Error %11.6f\n', n, fx);
108   end
109 end
110 options(8) = fx;
```

The first block of code (lines 4–8) ensures that the `options` vector is correctly treated. The argument `f` is then processed using the built-in MATLAB function `fcnchk` in line 12 so that string expressions and M-files are treated consistently.

Local variables representing numeric constants are initialised in lines 14–17. The value `TOL` is the maximum fractional precision in the search and is set to `sqrt(eps)` for the reasons discussed in Section 2.3.1. Relative precision cannot be used if the minimum is at, or very close to, zero. So the implementation ensures that the absolute precision for the line search is greater than the variable `TINY`.

The first step of line minimisation is to find a bracketing triple; the NETLAB function `minbrack` is discussed further in Section 2.3.3. Because of our assumption that `dir` is downhill, we know that a local minimum can be found in the direction of the vector `dir`. Both `linemin` and `minbrack` are written for functions of a single variable. In general, the argument `f` may be a function of many variables. To convert it to a one-dimensional function evaluated along a line, the NETLAB function `linef` is used. The key line of code in this function is

```
y = feval(fn, x+lambda.*d, varargin{:});
```

where the function f is evaluated (using the MATLAB function `feval`) at the point $x + \lambda d$ so that the line passes through x in direction d. The count of the number of function evaluations in `options(10)` is incremented by the total used in bracketing (line 21).

Brent's algorithm involves tracking six points, and the details of the manipulation of these points in the implementation makes the algorithm seem more complicated than is actually the case (Press *et al.*, 1992). These points are: `br_min` and `br_max`, which bracket the minimum; `x`, which is the current minimum; `w` and `v`, which are the point with the second least function value and the previous value of `w` respectively, and `u`, which is the point at which the function was evaluated most recently.

A parabolic interpolation step through the points `x`, `v` and `w` (2.17) is attempted in lines 41–48 provided `e`, the size of the step before last was sufficiently large, otherwise a golden section step is taken (65–73). The choice of the step before last, rather than the last step is entirely heuristic. The size of the step is given by `p/q`. The step is accepted (lines 50–51) if both

1. The step is no more than half `e`. This condition is inserted to ensure that the parabolic interpolation steps are becoming smaller. This is a necessary condition to ensure that the steps are actually converging.
2. The step remains within the bracket (`br_min`, `br_max`).

If the parabolic step is not acceptable, then a golden section step is taken instead (lines 52–57). In either case, the size of the step `d` must be sufficiently large; this is tested in lines 75–79. The rest of the function ensures that all the variables are correctly updated.

2.3.3 Bracketing the Minimum

Minimum bracketing is an essential prerequisite to line search. We are looking for the smallest possible bracket, so as to speed up the following search, but we don't want to use too many function evaluations when finding it. The NETLAB implementation in minbrack is based on ideas in Press *et al.* (1992):

```
[br_min, br_mid, br_max, num_evals] = minbrack(f, a, b, fa, varargin)
```

where f is the one-dimensional function, and a < b are initial guesses at the bracketing points. We assume that the minimum of f is definitely achieved at a point greater than a: when this function is called by linemin this is justified as we know that the search direction is downhill. The variable fa is the value of f at a: this is computed anyway at a higher level by many of the optimisation algorithms, so it is more efficient not to recompute it.

```
1   function  [br_min, br_mid, br_max, num_evals] = minbrack(f, ...
2                                   a, b, fa, varargin)
3
4   f = fcnchk(f, length(varargin));
5
6   phi = 1.6180339887499;
7   num_evals = 0;
8   TINY = 1.e-10;
9   max_step = 10.0;
10
11  fb = feval(f, b, varargin{:});
12  num_evals = num_evals + 1;
13
14  if (fb > fa)
15    c = b;
16    b = a + (c-a)/phi;
17    fb = feval(f, b, varargin{:});
18    num_evals = num_evals + 1;
19    while (fb > fa)
20      c = b;
21      b = a + (c-a)/phi;
22      fb = feval(f, b, varargin{:});
23      num_evals = num_evals + 1;
24    end
25  else
26    c = b + phi*(b-a);
27    fc = feval(f, c, varargin{:});
28    num_evals = num_evals + 1;
29    bracket_found = 0;
30
31    while (fb > fc)
32      r = (b-a).*(fb-fc);
33      q = (b-c).*(fb-fa);
34      u = b - ((b-c)*q - (b-a)*r)/ ...
35        (2.0*(sign(q-r)*max([abs(q-r), TINY])));
36      ulimit = b + max_step*(c-b);
37
```

```
38      if ((b-u)'*(u-c) > 0.0)
39        % Interpolant lies between b and c
40        fu = feval(f, u, varargin{:});
41        num_evals = num_evals + 1;
42        if (fu < fc)
43          % Have a minimum between b and c
44          br_min = b;  br_mid = u; br_max = c;
45          return;
46        elseif (fu > fb)
47          % Have a minimum between a and u
48          br_min = a; br_mid = c; br_max = u;
49          return;
50        end
51        u = c + phi*(c-b);
52      elseif ((c-u)'*(u-ulimit) > 0.0)
53        % Interpolant lies between c and limit
54        fu = feval(f, u, varargin{:});
55        num_evals = num_evals + 1;
56        if (fu < fc)
57          b = c; c = u; u = c + phi*(c-b);
58        else
59          bracket_found = 1;
60        end
61      elseif ((u-ulimit)'*(ulimit-c) >= 0.0)
62        % Limit parabolic u to maximum value
63        u = ulimit;
64      else
65        % Reject parabolic u and use golden section step
66        u = c + phi*(c-b);
67      end
68      if ~bracket_found
69        fu = feval(f, u, varargin{:});
70        num_evals = num_evals + 1;
71      end
72      a = b; b = c; c = u;
73      fa = fb; fb = fc; fc = fu;
74    end % while loop
75  end    % bracket found
76  br_mid = b;
77  if (a < c)
78    br_min = a; br_max = c;
79  else
80    br_min = c; br_max = a;
81  end
```

There are two cases treated by the algorithm:

1. $f(b) > f(a)$. Since the minimum is known to be greater than a, this implies that there must be a minimum between b and a, and a fortiori a bracket inside the interval $[a, b]$. We simply perform a golden section search within (a, b), keeping a fixed, until we find points b and c such that $a < b < c$ is a bracket. At each step of the process, $b \leq c$. If $f(b) > f(a)$,

we set $c = b$ and continue. Otherwise, the three points must form a bracket. This is implemented in lines 14–24.

2. $f(b) \leq f(a)$. This means that the third point of the bracket can be chosen to be greater than b. So we are searching for a point c such that $c > b$ and $f(c) > f(b)$ to complete the triplet. As an initial guess for c we take a golden section step outside the interval (a, b) in lines 26–27. If $f(c) > f(b)$, then we are done. Otherwise, we generate a test point u at the minimum of the parabola through a, b and c (lines 32–36). If u lies between b and c (lines 38–50) or if u lies beyond c but not beyond ulimit (lines 52–60), then it is possible that computing the function value at u will enable us to find a bracket. If a bracket is not found, then u is replaced by a golden section jump (line 51 or 57).

If we don't find a bracket, or if u is greater than ulimit then we replace u by a golden section extrapolation outside c (line 66). This is undesirable, since it increases the width of the initial bracket, so it is only done as a last resort. At the next iteration the triplet $(1, b, c)$ is replaced by (b, c, u) (lines 72–73).

2.4 Batch Gradient Descent

All of the multivariate optimisation techniques that we consider are iterative, i.e. we proceed towards the minimum x^* by a sequence of steps. On the jth step we take a step of length α_j in the direction d_j,

$$x_{j+1} = x_j + \alpha_j d_j. \tag{2.18}$$

Perhaps the simplest choice for d_j is to set it equal to $-g_j$, i.e. to go down the *steepest* downhill direction available at x_j. This is the approach taken by *gradient descent* algorithms (also known as *steepest descent*).

Using gradient descent guarantees that $f(x_{j+1}) < f(x_j)$, as long as the parameter α_j (called the *learning rate*) is chosen to be small enough. To see this, expand f around x_j using Taylor's theorem:

$$f(x_j + \alpha_j d_j) \simeq f(x_j) + \alpha_j g^T d_j. \tag{2.19}$$

With $d_j = -g_j$, this guarantees a reduction in f for small enough α_j. The tradeoff is that we need α_j to be small enough to ensure descent, but large enough to limit the number of steps needed to reach the minimum.

The NETLAB function graddesc implements a batch gradient descent algorithm. Gradient descent is typically very slow to converge. The reason for this is precisely that it always goes down the local gradient, and if the curvature of f (given by the Hessian) varies significantly with direction, then this gradient will not, in general, point towards the minimum. Even if the learning rate α is chosen to be small enough, successive steps tend to oscillate across 'valleys' in the function f. This tendency is reduced to some extent by including a *momentum* term (Bishop, 1995, Section 7.5.2). The modified formula is given by:

$$x_{j+1} = x_j - \alpha_j g_j + \mu \Delta x_{j-1}, \qquad (2.20)$$

where Δx_{j-1} is the change in x at the *previous* iteration. The value of μ should always be in the range $0 \le \mu \le 1$. The learning rate and momentum are passed to graddesc as options(18) and options(17) respectively. The following lines of code from graddesc implement the algorithm. Note that grad is the gradient, mu the momentum and eta the learning rate.

```
1    dx = mu*dxold - eta*grad;
2    x =  x + dx;
3    dxold = dx;
4    if fcneval
5       fold = fnew;
6       fnew = feval(f, x, varargin{:});
7       options(10) = options(10) + 1;
8    end
```

The variable dx represents the change in parameter space: the first line of this code fragment represents (2.20). The second line of code modifies the parameter vector x and the third line saves the change in dxold so that it can be used in the momentum term. The remainder of the fragment evaluates the function at the new point x: this is only done if it is necessary to test for termination or for storing the values.

It is possible to achieve a larger reduction in f at each step by carrying out a *line search* along the direction d_j to determine a local minimum instead of using a pre-determined learning rate α_j. We wish to find a step size α_j^* so that

$$\frac{\partial}{\partial \alpha_j} f(x_j + \alpha_j d_j) = 0 \qquad \text{at } \alpha_j = \alpha_j^*. \qquad (2.21)$$

By the chain rule, this implies that, if $g_{j+1} = \nabla f(x_{j+1})$, where $x_{j+1} = x_j + \alpha_j^* d_j$,

$$g_{j+1}^T d_j = 0. \qquad (2.22)$$

This implies that the new gradient vector g_{j+1}^T is orthogonal to the old search direction d_j. Thus each step is taken in a direction orthogonal to the previous one, and so this algorithm follows a characteristic zig-zag path. If the curvature of f is not spherical, there is no reason why taking orthogonal steps should yield fast convergence. This algorithm is implemented with the following code fragment taken from graddesc:

```
1  sd = - grad./norm(grad);    % New search direction.
2  fold = fnew;
3  [lmin, line_options] = feval('linemin', f, x, sd, fold, ...
```

```
4      line_options, varargin{:});
5   options(10) = options(10) + line_options(10);
6   x = xold + lmin*sd;
7   fnew = line_options(8);
```

In line 1 of the fragment, the search direction sd is normalised to have length 1. This is so that the bracketing function minbrack used by the line minimisation procedure can start with a sensible first guess. The line_options vector is used to pass the user-determined parameters to linemin. It is set, earlier in graddesc, to be the default set of option values. If other values are required, this line should be modified. Line 5 uses the return values from linemin to update the number of function evaluations in line_options(10). Line 6 updates the current point.

One further drawback of all gradient descent methods is that their behaviour is entirely dependent on the scaling of the variables. If we rescale each x-coordinate by a different amount, so that $X_i = \lambda_i x_i$, then

$$\frac{\partial f}{\partial X_i} = \frac{1}{\lambda_i}\frac{\partial f}{\partial x_i}, \tag{2.23}$$

and thus the direction of g can be altered arbitrarily by changing λ. As there is no obvious way of choosing λ *a priori*, the method is basically unsatisfactory. It is included in NETLAB for purposes of comparison and for historical reasons, rather than for serious use. Practical training of neural networks is nearly always much more efficient using the methods discussed in Sections 2.5, 2.6 and 2.7. There is also an *on-line* version of gradient descent specific to neural networks that is discussed in Section 2.8.2.

2.5 Conjugate Gradients

In Section 2.4 we showed that after a line minimisation, the new gradient is orthogonal to the line search direction (2.22). So, in steepest descent, search directions will always be orthogonal. One solution to this problem is to choose the next search direction so that we do not 'spoil' the minimisation that we have just carried out. If d_j represents the new direction, we want

$$\left[\frac{\partial}{\partial\alpha}\left(\nabla f(x_j + \alpha d_j)\right)\right]^T d_{j-1} = 0. \tag{2.24}$$

Using a second-order Taylor series expansion of f around x_j, we have, for $x = x_j + \alpha d_j$ and the Hessian matrix $H = \nabla\nabla f|_{x_j}$,

$$f(x) \approx f(x_j) + \nabla f(x_j)^T(x - x_j) + \frac{1}{2}(x - x_j)^T H(x - x_j)$$

$$= f(x_j) + \alpha\nabla f(x_j)^T d_j + \frac{\alpha^2}{2}d_j^T H d_j. \tag{2.25}$$

Similarly, expanding ∇f to first order around x_j,

$$\nabla f(x) = \nabla f(x_j) + H(x - x_j) \tag{2.26}$$

$$= \nabla f(x_j) + \alpha H d_j. \tag{2.27}$$

From this we conclude that

$$\frac{\partial}{\partial \alpha}(\nabla f(x)) = H d_j, \tag{2.28}$$

so for this to be perpendicular to d_{j-1} we require

$$d_j^T H d_{j-1} = 0. \tag{2.29}$$

We say that d_j is *conjugate* to d_{j-1}. If f is quadratic, then this relation holds for arbitrary values of α, since the second-order Taylor series expansion is exact and H is constant. Another way of viewing conjugacy is that we want the search directions to be orthogonal not with respect to the usual Euclidean inner product, but with respect to the inner product defined by the curvature of the function at the minimum. In this light, the requirement for conjugacy seems natural.

Because H is a symmetric matrix, in $\mathbb{R}^n$ we can always choose n mutually conjugate directions by selecting the eigenvectors of H. This is not a very efficient way of choosing conjugate directions, particularly if f is not quadratic and thus H depends on where it is evaluated, as then we would need to carry out a full eigen-decomposition of H at each step. The conjugate gradients algorithm is an iterative and efficient method for choosing successive mutually conjugate search directions.

Suppose that H is a symmetric positive-definite matrix. Define two sequences of vectors as follows:

1. $d_0 = g_0$ are any non-zero vectors.
2. At the jth step, set

$$g_{j+1} = g_j - \lambda_j H d_j \quad \text{and} \quad d_{j+1} = g_{j+1} + \gamma_j d_j$$

where λ_j and γ_j are chosen to make g_{j+1} and g_j orthogonal and d_{j+1} and d_j conjugate.

The Hestenes–Stiefel formula (Hestenes and Stiefel, 1952) defines

$$\lambda_j = \begin{cases} 0 & g_j^T H d_j = 0 \\ \frac{g_j^T g_j}{g_j^T H d_j} & \text{otherwise.} \end{cases} \tag{2.30}$$

$$\gamma_j = \begin{cases} 0 & d_j^T H d_j = 0 \\ \frac{-g_{j+1}^T H d_j}{d_j^T H d_j} & \text{otherwise.} \end{cases} \tag{2.31}$$

Then it can be shown that for $1 \leq i \neq j \leq n$

$$g_i^T g_j = 0, \qquad g_i^T d_j = 0, \quad \text{and} \quad d_i^T H d_j = 0, \tag{2.32}$$

so that the sequences of vectors g_i and d_i are pairwise orthogonal and conjugate respectively.

Once we know that equation (2.32) holds, we can obtain equivalent expressions for λ_j and γ_j, due to Polak (1971) and Ribiere:

$$\gamma_j = \frac{g_{j+1}^T g_{j+1}}{g_j^T g_j} = \frac{(g_{j+1} - g_j)^T g_{j+1}}{g_j^T g_j}, \tag{2.33}$$

and

$$\lambda_j = \frac{g_j^T d_j}{d_j^T H d_j}. \tag{2.34}$$

A third expression for γ_j is the Fletcher-Reeves formula

$$\gamma_j = \frac{g_{j+1}^T g_{j+1}}{g_j^T g_j}. \tag{2.35}$$

Using the vectors d_j as directions, with n line minimisations in exact arithmetic we reach the (global) minimum of a quadratic function f with Hessian H. However, in general, the Hessian is not constant and is expensive to compute. Fortunately, a remarkable result comes to our aid.

Theorem 2.5.1 *Let f be quadratic, and suppose that $g_j = -\nabla f(x_j)$. Let x_{j+1} be a local minimum of f along the line through x_j in the direction d_j, so that $x_{j+1} = x_j + \alpha^* d_j$. Then $g_{j+1} = -\nabla f(x_{j+1})$, where g_{j+1} is the vector computed at the kth step of the conjugate gradient algorithm.*

This theorem shows that by minimising exactly along the line, we do not need to know the Hessian to compute λ_j: we just set the new vector g_{j+1} equal to the negative gradient. (In addition, to start the induction, we must choose g_1 and h_1 to be the negative gradient at the starting point.)

All the expressions discussed in this section are equivalent for quadratic functions. If the function f is not quadratic, then n successive minimisations may not reach a local minimum. In such cases, it is common to restart the algorithm with the negative gradient evaluated at the last point reached. There is evidence that the Polak–Ribiere form of the algorithm (2.33) is more effective in such cases. If not much progress is being made, then g_j is approximately equal to g_{j+1} and hence γ_j is approximately zero. This means that d_{j+1} is set to point down the local gradient g_{j+1}, which is equivalent to starting the algorithm afresh.

This algorithm is implemented by the NETLAB function conjgrad, the key parts of which are shown below.

```
1  function [x, options, flog, pointlog] = conjgrad(f, x, ...
2                          options, gradf, varargin)
3
4  % Set up options for line search
5  line_options = foptions;
6  % Need a precise line search for success
7  if options(15) > 0
8    line_options(2) = options(15);
9  else
10   line_options(2) = 1e-4;
11 end
12 display = options(1);
13
14 nparams = length(x);
15 fnew = feval(f, x, varargin{:});
16 gradnew = feval(gradf, x, varargin{:});
17 d = -gradnew;           % Initial search direction
18 br_min = 0;
19 br_max = 1.0;   % Initial bracket length
20 tol = sqrt(eps);
21
22 while (j <= niters)
23
24   xold = x;
25   fold = fnew;
26   gradold = gradnew;
27
28   gg = gradold*gradold';
29   if (gg == 0.0)
30     options(8) = fnew;
31     return;
32   end
33
34   if (gradnew*d' > 0)
35     d = -d;
36     if options(1) >= 0
37       fprintf(1, ...
38           'Warning: search direction uphill in conjgrad\n');
39     end
40   end
41
42   line_sd = d./norm(d);
43   [lmin, line_options] = feval('linemin', f, xold, ...
44     line_sd, fold, line_options, varargin{:});
45   x = xold + lmin * line_sd;
46   fnew = line_options(8);
47
48   % Check for termination
49   if (max(abs(x - xold)) < options(2) & ...
50       max(abs(fnew - fold)) < options(3))
51     options(8) = fnew;
52     return;
53   end
```

```
54
55    gradnew = feval(gradf, x, varargin{:});
56    % Use Polak-Ribiere formula to update search direction
57    gamma = ((gradnew - gradold)*(gradnew)')/gg;
58    d = (d .* gamma) - gradnew;
59  end
```

The main steps are:

1. Computation of the search direction. We first calculate the gradient at the new point (line 16 initially, line 56 in iterative loop). The variable gradold is the gradient at the previous search point. Line 30 checks that it is non-zero in order to prevent division by zero in the Polak–Ribiere formula (2.33), which is calculated in lines 69–70.

2. Line minimisation. Lines 36–40 check that the current search direction is downhill. On rare occasions, rounding error may cause the search direction to move the function uphill, and this can break the function linemin. The line minimisation takes place in lines 42–46. Note the normalisation of the search direction vector to unit length in line 42.

2.6 Scaled Conjugate Gradients

The conjugate gradients algorithm uses line search in a very clever way to avoid having to calculate the Hessian matrix. However, the line search typically involves several additional function evaluations per step. In addition, the precision of the line search becomes another parameter which can effect the convergence of the algorithm. Møller's scaled conjugate gradients algorithm (Møller, 1993) provides a way of choosing 'nearly' conjugate search directions without performing a line search or calculating the Hessian. Practical experiments have shown that it can be an extremely efficient algorithm, outperforming both conjugate gradients and quasi-Newton algorithms when the cost of function and gradient evaluation is relatively small.

Recall from equation (2.34) that

$$\lambda_j = \frac{g_j^T d_j}{d_j^T H d_j}, \tag{2.36}$$

and that this was the only term involving the Hessian H. This expression for λ_j is also the step size α_j such that $f(x_j + \alpha_j d_j)$ is a local minimum (along the line d_j), as was proved in Theorem 2.5.1. It turns that we can compute an approximation to Hd_j relatively cheaply using a finite difference formula and use this to compute λ_j without a line minimisation. Let σ_0 be a small positive quantity and write

$$\sigma = \frac{\sigma_0}{\|d_j\|}. \tag{2.37}$$

From (2.27) we have

$$\nabla f(x_j + \sigma d_j) \approx \nabla f(x_j) + \sigma H d_j, \tag{2.38}$$

and so

$$H d_j \approx \frac{\nabla f(x + \sigma d_j) - \nabla f(x_j)}{\sigma}. \tag{2.39}$$

We define

$$\theta_j = d_j^T \left(\frac{\nabla f(x + \sigma d_j) - \nabla f(x_j)}{\sigma} \right) \approx d_j^T H d_j. \tag{2.40}$$

However, if the function f is not a quadratic form, then H may not be positive definite, and in this case the parameter update formula (2.36) may *increase* the function value.

This can be overcome by adding a non-negative multiple β_j of the unit matrix to the Hessian: $H + \beta_j I$. This gives rise to a revised update formula:

$$\lambda_j = \frac{g_j^T d_j}{d_j^T H d_j + \beta_j \| d_j \|^2}. \tag{2.41}$$

Note that if β_j is large, then the step size λ_j is small. This is an example of a *model trust region* approach, because the model (for the function) is trusted in a small region around the current search point. Another term for this type of algorithm is a *restricted step method*: the step size is restricted by the region of validity of a Taylor series expansion.

From Theorem 2.5.1, we know that setting $\beta_j = 0$ moves us to a minimum provided that

1. the function is a quadratic form, and
2. the Hessian is positive definite (or at least $d_j^T H d_j > 0$).

Consider the second of these conditions. Let

$$\delta_j = d_j^T H d_j + \beta_j \| d_j \|^2 . \tag{2.42}$$

If $\delta_j < 0$, then $d_j^T H d_j$ must be negative, and we need to increase β_j. Møller's original algorithm uses

$$\bar{\beta}_j = 2 \left(\beta_j - \frac{\delta_j}{\| d_j \|^2} \right). \tag{2.43}$$

Then we set

$$\bar{\delta}_j = \delta_j + (\bar{\beta}_j - \beta_j) \| d_j \|^2$$

$$= -\delta_j + \beta_j \| d_j \|^2$$

$$= -d_j^T H d_j > 0. \tag{2.44}$$

An alternative procedure is to put

$$\bar{\delta}_j = \beta_j \parallel d_j \parallel^2, \tag{2.45}$$

when it follows that

$$\bar{\beta}_j = \beta_j - \frac{\theta}{\parallel d_j \parallel^2}, \tag{2.46}$$

and so

$$\bar{\delta}_j = \theta \bar{\beta}_j \parallel d_j \parallel^2 . \tag{2.47}$$

Now consider the first condition. Let

$$\Delta_j = \frac{f(x_j) - f(x_j + \alpha_j d_j)}{f(x_j) - f_Q(x_j + \alpha_j d_j)}, \tag{2.48}$$

where f_Q is the local quadratic approximation to f along d_j given by

$$f_Q(x_j + \alpha_j d_j) = f(x_j) + \alpha_j d_j^T g_j + \frac{\alpha_j^2}{2} d_j^T H d_j. \tag{2.49}$$

If $\Delta_j \approx 1$, this is a good approximation and β_j can be decreased. However, if Δ_j is small, then β_j needs to be increased. Simplifying equation (2.48), we obtain

$$\Delta_j = \frac{2(f(x_j) - f(x_j + \alpha_j d_j))}{\alpha_j d_j^T d_j}, \tag{2.50}$$

which can be calculated using only the gradient and no higher order derivatives. The definition of Δ_j being 'small' is essentially heuristic. Values that have proved successful are:

$$\begin{cases} \Delta_j > 0.75 & \beta_{j+1} = \beta_j/2 \\ 0.25 < \Delta_j < 0.75 & \beta_{j+1} = \beta_j \\ \Delta_j < 0.25 & \beta_{j+1} = 4\beta_j \\ \Delta_j < 0 & \beta_{j+1} = 4\beta_j \text{ and take no step.} \end{cases} \tag{2.51}$$

Although the parameters 0.25, 0.75, etc. are arbitrary, the algorithm is not overly sensitive to changes in them. The search direction d_j can be updated using any of the formulae discussed in Section 2.5. In the NETLAB implementation, the Polak–Ribiere formula is used. A slightly simplified listing of scg follows.

```
1  function [x, options, flog, pointlog, scalelog] = ...
2    scg(f, x, options, gradf, varargin)
3
4  display = options(1);
```

```
 5  nparams = length(x);
 6
 7  sigma0 = 1.0e-4;
 8  fold = feval(f, x, varargin{:});   % Initial point
 9  fnow = fold;
10  options(10) = options(10) + 1;
11  gradnew = feval(gradf, x, varargin{:}); % Initial gradient.
12  gradold = gradnew;
13  options(11) = options(11) + 1;
14  d = -gradnew;                      % Initial search direction.
15  success = 1;
16  nsuccess = 0;                      % Number of successes.
17  beta = 1.0;                        % Initial scale parameter.
18  betamin = 1.0e-15;                 % Lower bound on scale.
19  betamax = 1.0e100;                 % Upper bound on scale.
20  j = 1;
21
22  % Main optimisation loop.
23  while (j <= niters)
24    % Calculate first and second directional derivatives.
25    if (success == 1)
26      mu = d*gradnew';
27      if (mu >= 0)
28        d = - gradnew;
29        mu = d*gradnew';
30      end
31      kappa = d*d';
32      if kappa < eps
33        options(8) = fnow;
34        return
35      end
36      sigma = sigma0/sqrt(kappa);
37      xplus = x + sigma*d;
38      gplus = feval(gradf, xplus, varargin{:});
39      options(11) = options(11) + 1;
40      theta = (d*(gplus' - gradnew'))/sigma;
41    end
42
43    % Increase effective curvature and evaluate step size alpha.
44    delta = theta + beta*kappa;
45    if (delta <= 0)
46      delta = beta*kappa;
47      beta = beta - theta/kappa;
48    end
49    alpha = - mu/delta;
50
51    % Calculate the comparison ratio.
52    xnew = x + alpha*d;
53    fnew = feval(f, xnew, varargin{:});
54    options(10) = options(10) + 1;
55    Delta = 2*(fnew - fold)/(alpha*mu);
56    if (Delta  >= 0)
57      success = 1;
```

```
58      nsuccess = nsuccess + 1;
59      x = xnew;
60      fnow = fnew;
61    else
62      success = 0;
63      fnow = fold;
64    end
65
66    if (success == 1)
67      if (max(abs(alpha*d)) < options(2) & ...
68          max(abs(fnew-fold)) < options(3))
69        options(8) = fnew;
70        return;
71      else
72        % Update variables for new position
73        fold = fnew;
74        gradold = gradnew;
75        gradnew = feval(gradf, x, varargin{:});
76        options(11) = options(11) + 1;
77        % If the gradient is zero then we are done.
78        if (gradnew*gradnew' == 0)
79          options(8) = fnew;
80          return;
81        end
82      end
83    end
84
85    % Adjust beta according to comparison ratio.
86    if (Delta < 0.25)
87      beta = min(4.0*beta, betamax);
88    end
89    if (Delta > 0.75)
90      beta = max(0.5*beta, betamin);
91    end
92
93    % Update search direction
94    if (nsuccess == nparams)
95      d = -gradnew;
96      nsuccess = 0;
97    else
98      if (success == 1)
99        gamma = (gradold - gradnew)*gradnew'/(mu);
100       d = gamma*d - gradnew;
101     end
102   end
103   j = j + 1;
104 end
```

Most of the algorithm startup is the same as conjgrad. The main difference is the scale parameter β_j, which is initialised in line 17. Upper and lower bounds for it are defined in lines 18–19 to ensure that the trust region remains reasonable throughout.

The variable mu contains the value of $d_j^T g_j$ (line 26). The check in lines 27–30 ensures that the search direction is downhill. If the gradient is close to zero in magnitude then the algorithm terminates (lines 32–35). The small test magnitude σ is computed in line 36 according to (2.37), and θ is computed in line 40 following (2.40). Line 44 calculates δ_j (2.42); if it is non-positive (line 45) the value is adjusted in lines 46–47 (2.45). Line 49 computes $\alpha_j = \lambda_j$ and this is then used (lines 52–54) to generate xnew (which is x_{j+1}).

Equation (2.50) is used in line 55 to calculate the comparison ratio. This is used to decide whether to accept the test point (lines 56–64). If the test point is accepted, then the convergence criteria are tested (lines 67–70) and the function and gradient values are updated (lines 72–82). Lines 86–91 update β following (2.51). Finally, the the search direction d is updated:

1. The new negative gradient vector gradnew is used to restart the algorithm if there have been nparams steps taken (line 95).
2. Otherwise, the Polak–Ribiere formula (2.33) is used (lines 99–100).

2.7 Quasi-Newton Methods

The basic idea behind Newton's method can be glimpsed in our expression for ∇f (2.27),

$$\nabla f(x) = \nabla f(x_j) + H(x - x_j), \tag{2.52}$$

where H represents $H|_{x_j}$, the Hessian of f evaluated at x_j. This equation is exact if f is a quadratic form. If x is a minimum, then

$$\nabla f(x) = 0 \quad \Rightarrow \quad H(x - x_j) = -\nabla f(x_j), \tag{2.53}$$

i.e. if we solve this linear equation for x, knowing the gradient and Hessian of f at x_j then we can find the minimum of f. Hence

$$x = H^{-1}(Hx_j - \nabla f(x_j))$$

$$= x_j - H^{-1}\nabla f(x_j). \tag{2.54}$$

We call the vector $H^{-1}\nabla f(x_j)$ the *Newton direction*. If f is quadratic, then the gradient ∇f will only lie along the Newton direction if the vector joining x_j and the minimum of f is along an eigenvector of f. This is another explanation for the poor performance of gradient descent optimisation.

This method is attractive in principle, but there are some practical problems with applying it directly.

1. Evaluation of the Hessian can be very demanding computationally. Furthermore, if f is not a quadratic form, then the Hessian is no longer constant, and depends on the point where it is evaluated.

2. Inverting the Hessian is also computationally demanding, and can be difficult if the matrix is singular or nearly so. If f is nearly flat in several dimensions, then H is ill-conditioned.
3. This method is actually applying the Newton–Raphson root finding method to the derivative of f: i.e. we are finding zeros of ∇f, so it is possible to find the wrong sort of critical point.
4. If the step we take is large (i.e. if x is a long way from x_j), then the local quadratic approximation may break down.

An alternative is to set up the iteration

$$x_{j+1} = x_j - \alpha_j S_j g_j. \tag{2.55}$$

This is a very general algorithm; if $S_j = H^{-1}$ then we have Newton's method, while if $S_j = I$ we have steepest descent with learning rate α_j. Motivated by (2.54), we choose S_j to be an approximation to the inverse Hessian. It is important that S_j be positive definite so that for small α_j we obtain a descent method.

The idea behind quasi-Newton methods is to construct an approximation G_j to the inverse Hessian using information gathered as the algorithm progresses, and to set $S_j = G_j$. As we have seen (2.52), for a quadratic optimisation problem we have the relationship

$$g_j - g_{j-1} = H(x_j - x_{j-1}). \tag{2.56}$$

Defining

$$p_j = x_j - x_{j-1} \quad \text{and} \quad v_j = g_j - g_{j-1}, \tag{2.57}$$

we see that (2.56) can be written as

$$v_j = Hp_j. \tag{2.58}$$

It is reasonable to demand that

$$G_{j+1}v_i = p_i \quad 1 \le i \le j. \tag{2.59}$$

After n linearly independent steps we would then have $G_{n+1} = H^{-1}$. For $j < n$ there are infinitely many possibilities for G_{j+1} satisfying (2.59). We shall focus on one of the most popular, the Broyden–Fletcher–Goldfarb–Shanno (or BFGS) update (Press et al., 1992). This is given by

$$G_{j+1} = G_j + \frac{p_j p_j^T}{p_j^T v_j} - \frac{(G_j v_j)(v_j^T G_j)}{v_j^T G_j v_j} + (v_j^T G_j v_j)u_j u_j^T, \tag{2.60}$$

where

$$u_j = \frac{p_j}{p_j^T v_j} - \frac{G_j v_j}{v_j^T G_j v_j}. \tag{2.61}$$

Simplifying, (2.60) reduces to the following form

$$G_{j+1} = G_j + \left(1 + \frac{v_j^T G_j v_j}{v_j^T p_j}\right) \frac{p_j p_j^T}{p_j^T v_j} - \frac{p_j v_j^T G_j + G_j v_j p_j^T}{p_j^T v_j}. \qquad (2.62)$$

This is a rank-2 correction to G_j constructed from the vectors p_j and $G_j v_j$.

There are three important properties of the BFGS update. Although they require exact line minimisation to be used, in practice the precision of the line search does not have to be as great as for the conjugate gradients algorithm to achieve good results. If f is quadratic:

1. All the Gs are symmetric. This is clear immediately as $G_1 = I$ is symmetric, and each update is symmetric.
2. All the Gs are positive definite. This implies that $d_j = G_j g_j$ is a descent direction.
3. The direction vectors $d_1, d_2, \ldots, d_j$ produced by the algorithm obey

$$d_i^T H d_j = 0 \qquad 1 \le i < k \le j \qquad (2.63)$$

$$G_{j+1} H d_i = d_i \qquad 1 \le i \le j. \qquad (2.64)$$

The third property shows that the d_js are H-conjugate and, since we successively minimise f in these directions, we see that the BFGS algorithm is a conjugate direction method; in fact with the choice of $H_1 = I$ and exact line search it is equivalent the standard conjugate gradients method.

The BFGS update is only one out of a large range of updates that can be considered. An earlier one was the Davidon–Fletcher–Powell DFP formula update:

$$G_{j+1} = G_j + \frac{p_j p_j^T}{p_j^T v_j} - \frac{(G_j v_j)(v_j^T G_j)}{v_j^T G_j v_j}. \qquad (2.65)$$

However, this has some disadvantages in practice and so the BFGS update is implemented in NETLAB.

A full Newton step may take the search outside the region where the quadratic approximation near the minimum is valid or even increase the function value. The remedy is to find a new search point at which the value of f is sufficiently reduced, so that

$$y_{j+1} = y_j + \alpha_j G_j \nabla f \qquad (2.66)$$

under the condition that

$$f(y_{j+1}) < f(y_j) + \epsilon \alpha_j \nabla f(y_j)^T d_j, \qquad (2.67)$$

where ϵ is a small positive quantity. If (2.67) is not satisfied by the Newton step, then a line search (which is much more computationally costly) is carried out.

This method is relatively tolerant of moderate precision on line searches, which is an advantage compared to conjugate gradients. Against this, quasi-Newton methods explicitly model the inverse Hessian, which requires $O(n^2)$ storage, while the conjugate gradients algorithm requires only $O(n)$, where n is the number of parameters. Typically, quasi-Newton methods are preferred for problems of small or intermediate size, while if the number of variables is in the hundreds, conjugate gradients or scaled conjugate gradients are more practical.

```
1   function [x, options, flog, pointlog] = quasinew(f, x, ...
2                                    options, gradf, varargin)
3
4   % Set up options for line search
5   line_options = foptions;
6   % Don't need a very precise line search
7   if options(15) > 0
8     line_options(2) = options(15);
9   else
10    line_options(2) = 1e-2;  % Default
11  end
12  % Minimal fractional change in f from Newton step
13  min_frac_change = 1e-4;
14
15  nparams = length(x);
16  fnew = feval(f, x, varargin{:});
17  options(10) = options(10) + 1;
18  gradnew = feval(gradf, x, varargin{:});
19  options(11) = options(11) + 1;
20  p = -gradnew;            % Search direction
21  hessinv = eye(nparams); % Initialise inverse Hessian to identity
22  j = 1;
23
24  while (j <= niters)
25    xold = x;
26    fold = fnew;
27    gradold = gradnew;
28
29    x = xold + p;
30    fnew = feval(f, x, varargin{:});
31
32    if (gradnew*p' >= 0)
33      p = -p;
34      if options(1) >= 0
35        fprintf(1, ...
36          'Warning: search direction uphill in quasinew\n');
37      end
38    end
39
40    % Does the Newton step reduce the f sufficiently?
41    if (fnew >= fold + min_frac_change * (gradnew*p'))
42      % Minimise along current search direction
43      [lmin, line_options] = feval('linemin', f, xold, p, fold, ...
```

```
44        line_options, varargin{:});
45        % Correct x and fnew to actual search point
46        x = xold + lmin * p;
47        p = x - xold;
48        fnew = line_options(8);
49      end
50
51      % Check for termination
52      if (max(abs(x - xold)) < options(2) & ...
53          max(abs(fnew - fold)) < options(3))
54        options(8) = fnew;
55        return;
56      end
57      gradnew = feval(gradf, x, varargin{:});
58      v = gradnew - gradold;
59      vdotp = v*p';
60
61      % Skip update to hessinv if fac not sufficiently positive
62      if (vdotp*vdotp > eps*sum(v.^2)*sum(p.^2))
63        Gv = (hessinv*v')';
64        vGv = sum(v.*Gv);
65        u = p/vdotp - Gv/vGv;
66        % Use BFGS update rule
67        hessinv = hessinv + (p'*p)/vdotp - ...
68          (Gv'*Gv)/vGv + vGv*(u'*u);
69      end
70      p = -(hessinv * gradnew')';
71
72      j = j + 1;
73    end
```

The setup of the algorithm is similar to that in conjgrad, though the default line search precision (line 10) is much less restrictive. The variable min_frac_change takes the role of ϵ in (2.67). The variable p, initialised in line 20, is used in place of both p_j and d_j since these vectors are both in the same direction.

The new test point is computed in line 29. Equation (2.67) is then used in line 41 to decide whether a line search step (lines 42–48) is needed. Note how fnew is updated using the options vector returned from linemin to avoid an unnecessary function evaluation. After the usual termination test (lines 51–55), the inverse Hessian approximation hessinv is updated. The variable v_j is computed in line 58, following (2.57). The remaining variables have been named to correspond with the update formula (2.62) (implemented in lines 67–68); for example Gv represents $G_j v_j$. The test in line 62 ensures that the update only occurs if $v_j^T d_j$ is sufficiently large not to cause large rounding errors, since it appears in the denominator of two expressions.

2.8 Optimisation and Neural Networks

The general purpose optimisation algorithms discussed in the rest of this chapter cannot be used directly with neural networks. In Section 2.8.1 we show how to use NETLAB neural networks with any optimisation algorithm with the standard interface by means of the function netopt. In Section 2.8.2 we introduce the on-line gradient descent algorithm, which is specific to neural networks.

2.8.1 General Purpose Optimisation Algorithms

The reason that the NETLAB optimisation functions cannot be applied to neural networks is that the functions assume that the adjustable parameters are contained in a single vector, while the NETLAB data structures for neural networks generally store each layer of weights in separate matrices and distinguish between inter-layer connections and bias weights. For example, the data structure for the MLP contains the following weight fields:

```
w1        % first-layer weight matrix
b1        % first-layer bias vector
w2        % second-layer weight matrix
b2        % second-layer bias vector
```

To apply the optimisation algorithms to this data structure, a 'wrapper' function netopt is supplied. For example, the following code fragment uses the scaled conjugate gradient algorithm to train a multi-layer perceptron contained in the data structure mlpnet, with input data train_in and target data train_out and options vector options:

```
[mlpnet, options]=netopt(mlpnet, options, train_in, train_out, 'scg');
```

More examples of its use can be found in many of the demonstration programs.

The netopt function will work with any data structure provided that the following conditions are met.

- The data structure contains a field type that contains a string prefixed to all the functions described below. In the example above, this field has the value 'mlp'.
- The function that computes the objective, or error, function is called <type>err, for example mlperr. This function should have the signature

  ```
  e = <type>err(net, x, t)
  ```

  where x represents the data inputs and t the corresponding targets.
- The function that computes the gradient of the objective function should have the name <type>grad, for example mlpgrad. This function should have the signature

  ```
  g = <type>err(net, x, t)
  ```

- There is a function <type>pak, for example mlppak, that packs all the component weight matrices in the data structure into one single vector that can be manipulated by the optimisation algorithms. This function should have the calling syntax

```
w = <type>pak(net)
```

- There should be an inverse <type>unpak to the packing function, for example mlpunpak, that unpacks a single parameter vector into its component weight matrices in a network data structure. This function should have the signature

```
out_net = <type>unpak(in_net, w)
```

where w is the parameter vector to be unpacked and in_net is used to determine all the fields in out_net except for the weights.

- Note that netopt can be used with any MATLAB optimisation algorithm with the same interface as those in NETLAB: this includes the functions in the MATLAB optimisation toolbox.

- To use a network to make Bayesian predictions with the evidence procedure using the NETLAB function fevbayes, the output activation function should be a string contained in the field outfn (see Chapter 9).

The netopt function makes heavy use of the string handling and variable argument list features provided by MATLAB.

```
1  function [net, options, varargout] = netopt(net, options, ...
2                                               x, t, alg);
3
4  optstring = [alg, '(''neterr'', w, options, ''netgrad'', net, ...
5                                               x, t)'];
6  w = netpak(net);
7  % Carry out optimisation
8  [s{1:nargout}] = eval(optstring);
9  w = s{1};
10 if nargout > 1
11   options = s{2};
12   % If there are additional arguments, extract them
13   nextra = nargout - 2;
14   if nextra > 0
15     for i = 1:nextra
16       varargout{i} = s{i+2};
17     end
18   end
19 end
20 % Pack the weights back into the network
21 net = netunpak(net, w);
```

The string optstring is constructed so that the correct optimisation algorithm is run when it is evaluated in line 8. For example, if the scaled conjugate gradients algorithm is specified, optstring has the form

```
scg('neterr', w, options, 'netgrad', net, x, t)
```

Note that the objective function and gradient function have the fixed names
neterr and netgrad. Both of these functions work in the same way: they
unpack the current weight vector into the network data structure and call
the appropriate error (or gradient) function, all based on the network type.
The key lines from neterr are

```
unpakstr = [net.type, 'unpak'];
errstr = [net.type, 'err'];
net = feval(unpakstr, net, w);
[s{1:nargout}] = feval(errstr, net, x, t);
```

The weights to be used as adjustable parameters by the optimisation
algorithm are extracted in line 6. The cell array s is used to hold the result
of calling the optimisation function (line 8). The varargout cell array is used
to pass back any return values from netopt that the optimisation routine
generates in addition to the location of the minimum (always s{1}) and the
options vector (always s{2}). These additional return values are extracted
in lines 13–18. This allows netopt to be used with algorithms even if they
return different information. A similar use of varargout is made in neterr
and netgrad.

2.8.2 On-line Gradient Descent

This algorithm is not general purpose since it assumes that the function to
be minimised is the sum of contributions from a set of patterns $E = \sum_n E^n$.
On-line gradient descent is a sequential version of gradient descent where the
error function gradient g_τ^n is evaluated for a single pattern at a time:

$$w_{\tau+1} = w_\tau - \alpha_\tau g_\tau^n + \mu \Delta w_{\tau-1}. \tag{2.68}$$

The interface to the NETLAB function olgd has, therefore, the following form:

```
net = olgd(net, options, x, t)
```

where x is the set of input patterns and t is the set of corresponding target
vectors. Because MATLAB works much more efficiently with vectorised operations, on-line algorithms are not very efficient, and olgd has been included
mainly for teaching purposes. Although it is an on-line algorithm, the number of iterations (as determined by options(14)) refers to passes through
the complete pattern set.

There are two different ways of drawing samples from the pattern set.
The default is to present each pattern in order (line 42 below)

```
pnum = 1:ndata;
```

The alternative (which has a better theoretical justificiation) is to present
them in a random order with replacement, so that every pattern has a probability of 1/ndata of being presented at each step (line 40 below).

```
pnum = ceil(rand(ndata, 1).*ndata);
```

The second method is used if options(5) is set to 1. By the Robbins–Monro theorem (Bishop, 1995, Section 2.4.1), the algorithm is guaranteed to converge to a local minimum if the momentum is zero and the learning rate is decreased at each step of the algorithm. The law

$$\alpha_\tau \propto \frac{1}{\tau} \tag{2.69}$$

is adequate for the application of the Robbins–Monro theorem, although such a choice leads to very slow convergence. In practice, a fixed value of α is often used as this generally leads to faster convergence. The learning rate decrease is controlled by the options(6) flag. Figure 2.4 compares on-line

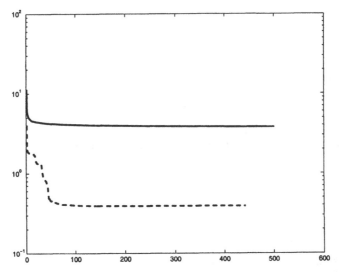

Fig. 2.4. Demonstration of on-line gradient descent. Learning curves for an MLP applied to a simple regression problem: on-line gradient descent (*solid line*) and scaled conjugate gradient (*dashed line*).

gradient descent with scaled conjugate gradient for training a neural network. Scaled conjugate gradient effectively converges after about 50 iterations, and to within machine precision after 443. On-line gradient descent is still in its initial plateau after 500 iterations and will clearly take several orders of magnitude longer than SCG to converge.

A potential advantage of sequential gradient descent is that, since it is a stochastic algorithm, there is the possibility that it may escape from local minima. However, given the orders of magnitude difference in training iterations, it is usually possible to use a deterministic algorithm from several initial parameter sets in a shorter time.

```
1   function [net, options, errlog, pointlog] = olgd(net, options, ...
2                                                 x, t)
3
4   % Learning rate: must be positive
5   if (options(18) > 0)
6     eta = options(18);
7   else
8     eta = 0.01;
9   end
10  % Save initial learning rate for annealing
11  lr = eta;
12  % Momentum term: allow zero momentum
13  if (options(17) >= 0)
14    mu = options(17);
15  else
16    mu = 0.5;
17  end
18
19  pakstr = [net.type, 'pak'];
20  unpakstr = [net.type, 'unpak'];
21  w = feval(pakstr, net);
22
23  fcneval = (display | options(3));
24
25  dwold = zeros(1, length(w));
26  fold = 0; % Must be initialised to perform termination test
27  ndata = size(x, 1);
28
29  if fcneval
30    fnew = neterr(w, net, x, t);
31    fold = fnew;
32  end
33
34  j = 1;
35  % Main optimisation loop.
36  while j <= niters
37    wold = w;
38    if options(5)
39      % Random order of patterns: with replacement
40      pnum = ceil(rand(ndata, 1).*ndata);
41    else
42      pnum = 1:ndata;
43    end
44    for k = 1:ndata
45      grad = netgrad(w, net, x(pnum(k),:), t(pnum(k),:));
46      if options(6)
47        % Let learning rate decrease as 1/t
48        lr = eta/((j-1)*ndata + k);
49      end
50      dw = mu*dwold - lr*grad;
51      w = w + dw;
52      dwold = dw;
53    end
```

```
54   if fcneval
55     fold = fnew;
56     fnew = neterr(w, net, x, t);
57   end
58   j = j + 1;
59   if (max(abs(w - wold)) < options(2) & ...
60       abs(fnew - fold) < options(3))
61     options(8) = fnew;
62     net = feval(unpakstr, net, w);
63     return;
64   end
65 end
66
67 if fcneval
68   options(8) = fnew;
69 else
70   % Return error on entire dataset
71   options(8) = neterr(w, net, x, t);
72   options(10) = options(10) + 1;
73 end
74
75 net = feval(unpakstr, net, w);
```

Because this algorithm uses the stochastic gradient, there is no need to calculate the error on the complete dataset to update the weights. Leaving aside the inefficiency in MATLAB of looping over the pattern set, calculating the pattern set error would roughly double the computational effort required for the algorithm, so it is done only if it must be either displayed or used in a termination criterion (line 23).

Line 45 computes g_τ^n and lines 50–51 evaluate (2.68). The learning rate update (2.69) is performed in line 48.

2.9 Worked Example: Constrained Optimisation

The methods treated so far have been concerned with minimising a function f either locally or globally in a Euclidean space $\mathbb{R}^n$. However, many practical optimisation problems place constraints on the search space. These can be of two types:

- Equality: $g(x) = 0$. These reduce the dimension of the search space.
- Inequality: $g(x) \leq 0$ or $g(x) < 0$. These reduce the 'volume' of the search space, but do not affect the dimension.

The area of search space where the constraints are satisfied is known as the *feasible region*. The unconstrained optimisation techniques described in this chapter cannot be applied directly to such problems. A relatively simple technique for tackling these problems (though it is not as reliable or as efficient as more advanced techniques: see Fletcher, 1987) is the *penalty function method*.

Suppose that we are minimising a function $f(x)$ subject to constraints $g_i(x) = 0$ or $g_i(x) \leq 0$ for $i = 1, \ldots, t$. We can construct a quadratic penalty function

$$P_Q(x, \rho) = f(x) + \frac{\rho}{2}\hat{g}(x)^T \hat{g}(x), \qquad (2.70)$$

where $\hat{g}$ contains *only* those constraints that are violated at x, and ρ is the *penalty parameter*.

The penalty term is continuously differentiable, but has discontinuous second derivatives where inequality constraints are exactly satisfied. A constrained minimum is likely to lie on the boundary of the feasible region (i.e. the region where the constraints are satisfied). This can potentially cause problems for optimisation algorithms that rely on second-order Taylor series expansions. To get round this problem we can consider the constraint $g_i(x) \leq 0$ to be violated only if $g_i(x) > -\epsilon$ for some small $\epsilon > 0$.

Under mild technical conditions, if $x^*(\rho)$ denotes an unconstrained minimum of P_Q (which may be found using one of the algorithms described in this chapter) and

$$x^* = \lim_{\rho \to \infty} x^*(\rho) \qquad (2.71)$$

then x^* is the constrained minimum of f. However, we cannot just choose a large value for ρ from the start. If the number of constraints is less than n, then the condition number of the Hessian at $x^*(\rho)$ becomes larger with increasing ρ. This is because the contours of P_Q become nearly parallel. Instead, it is more effective in practice to carry out several unconstrained minimisations for gradually increasing ρ, with each one starting at the point $x^*(\rho)$ where the previous one finished.

The effect of the penalty term is to create a local minimum near to x^* for sufficiently large ρ. For example, let $f(x) = x^3$ be minimised subject to the constraint $-(x + 1) \leq 0$. The true constrained minimum is at $x = -1$. The penalty function is

$$P_Q(x) = \begin{cases} x^3 & x \geq -1 \\ x^3 + \frac{\rho}{2}(x+1)^2 & x < -1. \end{cases} \qquad (2.72)$$

This is unbounded below for any ρ when $x \to -\infty$ and so an unconstrained minimisation algorithm may move outside the feasible region. For best results it is preferable to modify the algorithm to detect and, if possible, recover from unboundedness (though this is not done here). In addition, the starting point for search can be very important. In this example, there are three critical points: a point of inflexion at 0, a minimum at a point close to but less than -1, and a maximum at a point much less than -1. If the starting point is less than the maximum, then the minimisation algorithm is likely to head off to $-\infty$. This is illustrated in Fig. 2.5.

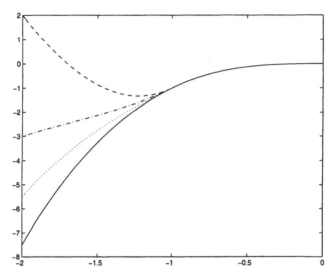

Fig. 2.5. Penalty function for different values of ρ. $\rho = 1$ (*solid line*), $\rho = 5$ (*dotted line*), $\rho = 10$ (*dash-dotted line*), $\rho = 20$ (*dashed line*).

In our simple implementation, we shall follow approximately the interface of the function `constr` in the MATLAB optimisation toolbox. We shall assume that the constraints are in the form $g(x) \le 0$. The user must write two M-files for any application. The M-file containing the function to be optimised should return two values: the objective function as a scalar, and the constraint values $g(x)$ as a row vector. The M-file containing the function gradient should return three values: the gradient of the objective function as a row vector, the gradient of the constraints as a matrix

$$\begin{bmatrix} \frac{\partial g_1}{\partial x_1} & \cdots & \frac{\partial g_c}{\partial x_1} \\ \cdots & \cdots & \cdots \\ \frac{\partial g_1}{\partial x_m} & \cdots & \frac{\partial g_c}{\partial x_m} \end{bmatrix} \tag{2.73}$$

and the constraint values (for consistency). For example, if we want to optimise Rosenbrock's function (2.6) subject to the constraint that $x_1^2 + x_2^2 - 1.5 \le 0$, the function M-file has the form

```
1  function [f, g] = testf(x)
2
3  f = rosen(x);
4  g = x*x' - 1.5;
```

where g denotes the constraints, and the gradient M-file has the form

```
1  function [fgrad, ggrad, g] = testgrad(x)
2
3  fgrad = rosegrad(x);
4  g = x*x' - 1.5;
5  ggrad = [2*x(1); 2*x(2)];
```

To write a general penalty function optimiser, there are three MATLAB functions to write: two of these, fcon and gradcon, calculate the penalty function and its gradient respectively (playing a similar role to linef when using the one-dimensional optimiser for line minimisation), and the third, optcon controls the optimisation process (in a similar way that netopt uses general purpose optimisers for NETLAB data models) for this pair of functions.

The function fcon computes the penalty function value with a given parameter ρ:

```
1  function y = fcon(x, fn, gradf, rho, varargin)
2
3  fn = fcnchk(fn, length(varargin));
4
5  % Evaluate function and constraints
6  [f, g] = feval(fn, x, varargin{:});
7  % Zero negative constraint values (as they are satisfied)
8  g = max(g, 0);
9  % Add penalty term
10 y = f + 0.5*rho*(g*g');
```

Note that it takes both the function fn and its gradient gradf as arguments. The reason for this is explained later.

The function gradcon computes the penalty function gradient with a given parameter ρ. A simple application of the chain rule to (2.70) shows that this gradient is given by

$$\nabla P_Q(x) = \nabla f + \rho(\hat{g}^T \nabla \hat{g}). \tag{2.74}$$

```
1  function gc = gradcon(x, fn, gradf, rho, varargin)
2
3  gradf = fcnchk(gradf, length(varargin));
4
5  % Evaluate gradient of function and constraints
6  [fgrad, ggrad, g] = feval(gradf, x, varargin{:});
7  % Zero negative constraint values (as satisfied)
8  g = max(g, 0);
9  % Add penalty term
10 gc = fgrad + rho*(g*ggrad');
```

The function optcon then passes fcon and gradcon to the scg optimiser with increasing values of ρ:

```
1  function [y, x] = optcon(x, fn, gradf)
2
3  options = foptions;
4
5  options(1) = 1;
6  options(2) = sqrt(eps);
7  options(3) = eps;
8  options(14) = 20;              % Number of training cycles.
9
10 rho = 5.0;
11 for i = 1:15
```

```
11  for i = 1:15
12    [x, options] = scg('fcon', x, options, 'gradcon', ...
13      fn, gradf, rho);
14    rho = rho * 2.0;
15  end
16  % Final blast of training to polish the result.
17  options(14) = 50;
18  [x, options] = scg('fcon', w, options, 'gradcon', ...
19    fn, gradf, rho);
20  y = options(8)
```

It is left as Exercise 2.10 to modify this function to provide a more generic tool. Note that the function fn and its gradient gradf are passed to fcon and gradcon by the optimiser scg. Both must be passed, since scg passes the same arguments to fcon and gradcon even though they only require fn and gradf respectively.

Exercises

2.1 ($\star$) Implement and compare Hestenes–Stiefel (2.31) and Fletcher–Reeves (2.35) with Polak–Ribiere search direction update methods in conjugate gradients. Evaluate the speed and accuracy of convergence on a simple function (such as Rosenbrock's) and training a neural network using netopt.

In all exercises where you implement alternative methods within existing optimisation algorithms, allow the user to switch between these methods using the options vector.

2.2 ($\star$) Compare Hestenes–Stiefel (2.31) and Fletcher–Reeves (2.35) with the Polak–Ribiere (2.33) search direction update method in scaled conjugate gradients.

2.3 ($\star$) Implement Møller's original method for updating β_j and δ_j (2.43) and (2.44) in scaled conjugate gradient and compare it with the NETLAB approach.

2.4 ($\star$) Evaluate the effect of using central differences in place of single-sided differences in the calculation of theta in scaled conjugate gradients.

2.5 ($\star\star$) Evaluate the effect on the performance of conjugate gradients of using different precision values in the line search. Compare the results with those for quasi-Newton methods on the same test problems.

2.6 ($\star\star$) The disadvantage for quasi-Newton methods over conjugate gradients is the requirement for storing the approximate inverse Hessian G_j which contains $\mathcal{O}(n^2)$ parameters. Shanno (1978) introduced a *limited memory BFGS* update method which requires only $\mathcal{O}(n)$ storage. The matrix G_j is replaced by the identity in the update formula (2.62). This leads to the following choice of search direction

$$d_j = -g_j + a p_j + b v_j \tag{2.75}$$

$$a = -\left(1 + \frac{v_j^T v_j}{v_j^T p_j}\right) \frac{p_j^T g_j}{p_j^T v_j} + \frac{v_j^T g_j}{p_j^T v_j} \tag{2.76}$$

$$b = \frac{p_j^T g_j^T}{p_j^T v_j}. \tag{2.77}$$

Implement this algorithm and compare its speed of convergence with conjugate gradients and the standard BFGS update.

2.7 $(\star)$ Implement the Davidon–Fletcher–Powell matrix update rule (2.65) in the quasi-Newton algorithm. Evaluate its effectiveness in comparison with BFGS.

2.8 $(\star\star)$ *Quickprop* (Fahlman, 1988) was an early heuristic scheme to improve the performance of gradient descent algorithms. It uses a local quadratic approximation to the function but on individual parameters, not in a multivariate sense as in conjugate gradients etc. At each step the parameters are moved to the minimum of the quadratic. This leads to the following expression for the update of parameter i at step τ:

$$\Delta x_i^{(\tau+1)} = \frac{g_i^{(\tau)}}{g_i^{(\tau-1)} - g_i^{(\tau)}} \Delta x_i^{(\tau)}. \tag{2.78}$$

The first step can be made using gradient descent. If the quickprop step (2.78) leads uphill, a gradient descent step can be substituted, and a bound on the maximum quickprop step is also needed. Implement this algorithm using the stochastic gradient and in a batch version and compare the effectiveness with olgd, graddesc and scg.

2.9 $(\star)$ Apply the constrained optimisation routine optcon to the version of Rosenbrock's function given as testf and testgrad. From the starting point $[-1.9, 2]$ you should reach the solution point $[0.9072, 0.8228]$.

2.10 $(\star\star)$ Extend the constrained optimisation function optcon given in the text to allow the options vector to control the process (for example, the number of iterations at each stage). Also allow the user to specify the algorithm used and a schedule for the parameter ρ as an argument. Use netopt as a model for how this can be achieved.

2.11 $(\star)$ Finding the roots, or zeros, of a function is related to function minimisation. There are several uses for a MATLAB function that finds the roots of a function of one variable later in the book. A root bracket is an interval (a, b) with the property that $f(a)$ and $f(b)$ have opposite signs (i.e. $f(a)f(b) < 0$). The simplest and most robust algorithm repeatedly bisects an interval (a_n, b_n) with a trial point x_n and sets the new interval to be (a_n, x_n) or (x_n, b_n) depending on the sign of $f(x_n)$. Write a function bisect that implements this algorithm. It should take the function as an argument and should allow the user to specify the maximum number of iterations and the termination criteria using the options vector. Test and evaluate your implementation by comparing it with the MATLAB function roots, which finds the roots of a polynomial.

2.12 ($\star\star$) The Newton–Raphson algorithm is a method of finding roots that converges faster than bisection. The algorithm assumes that f is twice continuously differentiable, and has a first-order Taylor series expansion near the root r. If x is an approximation to r and $h = r - x$ then

$$0 = f(r) = f(x + h) = f(x) + hf'(x) + \mathcal{O}(h^2). \tag{2.79}$$

If x is close to r, then h is small, and it is reasonable to ignore the $\mathcal{O}(h^2)$ term and solve the remaining equation for h. The solution is

$$h = \frac{-f(x)}{f'(x)}.$$

Of course, the new point $x + h$ probably will not be exactly equal to r, so we can proceed iteratively: start with x_0 and then define x_{n+1} inductively by

$$x_{n+1} = x_n - \frac{f(x_n)}{f'(x_n)}. \tag{2.80}$$

Implement this algorithm in MATLAB in a function newton with the following interface:

```
function root = newton(f, gradf, x, options)
```

Compare this algorithm with bisection for speed of convergence.

2.13 ($\star\star$) In Newton's algorithm we are replacing the function f by a linear approximation using the tangent line at the point x, as shown in Fig. 2.6. With this in mind, it is not hard to construct examples of functions where Newton's algorithm will diverge for certain starting points. Design and implement a test program to show this behaviour and compare the Newton and bisection test points.

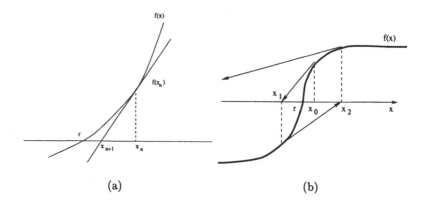

Fig. 2.6. (a) Geometric interpretation of Newton's method. (b) Example of divergence of Newton's method.

3. Density Modelling and Clustering

In this chapter we consider methods for modelling an unconditional probability density $p(x)$ given a finite set of unlabelled data points $x_1, \ldots, x_n$. These algorithms can be used to build classifier systems, but they are more commonly used for clustering, novelty detection, or as a means of training the hidden layer of RBF networks (Section 6.2). In addition, in Chapter 5, density models are combined with neural networks in the Mixture Density Network framework to provide a general purpose model for *conditional* density estimation.

The main approach to density estimation described in this chapter is the Gaussian mixture model (GMM). This model is classed as a *semi-parametric* estimation method since it defines a very general class of functional forms for the density model where the number of adaptive parameters can be increased in a systematic way (by adding more components to the model) so that the model can be made arbitrarily flexible. We shall also consider K-means clustering and the K-nearest-neighbour algorithm, which can be viewed as simple density models.

Some other NETLAB algorithms (in particular, the Generative Topographic Mapping (GTM) and mixture of Probabilistic Principal Component Analysers (PPCA)) can also be used for density modelling. The mixture of PPCA model implementation in NETLAB actually forms part of the GMM structure, but is discussed along with GTM and other visualisation models in Chapter 7. The principal functions described in this chapter are listed in Table 3.1.

3.1 Gaussian Mixture Models

In this section we introduce the basic theory of mixture models and the implementation of model creation and sampling.

3.1.1 Theory

In a mixture model, a probability density function is expressed as a linear combination of basis functions. A model with M components is written in the form

Table 3.1. Functions in this chapter.

Density Modelling	
demgmm1	Demonstration of EM training
demgmm2	Demonstration of GMM with spherical covariance
demgmm3	Demonstration of GMM with diagonal covariance
demgmm4	Demonstration of GMM with full covariance
demkmn1	Demonstration of K-means algorithm
demknn1	Demonstration of K-nearest-neighbour classifier
gmm	Create a Gaussian mixture model
gmmactiv	Compute the activations of a GMM
gmmem	EM training algorithm for GMM
gmminit	Initialise GMM from data
gmmpak	Combine all the parameters in a GMM into one vector
gmmpost	Compute the class posterior probabilities of a GMM
gmmprob	Compute the data probability for a GMM
gmmsamp	Sample from a GMM
gmmunpak	Separate a vector of GMM parameters into its components
kmeans	Trains a K-means model
knn	Create a K-nearest-neighbour classifier

$$p(\boldsymbol{x}) = \sum_{j=1}^{M} P(j) p(\boldsymbol{x}|j), \tag{3.1}$$

where the parameters $P(j)$ are called the *mixing coefficients* and the parameters of the *component density* functions $p(\boldsymbol{x}|j)$ typically vary with j. To be a valid probability density, a function must be non-negative everywhere and integrate to 1 over the whole space. By constraining the mixing coefficients

$$\sum_{j=1}^{M} P(j) = 1 \tag{3.2}$$

$$0 \le P(j) \le 1, \tag{3.3}$$

and choosing normalised density functions

$$\int p(\boldsymbol{x}|j) \, d\boldsymbol{x} = 1 \tag{3.4}$$

guarantees that the model does represent a density function.

The mixture model is a *generative* model and it is useful to consider the process of generating samples from the density it represents. First one of the components j is chosen at random with probability $P(j)$; thus we can view $P(j)$ as the *prior* probability of the jth component. Then a data point is generated from the corresponding density $p(\boldsymbol{x}|j)$. The corresponding *posterior* probabilities can be written, using Bayes' theorem, in the form

$$P(j|x) = \frac{p(x|j)P(j)}{p(x)}, \tag{3.5}$$

where $p(x)$ is given by (3.1). These posterior probabilities satisfy the constraints

$$\sum_{j=1}^{M} P(j|x) = 1 \tag{3.6}$$

$$0 \le P(j|x) \le 1. \tag{3.7}$$

It only remains to decide on the form of the component densities. In the

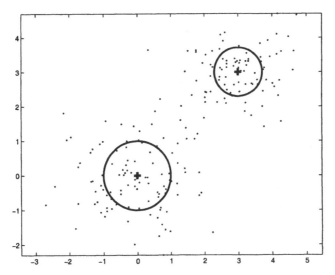

Fig. 3.1. Spherical covariance mixture model. Sampled data (*dots*), centres (*crosses*) and one standard deviation error bars (*lines*).

NETLAB implementation there are four options, each of which is a Gaussian distribution with a different form of covariance matrix. Thus each density is described by a mean vector μ of dimension d and a covariance matrix of the form:

Spherical The covariance matrix is a scalar multiple of the identity matrix, $\Sigma_j = \sigma_j^2 I$ so that

$$p(x|j) = \frac{1}{(2\pi\sigma_j^2)^{d/2}} \exp\left\{ -\frac{\|x - \mu_j\|^2}{2\sigma_j^2} \right\}. \tag{3.8}$$

An example of this model is shown in Fig. 3.1.

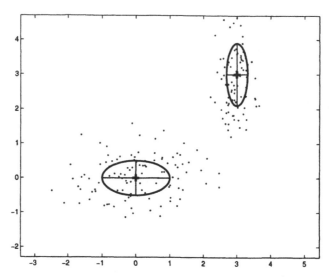

Fig. 3.2. Diagonal covariance mixture model. Sampled data (*dots*), centres (*crosses*), covariance axes (*thin lines*) and one standard deviation error bars (*thick lines*).

Diagonal The covariance matrix is diagonal

$$\Sigma_j = \text{diag}(\sigma_{j,1}^2, \ldots, \sigma_{j,d}^2) \tag{3.9}$$

and the density function is

$$p(x|j) = \frac{1}{(2\pi \prod_{i=1}^{d} \sigma_{j,i}^2)^{d/2}} \exp\left\{ -\sum_{i=1}^{d} \frac{(x_i - mu_{j,i})^2}{2\sigma_{j,i}^2} \right\}. \tag{3.10}$$

An example of this model is shown in Fig. 3.2.

Full The covariance matrix is allowed to be any positive definite $d \times d$ matrix Σ_j and the density function is

$$p(x|j) = \frac{1}{(2\pi)^{d/2}|\Sigma_j|^{1/2}} \exp\left\{ -\frac{1}{2}(x - \mu_j)^T \Sigma^{-1}(x - \mu_j) \right\}. \tag{3.11}$$

An example of this model is shown in Fig. 3.3.

PPCA The covariance matrix is the sum of two terms: one is diagonal in a q-dimensional subspace spanned by the first q principal components and the other is spherical. This corresponds to a probabilistic model for PCA, and is discussed further in Chapter 7.

Each of these models is a universal approximator, in that they can model any density function arbitrarily closely provided that they contain enough components (McLachlan and Basford, 1988). Usually a mixture model with

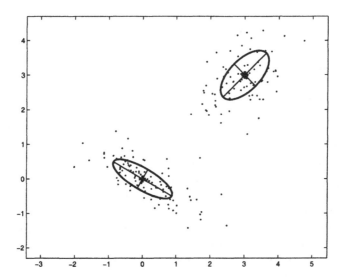

Fig. 3.3. Full covariance mixture model. Sampled data (*dots*), centres (*crosses*), covariance axes (*thin lines*) and one standard deviation error bars (*thick lines*).

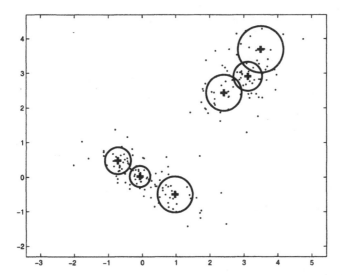

Fig. 3.4. Spherical covariance mixture model with six components fitted to the data sampled from the full covariance two-component model in Fig. 3.3. Sampled data (*dots*), centres (*crosses*) and one standard deviation error bars (*lines*).

full covariance matrices will need fewer components to model a given density, but each component has more adjustable parameters. Figure 3.4 shows how a mixture model with spherical covariance can model the distribution of a mixture model with full covariance but using twice as many components.

3.1.2 NETLAB Implementation

Model Creation

A Gaussian mixture model is created using the NETLAB function gmm, which has the syntax

```
mix = gmm(dim, ncentres, covarType)
```

where covarType is a string specifying the covariance structure. The possible choices are 'spherical', corresponding to (3.8), 'diag', corresponding to (3.10), 'full', corresponding to (3.11), and 'ppca', which represents mixtures of PPCA. The first two arguments specify the data dimension and the number of components respectively. The function gmm returns the network data structure mix, which has the following fields:

```
type          % string describing network type: always 'gmm'
nin           % number of inputs
ncentres      % number of components
covar_type    % covariance structure
nwts          % total number of parameters
priors        % component prior probabilities
centres       % component means
covars        % component covariances
```

The matrices have the following dimensions: priors is $1 \times$ ncentres; centres is ncentres$\times$nin. However, the dimension of covars depends on the covariance type:

Spherical $1 \times$ ncentres
Diagonal ncentres $\times$ nin
Full A three-dimensional array nin $\times$ nin $\times$ ncentres

The function is defined as follows (omitting material for PPCA):

```
1  function mix = gmm(dim, ncentres, covar_type)
2
3  if ncentres < 1
4    error('Number of centres must be greater than zero')
5  end
6  mix.type = 'gmm';
7  mix.nin = dim;
8  mix.ncentres = ncentres;
9  vartypes = {'spherical', 'diag', 'full', 'ppca'};
10 if sum(strcmp(covar_type, vartypes)) == 0
11   error('Undefined covariance type')
12 else
13   mix.covar_type = covar_type;
14 end
15
```

```
16  % Initialise priors to be equal and summing to one
17  mix.priors = ones(1,mix.ncentres) ./ mix.ncentres;
18  % Initialise centres
19  mix.centres = randn(mix.ncentres, mix.nin);
20  % Initialise all the variances to unity
21  switch mix.covar_type
22  case 'spherical'
23    mix.covars = ones(1, mix.ncentres);
24    mix.nwts = mix.ncentres + mix.ncentres*mix.nin + mix.ncentres;
25  case 'diag'
26    % Store diagonals of covariance matrices as rows in a matrix
27    mix.covars =  ones(mix.ncentres, mix.nin);
28    mix.nwts = mix.ncentres + mix.ncentres*mix.nin + ...
29      mix.ncentres*mix.nin;
30  case 'full'
31    % Store covariance matrices in a row vector of matrices
32    mix.covars = repmat(eye(mix.nin), [1 1 mix.ncentres]);
33    mix.nwts = mix.ncentres + mix.ncentres*mix.nin + ...
34      mix.ncentres*mix.nin*mix.nin;
35  end
```

The priors are initialised to 1/ncentres (line 17) and the centres (the means of the component densities) are initialised from a Gaussian distribution with zero mean and unit variance (line 19). The covariance matrices are all initialised to the identity matrix. For spherical covariance, this corresponds to a row vector of ones (line 23). For diagonal covariance, the jth diagonal is stored as the jth row in the matrix covars, and this is set initially to a vector of ones (line 27). For full covariance matrices, a three-dimensional array is set up with a nin × nin identity matrix in each location (line 32).

Sampling

There are several reasons why it can be useful to generate samples from a GMM (see also Chapter 8).

- A sample can be compared with the actual data to help decide whether the density function is a realistic model for the data.
- Suppose that in a prediction problem there are some input values missing for some data vectors. Simply filling in the missing values (using, for example, the mean of the corresponding variable) will often give biased predictions and underestimate the size of the error bars. Sampling from an unconditional density model can be used to generate many possible completions of the vectors with missing data, and a prediction can be made by averaging the predictions for each completion. This can be regarded as a simple Monte Carlo approximation to the correct treatment, which is to integrate over the missing variables weighted by the appropriate conditional distribution.
- It is easy to generate synthetic data from a GMM in order to test other algorithms. Because the true generating distribution is known, it is of-

ten possible to calculate the optimal decision boundary for a classification problem using Bayes' theorem. In addition, by selecting the number of components and the covariance matrices, it is possible to control the complexity of the problem in a systematic way.

Fortunately, it is straightforward to sample from a Gaussian distribution using the NETLAB function gsamp (see Section 8.2.2). This has syntax

```
x = gsamp(mu, covar, nsamp)
```

where mu is the mean, covar is the covariance (expressed as a full $d \times d$ matrix, and nsamp is the number of samples.

With this function available, sampling from a Gaussian mixture model proceeds in two steps:

1. Choosing a component to generate a sample from according to the prior probabilities $P(j)$.
2. Constructing the covariance matrix for that component from the information stored in the GMM data structure and then generating a sample using gsamp.

In the NETLAB implementation, gmmsamp, both the sample data and a matrix label denoting which component each data point came from are returned.

```
1   function [data, label] = gmmsamp(mix, n)
2
3   if n < 1
4     error('Number of data points must be positive');
5   end
6   priors = rand(1, n);
7   data = zeros(n, mix.nin);
8   if nargout > 1
9     label = zeros(n, 1);
10  end
11  cum_prior = 0;          % Cumulative sum of priors
12  total_samples = 0;      % Number of sampled points
13  for j = 1:mix.ncentres
14    num_samples = sum(priors >= cum_prior & ...
15      priors < cum_prior + mix.priors(j));
16    % Form a full covariance matrix
17    switch mix.covar_type
18      case 'spherical'
19        covar = mix.covars(j) * eye(mix.nin);
20      case 'diag'
21        covar = diag(mix.covars(j,:));
22      case 'full'
23        covar = mix.covars(:,:,j);
24    end
25    data(total_samples+1:total_samples+num_samples, :) = ...
26      gsamp(mix.centres(j,:), covar, num_samples);
27    if nargout > 1
28      label(total_samples+1:total_samples+num_samples) = j;
```

```
29    end
30    cum_prior = cum_prior + mix.priors();
31    total_samples = total_samples + num_samples;
32  end
```

Rather than sampling points individually, it is more efficient to loop over the components (line 13) and generate a sample from each component in turn. To ensure that the components are chosen randomly with the correct frequencies, we first generate n uniformly distributed random numbers in the interval $(0, 1)$ in line 6. The number of samples generated from component j (lines 14–15) is given by

$$\#\{y_j | P_c(i-1) \leq y_j < P_c(i)\}, \tag{3.12}$$

where y_j for $j = 1, \ldots, n$ are the samples from $U(0, 1)$, and P_c is the cumulative probability function for the prior probabilities

$$P_c(i) = \sum_{k=1}^{i} P(k). \tag{3.13}$$

The full covariance matrix is then formed in an appropriate way for the type of covariance and a call made to gsamp on line 25–26.

3.2 Computing Probabilities

It is useful to be able to compute three different probabilities for a Gaussian mixture model: the component likelihoods (or *activations*) $p(x|j)$, the data probability $p(x)$, and the component posterior probabilities $p(j|x)$. NETLAB provides the functions gmmactiv, gmmprob, and gmmpost for these calculations.

3.2.1 GMM Activations

The function gmmactiv computes the component likelihoods for each type of covariance function.

```
1   function a = gmmactiv(mix, x)
2
3   ndata = size(x, 1);
4   a = zeros(ndata, mix.ncentres);   % Preallocate matrix
5
6   switch mix.covar_type
7
8   case 'spherical'
9     % Calculate squared norm matrix, of dimension (ndata, ncentres)
10    n2 = dist2(x, mix.centres);
11    % Calculate width factors
```

```
12    wi2 = ones(ndata, 1) * (2 .* mix.covars);
13    normal = (pi .* wi2) .^ (mix.nin/2);
14    % Now compute the activations
15    a = exp(-(n2./wi2))./ normal;
16
17  case 'diag'
18    normal = (2*pi)^(mix.nin/2);
19    s = prod(sqrt(mix.covars), 2);
20    for j = 1:mix.ncentres
21      diffs = x - (ones(ndata, 1) * mix.centres(j, :));
22      a(:, j) = exp(-0.5*sum((diffs.*diffs)./(ones(ndata, 1) * ...
23        mix.covars(j, :)), 2)) ./ (normal*s(j));
24    end
25
26  case 'full'
27    normal = (2*pi)^(mix.nin/2);
28    for j = 1:mix.ncentres
29      diffs = x - (ones(ndata, 1) * mix.centres(j, :));
30      % Cholesky decomposition of covariance matrix for efficiency
31      c = chol(mix.covars(:, :, j));
32      temp = diffs/c;
33      a(:, j) = exp(-0.5*sum(temp.*temp,2))./(normal*prod(diag(c)));
34    end
35  end
```

The calculation for spherical covariance follows (3.8). The function dist2 computes the squared distance between x and the GMM centres mix.centres. Each row of the result corresponds to a data point and each column corresponds to a centre.

For a diagonal covariance matrix, line 21 computes $x - \mu_j$ as a matrix. Lines 22–23 then compute (3.10) for the jth centre.

For a full covariance matrix, in order to compute the quadratic form

$$(x - \mu_j)^T \Sigma^{-1} (x - \mu_j) \tag{3.14}$$

and the determinant $|\Sigma|$ it is more efficient to compute the Cholesky decomposition of $C^T C = \Sigma$ first. Then the quadratic form in (3.14) is equal to

$$((x - \mu_j)C^{-1}) .* ((x - \mu_j)C^{-1}) \tag{3.15}$$

and the determinant $|\Sigma|$ is equal to the product of the diagonal elements of C.

3.2.2 GMM Probabilities

The function gmmprob computes the probabilities of a dataset x using (3.1).

```
1  function prob = gmmprob(mix, x)
2
3  % Compute activations
```

```
4   a = gmmactiv(mix, x);
5   % Form dot product with priors
6   prob = a * (mix.priors)';
```

3.2.3 GMM Posteriors

The function gmmpost computes the posterior component probabilities given by (3.5).

```
 1  function [post, a] = gmmpost(mix, x)
 2
 3  ndata = size(x, 1);
 4  a = gmmactiv(mix, x);
 5
 6  post = (ones(ndata, 1)*mix.priors).*a;
 7  s = sum(post, 2);
 8  % Set any zeros to one before dividing
 9  s = s + (s==0);
10  post = post./(s*ones(1, mix.ncentres));
```

The function also optionally returns the activations a, as this is useful additional information for the EM training algorithm. If a data point x is a long way from all the mixture model centres, then it is possible that all the values

$$p(x|j)P(j) \tag{3.16}$$

are zero within rounding error. Then the sum of the values would also be zero, leading to an arithmetic exception when calculating (3.5). To avoid this, line 9 replaces any zero values by 1. This prevents any arithmetic errors, though the resulting posterior probabilities are zero for all components, and hence do not satisfy the constraint (3.6).

3.3 EM Training Algorithm

The method for determining the parameters of a Gaussian mixture model from a data set is based on maximising the data likelihood. It is convenient to recast the problem in the equivalent form of minimising the negative log likelihood of the data set

$$E = -\mathcal{L} = -\sum_{n=1}^{N} \log p(x^n), \tag{3.17}$$

which is treated as an error function. There are two practical difficulties with this minimisation problem. Firstly, the global minimum of E is $-\infty$. This is achieved when one of the Gaussian components collapses onto a data point so that $\mu_j = x$ and the corresponding variance tends to 0. To avoid this problem, the variance is checked at each iteration, and dangerously small values are replaced by larger ones. Secondly, there are often a large number of local minima which correspond to poor models of the true density function. A solution for this is to train models from many different starting points and to take care over the initialisation of the models (see Section 3.3.2).

Because the likelihood is a differentiable function of the parameters, it is possible to use a general purpose non-linear optimiser to find the minima of E. However, there are some advantages to using a specialised method, known as the *expectation-maximisation*, or EM, algorithm (Dempster *et al.*, 1977). This algorithm is simple to implement and understand, avoids the calculation and storage of derivatives, is usually faster to converge than general purpose algorithms, and can also be extended to deal with data sets where some points have missing values(Ghahramani and Jordan, 1994b). The ideas behind the algorithm have also been applied to many other probabilistic models, including hidden Markov models (Baum and Petrie, 1966; Baum and Sell, 1968; Rabiner, 1989) and Kalman filters. With the use of variational methods, the EM algorithm has recently been extended to provide upper bounds on the error function E for classes of so-called *probabilistic graphical models* where the exact calculation of E is computationally intractable (Jordan, 1998).

3.3.1 Algorithm Theory

The EM algorithm iteratively modifies the GMM parameters to decrease E. It is guaranteed to reduce E at each step until a local minimum is found. It is helpful to suppose that the data set was sampled from an (unknown) mixture model. If we knew which component each data point x^n had been sampled from, then it would be straightforward to estimate the model parameters. Let I_j denote the indices of the data points sampled from component j, and N the total number of data points. Then the prior $P(j)$ would be given by

$$P(j) = \frac{|I_j|}{N},$$ (3.18)

the mean μ_j by

$$\mu_j = \frac{1}{|I_j|} \sum_{i \in I_j} x^i,$$ (3.19)

and the covariance by a similar formula that depends on the form of the covariance matrix; for example, for spherical covariance

$$\sigma_j^2 = \frac{1}{d|I_j|} \sum_{i \in I_j} \|x^i - \mu_j\|^2.$$ (3.20)

Of course, we don't know which component generated each data point, so instead we consider a hypothetical *complete* data set in which each data point is labelled with the component that generated it. So, for each data point x^n, there is a corresponding random variable z^n, which is an integer in the range $1, \ldots, M$. We write y^n for the complete data point (x^n, z^n) and w for the parameters in the mixture model. The EM algorithm generates a sequence of estimates $w^{(m)}$ starting from the initial parameter set $w^{(0)}$.

First we write down the likelihood of a complete data point if $z = j$:

$$p((x, z = j)|w) = p(x|z = j, w)P(z = j|w) \tag{3.21}$$

$$= p(x|\theta_j)P(z = j|w), \tag{3.22}$$

where θ_j are the density function parameters (mean and variance) for component j. The likelihood of x can be obtained by marginalising over z which, since it is a discrete variable, is simply a matter of summing (3.22) over all its possible values:

$$p(x|w) = \sum_{j=1}^{M} P(z = j|w)p(x|\theta_j). \tag{3.23}$$

Comparing this with (3.1), we see that the probabilities $P(z = j|w)$ are playing the same role as the mixing coefficients.

Given a set of parameters $w^{(m)}$ we would like to use class labels z^n and (3.18), (3.19) and (3.20) to estimate the next set of parameters $w^{(m+1)}$. As we don't know the class labels, but do know their probability distribution, what we can do is to use the *expected* values of the class labels given the current parameters. We form the function $Q(w|w^{(m)})$ as follows:

$$Q(w|w^{(m)}) = E(\log p(y|w))p(z^n|x^n, w^{(m)}) \tag{3.24}$$

$$= \sum_{j=1}^{M} \sum_{n=1}^{N} [\log(p(x^n, z^n|w))] P(z^n = j|x^n, w^{(m)}) \tag{3.25}$$

$$= \sum_{j=1}^{M} \sum_{n=1}^{N} [\log P(j) + \log p(x^n|\theta_j)]P^{(m)}(j|x^n), \tag{3.26}$$

where

$$P^{(m)}(j|x^n) := P(z^n = j|x^n, w^{(m)}) = \frac{P^{(m)}(j)p(x^n|\theta_j^{(m)})}{\sum_{j=1}^{M} P^{(m)}(j)p(x^n|\theta_j^{(m)})} \tag{3.27}$$

is the expected posterior distribution of the class labels given the observed data. Note that $Q(w|w^{(m)})$ is a function of the parameters $P(j)$ and θ_j while $P^{(m)}(j)$ and $\theta_j^{(m)}$ are fixed values. The calculation of Q is the E-step of the algorithm. To compute the new set of parameter values $w^{(m+1)}$, we optimise $Q(w|w^{(m)})$, i.e.

$$w^{(m+1)} = \arg\max_{w} Q(w|w^{(m)}).$$ (3.28)

This is the M-step of the algorithm. For Gaussian mixture models, the optimisation can be carried out analytically. For more complicated models, this is not always possible, and we may have to be satisfied with an M-step that simply increases the value of Q (Neal and Hinton, 1993).

The M-step equations for the mixing coefficients and the component means are the same for all types of GMM in NETLAB. The mixing coefficients are found by introducing a Lagrange multiplier λ to enforce the constraint $\sum_j P(j) = 1$. We differentiate

$$Q + \lambda \left(\sum_{j=1}^{M} P(j) - 1 \right)$$ (3.29)

with respect to $P(j)$ and set the result to zero, yielding the update equation

$$P^{(m+1)}(j) = \frac{1}{N} \sum_{n=1}^{N} P^{(m)}(j|x^n).$$ (3.30)

This is a 'soft' version of (3.18). Differentiating Q with respect to the jth mean μ_j and setting the result to zero gives the update equation

$$\mu_j^{(m+1)} = \frac{\sum_{n=1}^{N} P^{(m)}(j|x^n)x^n}{\sum_{n=1}^{N} P^{(m)}(j|x^n)},$$ (3.31)

which is a soft version of (3.19).

The details of the M-step for the covariance parameters depend on the type of covariance structure, but the basic idea is the same in each case. We compute the covariance in the usual way but with the contribution from each data point weighted by $P^{(m)}(j|x^n)$. This follows from differentiating Q with respect to the covariance matrix parameters and setting the result to zero.

Spherical spherical covariance matrices We obtain a soft version of (3.20)

$$(\sigma_j^{(m+1)})^2 = \frac{1}{d} \frac{\sum_{n=1}^{N} P^{(m)}(j|x^n)\|x^n - \mu_j^{(m+1)}\|^2}{\sum_{n=1}^{N} P^{(m)}(j|x^n)}.$$ (3.32)

Diagonal diagonal covariance matrices The update equation is

$$(\sigma_{i,j}^{(m+1)})^2 = \frac{\sum_{n=1}^{N} P^{(m)}(j|x^n)(x_i^n - \mu_{i,j}^{(m+1)})^2}{\sum_{n=1}^{N} P^{(m)}(j|x^n)}.$$ (3.33)

Full The update equation is

$$\Sigma_j = \frac{\sum_{n=1}^{N} P^{(m)}(j|x^n)(x^n - \mu_j^{(m+1)})(x^n - \mu_j^{(m+1)})^T}{\sum_{n=1}^{N} P^{(m)}(j|x^n)}.$$ (3.34)

Because of (3.30), we can rewrite the denominator of the expressions for mean and covariance as

$$\sum_{n=1}^{N} P^{(m)}(j|x^n) = N P^{(m+1)}(j).$$ (3.35)

3.3.2 Initialisation

In the NETLAB implementation of EM, the initialisation of the model (which is contained in gmminit) is separated from the iterative part of the algorithm. This separation allows the user to continue to train a model in stages, evaluating it after each segment of training, and to experiment with different initialisation methods. A drawback of this choice is that there is some code duplication between gmminit and gmmem, which contains the iterative parameter update.

The initialisation is conceptually straightforward. A rough clustering of the data is performed using the K-means algorithm (see Section 3.5). Then each data point is assumed to belong to the closest cluster centre and the 'complete' data form of the calculations, (3.18), (3.19), and (3.20), are used to set the parameters using the data points assigned to each component.

```
1   function mix = gmminit(mix, x, options)
2
3   [ndata, xdim] = size(x);
4   GMM_WIDTH = 1.0;
5
6   % Use kmeans algorithm to set centres
7   options(5) = 1;
8   [mix.centres, options, post] = kmeans(mix.centres, x, options);
9   % Set priors depending on number of points in each cluster
10  cluster_sizes = max(sum(post, 1), 1);  % Ensure no prior is zero
11  mix.priors = cluster_sizes/sum(cluster_sizes); % Normalise priors
12
13  switch mix.covar_type
14  case 'spherical'
15     if mix.ncentres > 1
16        cdist = dist2(mix.centres, mix.centres);
17        cdist = cdist + diag(ones(mix.ncentres, 1)*realmax);
18        mix.covars = min(cdist);
19        mix.covars = mix.covars + GMM_WIDTH*(mix.covars < eps);
20     else
21        mix.covars = mean(diag(cov(x)));
22     end
23  case 'diag'
24     for j = 1:mix.ncentres
25        % Pick out data points belonging to this centre
26        c = x(find(post(:, j)),:);
27        diffs = c - (ones(size(c, 1), 1) * mix.centres(j, :));
28        mix.covars(j, :) = sum((diffs.*diffs), 1)/size(c, 1);
29        mix.covars(j, :) = mix.covars(j, :) + GMM_WIDTH.* ...
```

```
30              (mix.covars(j, :)<eps);
31      end
32    case 'full'
33      for j = 1:mix.ncentres
34        % Pick out data points belonging to this centre
35        c = x(find(post(:, j)),:);
36        diffs = c - (ones(size(c, 1), 1) * mix.centres(j, :));
37        mix.covars(:,:,j) = (diffs'*diffs)/(size(c, 1));
38        % Add GMM_WIDTH*Id to rank-deficient covariance matrices
39        if rank(mix.covars(:,:,j)) < mix.nin
40          mix.covars(:,:,j) = mix.covars(:,:,i) + ...
41            GMM_WIDTH.*eye(mix.nin);
42        end
43      end
44    end
45  end
```

The function gmminit takes three parameters: the mixture model mix, the data from which to initialise the model x, and the options vector used to control the K-means algorithm. In lines 7–8, the K-means algorithm (see Section 3.5) is used to move the centres to reflect the density of the data points. Line 7 ensures that the model centres are assigned to the first ncentres rows of the dataset *after* a random permutation by kmeans. This prevents any problems arising from an initially ordered dataset.

In lines 13–14 the mixing coefficients are set to the number of points in the corresponding cluster divided by the total number of data points subject to the condition that each value is at least $1/N$. This is necessary since otherwise the corresponding component will never be responsible for any data and all its parameters will be unchanged by the EM algorithm.

In the initial stages of the EM algorithm it is better if the covariance parameters are too large rather than too small (again, to ensure that each component is responsible for a reasonable fraction of the dataset), so small values are replaced by a parameter WIDTH which is set to the value 1 (line 4). This value has been chosen through practical experience, and a different value may be more appropriate on occasion. The method for initialising the covariances depends on the type:

Spherical If there is just one centre, then the covariance is set to the mean diagonal entry in the covariance matrix (line 24). Otherwise, the ith covariance is set to the squared distance to the nearest different centre. Any covariance that is less than machine precision eps is set to WIDTH (line 22).

Diagonal Line 29 picks out the data points closest to the jth centre. The covariance is then computed as in (3.33) with a hard responsibility (i.e. 1 for the closest centre and 0 for the others). In lines 32–33, all values less than eps are replaced by WIDTH.

Full Line 38 picks out the data points closest to the jth centre. The covariance is then computed as in (3.34) with a hard responsibility (lines

39–40). In lines 42–44 if the covariance matrix does not have full rank, a multiple of the identity matrix is added to ensure that the matrix does have full rank.

3.3.3 NETLAB EM Implementation

The function gmmem implements the EM algorithm for Gaussian mixture models:

```
1   function [mix, options, errlog] = gmmem(mix, x, options)
2
3   [ndata, xdim] = size(x);
4
5   display = options(1);
6   store = 0;
7   if (nargout > 2)
8     store = 1;    % Store the error values to return them
9     errlog = zeros(1, niters);
10  end
11  test = 0;
12  if options(3) > 0.0
13    test = 1;    % Test log likelihood for termination
14  end
15
16  check_covars = 0;
17  if options(5) >= 1
18    disp('check_covars is on');
19    check_covars = 1;    % Ensure covariances don't collapse
20    MIN_COVAR = eps;    % Min. singular value of covariance
21    init_covars = mix.covars;
22  end
23
24  % Main loop of algorithm
25  for n = 1:niters
26
27    % Calculate posteriors based on old parameters
28    [post, act] = gmmpost(mix, x);
29
30    % Calculate error value if needed
31    if (display | store | test)
32      prob = act*(mix.priors)';
33      % Error value is negative log likelihood of data
34      e = - sum(log(prob));
35      if store
36        errlog(n) = e;
37      end
38      if display > 0
39        fprintf(1, 'Cycle %4d  Error %11.6f\n', n, e);
40      end
41      if test
42        if (n > 1 & abs(e - eold) < options(3))
43          options(8) = e;
44          return;
```

```
45        else
46          eold = e;
47        end
48      end
49    end
50
51    % Adjust the new estimates for the parameters
52    new_pr = sum(post, 1);
53    new_c = post' * x;
54
55    % Now move new estimates to old parameter vectors
56    mix.priors = new_pr ./ ndata;
57    mix.centres = new_c ./ (new_pr' * ones(1, mix.nin));
58
59    switch mix.covar_type
60    case 'spherical'
61      n2 = dist2(x, mix.centres);
62      for j = 1:mix.ncentres
63        v(j) = (post(:,j)'*n2(:,j));
64      end
65      mix.covars = ((v./new_pr))./mix.nin;
66      if check_covars
67        % Ensure that no covariance is too small
68        for j = 1:mix.ncentres
69          if mix.covars(j) < MIN_COVAR
70            mix.covars(j) = init_covars(j);
71          end
72        end
73      end
74    case 'diag'
75      for j = 1:mix.ncentres
76        diffs = x - (ones(ndata, 1) * mix.centres(j,:));
77        mix.covars(j,:) = sum((diffs.*diffs).*(post(:,j)* ...
78          ones(1, mix.nin)), 1)./new_pr(j);
79      end
80      if check_covars
81        % Ensure that no covariance is too small
82        for j = 1:mix.ncentres
83          if min(mix.covars(j,:)) < MIN_COVAR
84            mix.covars(j,:) = init_covars(j,:);
85          end
86        end
87      end
88    case 'full'
89      for j = 1:mix.ncentres
90        diffs = x - (ones(ndata, 1) * mix.centres(j,:));
91        diffs = diffs.*(sqrt(post(:,j))*ones(1, mix.nin));
92        mix.covars(:,:,j) = (diffs'*diffs)/new_pr(j);
93      end
94      if check_covars
95        % Ensure that no covariance is too small
96        for j = 1:mix.ncentres
97          if min(svd(mix.covars(:,:,j))) < MIN_COVAR
```

```
98              mix.covars(:,:,j) = init_covars(:,:,j);
99          end
100       end
101     end
102   end
103 end
104
105 options(8) = -sum(log(gmmprob(mix, x)));
106 if (display >= 0)
107   disp('Warning: Max. number of iterations has been exceeded');
108 end
```

The first important section of the function is in lines 17–22. If options(5) is set to 1, then the algorithm checks at each iteration if any of the covariance matrices have collapsed to small values (the threshold is given by the variable MIN_COVAR which is set to machine precision in line 20). If this occurs, the corresponding covariance matrix is set to its initial value; the relevant matrices are stored in init_covars. It is nearly always a good idea to use this feature, since usually if a covariance matrix does collapse, the computation of the next iteration of the algorithm fails due to underflow and the parameters of the model are no longer floating point numbers. (This is *not* the default option in order to maintain backwards compatibility of the software.)

Line 28 is the E-step, calculating the component posterior probabilities following (3.27). Line 52 computes the new mixing coefficients (3.30); line 53 does the same for the component means (3.31). These values are stored in the mixture data structure mix in lines 56–57. The remainder of the function is concerned with updating the covariance matrices: spherical in lines 61–65 (3.32); diagonal in lines 75–79 (3.33); full in lines 89–93 (3.34). In each case, provided that option(5) has been selected, the covariance is reset to its original value if it has collapsed to less than MIN_COVAR.

3.4 Demonstrations of GMM

There are several demonstration programs of GMM provided by NETLAB, in order to illustrate the different capabilities of the different covariance matrix types. Here we will only discuss in detail a selection of these programs.

3.4.1 EM Algorithm

The program demgmm1 is designed to illustrate the workings of the EM training algorithm, and in particular the nature of the E and M steps. A small two-dimensional dataset of 40 points is generated, with 20 points from each of two spherical Gaussians, with means $(0.3, 0.3)$ and $(0.7, 0.7)$ respectively and common variances 0.01.

```
1 randn('state', 0); rand('state', 0);
2 gmix = gmm(2, 2, 'spherical');
```

```
3   ndat1 = 20; ndat2 = 20;
4   ndata = ndat1+ndat2;
5   gmix.centres =  [0.3 0.3; 0.7 0.7];
6   gmix.covars = [0.01 0.01];
7   x = gmmsamp(gmix, ndata);
```

A two-component mixture model with spherical covariance structure is created with poorly chosen initial parameters so as to make the effect of the EM algorithm more visible.

```
8    ncentres = 2; input_dim = 2;
9    mix = gmm(input_dim, ncentres, 'spherical');
10   mix.centres = [0.2 0.8; 0.8, 0.2];
11   mix.covars = [0.01 0.01];
```

The model is plotted with each component represented by a circle centred on its mean with radius of one standard deviation.

```
12   ncirc = 30; theta = linspace(0, 2*pi, ncirc);
13   xs = cos(theta); ys = sin(theta);
14   xvals = mix.centres(:, 1)*ones(1,ncirc) + sqrt(mix.covars')*xs;
15   yvals = mix.centres(:, 2)*ones(1,ncirc) + sqrt(mix.covars')*ys;
```

At each E-step, the responsibility of each component for each data point is calculated (line 16) and then represented by a colour mixing red and blue: red represents the first component and blue the second (line 17: MATLAB colours are given by RGB values).

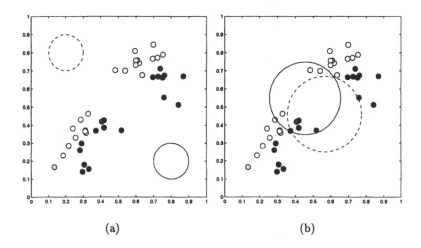

(a)   (b)

Fig. 3.5. EM training of two-component model. Circles show one standard deviation around component means 1 (*solid line*) and 2 (*dashed line*). Training data (*circles*) are shaded with responsibility of component 1 on a grey scale with $p(C_1|x) = 1$ as white. (a) First E-step. (b) First M-step.

```
16   post = gmmpost(mix, x);
17   dcols = [post(:,1), zeros(ndata, 1), post(:,2)];
18   delete(hd);
19   for i = 1 : ndata
20     hd(i) = plot(x(i, 1), x(i, 2), 'color', dcols(i,:), ...
21                  'marker', '.', 'markersize', 30);
22   end
```

The result of the M-step can be found by calling gmmem for a single iteration
and then plotting the result as in lines 12–15. This is shown in Fig. 3.5.

```
23   options = foptions;
24   options(14) = 1; % A single iteration
25   options(1) = -1; % Switch off all messages, including warning
26   mix = gmmem(mix, x, options);
27   delete(hc);
28   xvals = mix.centres(:, 1)*ones(1,ncirc) + sqrt(mix.covars')*xs;
29   yvals = mix.centres(:, 2)*ones(1,ncirc) + sqrt(mix.covars')*ys;
30   hc(1)=line(xvals(1,:), yvals(1,:), 'color', 'r');
31   hc(2)=line(xvals(2,:), yvals(2,:), 'color', 'b');
```

The demonstration then continues by alternating E- and M-steps until the
model converges. Further steps towards convergence are shown in Fig. 3.6.
After the component centres are pulled together towards the middle of the
data, they gradually move apart from iterations 3 to 6.

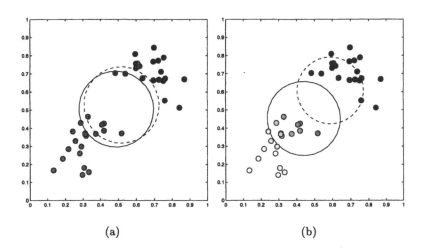

(a)   (b)

Fig. 3.6. EM training of two-component model. Circles show one standard deviation around component means 1 (*solid line*) and 2 (*dashed line*). Training data (*cir-
cles*) are shaded with responsibility of component 1 on a grey scale with $p(C_1|x) = 1$
as white. (a) After three EM steps. (b) After six EM steps.

3.4.2 Density Modelling

While the program described in Section 3.4.1 is useful in order to understand the EM algorithm, it is not the way in which a Gaussian mixture model should be trained in practice. The two principal changes to be made are to initialise the model in a more sensible way and to run the EM algorithm for more than a single iteration at a time. These changes are illustrated in demgmm2, where a model is trained on data that is sampled from a mixture of three Gaussians.

```
1   [data, datac, datap, datasd] = dem2ddat(ndata);
2   fh1 = figure;
3   plot(data(:, 1), data(:, 2), 'o')
4   set(gca, 'Box', 'on')
5   % Set up mixture model
6   ncentres = 3;
7   input_dim = 2;
8   mix = gmm(input_dim, ncentres, 'spherical');
9
10  options = foptions;
11  options(14) = 5;          % Just 5 iterations of k-means
12  % Initialise the model parameters from the data
13  mix = gmminit(mix, data, options);
14
15  % Set up vector of options for EM trainer
16  options = zeros(1, 18);
17  options(1)  = 1;          % Prints out error values.
18  options(14) = 10;         % Max. Number of iterations.
19  [mix, options, errlog] = gmmem(mix, data, options);
20
21  % Plot the result
22  x = -4.0:0.2:5.0; y = -4.0:0.2:5.0;
23  [X, Y] = meshgrid(x,y);
24  X = X(:); Y = Y(:);
25  grid = [X Y];
26  Z = gmmprob(mix, grid);
27  Z = reshape(Z, length(x), length(y));
28  c = mesh(x, y, Z);
29
30  hp1 = plot(data(:, 1), data(:, 2), 'bo');
31  axis('equal');
32  hold on
33  hp2 = plot(mix.centres(:, 1), mix.centres(:,2), 'g+');
34
35  angles = 0:pi/30:2*pi;
36  for i = 1 : mix.ncentres
37    x_circle = mix.centres(i,1)*ones(1, length(angles)) + ...
38      sqrt(mix.covars(i))*cos(angles);
39    y_circle = mix.centres(i,2)*ones(1, length(angles)) + ...
40      sqrt(mix.covars(i))*sin(angles);
41    plot(x_circle, y_circle, 'r')
42  end
```

The model is initialised in lines 10–13 using data, the matrix of training data. Because this involves training a K-means clustering model, the function is controlled by an options vector. It is not worth using too many iterations of K-means, since its purpose is to get reasonable values for the parameters of the GMM that can then be improved by EM.

Once the initialisation is complete, the model can be trained using EM. On this relatively simple problem, EM converges very rapidly, and just 10 iterations are needed for a good model.

The remainder of the program plots the resulting model in two different ways. Lines 22–28 produce a mesh plot of the density function of the trained model. The density values for the grid of points are computed in line 26 using gmmprob. Lines 30 to the end plot the means (as crosses) and one standard deviation contours (as red circles).

3.5 K-means Clustering

The K-means algorithm is a method for finding K vectors μ_j (for $j = 1, \ldots, K$) that represent an entire dataset. The data is considered to be partitioned into K clusters, with each cluster represented by its mean vector and each data point assigned to the cluster with the closest vector.

Although this is an unsupervised learning method, the resulting clusters do not form a density model. However, the K-means algorithm converges quickly, and as such is used to initialise other models so that more sophisticated training algorithms can be started closer to the eventual solution. For example, the initialisation of Gaussian mixture models uses K-means to form an initial partition of the data and assign the model parameters from this partition. K-means can also be used to determine the basis function parameters for RBF networks.

3.5.1 Algorithm and NETLAB Implementation

The K-means algorithm works iteratively. At each stage, the N data points x^n are partitioned into K disjoint clusters S_j each containing N_j data points. The error function that is minimised is the total within-cluster-sum-of-squares:

$$E = \sum_{j=1}^{K} \sum_{n \in S_j} \|x^n - \mu_j\|^2, \tag{3.36}$$

where μ_j is the centre of the jth cluster, given by the mean of the data points belonging to the cluster:

$$\mu_j = \frac{1}{N_j} \sum_{n \in S_j} x^n. \tag{3.37}$$

The initial partition of the data is at random. Then the following two steps are iterated until there is no further change to the error E.

1. The mean vectors for each cluster are calculated using (3.37).
2. Each data point is assigned to the cluster containing the closest mean vector.

This algorithm can be viewed as the limit of the EM algorithm for a Gaussian mixture model where each kernel is spherical with vanishingly small variance. The first of these steps is equivalent to the M-step, updating the kernel mean, while the second is equivalent to the E-step, assigning a responsibility for each data point (though instead of the 'soft' probabilistic responsibility of the GMM, it is a hard 0–1 value). More details can be found in (Bishop, 1995, Section 5.9).

Since the algorithm is iterative, the NETLAB implementation uses the standard options vector to control it. The only non-standard option is the 5th entry, which controls whether the initial set of centres should be taken from the argument list or randomly selected from the data (lines 8–12). The following listing is a shortened version of the NETLAB function kmeans.

```
1   function [centres, options, post, errlog] = ...
2                        kmeans(centres, data, options)
3
4   [ndata, data_dim] = size(data);
5   [ncentres, dim] = size(centres);
6
7   % Check if centres need to be initialised from data
8   if (options(5) == 1)
9     perm = randperm(ndata);
10    perm = perm(1:ncentres);
11    centres = data(perm, :);
12  end
13  id = eye(ncentres);
14
15  for n = 1:niters
16    old_centres = centres;
17
18    d2 = dist2(data, centres);
19    [minvals, index] = min(d2', [], 1);
20    post = id(index,:);
21
22    num_points = sum(post, 1);
23    for j = 1:ncentres
24      if (num_points(j) > 0)
25        centres(j,:)=sum(data(find(post(:,j)),:), 1)/num_points(j);
26      end
27    end
28
29    e = sum(minvals);
30    if options(1) > 0
31      fprintf(1, 'Cycle %4d  Error %11.6f\n', n, e);
32    end
```

```
33
34    if n > 1
35      % Test for termination
36      if max(max(abs(centres - old_centres))) < options(2) & ...
37          abs(old_e - e) < options(3)
38        options(8) = e;
39        return;
40      end
41    end
42    old_e = e;
43  end
```

Line 18 computes d2, the squared distance between all the data points and the current set of centres. d2 is used to construct post, a matrix which contains the 'hard' responsibilities for each data point (lines 19–20), so all entries in row i are zero except for a 1 in the column corresponding to the index of the nearest centre. Lines 22–27 compute the new set of centres following (3.37), and line 29 computes E as in (3.36).

3.5.2 Demonstration Program

The demonstration program for K-means simply shows how it can be used to find cluster centres in the same two-dimensional dataset as used for demgmm2.

```
1   % Generate data, fixing seeds for reproducible results
2   ndata = 250;
3   randn('state', 42);
4   rand('state', 42);
5   data = dem2ddat(ndata);
6
7   % Randomise data order
8   data = data(randperm(ndata),:);
9
10  % Plot the data
11  fh1 = figure;
12  plot(data(:, 1), data(:, 2), 'o')
13
14  % Set up cluster model
15  ncentres = 3;
16  centres = zeros(ncentres, 2);
17
18  % Set up vector of options for kmeans trainer
19  options = foptions;
20  options(1)  = 1;        % Prints out error values.
21  options(5) = 1;
22  options(14) = 10;       % Max. number of iterations.
23
24  % Train the centres from the data
25  [centres, options, post] = kmeans(centres, data, options);
```

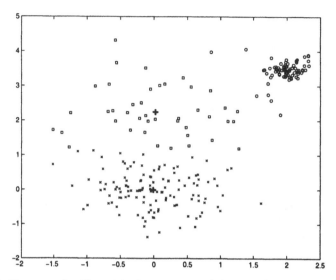

Fig. 3.7. *K*-means classifier with cluster centres (*plus signs*). Model classification: class 1 (*crosses*), class 2 (*squares*), class 3 (*circles*).

This model can be used as a simple classification technique by assigning each vector to the class of its closest centre. This is done by finding the index of the winning centre from the post matrix.

```
26  % Find the winning centre for each point
27  [tempi, tempj] = find(post);
28  figure(2);
29  hold on
30  for i = 1:3
31     % Select data points closest to ith centre
32     thisX = data(tempi(tempj == i), 1);
33     thisY = data(tempi(tempj == i), 2);
34     hp(i) = plot(thisX, thisY, colours(i,:));
35  end
36  legend('Class 1', 'Class 2', 'Class 3', 2)
37  hold on
38  plot(centres(:, 1), centres(:,2), 'k+', 'LineWidth', 2, ...
39     'MarkerSize', 8)
40  hold off
```

The results of this classifier are shown in Fig. 3.7.

3.6 *K*-nearest-neighbour

The *K*-nearest-neighbour algorithm is a very simple method for classification which can also be used as a crude density estimate. Despite the simplicity of the algorithm, it often performs very well and is an important benchmark method. One drawback is that all the training data must be stored.

Suppose that there are c classes. For a new pattern x we compute the distances to all the training examples and select a subset S_K consisting of the K closest. Let k_i be the frequency of the ith class in S_K. Then we assign x to the class C_m with the greatest frequency:

$$k_m \geq k_i \qquad \text{for } i = 1, \ldots, c. \tag{3.38}$$

If there is a tie (i.e. $k_m = k_n$ for $m \neq n$), then there are several possible strategies to choose a class. The one implemented in NETLAB is simply to choose at random from the winning classes.

For the case $K = 1$, the nearest-neighbour algorithm, the decision boundaries are piecewise linear, while larger values of K give smoother boundaries. A very important property of the nearest-neighbour algorithm is that its asymptotic error rate e is no worse than twice the Bayesian optimal rate e^*. More precisely (Cover and Hart, 1967),

$$e^* \leq e \leq e^* \left(2 - \frac{ce^*}{c-1}\right). \tag{3.39}$$

It is also clear that the error rate of the nearest-neighbour algorithm on the training set is 0, unless there are identical points with different classifications.

3.6.1 Algorithm and NETLAB Implementation

The NETLAB implementation of the K-nearest-neighbour algorithm involves just two functions, since training the model simply consists of storing the training data: knn sets up the model structure, and knnfwd classifies data.

The complete definition of the model data structure is given in Table 3.2. These fields are initialised by the function knn. We assume that the training

Table 3.2. Fields in the knn data structure.

type	Type (always 'knn')
nin	Dimension of input space
nout	Number of classes
k	Number of neighbours to consider
tr_in	Training data inputs
tr_targets	Training data targets

targets are represented by a 1-of-c encoding, where c is the number of classes (the variable nout).

```
1  function net = knn(nin, nout, k, tr_in, tr_targets)
2
3  net.type = 'knn';
4  net.nin = nin;
5  net.nout = nout;
6  net.k = k;
7  net.tr_in = tr_in;
8  net.tr_targets = tr_targets;
```

The classification function knnfwd is rather more interesting. It returns two matrices, y and l, each of which contains one row per example in the dataset presented. The matrix y has one column per class, and the ijth entry counts how many of the K training examples nearest to the ith example belonged to the jth class. The matrix l has one column, and the ith entry gives the index (counting from one) of the 'winning' class for the ith example, using a random selection to break ties.

```
1  function [y, l] = knnfwd(net, x)
2
3  ntest = size(x, 1);            % Number of input vectors.
4  nclass = size(net.tr_targets, 2);   % Number of classes.
5
6  distsq = dist2(net.tr_in, x);
7  [vals, kind] = sort(distsq);
8  y = zeros(ntest, nclass);
9
10 for k=1:net.k
11   y = y + net.tr_targets(kind(k,:),:);
12 end
13
14 if nargout == 2
15   [temp, l] = max((y + 0.1*rand(size(y))), [], 2);
16 end
```

Line 6 computes the squared distances between the training inputs and the current dataset x. The ijth entry of distsq represents the squared distance between the ith example in tr_in and the jth example in x. These distances are sorted in line 7, so that the ijth entry of kind gives the index in tr_in of the ith nearest neighbour to the jth pattern in x. (The sorted matrix vals is of no interest.)

The loop in lines 10–12 increments the count matrix y for the class of the kth nearest neighbour (assuming that the training targets have a 1-of-c encoding). The final three lines set l to be the column index of the maximal count for each example, while adding 0.1*rand(size(y)) ensures (with probability one) that no two counts can be the same but that only ties are affected.

3.6.2 Demonstration Program

The demonstration program classifies the same two-dimensional dataset as is used for K-means (see Section 3.5.2). The training examples are the centres of the generating Gaussian mixture model (line 22).

```
 1  % Generate the test data
 2  ndata = 250;
 3  randn('state', 42);
 4  rand('state', 42);
 5  [data, c] = dem2ddat(ndata);
 6
 7  % Randomise data order
 8  data = data(randperm(ndata),:);
 9  fh1 = figure;
10  plot(data(:, 1), data(:, 2), 'o')
11  hold on
12  hp1 = plot(c(:, 1), c(:,2), 'k+')
13  hold off
14
15  % Use centres as training data
16  train_labels = [1, 0, 0; 0, 1, 0; 0, 0, 1];
17
18  % Label the test data up to kmax neighbours
19  kmax = 1;
20  net = knn(2, 3, kmax, c, train_labels);
21  [y, l] = knnfwd(net, data);
22
23  % Plot the result
24  fh2 = figure;
25  colors = ['b.'; 'r.'; 'g.'];
26  for i = 1:3
27    thisX = data(l == i,1);
28    thisY = data(l == i,2);
29    hp(i) = plot(thisX, thisY, colors(i,:));
30    if i == 1
31      hold on
32    end
33  end
```

3.7 Worked Examples

In this section we show how the models introduced in this chapter can be used for tasks that arise in pattern recognition applications. The first of these is classification and the second is novelty detection.

3.7.1 Classification with Density Models

Suppose that a dataset contains examples from c classes $C_1, \ldots, C_c$. The most general approach to classifying these examples is to use the posterior probabilities of class membership $P(C_k|x)$. One way to build a classifier is to develop a model that estimates the posterior probabilities directly; this can be done using non-linear output nodes with a neural network (see Chapters 4 and 5). An alternative is to use a set of density estimators and Bayes' theorem.

First we build a density model for each class in turn: this estimates $p(x|\mathcal{C}_k)$ by training the model only on data from class $\mathcal{C}_k$. Then we write Bayes' theorem in the form

$$P(\mathcal{C}_k|x) = \frac{p(x|\mathcal{C}_k)P(\mathcal{C}_k)}{p(x)}, \tag{3.40}$$

where the unconditional density (or normalisation constant) $p(x)$ is given by the sum of the numerator over all classes:

$$p(x) = \sum_{k=1}^{c} p(x|\mathcal{C}_k)P(\mathcal{C}_k). \tag{3.41}$$

This ensures that the estimated posterior probabilities sum to one. The prior probability $P(\mathcal{C}_k)$ is simply given by the fraction of examples from class $\mathcal{C}_k$ in the training set.

If we only want to use the model as a classifier (and don't require estimates of the class-conditional probabilities $p(\mathcal{C}_k|x)$), then it is sufficient to consder the terms

$$P(\mathcal{C}_k|x) = p(x|\mathcal{C}_k)P(\mathcal{C}_k), \tag{3.42}$$

since the denominator $p(x)$ is the same for all classes.

The script demgmmc shows how the method can be applied to some toy two-dimensional data.

```
1   % DEMGMMC Demo of GMM used for classification
2
3   % Work with 2-d data
4   nin = 2;
5   % Fix the seeds
6   rand('state', 4231);
7   randn('state', 4231);
8   % Generate the training data: this follows demmlp2
9   n=200; % Number of data points
10
11  % Set up mixture model: 2d data with three centres
12  % Class 1 is first centre, class 2 from the other two
13  mix = gmm(nin, 3, 'full');
14  mix.priors = [0.5 0.25 0.25];
15  mix.centres = [0 -0.1; 1 1; 1 -1];
16  mix.covars(:,:,1) = [0.625 -0.2165; -0.2165 0.875];
17  mix.covars(:,:,2) = [0.2241 -0.1368; -0.1368 0.9759];
18  mix.covars(:,:,3) = [0.2375 0.1516; 0.1516 0.4125];
19
20  [data, label] = gmmsamp(mix, n);
21
```

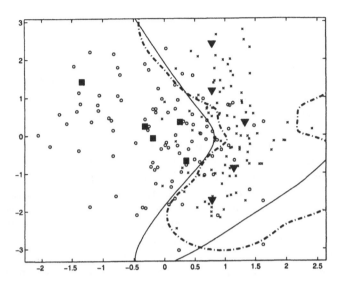

Fig. 3.8. Classification with Gaussian mixture models. 200 data points are drawn from class 1 (*circles*) and class 2 (*crosses*). The centres of mixture models trained on class 1 (*large squares*) and class 2 (*large triangles*) are show with the decision boundary (*dash-dotted line*). The optimal decision boundary (*solid line*) was found by applying Bayes' theorem to the generating distributions.

```
22  % Now fit a mixture of Gaussians to each class. Use spherical
23  % Gaussians as we assume we don't know the data structure.
24  ncentres = 5;  % Use 5 kernels
25  mix1 = gmm(nin, ncentres, 'spherical');
26  mix2 = gmm(nin, ncentres, 'spherical');
27
28  % Initialise models
29  options = foptions;
30  options(14) = 5;        % Just use 5 iterations of k-means
31  % Initialise the model parameters from the data
32  mix1 = gmminit(mix1, data(label==1, :), options);
33  mix2 = gmminit(mix2, data(label>1, :), options);
34
35  % Now train each model
36  options(1) = 1;  % Print error values
37  options(5) = 1;  % Prevent collapse of variances
38  options(14) = 15; % Number of iterations
39  mix1 = gmmem(mix1, data(label==1, :), options);
40  mix2 = gmmem(mix2, data(label>1, :), options);
41
42  % Estimate class priors
43  p_1 = sum(label==1)/n;
44
45  % Generate test data
46  [test, test_label] = gmmsamp(mix, n);
47  test_probs=[gmmprob(mix1,test).*p_1 gmmprob(mix2,test).*(1-p_1)];
```

```
48  % Convert to 1 of N encoding
49  target = [test_label==1 test_label>1];
50
51  fh1 = conffig(test_probs, target);
```

The dataset data is generated from a mixture model mix of three full covariance Gaussians (lines 13–20), and it is assumed that the first kernel is class C_1, and the second and third kernels are class C_2. (The use of multiple kernels for the second class ensures that the decision boundary is non-linear.) The mixing coefficients are set so that both classes have equal priors.

The classification model contains two Gaussian mixture models, mix1 and mix2, which are constructed on lines 25–26. Each consists of five kernels with spherical covariance structure: the mismatch between this and the original generator of the data is deliberate. The training data for mix1 is selected from data by the expression data(label==1, :) which picks out those rows that came from the first kernel of mix (see lines 32 and 39). The two models are initialised and trained in the usual way in lines 28–40. In line 43, the prior probability for class C_1 is estimated by counting the fraction of training points with label 1.

The classification model is tested by generating another 200 points from mix (line 46). The prediction from the model is generated (line 47) using (3.42). The final few lines of the demonstration create a figure containing the confusion matrix for this classifier. The results of this classifier compared with the optimal Bayesian classifier (which uses the true model mix in a similar way) are shown in Fig. 3.8. The accuracy of the mixture models is 84% compared to 85.5% for the optimal classifier using Bayes' rule applied to the known generating distribution.

3.7.2 Novelty Detection

All empirical (i.e. data-based) models will only give reliable results in operation when the data is similar to the training set. The statistical interpretation of this statement is that the data should have a similar probability distribution to that in the training set. For example, if a model $f(x)$ with one input is trained on data that lies in the interval $[0, 1]$, its output is unlikely to be accurate if $x = 1.5$.

Although it is easy enough with one-dimensional data to decide if the model is interpolating (the input lies in the range it was trained on) or extrapolating (the input lies outside this range), it is much harder if the input is multi-dimensional. A general approach to this problem is to model the *unconditional* data density $p(x)$ for the training data. We can then monitor the likelihood of input patterns during operation and compare them with the range of likelihoods in the training set (Bishop, 1994; Tarassenko, 1995). Any values that fall well outside this range are probably due to novel inputs, and the corresponding model output should not be relied upon.

In fact, many condition monitoring problems are best tackled with a novelty detection approach. For example, suppose that the task is to decide when an engine is not operating correctly. Typically there will be very large quantities of data when the engine is working correctly, and very little or no data for it operating in a faulty condition. In addition, there are often many different types of fault that can occur, so it is infeasible to gather sufficient quantities of data for each fault (and combination of faults) that might be present. An alternative approach is to train a density model on the normal data so that it can recognise when the engine is working correctly, and to treat any significant deviation from this model as a potential fault that requires further investigation.

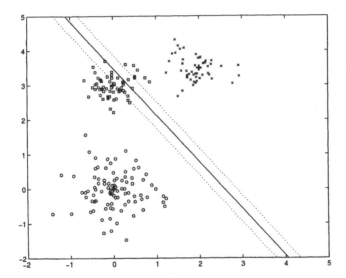

Fig. 3.9. Synthetic test dataset used in demonstration of novelty detection. Linear classifier trained on classes 1 (*crosses*) and 3 (*circles*), omitting data from class 2 (*squares*). Crosses show the centres of the mixture components used to generate the data. Decision boundary (*solid line*) and 0.1 and 0.9 probability levels (*dotted lines*) also shown.

The technique is illustrated by the `novel` script:

```
1  % NOVEL Demonstrate novelty detection
2  % Generate the data, fixing seeds for reproducible results
3  ntrain = 300;
4  ntest = 200;
5  randn('state', 42);
6  rand('state', 42);
7
8  mix = gmm(2, 3, 'spherical');
9  mix.centres = [2.0 3.5; 0 3; 0 0];
```

```
10  mix.priors = [0.3 0.3 0.4];
11  mix.covars = [0.15 0.1 0.3];
12
13  [tr_data, tr_labels] = gmmsamp(mix, ntrain);
14  % Remove class 2 from training data
15  tr_data = tr_data((tr_labels~=2), :);
16
17  tr_labels = tr_labels((tr_labels~=2));
18  tr_targets = (tr_labels==1);
19
20  net = glm(2, 1, 'logistic');
21  options = foptions;
22  options(1) = 1;
23  options(14) = 10;
24  net = glmtrain(net, options, tr_data, tr_targets);
25
26  mixn = gmm(2, 2, 'spherical');
27  options = foptions;
28  options(14) = 5;
29  mixn = gmminit(mixn, tr_data, options);
30  options(1) = 1;
31  options(5) = 1;
32  options(14) = 10;
33  mixn = gmmem(mixn, tr_data, options);
34  hist_levels = -10:1:0;
35  [n, x] = hist(log(gmmprob(mixn, tr_data)), hist_levels);
36  bp1 = bar(x, n);
37
38  [te_data, te_labels] = gmmsamp(mix, ntest);
39  te_pred = glmfwd(net, te_data((te_labels==2), :));
40  [n, x] = hist(log(gmmprob(mixn, te_data((te_labels==2), :))), ...
41    hist_levels);
42  bp2 = bar(x, n);
```

In this synthetic example, lines 8–11 set up a mixture model mix with three components, and line 13 generates some data from mix. Before using this data for training, all the examples from class 2 are removed (line 15), and the labels converted to a 0–1 encoding (lines 17–18). A simple linear classifier net is created (line 20) and trained (lines 21–24) on this data (see Fig. 3.9).

A mixture model mixn is trained to provide novelty detection in lines 26–33. The histogram of typical log probability values for the training set is created in lines 34–36.

An independent test set is sampled from the same distribution as the training data (line 38), and the classifier makes its predictions in line 39. Figure 3.10(b) shows that the outputs for class 2 examples, which were *not* included in the training data, are mostly close to 0 or 1, so that the model does not diagnose these unreliable predictions. However, the histogram of log probability for the class 2 examples (lines 40–42 and Fig. 3.10(a)) shows very little overlap with that for the training data, and this would allow most of the predictions made on these novel inputs to be rejected.

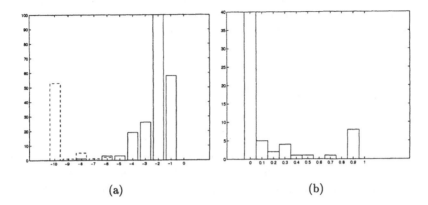

(a)   (b)

Fig. 3.10. Demonstration of novelty detection. (a) Histogram of log probability of training set (*solid lines*) and log probability of class 2 examples from test set (*dashed lines*). (b) Histogram of linear classifier outputs on class 2 examples from test set.

Exercises

3.1 (⋆) Compare the speed of convergence of the EM algorithm using random parameter initialisation and K-means initialisation.

3.2 (⋆⋆⋆) Extend the EM algorithm implementation to deal with missing values in the data set. These values are conventionally represented by not-a-number NaN values in MATLAB.

Denote the missing and observed data by x_m^n and x_o^n respectively. Then the log-likelihood of the parameters θ_j given $y^n = (x_o^n, x_m^n, z^n)$ can be written

$$\mathcal{L}(\theta|y^n) = \sum_{n=1}^{N} \sum_{j=1}^{M} z_j^n \Big[\frac{n}{2} \log 2\pi + \frac{1}{2} \log |\Sigma_j|$$

$$- \frac{1}{2}(x_o^n - \mu_{j,o})^T \Sigma_j^{-1,oo}(x_o^n - \mu_{j,o})$$ (3.43)

$$- (x_o^n - \mu_{j,o})^T \Sigma_j^{-1,om}(x_m^n - \mu_{j,m})$$

$$- \frac{1}{2}(x_m^n - \mu_{j,m})^T \Sigma_j^{-1,mm}(x_m^n - \mu_{j,m})\Big],$$

where the superscript $(-1, om)$ denotes taking the matrix inverse followed by extracting the submatrix corresponding to observed versus missing variables. If a spherical or diagonal covariance matrix is used, then all cross terms in the covariance (and its inverse) are zero.

The E-step involves taking the expectation of (3.43) to compute three values: $E(z_j^n|x_o^n, w^{(t)})$, $E(z_j^n x_m^n|x_o^n, w^{(t)})$, $E(z_j^n x_n^m (x_m^n)^T|x_o^n, w^{(t)})$ (where t is used to index the iteration number). To compute these expectations we define

$$\hat{x}_{j,m}^n = E\left[x_m^n|z_{ij} = 1, x_o^n, w^{(m)}\right] = \mu_{j,m} + \Sigma_j^{mo}(\Sigma_j^{oo})^{-1}(x_o^n - \mu_{j,o}),$$

(3.44)

which is the least-squares regression of x_m^n on x_o^n from the jth kernel. Only the first term on the right-hand side contributes for spherical and diagonal covariance matrices. Then the three E-step terms are given by

$$E(z_j^n|x_o^n, w^{(m)}) = P^{(t)}(j|x_o^n)$$

(3.45)

$$E(z_j^n x_m^n|x_o^n, w^{(m)}) = P^{(t)}(j|x_o^n)\hat{x}_{j,m}^n$$

(3.46)

$$E(z_j^n x_n^m (x_m^n)^T|x_o^n, w^{(m)}) =$$

$$P^{(t)}(j|x_o^n)(\Sigma_j^{mm} - \Sigma_j^{(mo)}(\Sigma_j^{oo})^{-1}(\Sigma_j^{mo})^T + \hat{x}_{j,m}^n(\hat{x}_{j,m}^n)^T).$$

(3.47)

The M-step uses these values in the standard update equations to reestimate mixing coefficients, means and covariances (Ghahramani and Jordan, 1994a). So the values of $\hat{x}_{j,m}^n$ are substituted for the missing values of x^n in (3.31), (3.32) and (3.33) while the values of the bracketed term are substituted in (3.47).

3.3 ($\star\star$) Write a function to train a kernel density estimator using the GMM framework provided by NETLAB. The functional form of a kernel density estimator containing N kernels is

$$p(x) = \frac{1}{N}\sum_{n=1}^{N}\phi_n(x),$$

(3.48)

where ϕ_n is a density function that is 'centred' on the nth data point. It can easily be shown that under these conditions, p is also a density function. A common choice for ϕ is a multivariate Gaussian:

$$\phi(x) = \frac{1}{(2\pi\sigma^2)^{d/2}}\exp\left\{-\frac{\|x - x^n\|^2}{2\sigma^2}\right\},$$

(3.49)

where x^n runs over the entire training set. This has the same form as a Gaussian mixture model with spherical covariance where the mixing coefficients are all equal, the means are given by the data points, and the only adjustable parameter is the covariance σ^2, also known as the smoothing parameter.

The smoothing parameter is usually chosen by cross-validation: it is set to a selection of values and the likelihood of a validation set is used to determine the best one.

3.4 ($\star$) Use the algorithm you have developed in question 3.3 to investigate the effect of the smoothing parameter on the fitted distribution. This is most easily visualised with 1-d or 2-d data. Generate a random sample of training and validation data from a distribution (e.g. a mixture of Gaussians). Plot the density function of a kernel estimator for a range of different values of σ^2 and show that when σ is large, the density is over-smooth, while when σ is small, the density is too noisy and approaches a set of delta functions on the training data points.

3.5 ($\star\star$) Extend the example of GMM used for classification to a robust NETLAB model gmmc. You will need to write three functions.

- Create the data structure
  `function mixc = gmmc(nin, nclasses, ncentres, covar_type)`
  (you may assume that all the mixture models have the same structure). The data structure should hold an array of mixture models, one for each class, and an array of class priors.

- Train the model
  `function mixc = gmmcem(mixc, x, t, options)`
  where x is the input data, t are the targets, assumed to use a 1-of-c encoding, and `options` is the usual options vector. You may make the simplifying assumption that this function will carry out the model initialisation using gmminit. Alternatively, for more flexibility, you can write a function gmmcinit to perform this separately.

- Run the model
  `function [y, p] = gmmcfwd(mixc, x)`
  to generate un-normalised probabilities y and normalised probabilities p if there are two output arguments.

3.6 ($\star$) Write a demonstration program for K-means that mirrors demgmm1 for the GMM.

3.7 ($\star\star\star$) Explore empirically the behaviour of the K-nearest-neighbour algorithm as K varies. Generate data from a mixture of Gaussians and use Bayes' theorem to draw the optimal decision boundary. Train K-nearest-neighbour models for different values of K and show that there is an optimal value of K for which the decision boundary for the model lies closest to the Bayes boundary.

3.8 ($\star\star$) The K-nearest-neighbour density at a point x is computed as follows. Find the smallest r so that the sphere $\mathcal{S}_x$ of radius r centred on x contains K training examples. If there are N examples in the training dataset and the volume of $\mathcal{S}_x$ is V, then the density estimate is

$$p(x) = \frac{K}{NV}. \tag{3.50}$$

This is not a true density function, since there is no guarantee that it integrates to 1, but it can be used as a relative density measure.

Implement a function knnprob(net, x) that computes this measure for a K-nearest-neighbour data structure net and dataset x. If the dataset has dimension d, the volume V is given by

$$V = \frac{2\pi^{(d/2)} r^d}{\Gamma(d/2)d},\tag{3.51}$$

where $\Gamma(x)$ is the gamma function defined by

$$\Gamma(x) = \int_0^\infty t^{x-1} \exp(-t)\, dt,\tag{3.52}$$

and available as the MATLAB function gamma.

4. Single Layer Networks

Single layer networks implement the well known statistical techniques of linear regression and generalised linear models. In NETLAB these models are given the generic title of Generalised Linear Models (GLMs) with the abbreviation glm. These models consist of a linear combination of the input variables, in which the coefficients are the parameters of the model, followed by an activation function appropriate to the type of data being modelled.

Once the error function and its gradient have been computed, such models can be trained with non-linear optimisation algorithms in the same way as other neural networks. However, it is also possible to take advantage of the linear (or near-linear) structure of the network and use a particularly efficient special purpose training algorithm known as iterated re-weighted least squares (IRLS), which is implemented in NETLAB. It is always useful to apply a (generalised) linear model to a dataset to provide a benchmark for more sophisticated methods. Because of their simplicity, they rarely overfit the training data, and they also have the advantage of being extremely fast to train.

The demonstration programs in this chapter show how generalised linear models can be applied to classification problems. The worked example is a robust method for regularising linear regression models by controlling the magnitude of the weight vector. The principal functions described in this chapter are listed in Table 4.1.

4.1 The Single Layer Feed-forward Network

We shall denote the input values to the network by x_i where $i = 1, \ldots, d$. The network forms c linear combinations of these inputs (where c is the number of outputs) to give a set of intermediate variables a_j,

$$a_j = \sum_{i=1}^{d} w_{ji}^{(1)} x_i + b_j^{(1)} \qquad j = 1, \ldots, c, \tag{4.1}$$

with one variable a_j associated with each output unit. Here $w_{ji}^{(1)}$ represents the elements of the weight matrix and $b_j^{(1)}$ are the bias parameters.

Table 4.1. Functions in this chapter.

GLM Functions	
demglm1	Demonstration of GLM on two-class problem
demglm2	Demonstration of GLM on three-class problem
glm	Create a single layer feed-forward network
glmbkp	Backpropagate error gradient through network
glmderiv	Evaluate derivatives of network outputs
glmerr	Evaluate error function
glmfwd	Forward propagation
glmgrad	Evaluate error gradient
glmhess	Evaluate the Hessian matrix
glminit	Initialise the weights
glmpak	Combine weights and biases into one parameter vector
glmtrain	Iterated re-weighted least squares training algorithm
glmunpak	Separate parameter vector into weight and bias matrices

The variables a_j are then transformed by the activation functions of the output layer to give output values y_j. NETLAB implements three different activation functions. For regression problems an appropriate choice is the linear function of the form

$$y_j = a_j. \tag{4.2}$$

For classification problems involving multiple independent attributes we use independent logistic sigmoidal activation functions applied to each of the outputs independently, so that

$$y_j = \frac{1}{1 + \exp(-a_j)}. \tag{4.3}$$

Finally, for the more usual kind of classification problem in which we have a set of c mutually exclusive classes, we use the softmax activation function of the form

$$y_j = \frac{\exp(a_j)}{\sum_{j'} \exp(a_{j'})}. \tag{4.4}$$

For each of these choices of activation function there is a corresponding choice of error function, which is discussed in Section 4.2.

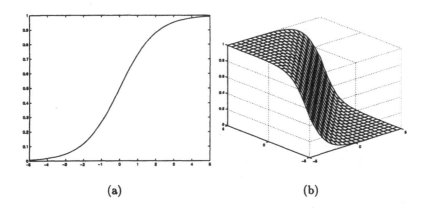

(a)   (b)

Fig. 4.1. Output activation functions. (a) Logistic sigmoid. (b) Softmax.

4.1.1 NETLAB Implementation

Network Creation and Initialisation

A GLM is created using the NETLAB function glm, which has the calling syntax

```
net = glm(nin, nout, outfunc, prior, beta);
```

where outfunc is a string specifying the output-unit activation function. Possible choices are 'linear', 'logistic' and 'softmax' corresponding to (4.2), (4.3), and (4.4) respectively. In order to specify the network architecture, the user must provide values for the number of inputs and the number of output units. The prior and beta arguments are optional, and will be discussed in more detail in the context of the Bayesian viewpoint in Chapter 9. The function glm returns the network data structure net, which has the following fields:

```
type    % string describing network type: always 'glm'
nin     % number of inputs
nout    % number of outputs
nwts    % total number of weights and biases
outfn   % string describing the output unit activation function
w1      % first-layer weight matrix
b1      % first-layer bias vector
```

The matrices have the following dimensions: w1 is nin × nout; b1 is 1 × nout.

```
1  function net = glm(nin, nout, outfunc, ...
2                      prior, beta)
3  net.type = 'glm';
4  net.nin = nin;
5  net.nout = nout;
```

```
 6  net.nwts = (nin + 1)*nout;
 7
 8  outfns = {'linear', 'logistic', 'softmax'};
 9
10  if sum(strcmp(outfunc, outfns)) == 0
11    error('Undefined activation function. Exiting.');
12  else
13    net.outfn = outfunc;
14  end
15
16  if nargin > 3
17    if isstruct(prior)
18      net.alpha = prior.alpha;
19      net.index = prior.index;
20    elseif size(prior) == [1 1]
21      net.alpha = prior;
22    else
23      error('prior must be a scalar or structure');
24    end
25  end
26
27  net.w1 = randn(nin, nout)/sqrt(nin + 1);
28  net.b1 = randn(1, nout)/sqrt(nin + 1);
29
30  if nargin == 5
31    net.beta = beta;
32  end
```

The total number of weights is computed in line 6. To prevent the user from specifying an unsupported activation function, lines 8–14 test that the string matches one of the three permissible values.

The weights are initialised by random selection from a zero mean, unit variance isotropic Gaussian where the variance is scaled by the fan-in of the hidden or output units as appropriate. This is accomplished by lines 27–28. The seed for the random weight initialisation can be set by calling

```
randn('state', s);
```

where s is the seed value, prior to invoking glm. Lines 16–25 and 30–32 are concerned with setting up priors for the Bayesian framework, and are discussed in more detail in Chapter 9.

The function glminit can be used to initialise all the weights from a zero mean isotropic Gaussian distribution with covariance sigma as follows:

```
net = glminit(net, 1/sigma);
```

The relevant lines of the function are

```
1  function net = glminit(net, prior)
2
3  elseif size(prior) == [1 1]
4    w = randn(1, net.nwts).*sqrt(1/prior);
5  end
6  net = glmunpak(net, w);
```

where the function glmunpak separates the row vector w into its component weight and bias matrices as discussed in Section 4.1.1. More elaborate forms of initialisation are discussed in the context of the Bayesian viewpoint in Chapter 9.

Manipulating Weights

By defining separate matrices for the weights and biases, we ensure that the equations for forward propagation and gradient calculations take on a simple form. This representation, however, is not always convenient: if we train the network with a general purpose optimisation algorithm, then it is preferable to consider all the parameters (weights and biases) in the model as a single vector. The separate matrices can be packed into a single row vector using the function glmpak. The key line is

```
w = [net.w1(:)', net.b1];
```

The : operator takes a matrix and converts it to a column vector: the transpose operator then creates a row vector of length nin × nout.

To change representation in the opposite direction and convert a row vector w into the corresponding weight and bias matrices requires knowledge of the network data structure net and is performed by the function glmunpak

```
net = glmunpak(net, w)
```

After checking that the weight vector w has the correct size for the specified network data structure, the component weight matrices are extracted from w and resized appropriately:

```
1   function net = glmunpak(net, w)
2
3   if net.nwts ~= length(w)
4     error('Invalid weight vector length')
5   end
6
7   nin = net.nin;
8   nout = net.nout;
9   net.w1 = reshape(w(1:nin*nout), nin, nout);
10  net.b1 = reshape(w(nin*nout + 1: (nin + 1)*nout), 1, nout);
```

4.1.2 Forward Propagation

A dataset consists of input vectors x_n with components x_{ni} where $n = 1, \ldots, N$. The number of data points is denoted ndata, and the input vectors form the rows of a matrix x of dimensions ndata × nin. The function glmfwd performs batch forward propagation of a matrix of input vectors through the network and has the following syntax

```
y = glmfwd(net, x);
```

The output matrix y has dimensions ndata × nout. The function glmfwd has an additional optional return argument of the form

```
[y, a] = glmfwd(w, np, x);
```

where a contains the activations a_j of the output units corresponding to (4.1).

```
1   function [y, a] = glmfwd(net, x)
2
3   ndata = size(x, 1);
4   a = x*net.w1 + ones(ndata, 1)*net.b1;
5
6   switch net.outfn
7     case 'linear'      % Linear outputs
8       y = a;
9     case 'logistic'    % Logistic outputs
10      maxcut = -log(eps);
11      mincut = -log(1/realmin - 1);
12      a = min(a, maxcut);
13      a = max(a, mincut);
14      y = 1./(1 + exp(-a));
15    case 'softmax'     % Softmax outputs
16      nout = size(a,2);
17      maxcut = log(realmax) - log(nout);
18      mincut = log(realmin);
19      a = min(a, maxcut);
20      a = max(a, mincut);
21      temp = exp(a);
22      y(y<realmin) = realmin;
23      y = temp./(sum(temp, 2)*ones(1,nout));
24    otherwise
25      error(['Unknown activation function ', net.outfn]);
26  end
```

The forward propagation of the input data through the network is performed by line 4, and this is followed by the application of the appropriate activation function defined by net.outfn.

- The linear activation function simply copies the activation a to the output y (line 8).
- The logistic output function is given by

$$y = \frac{1}{1 + \exp(-a)}. \tag{4.5}$$

Care is taken in the computation of the logistic function to ensure that when computing the error function, the function log is always passed a value within its domain and that the result does not overflow a double precision representation. The computation of y in glmfwd is made compatible with that in glmerr, which is explained in Section 4.2. This requires not only that $\log y$ is computable, but also $\log(1 - y)$.

- For multi-class problems, the softmax activation function (4.4) is used. Similar precautions to those used for the logistic function are necessary to prevent overflow or taking a logarithm of zero when computing the error function.

4.2 Error Functions

The most general information about the target vector t for inputs x is given by the conditional density $p(t|x)$. We assume that each of the c outputs are independent (except for the softmax activation function), so that

$$p(t|x) = \prod_{k=1}^{c} p(t_k|x). \tag{4.6}$$

We model each target variable t_k by a deterministic function $y_k(x; w)$, where w is the set of weight parameters in the neural network mapping, with added stochastic noise ϵ_k.

$$t_k = y_k(x; w) + \epsilon_k. \tag{4.7}$$

For each of the functions available as the output of a GLM in NETLAB there is a corresponding *canonical* error function, which represents the negative log likelihood of the data under a certain choice of noise model ϵ_k. We assume that each data point (x^n, t^n) is i.i.d., that is drawn independently from a fixed distribution, so

$$p(t^1, \ldots, t^N | x^1, \ldots, x^N) = \prod_{n=1}^{N} p(t^n | x^n), \tag{4.8}$$

and thus

$$E = -\log p(t^1, \ldots, t^N | x^1, \ldots, x^N)$$

$$= -\sum_{n=1}^{N} \log p(t^n | x^n). \tag{4.9}$$

The NETLAB function glmerr computes this error function for each noise model as determined by the net.outfn field.

If we choose a Gaussian noise model ϵ_k with zero mean and constant variance σ^2

$$p(\epsilon_k) = \frac{1}{(2\pi\sigma^2)^{1/2}} \exp\left(-\frac{\epsilon_k^2}{2\sigma^2}\right), \tag{4.10}$$

this leads to a conditional distribution with an input-dependent mean and constant variance:

$$p(t_k | \boldsymbol{x}) = \frac{1}{(2\pi\sigma^2)^{1/2}} \exp\left(-\frac{\{y_k(\boldsymbol{x}; \boldsymbol{w}) - t_k\}^2}{2\sigma^2}\right). \tag{4.11}$$

If we take logs and ignore terms that do not depend on the network function y_k, we arrive at the sum-of-squares error function

$$E = \frac{1}{2}\sum_{n=1}^{N}\sum_{k=1}^{c}\{y_k(\boldsymbol{x}_n; \boldsymbol{w}) - t_{nk}\}^2. \tag{4.12}$$

It can also be useful to *regularise* the model to prevent any weights becoming too large; we shall see this again when we consider MLP and RBF networks. This means that a *weight decay* penalty term is added to the error function, which becomes

$$E_r = E + \alpha\sum w_i^2, \tag{4.13}$$

where the regularisation parameter α is non-negative. (Clearly if $\alpha = 0$ we are left with the normal sum-of-squares error function.) This is implemented in NETLAB by setting the field net.alpha to the required value. The optimal value of α is usually found by cross-validation, which involves reserving a validation dataset to evaluate the error E of models trained using a range of different values of α and selecting the value of α that gives the smallest E. In the linear regression framework, this is known as *ridge regression*. It can be viewed as a special case of a zero mean Gaussian prior over the weights in a Bayesian setting.

While the sum-of-squares error function is appropriate for regression, for classification problems it is often advantageous to optimise the network outputs to represent the posterior probabilities of each class (Bishop, 1995). Let us first consider a problem with two classes. The target variable is binary, and a Gaussian noise model does not provide a good description of its distribution. We use a single output y, which represents the posterior probability $P(C_1 | \boldsymbol{x})$, so the posterior probability of class C_2 is $P(C_2 | \boldsymbol{x}) = 1 - y$. The target coding scheme is $t = 1$ if the input vector belongs to class C_1 and $t = 0$ if it belongs to class C_2. Instead of a Gaussian, we use a Bernoulli random variable for the conditional distribution:

$$p(t | \boldsymbol{x}) = y(\boldsymbol{x}; \boldsymbol{w})^t (1 - y(\boldsymbol{x}; \boldsymbol{w}))^{(1-t)}. \tag{4.14}$$

Taking the negative logarithm of this and summing over the entire pattern set yields the *cross-entropy* error function

$$E = -\sum_n \{t^n \ln y^n + (1 - t^n)\ln(1 - y^n)\}. \tag{4.15}$$

This definition can be extended to problems where there are c attributes, each of which is present or absent independently. Then each target variable

t_k is binary and has a Bernoulli distribution. Because the target variables are independent, their joint distribution decomposes as in (4.6) and the resulting error function is given by

$$E = -\sum_n \sum_{k=1}^{c} \{t_k^n \ln y_k^n + (1 - t_k^n) \ln(1 - y_k^n)\}. \tag{4.16}$$

The final case to consider is where we have a single target variable with c mutually exclusive classes and $c > 2$. The network has a single output variable y_k for each class, and the target data has a 1-of-c coding, so that $y_k^n = \delta_{kl}$ if the nth pattern belongs to class C_l. The probability of observing this particular target, given an input vector x^n, is $P(C_l|x^n) = y_l(x_l^n; w_l^n)$. The conditional distribution for this pattern can be written as

$$p(t^n|x^n) = \prod_{k=1}^{c} (y_k^n)^{t_k^n}. \tag{4.17}$$

If we compute the likelihood of the data, and take the negative logarithm as before, we obtain the *entropy* error function:

$$E = -\sum_n \sum_{k=1}^{c} t_k^n \ln y_k^n. \tag{4.18}$$

A clear benefit from using the logistic and softmax outputs on classification problems is that the network outputs can be treated directly as estimates of class-conditional probabilities $P(C_k|x)$ since they conform to the requirements for being probabilities. This allows us to

- Combine the outputs of several models; by averaging their predictions we still have estimates of the class conditional probabilities.
- Make minimum risk classification by weighting a misclassification cost function by network predictions.
- Apply a rejection threshold so that if all the posterior probabilities fall below a threshold, then no classification is made.

See (Bishop, 1995, Chapter 6) for more details. These error functions are implemented in the NETLAB function glmerr.

```
1   function [e, edata, eprior, y, a] = glmerr(net, x, t)
2
3   [y, a] = glmfwd(net, x);
4
5   switch net.outfn
6      case 'linear'          % Linear outputs
7         edata = 0.5*sum(sum((y - t).^2));
8      case 'logistic'        % Logistic outputs
9         edata = - sum(sum(t.*log(y) + (1 - t).*log(1 - y)));
10     case 'softmax'         % Softmax outputs
```

```
11      edata = - sum(sum(t.*log(y)));
12    otherwise
13      error(['Unknown activation function ', net.outfn]);
14 end
15
16 [e, edata, eprior] = errbayes(net, edata);
```

The first step is to forward propagate the inputs through the model (line 3). Each output activation function then requires a different error calculation.

- The sum of squares error (4.12) can be calculated in a single matrix operation (line 7).
- We have to take a little care over the NETLAB implementation of the cross-entropy error function to avoid numerical difficulties. If MATLAB takes the log of zero, the result is -Inf and a warning message is generated. This is clearly not very user friendly. To avoid this, we ensure that the log function is always passed a value within its domain. Using the logistic output function

$$y = \frac{1}{1 + \exp(-a)}, \tag{4.19}$$

to ensure that log(1-y) is computable, we require

$$1 + \exp(-a) \geq 1, \tag{4.20}$$

which implies that

$$\exp(-a) \geq \text{eps} \quad \Longrightarrow \quad a \leq -\ln(\text{eps}). \tag{4.21}$$

To ensure that log(y) is computable, we require $y > 0$, which implies that $y \geq \text{realmin}$, and hence that

$$\frac{1}{1 + \exp(-a)} \geq \text{realmin}$$

$$\Longleftrightarrow \exp^{-a} \leq \frac{1}{\text{realmin}} - 1$$

$$\Longleftrightarrow a \geq -\log\left(\frac{1}{\text{realmin}} - 1\right). \tag{4.22}$$

These two conditions are enforced in glmfwd by recomputing y after upper ((4.21) and line 12) and lower ((4.22) and line 13) thresholds have been applied to a. This is then used to compute (4.16) in line 9 of glmerr.

- When computing the entropy error function in NETLAB, we have to guard against taking overflow in the exponential sum and taking a logarithm of zero. The former is achieved most easily in glmfwd by thresholding

$$e^{a_j} < \frac{\text{realmax}}{\text{nout}} \tag{4.23}$$

which is equivalent to

$$a_j < \log(\text{realmax}) - \log(\text{nout}), \tag{4.24}$$

which is enforced by line 17. Line 18 ensures that $e^{a_j} > 0$, as with the logistic function. The softmax function is then applied (lines 21–22), in order to compute y^n Finally, the cross-entropy error function is computed, with y bounded away from zero, in line 11 of glmerr.

The final line of the function glmerr is concerned with regularisation terms, and will be discussed further in Chapter 9.

4.3 Error Gradient Calculation

The NETLAB error gradient function for generalised linear models is glmgrad. The first step in evaluating the error derivatives is to perform a forward propagation for the complete data set in order to evaluate the activations y_k^n of the output units for each pattern n in the data set. Because of the canonical choice of the error function and its corresponding activation function, the partial derivative of the error with respect to a_k^n is the same for all three error functions (Bishop, 1995):

$$\frac{\partial E^n}{\partial a_k} = y_k^n - t_k^n. \tag{4.25}$$

Thus, in order to evaluate the derivatives of E with respect to the weight and bias parameters we first evaluate the quantities δ_k^n given by

$$\delta_k^n = y_k^n - t_k^n, \tag{4.26}$$

which represent 'errors' for the output units on pattern n. Here y_k^n denotes $y_k(w; x^n)$.

The derivatives of E with respect to the weights are given by

$$\frac{\partial E}{\partial w_{kj}^{(1)}} = \sum_{n=1}^{N} \delta_k^n x_j^n, \tag{4.27}$$

while the derivatives for the biases are given by

$$\frac{\partial E}{\partial b_k^{(1)}} = \sum_{n=1}^{N} \delta_k^n. \tag{4.28}$$

The NETLAB function glmgrad is implemented as follows:

```
1  function [g, gdata, gprior] = glmgrad(net, x, t)
2
3  y = glmfwd(net, x);
4  delout = y - t;
5
6  gw1 = x'*delout;
7  gb1 = sum(delout, 1);
8  gdata = [gw1(:)', gb1];
9  [g, gdata, gprior] = gbayes(net, gdata);
```

The first two steps are implemented by lines 3–4. Note that for some optimisation algorithms there is some loss of efficiency in doing a forward propagation as part of the gradient evaluation since in the optimisation this may have been preceded by another forward propagation using the same weight values to compute the error with glmerr. This inefficiency is more than compensated for by the resulting code simplicity and modularity, as discussed in the Preface.

Equations (4.27) and (4.28) are implemented in lines 6–7. The derivative terms are then combined to obtain a single gradient vector in line 8, so that each component of gdata contains the derivative of E with respect to the corresponding component of the weight vector w. The ordering of the weights is the same as that used in glmpak.

Line 9 modifies the error gradient to include regularisation terms, and will be discussed further in Chapter 9.

4.4 Evaluating Other Derivatives

In this section we show how other derivatives of a GLM can be computed. These are the derivatives of the network *outputs* with respect to the weights, and the matrix of the second derivatives of the error function.

4.4.1 Network Activation Derivatives

First we consider the problem of evaluating the derivatives of the network output activations with respect to the weights and biases

$$\frac{\partial A}{\partial w_{ji}}. \tag{4.29}$$

These derivatives are required in Section 9.5 to evaluate error bars on network regression predictions in a Bayesian framework. As the notation indicates, the result of this procedure is a three-dimensional array (since there are k outputs) and there is a term for each of N data points. Thus the array has dimension $N \times W \times k$, where W is the total number of network weights. The NETLAB function glmderiv computes these derivatives.

```
1  function g = glmderiv(net, x)
2
3  ndata = size(x, 1);
4  g = zeros(ndata, net.nwts, net.nout);
5
6  for n = 1:ndata
7    % Weight matrix w1
8    g(n, 1:net.nin*net.nout, :) = kron(eye(net.nout), (x(n, :))');
9    % Bias term b1
10   g(n, net.nin*net.nout+1:end, :) = eye(net.nout);
11 end
```

The derivative of the kth output is given simply by the input vector, augmented by a 1 for the bias unit, in the coordinates corresponding to the fan-in weights for the output unit, with zeros elsewhere. The loop from lines 6–11 computes the result for each input vector in turn. Because the weights are arranged in two matrices, w1 and b2, this requires a little care in the implementation. For concreteness, suppose that the model has three inputs and two outputs, and that the input vector x is $(1, 2, 3)$. Then line 8 creates a matrix

$$
G_{w1} = \begin{bmatrix} 1 & 0 \\ 2 & 0 \\ 3 & 0 \\ 0 & 1 \\ 0 & 2 \\ 0 & 3 \end{bmatrix}
\tag{4.30}
$$

which contains the gradient with respect to w1, since the first three weights are the fan-in for output 1 and the next three are the fan-in for output 2 using the standard ordering given by glmpak. Line 10 adds the matrix

$$
G_{b1} = \begin{bmatrix} 1 & 0 \\ 0 & 1 \end{bmatrix}
\tag{4.31}
$$

to the bottom of G_{w1}. G_{b1} contains the gradient with respect to b1, and the bias weights for the outputs are placed in order.

4.4.2 The Hessian Matrix

The second derivatives of the error function, given by

$$
\frac{\partial^2 E}{\partial w_{ji} \partial w_{lk}},
\tag{4.32}
$$

form the elements of the Hessian matrix H, which plays an important role in the theory and applications of generalised linear models. As well as the techniques discussed in Section 5.5, the Hessian is needed for the IRLS training algorithm.

Because of the nearly linear structure of the GLM, it is relatively straightforward to evaluate the Hessian directly. Let X denote the data matrix augmented with a column of 1s. Then the Hessian matrix for the linear regression model is equal to

$$X^T X. \tag{4.33}$$

The Hessian of a single-output logistic model (Hastie and Tibshirani, 1990) is equal to

$$X^T \Pi X. \tag{4.34}$$

Π is a diagonal *weight* matrix whose elements are $p^{(n)}(1 - p^{(n)})$, where $p^{(n)}$ is the model output for the nth pattern. The case of softmax regression is a little more complicated (and not so well documented in the literature). The gradient and Hessian for a single input pattern x are given by

$$\frac{\partial^2 \mathcal{L}}{\partial w_{ki} \partial w_{lj}} = (p_l \delta_{kl} - p_l p_k) x_i x_j. \tag{4.35}$$

These computations are implemented in the function glmhess. A slight complication is that the equations given above are correct when the model weights are arranged so that all the weights belonging to the fan-in of a given output unit are together, so that the bias for that unit follows directly after the weights connecting the input pattern to the output unit. The glm data structure is organised differently: the input to output weights are contained in a matrix w1 which is separate from the bias weights in b1. Hence the values given by (4.33) and (4.34) need to be reordered to correspond to the order of weights in the GLM data structure. This is accomplished by the sub-function rearrange_hess.

The full specification of the function glmhess is

```
function [h, hdata] = glmhess(net, x, t, hdata)
```

The return value h is the full Hessian matrix including contributions from regularisation terms, while dh is the data-dependent part of the Hessian. The first of these will be discussed further in Chapter 9, while we only consider the second in this section. The optional parameter hdata is used if the function is only called to update the regularisation contribution to the Hessian; this will also be discussed further in Chapter 9.

```
1  function [h, hdata] = glmhess(net, x, t, hdata)
2
3  ndata = size(x, 1);
4  nparams = net.nwts;
5  nout = net.nout;
6  p = glmfwd(net, x);
7  inputs = [x ones(ndata, 1)];
8
9  if nargin == 3
```

```
10    hdata = zeros(nparams);   % Data Hessian matrix
11    switch net.outfn
12    case 'linear'
13      out_hess = [x ones(ndata, 1)]'*[x ones(ndata, 1)];
14      for j = 1:nout
15        hdata = rearrange_hess(net, j, out_hess, hdata);
16      end
17    case 'logistic'
18      e = ones(1, net.nin+1);
19      link_deriv = p.*(1-p);
20      out_hess = zeros(net.nin+1);
21      for j = 1:nout
22        inputs = [x ones(ndata, 1)].*(sqrt(link_deriv(:,j))*e);
23        out_hess = inputs'*inputs;   % Hessian for this output
24        hdata = rearrange_hess(net, j, out_hess, hdata);
25      end
26    case 'softmax'
27      bb_start = nparams - nout + 1;  % Start of bias block
28      ex_hess = zeros(nparams); % Contribution from each example
29      for m = 1:ndata
30        X = x(m,:)'*x(m,:);
31        a = diag(p(m,:))-((p(m,:)')*p(m,:));
32        ex_hess(1:nparams-nout,1:nparams-nout) = kron(a, X);
33        ex_hess(bb_start:nparams, bb_start:nparams) = ...
34            a.*ones(net.nout, net.nout);
35        temp = kron(a, x(m,:));
36        ex_hess(bb_start:nparams, 1:nparams-nout) = temp;
37        ex_hess(1:nparams-nout, bb_start:nparams) = temp';
38        hdata = hdata + ex_hess;
39      end
40    otherwise
41      error(['Unknown activation function ', net.outfn]);
42    end
43    end
44    [h, hdata] = hbayes(net, hdata);
45
46    function hdata = rearrange_hess(net, j, out_hess, hdata)
47
48    bb_start = net.nwts - net.nout + 1; % Start of bias block
49    ob_start = 1+(j-1)*net.nin;      % Start of block for jth output
50    ob_end = j*net.nin;               % End of block for jth output
51    b_index = bb_start+(j-1);        % Index of bias weight
52    % Put input weight block in right place
53    hdata(ob_start:ob_end, ob_start:ob_end) = ...
54                        out_hess(1:net.nin, 1:net.nin);
55    % Put second derivative of bias weight in right place
56    hdata(b_index, b_index) = out_hess(net.nin+1, net.nin+1);
57    % Put cross terms (input weight v bias weight) in right place
58    hdata(b_index, ob_start:ob_end) = out_hess(net.nin+1,1:net.nin);
59    hdata(ob_start:ob_end, b_index) = out_hess(1:net.nin, net.nin+1);
60
61    return
```

In lines 6–7 the inputs x are propagated forward through the model and the augmented input matrix X is computed in the matrix inputs. The main body of glmhess is separated into three cases depending on the output activation function.

- The linear case computes (4.33) and rearranges the matrix (lines 13–16).
- For the logistic function, we use (4.34) to compute the Hessian for each output in turn, rearranging the resulting partial derivatives as we go (lines 18–25). This works since each output is independent of all the others, so all the cross terms in the Hessian are zero.
- For the softmax function, we compute the contribution to the Hessian from each example in turn, and sum up all the values (lines 28–39). This is obviously considerably less efficient than the procedures for linear and logistic regression, but it is forced upon us by the more complex nature of the Hessian in this case. The outputs of the softmax model are definitely not independent. Because the calculation is carried out for all outputs at once, the function rearrange_hess cannot be used here, and some special purpose code is introduced.
  Before the main loop of the calculation, the start of the bias weights block (introduced to make the rearrangement easier to follow) is computed and the matrix ex_hess which holds the contribution to the Hessian from a single example is pre-allocated. In the main loop through each data point, the contributions to the Hessian from the dataset inputs and from the bias weights are computed (lines 30–31) and rearranged appropriately (lines 32–34). Then the cross terms

$$\frac{\partial^2 \mathcal{L}}{\partial w_{ki} \partial w_{lj}}, \tag{4.36}$$

where one of w_{ki} and w_{lj} belongs to the input weights and one belongs to the bias weights, are calculated (line 35) and rearranged (lines 36–37).

4.5 Iterated Re-weighted Least Squares Training

Because of the linear or near-linear structure of GLMs, there are considerable efficiencies to be gained through the use of a special purpose training algorithm, as provided by the function glmtrain, instead of general purpose non-linear optimisation algorithms. The interface to this function has the form

```
[net, options] = glmtrain(net, options, x, t)
```

where net is a GLM data structure, options is the usual vector for controlling optimisation routines, and x and t are the input and target data respectively.

For linear regression, maximum likelihood is equivalent to minimising the quadratic form

$$(Y - Xw)^T(Y - Xw) \qquad (4.37)$$

with respect to w, where X is the data matrix and Y is the target matrix. Equating the derivative to zero yields the *normal* equations

$$(X^T X)w = X^T Y \qquad (4.38)$$

which can be solved efficiently by computing the pseudo-inverse $X^\dagger$ of X and setting $w = X^\dagger Y$. This is numerically more stable than computing the inverse of the square matrix $X^T X$ explicitly.

Maximum likelihood for both *generalised* linear models we are considering does not lead to a quadratic form, and so the resulting equations cannot be solved directly and iterative methods are used instead. Let $\mathcal{L}$ denote the log likelihood and $H = (\partial^2 \mathcal{L}/\partial w \partial w^T)$ the Hessian of $\mathcal{L}$. The *Fisher scoring* method updates the parameter estimates w at the rth step by

$$w_{r+1} = w_r - \{E[H]\}^{-1} \frac{\partial \mathcal{L}}{\partial w}. \qquad (4.39)$$

This is the same as the Newton–Raphson algorithm, as can be seen by comparing it with (2.54), except that the expected value of the Hessian replaces the Hessian. For the canonical link functions, the Hessian coincides with its expected value. Normally taking a full Newton step is not a good idea, as it is easy to overshoot the minimum. However, there are two special features of the generalised linear model that make this procedure work well in practice: the log likelihood of logistic models has a single maximum, and it is possible to initialise the parameter w reasonably close to the maximum. Figure 4.2 shows the improvement in efficiency that can be gained using IRLS instead of general purpose non-linear optimisation algorithms. It shows that a large part of the speed-up is due to the improved initialisation of the parameters.

The Hessian of the logistic model is equal to $X^T \Pi X$ (4.34) and the gradient is equal to $X^T \Pi e$, where the nth row of e is given by

$$e^{(n)} = (y^{(n)} - \pi^{(n)})/f'(a^{(n)}). \qquad (4.40)$$

We form the variable $z_r = Xw_r + e$, which is the linearisation of the activation function around the current value of the mean. Then the equation (4.39) reduces to:

$$(X^T \Pi_r X)w_{r+1} = X^T \Pi_r z_r, \qquad (4.41)$$

which is the normal form equation for a *least squares* problem with input matrix $X^T \Pi_r^{1/2}$ and dependent variables $\Pi_r^{1/2} z_r$. The 'weights' Π (not to be confused with the model weights, or parameters, w) change at each iteration, since they are a function of the parameters w_r. Multiple logistic outputs correspond to independent Bernoulli noise variables, so each output and its fan-in parameters can be treated independently, with its own weight

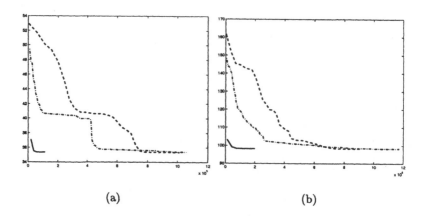

(a)   (b)

Fig. 4.2. Demonstration of GLM training algorithms. Graphs show error plotted against flop count for IRLS (*solid line*), scaled conjugate gradients (*dash-dotted line*) and quasi-Newton (*dashed line*). (a) Logistic regression with single output. (b) Softmax regression with three outputs.

matrix Π. The uniqueness of the maximum of $\mathcal{L}$ was shown in Auer *et al.* (1996).

The reduction of the Newton step to the normal form equation (4.41) depends on being able to find a square root of Π (which is easy in this case, as it is non-negative diagonal), and compute $X^T \Pi^{1/2}$ efficiently (which can be done without a full matrix multiplication, again because Π is diagonal). We initialise the procedure by using the values $(y^{(n)} + 0.5)/2.0$ as a first estimate for $\pi^{(n)}$ and from this, deriving the other quantities needed.

The case of multiple logistic, or softmax regression, is a little more complicated. The gradient and Hessian for a single input pattern x are given by

$$\frac{\partial \mathcal{L}}{\partial w_{ki}} = (p_k - y_k)x_i \qquad \frac{\partial^2 \mathcal{L}}{\partial w_{ki}\partial w_{lj}} = (p_l \delta_{kl} - p_l p_k)x_i x_j. \qquad (4.42)$$

To show that there is a unique maximum, it is sufficient to prove that the Hessian H is positive semi-definite. If v is an arbitrary vector, and we write $C = (p_l \delta_{kl} - p_l p_k)$, then

$$v^T H v = v x C x^T v = (x^T v)^T C (x^T v) \geq 0 \qquad (4.43)$$

since C is the covariance matrix of the multinomial distribution and is therefore positive semi-definite. However, when we write the Hessian in the form $\Xi^T \Pi \Xi$, where Ξ is the $(mn) \times (mp)$ block matrix containing m copies of X along the diagonal (and p is the input dimension), the matrix Π is an $m \times m$ block matrix, where each block is an $n \times n$ diagonal matrix containing the corresponding entries from C for each input pattern. Π is no longer diagonal; to compute its square root, we need to find a Cholesky decomposition of C. However, because C has m^2 non-zero entries, it is no longer clear that this representation of the problem offers practical advantage.

NETLAB implements two alternative algorithms. In the first we calculate the exact Hessian by summing terms given by equation (4.42) for each row in the dataset, using the function glmhess. The resulting matrix is usually very ill-conditioned, but using singular value decomposition, it is numerically tractable to solve the original Fisher scoring equation (4.39). Alternatively, in a simplified algorithm, we can treat each output as independent, which yields the same update rule as for the logistic model (this is no surprise, since the marginal distribution for a single output in a multiple logistic model is binomial with probability p_i), although this is not a good approximation to the true Hessian. In practice, this second algorithm converges more quickly than the exact procedure, but to a larger error value. It is also less numerically trustworthy and should be used with care. The selection between these two algorithms in glmtrain is determined by options(5). The default value (0), uses the exact Hessian algorithm, while the alternative value (1), uses the approximate algorithm. In either case, we initialise the parameters using the same procedure as for logistic regression, by treating each output independently.

These components are put together in glmtrain as follows:

```
1   function [net, options] = glmtrain(net, options, x, t)
2
3   display = options(1);
4   % Do we need to test for termination?
5   test = (options(2) | options(3));
6
7   ndata = size(x, 1);
8   inputs = [x ones(ndata, 1)];
9
10  if strcmp(net.outfn, 'linear')
11    if ~isfield(net, 'alpha')
12      temp = inputs\t;
13    elseif size(net.alpha == [1 1])
14      hessian = inputs'*inputs + net.alpha*eye(net.nin+1);
15      temp = pinv(hessian)*(inputs'*t);
16    else
17      error('Only scalar alpha allowed');
18    end
19    net.w1 = temp(1:net.nin, :);
20    net.b1 = temp(net.nin+1, :);
21    % Store error value in options vector
22    options(8) = glmerr(net, x, t);
23    return;
24  end
25
26  e = ones(1, net.nin+1);
27  for n = 1:options(14)
```

```
28    switch net.outfn
29      case 'logistic'
30        if n == 1
31          % Initialise model
32          p = (t+0.5)/2;
33          act = log(p./(1-p));
34        end
35        link_deriv = p.*(1-p);
36        weights = sqrt(link_deriv); % sqrt of weights
37        if (min(min(weights)) < eps)
38          fprintf(1, 'Warning: ill-conditioning in glmtrain\n')
39          return
40        end
41        z = act + (t-p)./link_deriv;
42        % Treat each output independently
43        for j = 1:net.nout
44          indep = inputs.*(weights(:,j)*e);
45          dep = z(:,j).*weights(:,j);
46          temp = indep\dep;
47          net.w1(:,j) = temp(1:net.nin);
48          net.b1(j) = temp(net.nin+1);
49        end
50        [err, edata, eprior, p, act] = glmerr(net, x, t);
51        if n == 1
52          errold = err;
53          wold = netpak(net);
54        else
55          w = netpak(net);
56        end
57      case 'softmax'
58        if n == 1
59          % Initialise model: ensure that row sum of p is one
60          % no matter how many classes there are
61          p = (t + (1/size(t, 2)))/2;
62          act = log(p./(1-p));
63        end
64        if options(5) == 1 | n == 1
65          link_deriv = p.*(1-p);
66          weights = sqrt(link_deriv); % sqrt of weights
67          if (min(min(weights)) < eps)
68            fprintf(1, 'Warning: ill-conditioning in glmtrain\n')
69            return
70          end
71          z = act + (t-p)./link_deriv;
72          % Treat each output independently
73          for j = 1:net.nout
74            indep = inputs.*(weights(:,j)*e);
75            dep = z(:,j).*weights(:,j);
76            temp = indep\dep;
77            net.w1(:,j) = temp(1:net.nin);
78            net.b1(j) = temp(net.nin+1);
79          end
80          [err, edata, eprior, p, act] = glmerr(net, x, t);
```

```
81              if n == 1
82                 errold = err;
83                 wold = netpak(net);
84              else
85                 w = netpak(net);
86              end
87           else
88              % Exact method of calculation after w first initialised
89              Hessian = glmhess(net, x, t);
90              temp = p-t;
91              gw1 = x'*(temp);
92              gb1 = sum(temp, 1);
93              gradient = [gw1(:)', gb1];
94              deltaw = -gradient*pinv(Hessian);
95              w = wold + deltaw;
96              net = glmunpak(net, w);
97              [err, edata, eprior, p] = glmerr(net, x, t);
98           end
99
100       otherwise
101          error(['Unknown activation function ', net.outfn]);
102       end
103       if options(1)
104         fprintf(1, 'Cycle %4d Error %11.6f\n', n, err)
105       end
106       % Test for termination
107       if err >  errold
108         errold = err;
109         w = wold;
110         options(8) = err;
111         fprintf(1, 'Error has increased: terminating\n')
112         return;
113       end
114       if test & n > 1
115         if (max(abs(w - wold)) < options(2) & ...
116             abs(err-errold) < options(3))
117           options(8) = err;
118           return;
119         else
120           errold = err;
121           wold = w;
122         end
123       end
124   end
125
126   options(8) = err;
127   if (options(1) >= 0)
128     disp('Warning: Maximum number of iterations has been exceeded');
129   end
```

The first step in the computation, after the usual processing of the options vector, is to add a column of ones to the input data to represent the bias unit (line 8).

The implementation of linear regression in `glmtrain` is straightforward. If there is no weight decay parameter α, then (4.38) is solved (line 12) by using the left division operator supplied by MATLAB. (This is slightly more efficient than computing a pseudo-inverse, and is nearly as numerically trustworthy.) If there is a weight decay parameter, then the normal form equations are evaluated (line 14)

$$(X^T X + \alpha I)w = X^T t \tag{4.44}$$

where X denotes the extended input matrix including the bias term. This equation is solved in line 15. The weights are then unpacked into the network data structure in lines 19–20.

For the non-linear output activation functions, an iterative algorithm is required (line 27). The code switches depending on the output activation function.

- The initialisation for logistic regression is carried out by lines 31–33. The square root of the weight matrix (stored as the variable `weights`) is calculated in lines 35–36. In rare cases, `weights` may be so ill-conditioned that the floating point solution of the normal equations contains infinite values. To prevent this, the smallest entry in `weights` is tested, and if it is too small, the algorithm terminates (lines 37–39). The linearised outputs are computed in line 41, and then, for each output in turn, the weighted normal equations are solved in lines 43–49, with the weights given by the corresponding *column* of `temp`, and the relevant weights in the GLM data structure are set. The error value at the new weights is then calculated in line 50, in order to test the termination criteria later in the function. The outputs p and activations `act` are needed for the next iteration of the IRLS algorithm.
- Recall that there are two variants of IRLS implemented for softmax outputs, but that both are initialised in the same way, assuming that the outputs are independent. The approximate algorithm (lines 64–87) is essentially the same as the algorithm for logistic outputs.
In the exact algorithm, the first step is to compute the Hessian (line 88) and gradient (given by (4.42)) of the model (lines 89–93). The Fisher score equation (4.39) can be rewritten as

$$w_{r+1} - w_r = - \{E[H]\}^{-1} \frac{\partial \mathcal{L}}{\partial w}. \tag{4.45}$$

In this form, it is numerically unstable, so the safest procedure in MATLAB is to calculate the pseudo-inverse of the Hessian as in line 94, and use this to update the weights (line 95). The weights are replaced in the network data structure (line 96) so that `glmhess` is called with the updated weights. The error and outputs are computed, but we don't need the activations, as the linearised outputs z_r are not used in this version of IRLS.

4.6 Demonstration Programs

The two demonstration programs demglm1 and demglm2 show the application of Generalised Linear Models to classification problems where the target variable has two and three classes respectively. In both programs, each class is generated from a spherical Gaussian, and there are two input variables so that the decision boundaries can be plotted.

4.6.1 Two-class Problem

Whatever the complexities in the detail of training a GLM, applying them is straightforward. There are four standard steps:

1. loading the training data;
2. creating and initialising the network;
3. training the network;
4. loading the test data and making predictions.

This section looks at each step in turn, using a simplified version of demglm1 to illustrate the process.

1. The two-dimensional data is sampled from a Gaussian mixture model using a call to gmmsamp.

   ```
   1   % Generate data from two classes in 2d
   2   input_dim = 2;
   3
   4   % Fix seeds for reproducible results
   5   randn('state', 42);
   6   rand('state', 42);
   7
   8   ndata = 100;
   9   mix = gmm(2, 2, 'spherical');
   10  mix.priors = [0.4 0.6];                % Cluster priors
   11  mix.centres = [2.0, 2.0; 0.0, 0.0];    % Cluster centres
   12  mix.covars = [0.5, 1.0];
   13
   14  [data, label] = gmmsamp(mix, ndata);
   15  targets = label - ones(ndata, 1);
   ```

   The labels are 1 and 2 for each of the classes; these are converted to targets encoded as 0 and 1 (line 15).
2. Because the target variable has a 0–1 encoding for two classes, a logistic regression model with a single output is appropriate. It is initialised as follows:

   ```
   16  net = glm(input_dim, 1, 'logistic');
   ```
3. The model is trained with five iterations of the IRLS algorithm.

```
17   options = foptions;
18   options(1) = 1;  % Print error values
19   options(14) = 5;
20   net = glmtrain(net, options, data, targets);
```

4. To evaluate the model on a set of test data x_test with targets t_test, the following code fragment can be used to compute and display a confusion matrix.

```
y_test = glmfwd(net, x_test);
conffig(y_test, t_test);
```

In demglm1, the results are shown in a more elaborate graphical manner. The outputs of the trained model are computed for a fine mesh of input data, and the results put in the matrix Z (line 27).

```
21   x = -4.0:0.2:5.0;
22   y = -4.0:0.2:5.0;
23   [X, Y] = meshgrid(x,y);
24   X = X(:);
25   Y = Y(:);
26   grid = [X Y];
27   Z = glmfwd(net, grid);
28   Z = reshape(Z, length(x), length(y));
```

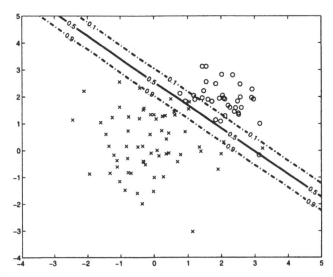

Fig. 4.3. Demonstration of logistic regression. Data belongs to class 1 (*circles*) or class 2 (*crosses*). Probability contours $P(C_1|x)$ at 0.5 (*solid line*), 0.1 and 0.9 (*dash-dotted line*).

These values are then used to generate a contour plot of the model output, which represents an estimate of the posterior class probability for class 1, at the values 0.1, 0.5 and 0.9.

```
29  v = [0.1 0.5 0.9];
30  [c, h] = contour(x, y, Z, v);
```

The contour for the value 0.5 represents the optimal decision boundary if misclassification costs for the two classes are equal. Note that all contours are linear (see Fig. 4.3).

4.6.2 Three-class Problem

In the program demglm2, a softmax model is applied to a three-class problem in a similar way to the logistic model used in demglm1.

1. The data is generated with a call to gmmsamp. The targets have a 1-of-N encoding for the three classes (line 8):

```
1  mix = gmm(2, 3, 'spherical');
2  mix.priors = [0.4 0.3 0.3];
3  mix.centres = [2, 2; 0.0, 0.0; 1, -1];
4  mix.covars = [0.5 1.0 0.6];
5
6  [data, label] = gmmsamp(mix, ndata);
7  id = eye(3);
8  targets = id(label,:);
```

2. A softmax regression model with three outputs is appropriate (as the data contains three classes). The model is initialised as follows:

```
9  net = glm(input_dim, size(targets, 2), 'softmax');
```

3. The model is trained with five iterations of the IRLS algorithm.

```
10  options = foptions;
11  options(1) = 1;    % Print error values
12  options(14) = 5;
13  net = glmtrain(net, options, data, targets);
```

By leaving options(5) at its default value (0), we ensure that the exact Hessian is used in the IRLS algorithm. In most cases, this provides better results than the approximate algorithm.

4. Again, a graphical representation of the results is given. The outputs of the model are computed for a fine mesh of input data, and the results put in the matrix Z.

```
14  x = -4.0:0.2:5.0;
15  y = -4.0:0.2:5.0;
16  [X, Y] = meshgrid(x,y);
17  X = X(:);
18  Y = Y(:);
19  grid = [X Y];
20  Z = glmfwd(net, grid);
```

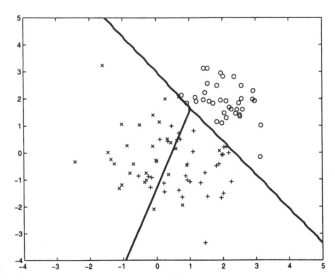

Fig. 4.4. Demonstration of softmax regression. Data belongs to class 1 (*circles*), class 2 (*crosses*) or class 3 (*plus signs*). Decision boundaries (*solid line*) shown where two posterior class probabilities are equal.

These values are then used to generate a plot of the predicted class (i.e. the one with the maximum posterior probability) at each point of the mesh. The classes are given the colours blue, red and green respectively.

```
21  [foo , class] = max(Z');
22  class = class';
23  colors = ['b.'; 'r.'; 'g.'];
24  for i = 1:3
25    thisX = X(class == i);
26    thisY = Y(class == i);
27    h = plot(thisX, thisY, colors(i,:));
28    set(h, 'MarkerSize', 8);
29  end
```

This plot (Fig. 4.4) clearly shows the linear nature of the decision boundary.

4.7 Worked Example: Training Regularised Models

We have seen how weight decay can be introduced into linear regression by solving the normal form equations (4.44)

$$(X^T X + \alpha I)w = X^T t. \tag{4.46}$$

However, the drawback of writing the equations in this form is that the product $X^T X$ is inherently ill-conditioned. Although the regularisation constant α restores matters to a degree, it is preferable to work directly with X.

Equation (4.46) is the normal equation formulation for the ridge regression problem of finding the minimum value of

$$\min_{w} \left[\|Xw - t\|^2 + \alpha\|w\|^2 \right].$$ (4.47)

It is also related to the constrained least squares problem

$$\min_{\|w\|\leq\lambda} \|Xw - t\|.$$ (4.48)

An efficient and robust method of solving this latter problem is given by Golub and van Loan (1996) (Algorithm 12.1):

1. Compute the SVD of $X = U\Sigma V^T$, save $V = [v_1, \ldots, v_n]$ and form $t = U^T t$.
2. Set $r = \text{rank}(X)$. This can be based on the singular values, σ_i, excluding those of small absolute value (see the exercises).
3. If

$$\sum_{i=1}^{r} \left(\frac{t_i}{\sigma_i} \right)^2 > \lambda^2$$ (4.49)

then find α^* such that

$$\sum_{i=1}^{r} \left(\frac{\sigma_i t_i}{\sigma_i^2 + \alpha^*} \right)^2 = \lambda^2$$ (4.50)

and set

$$w = \sum_{i=1}^{r} \left(\frac{\sigma_i t_i}{\sigma^2 + \alpha^*} \right) v_i.$$ (4.51)

4. Else set

$$w = \sum_{i=1}^{r} \left(\frac{t_i}{\sigma_i} \right) v_i.$$ (4.52)

The value α^* is the Lagrange multiplier for the constrained problem (4.48), and it is precisely the value of α in the ridge regression problem (4.47). To find α^* we need to find the zeros of

$$\phi(\alpha) = \sum_{i=1}^{r} \left(\frac{\sigma_i t_i}{\sigma_i^2 + \alpha^*} \right)^2 - \lambda^2.$$ (4.53)

By the condition (4.49), we know that $\phi(0) > 0$ and it is easy to show, by differentiating ϕ, that it decreases monotonically for $\alpha > 0$, and hence has a unique root α^*. This can be found using any standard root finding algorithm, such as Newton's method.

However, although the constrained minimisation and ridge regression views are equivalent, because there is no analytic solution for $\phi(\alpha)$, we cannot work out what value of λ gives rise to the value of α used in weight decay. Instead, we can use the constrained minimisation approach to ensure that the solution weight vector has norm less than a given constant λ, which is a different form of regularisation. The advantages of using this algorithm are that it is better conditioned than the normal form equation approach and that any dependence amongst the inputs can be removed by choosing the rank r carefully.

The function clsmin implements this algorithm:

```
1   function w = clsmin(X, t, max_cond, lambda)
2
3   % Compute the economy SVD of X
4   [U, S, V] = svd(X, 0);
5   nrows = size(V, 1);
6   t = U' * t;
7
8   % Compute approximate rank of A by considering ratio of first to
9   % subsequent singular values
10  D = diag(S);
11  temp = find((D./D(1)) > max_cond);
12  approx_rank = max(1, temp(end));
13  disp(['Approximate rank of X is ', num2str(approx_rank)]);
14
15  % Now factor in the constraint: we assume that the singular
16  % values are sorted
17  sol_coords = (t./D);
18  sol_coords = (sol_coords(1:approx_rank));
19  if sum(sol_coords.*sol_coords) <= lambda*lambda
20      % Solution found
21  else
22      % Constraint comes into play; need to find Lagrange
23      % multiplier using Newton's root finding algorithm
24      D = D(1:approx_rank);
25      t = t(1:approx_rank);
26      alpha = 0.0;  % Start search at zero
27      options(14) = 20;  % Number of iterations
28      options(3) = 1e-5; % Search precision in function direction
29      % Use zero tolerance on x axis in case lambda is very small
30      alpha = newton('clsroot', 'clsgrad', alpha, options, ...
31                     D, t, lambda);
32      sol_coords = (D.*t)./(D.*D + alpha);
33  end
34  w = sum((ones(nrows, 1)*sol_coords').*V(:, 1:approx_rank), 2);
```

Lines 4–6 implement step 1. The economy SVD computes only the first n columns of U (where X is $m \times n$) rather than the full $m \times m$ matrix, which would require an excessive quantity of memory for large datasets. Step 2 is implemented in lines 10–13. The ratio of each singular value to the largest (assumed to be the first) is compared with the maximum condition number specified as the third argument, and the approximate rank r is set to be the index of the last sufficiently large singular value. The function `newton` implements the Newton–Raphson root-finding algorithm (see Exercise 2.12).

The condition (4.49) is evaluated in line 19. If it is false, then step 4 is performed (line 34). Otherwise it is necessary to find the root of ϕ (lines 30–1). The M-file `clsroot` computes ϕ:

```
1  function y = clsroot(alpha, sigma, b, lambda)
2  %
3  y = sum(((((sigma.*b))./(sigma.*sigma+alpha)).^2)-lambda*lambda;
```

and the function `clsgrad` computes the gradient ϕ':

```
1  function g = clsgrad(alpha, sigma, b, lambda)
2  numerator = ((sigma.*b)).*(sigma.*b);
3  denominator = (sigma.*sigma + alpha).^3;
4  g = -2*sum(numerator./denominator);
```

We can apply `clsmin` to a toy linear regression problem in the following way:

```
1  %CLSGLM  Test clsmin on glm training
2  rand('state', 42);
3  randn('state', 42);
4
5  ndata = 40;
6  nin = 2;
7  x = randn(ndata, 1);
8  x = [x, x+1e-6*randn(ndata, 1)];
9  t = 3*x(:, 1) + 2*x(:, 2) + 1.0;
10
11  net = glm(nin, 1, 'linear');
12  options = foptions;
13  net2 = glmtrain(net, options, x, t);
14
15  X = [x, ones(ndata, 1)];
16  w = clsmin(X, t, 1e-4, sqrt(13.8));
17  net3 = glmunpak(net, w);
```

The conventionally trained model net2 has a weight vector very nearly equal to $(3, 2, 1)$, as would be expected from the form of the relationship between x and t (line 9). This weight vector has norm 14. The input data has effective rank of 2, since the condition number limit is set to greater than the noise level on the second input variable (10^{-4} compared with 10^{-6}; see line 8) and the network net3 has a weight vector given by $(2.5, 2.5, 1)$, which has norm $13.5 < 13.8$, so the root-finding algorithm was not required. The error of the two networks on the training data is 5.331×10^{-30} and 4.470×10^{-12}.

For networks with more than one output, this algorithm should be applied to each target vector in turn, putting the result in the appropriate fan-in weights.

Exercises

4.1 ($\star\star$) Compare the efficiency of `glmtrain` with general purpose non-linear optimisation algorithms in terms of flops and time. For example, to use scaled conjugate gradient to train a GLM **net**, the following call may be used:

```
[net, options] = netopt(net, options, data, targets, 'scg');
```

You should compare the algorithms for both logistic and softmax models. In both cases you should use some datasets that can be linearly separated, and some datasets that cannot.

4.2 ($\star\star$) Investigate the convergence of the IRLS training algorithm by plotting the decision boundary after each iteration for a two-dimensional input dataset. By editing a local copy of `glmtrain`, compare this with a network initialised with random weights rather than the special purpose initialisation implemented in NETLAB.

4.3 ($\star$) For normally distributed classes with equal covariances, a linear model gives the optimal discriminant in the sense that it gives the Bayesian decision boundary. Verify this result empirically for both logistic and softmax regression.

4.4 ($\star\star$) Extend weight decay training using the normal form equations in IRLS to logistic and softmax regression. Compare the results with networks trained using non-linear optimisers on the same data.

4.5 ($\star$) Investigate the behaviour of the constrained least squares minimisation `clsmin` as the constraint and conditioning threshold are varied in `clsglm`.

4.6 ($\star\star$) Implement a constrained least squares minimisation option for `glmtrain`. You will need to extend the approach described in Section 4.7 to deal with multiple outputs.

4.7 ($\star\star\star$) In step 1 of the constrained least squares algorithm (Section 4.7) the effective rank of X was determined by excluding the small singular values, which is appropriate when the inputs are affected by noise. However, rank deficiency in X may also be caused by redundant inputs. A robust method of selecting a non-redundant set of inputs is given by Golub and van Loan (1996) (Algorithm 12.2.1).

1. Compute the SVD of $X = U \Sigma V^T$, and save $V = [v_1, \ldots, v_n]$.
2. Set $r = \text{rank}(X)$. This can be based on the singular values, σ_i, excluding those of small absolute value.
3. Apply the economy QR algorithm with column pivoting (see the MATLAB function qr for details):

$$Q^T V(:, 1 : r) P = [R_{11} \ R_{12}], \tag{4.54}$$

where P is a permutation matrix. Set $XP = [X_1 \ X_2]$ with $X_1 \in \mathbb{R}^{m \times r}$ and $X_2 \in \mathbb{R}^{m \times (n-r)}$.

4. Find the least squares solution $z \in \mathbb{R}^r$ to $\|t - X_1 z\|$.
5. Compute

$$w = P \begin{bmatrix} z \\ 0 \end{bmatrix}. \tag{4.55}$$

Implement this algorithm, using `clsmin` for step 4 and test it on input data where there are known dependencies and levels of input noise.

4.8 $(\star\star)$ The conditioning of a least squares problem can often be improved with the use of *column balancing*. This means rescaling each column of the matrix so that it has (Euclidean) length 1. Implement a function `colbal` with syntax

`function [A, cw] = colbal(A)`

where c (`cw`) is the vector of weights each column of A were divided by.

4.9 $(\star\star\star)$ Combining subset selection with column balancing is easy: we simply divide each element of the solution w by the corresponding column weight. However, the constrained least squares algorithm must be made more sophisticated. We now solve the regularised least squares problem

$$\min \|Xw - t\| \quad \text{subject to} \quad \|Cw\| \leq \lambda. \tag{4.56}$$

This can be done with the following algorithm based on Golub and van Loan (1996) Section 12.1.1.
1. Compute the generalised SVD of X and C:

$$X = U \Sigma Y^T \quad \text{and} \quad C = V \Gamma Y^T. \tag{4.57}$$

The MATLAB function `gsvd` can be used for this. Set $t = U^T t$.
2. Set $r = \mathrm{rank}(X)$ as in `clsmin`.
3. If

$$\sum_{i=1}^{r} \left(\frac{\gamma_i t_i}{\sigma_i} \right)^2 > \lambda^2 \tag{4.58}$$

then find α^* such that

$$\sum_{i=1}^{r} \left(\frac{\sigma_i t_i}{\sigma_i^2 + \alpha^* \gamma_i^2} \right)^2 = \lambda^2 \tag{4.59}$$

and set

$$w_1 = \sum_{i=1}^{r} \left(\frac{\sigma_i t_i}{\sigma_i^2 + \alpha^* \gamma_i^2} \right) v_i. \tag{4.60}$$

4. Else set

$$w_1 = \sum_{i=1}^{r} \left(\frac{\gamma_i t_i}{\sigma_i} \right) v_i. \tag{4.61}$$

5. Set $w_2 = (Y^T)^{-1} w_1$.

Implement and test this algorithm on data containing redundant inputs, noise and where inputs have widely varying measurement scales. Compare the results with `glmtrain` and all the simpler algorithms you have developed.

5. The Multi-layer Perceptron

The multi-layer perceptron (MLP) is probably the most widely used architecture for practical applications of neural networks. In most cases the network consists of two layers of adaptive weights with full connectivity between inputs and hidden units, and between hidden units and outputs. This two-layer architecture is the one implemented in NETLAB. It is capable of *universal approximation* in the sense that it can approximate to arbitrary accuracy any continuous function from a compact region of input space provided the number of hidden units is sufficiently large and provided the weights and biases are chosen appropriately (Hornik *et al.*, 1989; Stinchecombe and White, 1989; Hornik, 1991). In practice, this means that provided there is enough data to estimate the network parameters, an MLP can model any smooth function.

For many applications, there will be no compelling reason to consider more general architectures. If special models are required they can be implemented using the general framework described in this chapter, and this provides a more satisfactory solution than attempting to provide a general purpose implementation with extensive functionality, most of which will never be used. An example of how the architecture can be extended to include direct connections from inputs to outputs is given in Section 5.8. The standard NETLAB implementation of the MLP also includes support for a Bayesian treatment of regularisation. This is not discussed in detail in this chapter, so some of the functions below are also analysed in Chapter 9.

In this chapter (Section 5.7) we also discuss an extension to the MLP that can be used for modelling general conditional probability densities. This is the Mixture Density Network (MDN). All the functions discussed in this chapter are listed in Table 5.1.

5.1 The Two-layer Feed-forward Network

5.1.1 Definition

As usual we shall denote the input values to the network by x_i where $i = 1, \ldots, d$. The first layer of the network forms M linear combinations of these inputs to give a set of intermediate activation variables $a_j^{(1)}$

Table 5.1. Functions in this chapter.

MLP Functions	
demmlp1	Demonstration of MLP regression
demmlp2	Demonstration of MLP classification
mlp	Create a two-layer MLP
mlpbkp	Backpropagate error gradient through network
mlpderiv	Evaluate derivatives of network outputs with respect to weights
mlperr	Evaluate error function
mlpfwd	Forward propagation
mlpgrad	Evaluate error gradient
mlphdotv	Evaluate the product of the data Hessian with a vector
mlphess	Evaluate the Hessian matrix
mlpinit	Initialise the weights
mlppak	Combine weights and biases into one parameter vector
mlpunpak	Separate parameter vector into weight and bias matrices

MDN Functions	
demmdn1	Demonstration of MDN regression
mdn	Create a Mixture Density Network
mdn2gmm	Convert an MDN mixture structure to an array of GMMs
mdndist2	Calculate squared distance from mixture centres to data
mdnerr	Evaluate error function
mdnfwd	Forward propagation
mdngrad	Evaluate error gradient
mdninit	Initialise the weights
mdnpak	Combine weights and biases into one parameter vector
mdnpost	Compute the posterior probability for each MDN component
mdnprob	Compute the data probability likelihood for MDN
mdnunpak	Separate parameter vector into weight and bias matrices

$$a_j^{(1)} = \sum_{i=1}^{d} w_{ji}^{(1)} x_i + b_j^{(1)} \qquad j = 1, \ldots, M, \tag{5.1}$$

with one variable $a_j^{(1)}$ associated with each hidden unit. Here $w_{ji}^{(1)}$ represents the elements of the first-layer weight matrix and $b_j^{(1)}$ are the bias parameters associated with the hidden units.

The variables $a_j^{(1)}$ are then transformed by the non-linear activation functions of the hidden layer. Here we restrict attention to tanh activation functions. The outputs of the hidden units are then given by

$$z_j = \tanh(a_j^{(1)}) \qquad j = 1, \ldots, M, \tag{5.2}$$

which has the property that

$$\frac{dz_j}{da_j^{(1)}} = (1 - z_j^2). \tag{5.3}$$

The z_j are then transformed by the second layer of weights and biases to give second-layer activation values $a_k^{(2)}$

$$a_k^{(2)} = \sum_{j=1}^{M} w_{kj}^{(2)} z_j + b_k^{(2)} \qquad k = 1, \ldots, c, \tag{5.4}$$

where c is the total number of outputs.

Finally, these values are passed throught the output-unit activation function to give output values y_k where $k = 1, \ldots, c$. Here we shall consider three forms of activation function. For regression problems an appropriate choice is the linear function of the form

$$y_k = a_k^{(2)}. \tag{5.5}$$

For classification problems involving multiple independent attributes we consider logistic sigmoidal activation functions applied to each of the outputs independently, so that

$$y_k = \frac{1}{1 + \exp(-a_k^{(2)})}. \tag{5.6}$$

Finally, for the more usual kind of classification problem in which we have a set of c mutually exclusive classes, we use the softmax activation function of the form

$$y_k = \frac{\exp(a_k^{(2)})}{\sum_{k'} \exp(a_{k'}^{(2)})}. \tag{5.7}$$

For each of these choices of activation function there is a corresponding choice of error function used to train the network, as we shall discuss in Section 5.2.

The structure of the network is shown in Fig. 5.1. It is possible to absorb the bias parameters into the weight matrices by introducing an extra input and an extra hidden unit, both of which have fixed values of +1 (Bishop, 1995). However, for the purposes of implementation within NETLAB it is more convenient to keep the weights and biases separate. The next three subsections describe how the basic network functions are implemented in NETLAB.

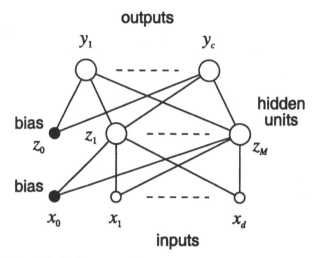

Fig. 5.1. Architecture of a two-layer feed-forward network.

5.1.2 Network Creation and Initialisation

An MLP network is created and its weights randomly initialised using the
NETLAB function mlp, which has the syntax

```
net = mlp(nin, nhidden, nout, outfunc, prior, beta);
```

where outfunc is a string specifying the output-unit activation function.
Possible choices are 'linear', corresponding to (5.5), 'logistic', corresponding to (5.6), and 'softmax', corresponding to (5.7). In order to specify
the network architecture, the user must provide values for the number of inputs, the number of hidden units, and the number of output units. The prior
and beta arguments are optional, and will be discussed in more detail in the
context of the Bayesian viewpoint in Chapter 9. The function mlp returns
the network data structure net, which has the following fields:

```
type      % string describing network type: always 'mlp'
nin       % number of inputs
nhidden   % number of hidden units
nout      % number of outputs
nwts      % total number of weights and biases
outfn     % string describing the output unit activation function
w1        % first-layer weight matrix
b1        % first-layer bias vector
w2        % second-layer weight matrix
b2        % second-layer bias vector
```

The matrices have the following dimensions: w1 is nin × nhidden; b1 is 1 ×
nhidden; w2 is nhidden × nout; b2 is 1 × nout. The function is implemented
as follows:

```
1   function net = mlp(nin, nhidden, nout, outfunc, ...
2                        prior, beta)
3   net.type = 'mlp';
4   net.nin = nin;
5   net.nhidden = nhidden;
6   net.nout = nout;
7   net.nwts = (nin + 1)*nhidden + (nhidden + 1)*nout;
8   outfns = {'linear', 'logistic', 'softmax'};
9   if sum(strcmp(outfunc, outfns)) == 0
10    error('Undefined activation function. Exiting.');
11  else
12    net.outfn = outfunc;
13  end
14
15  if nargin > 4
16    if isstruct(prior)
17      net.alpha = prior.alpha;
18      net.index = prior.index;
19    elseif size(prior) == [1 1]
20      net.alpha = prior;
21    else
22      error('prior must be a scalar or a structure');
23    end
24  end
25
26  net.w1 = randn(nin, nhidden)/sqrt(nin + 1);
27  net.b1 = randn(1, nhidden)/sqrt(nin + 1);
28  net.w2 = randn(nhidden, nout)/sqrt(nhidden + 1);
29  net.b2 = randn(1, nout)/sqrt(nhidden + 1);
30
31  if nargin == 6
32    net.beta = beta;
33  end
```

The total number of weights is computed by line 7. To prevent the user from specifying an unsupported activation function, lines 8–13 test that the string matches one of the three permissible values.

The weights are initialised by random selection from a zero mean, unit variance isotropic Gaussian where the variance is scaled by the fan-in of the hidden or output units as appropriate. This is accomplished by lines 26–29. The seed for the random weight initialisation can be set by calling

```
randn('state', s)
```

where s is the seed value, prior to invoking mlp. Lines 15–24 and 31–33 are concerned with setting priors for the Bayesian framework, and are discussed in Chapter 9.

The function mlpinit can be used to initialise all the weights from a zero mean isotropic Gaussian distribution with covariance 1/prior as follows:

```
1   net = mlpinit(net, prior);
2
3   % Bayesian material omitted
```

```
4  elseif size(prior) == [1 1]
5    w = randn(1, net.nwts).*sqrt(1/prior);
6
7  net = mlpunpak(net, w);
```

where the function mlpunpak separates the row vector w into its component weight and bias matrices as discussed in Section 5.1.3. For example, the command

```
net = mlpinit(net, 10);
```

initialises the weights in network randomly from a Gaussian with covariance 0.1. More elaborate forms of initialisation are discussed in the context of the Bayesian viewpoint in Chapter 9.

5.1.3 Manipulating Weights

By defining separate matrices and vectors for the first- and second-layer weights and biases, the forward and backward propagation equations take a very simple form in NETLAB. This representation, however, is not always convenient: if we train the network with a general purpose optimisation algorithm, then it is preferable to consider all the parameters (weights and biases) in the model as a single vector. The separate matrices can be packed into a single row vector using the function mlppak. The key line is

```
w = [net.w1(:)', net.b1, net.w2(:)', net.b2];
```

Here the : operator takes a matrix and converts it to a column vector by concatenating successive columns. Thus net.w1(:) consists of a column vector of length nin × nhidden, and net.w1(:)' is the corresponding row vector. The vectors from the different groups of parameters in the network are then concatenated to form the single row vector w. This has length net.nwts.

It is also necessary to change representation in the opposite direction and to convert w into the corresponding weight matrices and bias vectors. This requires knowledge of the network data structure net and is performed by the function mlpunpak

```
net = mlpunpak(net, w)
```

After checking that the weight vector w has the correct size for the specified network data structure, the component weight matrices are extracted from w:

```
1  function net = mlpunpak(net, w)
2  if net.nwts ~= length(w)
3    error('Invalid weight vector length')
4  end
5
6  nin = net.nin;
7  nhidden = net.nhidden;
8  nout = net.nout;
9
```

```
10  mark1 = nin*nhidden;
11  net.w1 = reshape(w(1:mark1), nin, nhidden);
12  mark2 = mark1 + nhidden;
13  net.b1 = reshape(w(mark1 + 1: mark2), 1, nhidden);
14  mark3 = mark2 + nhidden*nout;
15  net.w2 = reshape(w(mark2 + 1: mark3), nhidden, nout);
16  mark4 = mark3 + nout;
17  net.b2 = reshape(w(mark3 + 1: mark4), 1, nout);
```

If the return value is distinct from the input net argument, for example,

```
net2 = mlpunpak(net, w);
```

then all the fields of net are copied across to net2 and the weights in net2 are taken from w. In this case the values in net are unaffected.

5.1.4 Forward Propagation

Here we consider the problem of computing the MLP network output for batch data. A dataset consists of input vectors x_n with components x_{ni} where $n = 1, \ldots, N$. In NETLAB the number of data points is denoted ndata, and the input vectors form the rows of a matrix x of dimensions ndata $\times$ nin. The function mlpfwd performs batch forward propagation of a matrix of input vectors through the network and has the following syntax

```
y = mlpfwd(net, x);
```

The output matrix y has dimensions ndata $\times$ nout. The function mlpfwd has additional optional return arguments of the form

```
[y, z, a] = mlpfwd(net, x);
```

where z is a matrix of size ndata*nhidden containing the hidden unit values corresponding to (5.2), and a contains the summed inputs into the output units corresponding to (5.4).

```
1   function [y, z, a] = mlpfwd(net, x)
2
3   ndata = size(x, 1);
4   z = tanh(x*net.w1 + ones(ndata, 1)*net.b1);
5   a = z*net.w2 + ones(ndata, 1)*net.b2;
6
7   switch net.outfn
8     case 'linear'      % Linear outputs
9       y = a;
10    case 'logistic'    % Logistic outputs
11      maxcut = -log(eps);
12      mincut = -log(1/realmin - 1);
13      y = 1./(1 + exp(-a));
14    case 'softmax'     % Softmax outputs
15      maxcut = log(realmax) - log(nout);
16      mincut = log(realmin);
17      a = min(a, maxcut);
18      a = max(a, mincut);
```

```
19      temp = exp(a);
20      y = temp./(sum(temp, 2)*ones(1,nout));
21      y = 1./(1 + exp(-a));
22   end
```

The forward propagation of the input dataset through the network is performed by in lines 3–5, which are followed by the application of the appropriate activation function, as determined by net.outfn. The code to perform this (in lines 7–22) is identical to that used in GLMs (see glmfwd in Section 4.1.2).

5.2 Error Functions and Network Training

The goal of training a network is to model the underlying generator of the data in order to make the best possible predictions when new input data is presented. The most general information about the target vector t for inputs x is given by the conditional density $p(t|x)$. For each of the functions available as the output of an MLP in NETLAB there is a corresponding *canonical* error function, which represents the negative log likelihood of the data under a certain choice of ϵ_k. The choice of error function corresponding to the network output activation function is the same as for the Generalised Linear Model in Section 4.2.

For all error functions, the first step is a forward propagation of the inputs through the network using mlpfwd. The remainder of the function mlperr is identical to glmerr.

5.3 Error Gradient Calculation

Back-propagation is a general technique for evaluating derivatives of functions defined in terms of multi-layer feed-forward networks. The most common application involves the evaluation of derivatives of an error function with respect to the network weights and biases. It is based on successive application of the chain rule of partial derivatives and leads to an algorithm in which 'error' signals (strictly speaking, error derivatives) are propagated backward through the network starting from the output units. A key feature of the back-propagation approach is that it allows the required derivatives to be evaluated in $\mathcal{O}(NW)$ computational steps, where N is the total number of patterns and W is the total number of parameters in the network. This compares with $\mathcal{O}(NW^2)$ steps if numerical differentiation is used (see Exercise 5.2).

The general formalism of error back-propagation is described in Bishop (1995). Here we consider the task of evaluating the derivatives of each of the three NETLAB MLP error functions with respect to the network parameters for a two-layer feed-forward network.

The first step in evaluating the error derivatives is to perform a forward propagation for the complete data set in order to evaluate the activations z_j^n of the hidden units and the activations y_k^n of the output units for each pattern n in the data set. Because of the canonical choice of the error function and its corresponding activation function, we find that for all three error functions, the partial derivative of the error with respect to $a_k^{(2)n}$, the output activations, is the same:

$$\frac{\partial E^n}{\partial a_k^{(2)n}} = y_k^n - t_k^n. \tag{5.8}$$

Thus, in order to evaluate the derivatives of E with respect to the weight and bias parameters we first evaluate the quantities $\delta_k^{(2)n}$ given by

$$\delta_k^{(2)n} = y_k^n - t_k^n, \tag{5.9}$$

which represent 'errors' for the output units on pattern n. Here y_k^n denotes $y_k(\boldsymbol{w}; \boldsymbol{x}^n)$. The derivatives of E with respect to the second-layer weights are given by

$$\frac{\partial E}{\partial w_{kj}^{(2)}} = \sum_{n=1}^{N} \delta_k^{(2)n} z_j^n, \tag{5.10}$$

while the derivatives for the output-unit biases are given by

$$\frac{\partial E}{\partial b_k^{(2)}} = \sum_{n=1}^{N} \delta_k^{(2)n}. \tag{5.11}$$

In order to find the corresponding derivatives for the first-layer parameters, the 'errors' $\delta_k^{(2)n}$ must first be back-propagated through the second-layer weights to obtain 'error' signals for the hidden units. The back-propagation equations take the form

$$\delta_j^{(1)n} = g'(a_j^{(1)n}) \sum_{k=1}^{c} w_{kj}^{(2)} \delta_k^{(2)n} \tag{5.12}$$

$$= (1 - (z_j^n)^2) \sum_{k=1}^{c} w_{kj}^{(2)} \delta_k^{(2)n}, \tag{5.13}$$

where the sum runs over all output units. Here we have used the fact that the hidden unit activation functions are given by the hyperbolic tangent $z(a) = g(a) = \tanh(a)$ and hence the derivatives of the hidden unit activations are given by $g'(a) = 1 - \tanh^2(a) = 1 - z^2(a)$. The derivatives with respect to the first-layer weights are then given by

$$\frac{\partial E}{\partial w_{ji}^{(1)}} = \sum_{n=1}^{N} \delta_j^{(1)n} x_j^n,$$ (5.14)

while the derivatives for the hidden unit biases are given by

$$\frac{\partial E}{\partial b_j^{(1)}} = \sum_{n=1}^{N} \delta_j^{(1)n}.$$ (5.15)

The NETLAB implementation of mlpgrad is then quite simple

```
1  function [g, gdata, gprior] = mlpgrad(net, x, t)
2
3  [y, z] = mlpfwd(net, x);
4  delout = y - t;
5  gdata = mlpbkp(net, x, z, delout);
6
7  [g, gdata, gprior] = gbayes(net, gdata);
```

Lines 3–4 compute the output deltas as in equations (5.8) and (5.9). Because the back-propagation of error signals is common to several functions requiring gradient calculations, this is encapsulated in the NETLAB function mlpbkp. Line 7 modifies the error gradient to include regularisation terms, and will be discussed further in Chapter 9.

The NETLAB implementation of mlpbkp runs as follows

```
1  function g = mlpbkp(net, x, z, deltas)
2
3  % Evaluate second-layer gradients.
4  gw2 = z'*deltas;
5  gb2 = sum(deltas, 1);
6
7  % Now do the backpropagation.
8  delhid = deltas*net.w2';
9  delhid = delhid.*(1.0 - z.*z);
10
11  % Finally, evaluate the first-layer gradients.
12  gw1 = x'*delhid;
13  gb1 = sum(delhid, 1);
14
15  g = [gw1(:)', gb1, gw2(:)', gb2];
```

The error derivatives for each of the groups of weights are denoted by gw1 for the derivatives corresponding to the first-layer weight matrix w1 and so on. From (5.10) and (5.11) we derive lines 4–5. Next, the δ_k^n are back-propagated using the transpose of the second-layer weight matrix to give the $\delta_j^{(1)n}$ using (5.13). This is achieved in lines 8–9. Finally, from (5.14) and (5.15), the derivatives of the error function with respect to the first-layer weights and hidden unit biases are obtained using 12–13. The various derivative terms are then combined to obtain a single gradient vector in line 15, so that each component of g contains the derivative of E with respect to the corresponding component of the weight vector $\mathbf{w}$. The ordering of the weights is the same as that used in mlppak.

5.4 Evaluating other Derivatives

The standard back-propagation procedure described in Section 5.3 allows the derivatives of an error function with respect to the network weights and biases to be evaluated efficiently. There are often situations in which we are interested in other derivatives. For example, the second derivatives of an error function make up the elements of the Hessian matrix, which forms the topic of Section 5.5. The derivatives of the network *outputs* with respect to the input values form the elements of the *Jacobian* matrix. Design and testing of a MATLAB script to evaluate the Jacobian is discussed in Exercise 5.3.

Here we consider the problem of evaluating the derivatives of the network output activations with respect to the weights and biases

$$\frac{\partial a^{(2)}}{\partial w_{ji}}. \tag{5.16}$$

These derivatives are required in Section 9.5 to evaluate error bars on network predictions in a Bayesian framework. Since a is a vector, the result of this procedure is a three-dimensional array. Using the results of Section 5.3, we see that to calculate the partial derivatives in (5.16), it is sufficient to compute the 'errors'

$$\frac{\partial a_k^{(2)}}{\partial a_j^{(2)}} = \delta_{kj}, \tag{5.17}$$

where δ_{kj} is the Kronecker delta, and then use back-propagation.

The NETLAB function which computes the required derivatives is called mlpderiv.

```
1  function g = mlpderiv(net, x)
2
3  [y, z] = mlpfwd(net, x);
4  ndata = size(x, 1);
5
6  g = zeros(ndata, net.nwts, net.nout);
7  for k = 1 : net.nout
8    delta = zeros(1, net.nout);
9    delta(1, k) = 1;
10   for n = 1 : ndata
11     g(n, :, k) = mlpbkp(net, x(n, :), z(n, :), delta);
12   end
13  end
```

The first stage of the computation is to perform a forward propagation for the complete data set using mlpfwd. The derivatives are stored in a three-dimensional array g which is pre-sized (for efficiency) in line 6. The matrix g(:, :, k) is the gradient for output k. It is computed by lines 10–12.

5.5 The Hessian Matrix

The second derivatives of the error function, given by

$$\frac{\partial^2 E}{\partial w_{ji} \partial w_{lk}}, \tag{5.18}$$

form the elements of the Hessian matrix H, which is a square matrix of dimension $W \times W$, where W is the number of weights. This matrix plays an important role in several applications of MLP networks, including:

1. The inverse of the Hessian can be used to identify the least significant weights in a network as part of a pruning algorithm.
2. The inverse of the Hessian is used to assign error bars to network predictions (Section 9.5).
3. Suitable values for regularisation parameters can be determined from the eigenvalues of the Hessian (Section 9.4).
4. The determinant of the Hessian is used in evaluating the relative probability of different models (Section 9.4).

An extension of the technique of back-propagation can be used to evaluate the Hessian exactly. This is implemented in NETLAB in the function mlphess. For greater flexibility, the Hessian is not evaluated directly but instead an algorithm that computes the product of the Hessian and an arbitrary vector is used. We therefore look at this algorithm, and the NETLAB function mlphdotv that implements it, first.

5.5.1 Fast Multiplication by the Hessian

In some applications where the Hessian is required, the quantity of interest is not the Hessian matrix H itself, but the product of H and a vector v of dimension W. Since the evaluation of the Hessian takes $\mathcal{O}(W^2)$ operations, and the vector $v^T H$ has only W elements, we can hope to find an efficient algorithm for evaluating $v^T H$ directly in only $\mathcal{O}(W)$ operations. The $\mathcal{R}$-propagation due to Pearlmutter (1994) is such an algorithm, and has the additional attraction that the structure of the equations is very similar to those for standard forward and backward propagation for derivatives.

We first note that

$$v^T H \equiv v^T \nabla(\nabla E). \tag{5.19}$$

Thus, to compute $v^T H$, we write down the standard forward and backward propagation equations for ∇E and apply the differential operator $v^T \nabla$. Following Pearlmutter, we use the notation $\mathcal{R}\{\cdot\}$ for this operator. We use the usual rules of calculus, together with the identity

$$\mathcal{R}\{w\} = v, \tag{5.20}$$

where w represent the weights. Acting on the forward propagation equations (5.1), (5.2) and (5.4) with the $\mathcal{R}\{\cdot\}$ operator, we obtain a set of forward propagation equations of the form

$$\mathcal{R}\{a_j^{(1)}\} = \sum_i v_{ji} x_i \tag{5.21}$$

$$\mathcal{R}\{z_j\} = g'(a_j^{(1)}) \mathcal{R}\{a_j^{(1)}\} \tag{5.22}$$

$$\mathcal{R}\{a_k^{(2)}\} = \sum_j w_{kj} \mathcal{R}\{z_j\} + \sum_j v_{kj} z_j, \tag{5.23}$$

where v_{ji} is the element of v that corresponds to w_{ji}. The quantities $\mathcal{R}\{a_j^{(1)}\}$, $\mathcal{R}\{z_j\}$, and $\mathcal{R}\{a_k^{(2)}\}$ are new variables that are computed by $\mathcal{R}$-forward propagation with these equations. The quantities $\mathcal{R}\{y_k\}$ are given by

$$\mathcal{R}\{y_k\} = \mathcal{R}\{a_k^{(2)}\}, \tag{5.24}$$

for linear outputs,

$$\mathcal{R}\{y_k\} = y_k(1 - y_k) \mathcal{R}\{a_k^{(2)}\}, \tag{5.25}$$

for logistic outputs, and

$$\mathcal{R}\{y_k\} = y_k \mathcal{R}\{a_k^{(2)}\} - y_k \sum_{k'} y_{k'} \mathcal{R}\{a_{k'}^{(2)}\}, \tag{5.26}$$

for softmax outputs. Because of the choice of a canonical error function for each output activation function, we have a single set of back-propagation equations (5.9) and (5.13) to which we apply the $\mathcal{R}\{\cdot\}$-operator to obtain a set of $\mathcal{R}$-backward propagation equations:

$$\mathcal{R}\{\delta_k^{(2)}\} = \mathcal{R}\{y_k\} \tag{5.27}$$

$$\mathcal{R}\{\delta_j^{(1)}\} = g''(a_j^{(1)}) \mathcal{R}\{a_j\} \sum_k w_{kj} \delta_k + g'(a_j^{(1)}) \sum_k v_{kj} \delta_k$$

$$+ g'(a_j^{(1)}) \sum_k w_{kj} \mathcal{R}\{\delta_k\}. \tag{5.28}$$

Finally, we have the equations for the gradient with respect to the first- and second-layer weights (5.14) and (5.10). Acting on these with the $\mathcal{R}\{\cdot\}$-operator, we obtain expressions for the product $\boldsymbol{v}^T \boldsymbol{H}$ we are interested in:

$$\mathcal{R}\left\{\frac{\partial E}{\partial w_{kj}}\right\} = \mathcal{R}\{\delta_k\}z_j + \delta_k\,\mathcal{R}\{z_j\} \tag{5.29}$$

$$\mathcal{R}\left\{\frac{\partial E}{\partial w_{ji}}\right\} = x_i\,\mathcal{R}\{\delta_j^{(1)}\}. \tag{5.30}$$

The following listing gives the implementation of this algorithm in the function mlphdotv.

```
1   function hdv = mlphdotv(net, x, t, v)
2
3   ndata = size(x, 1);
4   [y, z] = mlpfwd(net, x);
5   zprime = (1 - z.*z);
6   zpprime = -2.0*z.*zprime;
7   vnet = mlpunpak(net, v);
8
9   % Do the R-forward propagation.
10  ra1 = x*vnet.w1 + ones(ndata, 1)*vnet.b1;
11  rz = zprime.*ra1;
12  ra2 = rz*net.w2 + z*vnet.w2 + ones(ndata, 1)*vnet.b2;
13
14  switch net.outfn
15    case 'linear'
16      ry = ra2;
17    case 'logistic'
18      ry = y.*(1 - y).*ra2;
19    case 'softmax'
20      nout = size(t, 2);
21      ry = y.*ra2 - y.*(sum(y.*ra2, 2)*ones(1, nout));
22    otherwise
23      error(['Unknown activation function ', net.outfn]);
24  end
25
26  delout = y - t;
27  delhid = zprime.*(delout*net.w2');
28  rdelhid = zpprime.*ra1.*(delout*net.w2') + ...
29            zprime.*(delout*vnet.w2') + zprime.*(ry*net.w2');
30  hw1 = x'*rdelhid;
31  hb1 = sum(rdelhid, 1);
32  hw2 = z'*ry + rz'*delout;
33  hb2 = sum(ry, 1);
34
35  hdv = [hw1(:)', hb1, hw2(:)', hb2];
```

The first key step is a standard forward propagation through the network (line 4). The first and second derivatives of the hidden unit activations $g'(a_j^{(1)})$ and $g''(a_j^{(1)})$ are then computed in lines 5–6. The tanh function used means that both of these are efficiently computed in terms of $z_j = g(a_j^{(1)})$. In order to carry out the $\mathcal{R}$-forward propagation, it is convenient to convert the vector v into matrices corresponding to the two layers of weight matrices and bias vectors in net. This is achieved by a call to mlpunpak in line 7, where vnet contains the result of the conversion, which can be accessed as component fields vnet.w1 etc. The $\mathcal{R}$-forward propagation equations are implemented by lines 10–24. using variables ra1, rz, ra2, and ry, corresponding to $\mathcal{R}\{a_j^{(1)}\}$, $\mathcal{R}\{z_j\}$, $\mathcal{R}\{a_k^{(2)}\}$ and $\mathcal{R}\{y_k\}$.

We introduce the variable rdelhid, corresponding to $\mathcal{R}\{\delta_j^{(1)}\}$ for the $\mathcal{R}$-backward propagation given by (5.28), in lines 26–29. Line 30 implements (5.30) and line 32 implements (5.29). Finally, we merge the components of $v^T H$ into one vector hdv in line 35.

5.5.2 NETLAB Implementation

The full specification of the function mlphess is

```
[h, dh] = mlphess(net, x, t, dh)
```

where the return value h is the full Hessian matrix including contributions from regularisation terms calculated using hbayes, while dh is the data-dependent part of the Hessian. The first of these will be discussed further in Chapter 9, while we consider only the second in this section. Its computation is performed by a sub-function datahess which, as for all sub-functions, is only accessible from within the file mlphess.m where it is defined.

```
1  function hdata = datahess(net, x, t)
2
3  hdata = zeros(net.nwts, net.nwts);
4  for v = eye(net.nwts);
5    hdata(find(v),:) = mlphdotv(net, x, t, v);
6  end
7  return
```

The data-dependent part of the Hessian hdata is pre-allocated to the correct size for efficiency in line 3. To evaluate hdata, we compute its product with net.nwts column identity vectors v of the form $(0, 0, \ldots, 0, 1, 0, \ldots, 0)^T$ using the function mlphdotv in lines 4–6. The loop is executed nwts times, once for each column of the identity matrix v.

5.6 Demonstration Programs

There are two basic demonstration programs for the MLP: demmlp1 uses an MLP for a simple regression problem, while demmlp2 illustrates the use of an MLP for classification. For demonstrations of the Hessian and other derivatives, see Section 9.8.

5.6.1 Regression Demonstration

The demmlp1 program shows how easy it is to use the NETLAB implementation of the MLP to solve standard problems. The process can be divided into four stages:

1. loading the training data;
2. creating and initialising the network;
3. training the network;
4. loading the test data and making predictions.

We now look at the details of each stage in turn.

1. The data set used in demmlp1 is the standard noisy sine wave with input matrix x and target matrix t.

```
1  ndata = 20;                % Number of data points.
2  noise = 0.2;               % Noise standard deviation.
3  x = [0:1/(ndata - 1):1]';
4  randn('state', 1);
5  t = sin(2*pi*x) + noise*randn(ndata, 1);
```

2. The network data structure net is created by a call to mlp:

```
6  nin = 1;                   % Number of inputs.
7  nhidden = 3;               % Number of hidden units.
8  nout = 1;                  % Number of outputs.
9  alpha = 0.01;              % Coefficient of weight-decay prior.
10 net = mlp(nin, nhidden, nout, 'linear', alpha);
```

3. To train the network, the options vector is set up and the function netopt is called with the scaled conjugate gradient algorithm.

```
11 options = zeros(1,18);
12 options(1) = 1;            % Display error values.
13 options(14) = 100;         % Number of training cycles.
14 [net, options] = netopt(net, options, x, t, 'scg');
```

The netopt function calls mlperr and mlpgrad through the neterr and netgrad mechanism.

4. The final task is to plot the function implemented by the trained network. This is performed using mlpfwd to compute the network outputs y at a regular grid of values contained in the matrix plotvals:

```
15 plotvals = [0:0.01:1]';
16 y = mlpfwd(net, plotvals);
```

The resulting graph is shown in Fig. 5.2.

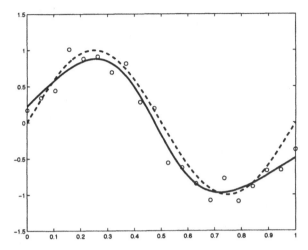

Fig. 5.2. Example of a simple regression problem, produced by the demonstration script demmlp1. Training data (*circles*) and generating function (*dashed line*) are plotted with network prediction (*solid line*).

5.6.2 Classification Demonstration

Although the classification demonstration demmlp2 is a considerably more complicated piece of software than demmlp1, this is more due to the large number of different graphs generated than any inherent difficulty in the use of the neural network. The core of the software is very similar to that in demmlp1 but with the linear output activation functions replaced by non-linear functions (in mlp) that are more appropriate for classification problems. The aim of the demonstration is to show how an MLP can model a non-linear decision boundary and accurately approximate the optimal Bayesian decision rule. Again, there are four main steps in the process.

1. The training data is generated from a Gaussian mixture model with three centres: the first of these is assigned to class 1, and the other two are assigned to class 2. The data is two-dimensional, so that the results can be easily visualised.

```
1  n=200;
2  mix = gmm(2, 3, 'full');
3  mix.priors = [0.5 0.25 0.25];
4  mix.centres = [0 -0.1; 1 1; 1 -1];
5  mix.covars(:,:,1) = [0.625 -0.2165; -0.2165 0.875];
6  mix.covars(:,:,2) = [0.2241 -0.1368; -0.1368 0.9759];
7  mix.covars(:,:,3) = [0.2375 0.1516; 0.1516 0.4125];
8  [data, label] = gmmsamp(mix, n);
```

The choice of these parameters ensures that each class has the same prior probability and that the optimal decision boundary between the two classes is non-linear. Because the true generator of the data is known and has a simple form, we can compute analytically, using Bayes' theorem, the class conditional probabilities $p(x|j)$ (the variable px_j), unconditional density $p(x)$ (px) and posterior class probabilities $P(C_1|x)$ (p1_x) and $P(C_2|x)$ (p2_x). The optimal decision boundary is the line $P(C_1|x) = P(C_2|x) = 0.5$, assuming equal misclassification costs. In the following lines of code X and Y are the x- and y-coordinates respectively for a 2d grid of points in the region of interest.

```
 9  px_j = gmmactiv(mix, [X(:) Y(:)]);
10  px=reshape(px_j*(mix.priors)',size(X));
11  post = gmmpost(mix, [X(:) Y(:)]);
12  p1_x = reshape(post(:, 1), size(X));
13  p2_x = reshape(post(:, 2) + post(:, 3), size(X));
```

2. The second step is to set up and initialise the network. The network is constructed with a logistic output function (suitable for a two-class problem) with the following lines.

```
14  nhidden=6; nout=1;
15  alpha = 0.2;    % Weight decay
16  net = mlp(2, nhidden, nout, 'logistic', alpha);
```

3. We now train an MLP on the data sample data and target. The network is then trained for 60 cycles using the quasi-Newton algorithm:

```
17  target=[label==1]; % Convert targets to 0-1 encoding
18  options = foptions; options(14) = 60;
19  [net] = netopt(net, options, data, target, 'quasinew');
```

4. The outputs of the network are then computed for a fine mesh of input data:

```
20  yg = mlpfwd(net, [X(:) Y(:)]);
21  yg = reshape(yg(:,1),size(X));
```

This matrix represents the network's estimate of $p(C_1|x)$. We can now plot the training data with the decision boundaries for the optimal rule and the MLP superimposed. The threshold on the posterior probability for the decision boundary is 0.5, since there are two classes.

```
22  plot(data((label==1),1), data(label==1,2),'r.', ...
23         'MarkerSize', PointSize)
24  plot(data((label>1),1), data(label>1,2),'y.', ...
25         'MarkerSize', PointSize)
26  % Bayesian decision boundary
27  [cB, hB] = contour(xrange,yrange,p1_x,[0.5 0.5],'b-');
28  % MLP decision boundary
29  [cN, hN] = contour(xrange,yrange,yg,[0.5 0.5],'r-');
```

This graph is shown as Fig. 5.3. To compare the generalisation performance of the MLP with the Bayesian decision rule, labelled test data is generated from the same mixture model:

```
30  [testdata testlabel] = gmmsamp(mix, n);
31  testlab=[testlabel==1 testlabel>1];
```

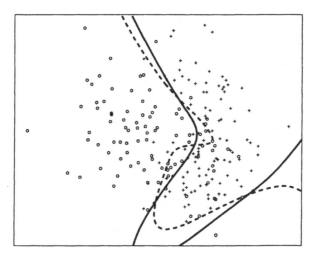

Fig. 5.3. Training set comparison of MLP (*dashed line*) and Bayesian decision rule (*solid line*). Data belongs to class 1 (*circles*), or class 2 (*crosses*).

The posterior probabilities of the test data are computed, and the resulting confusion matrix calculated, by the following lines of code.

```
32  tpx_j = gmmpost(mix, data);
33  Bpost = [tpx_j(:,1), tpx_j(:,2)+tpx_j(:,3)];
34  [Bcon Brate] = confmat(Bpost, [label==1 label>1]);
```

The decision boundaries for the two classifiers are plotted for the test data, as shown in Fig. 5.4. Finally, the performance of the MLP is compared with the optimal rule using a confusion matrix.

```
35  % Compute network classification
36  yt = mlpfwd(net, testdata);
37  % Convert single output to posteriors for both classes
38  testpost = [yt 1-yt];
39  [C trate]=confmat(testpost,[testlabel==1 testlabel>1]);
```

The NETLAB function confmat requires the probabilities for each of the classes as the columns of its first argument. Since yt contains $p(C_1|x)$, $p(C_2|x)$ is given by 1-yt.

5.7 Mixture Density Networks

We have viewed the aim of training an MLP as that of modelling the statistical properties of the data generator, expressed in terms of the conditional density function $p(t|x)$. For the three output activation/error function pairs we have considered so far, these distributions are: a Gaussian with global

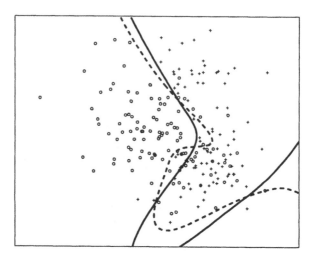

Fig. 5.4. Test set comparison of MLP (*dashed line*) and Bayesian decision rule (*solid line*). Data belongs to class 1 (*circles*), or class 2 (*crosses*).

variance parameter and x-dependent mean with linear outputs and sum-of-squares error function; a Bernoulli distribution with logistic output and cross-entropy error function; and a multinomial distribution with softmax output and entropy error function. However, if the data has a complex structure, for example it is a one-to-many mapping, then none of these choices may be adequate. For example, Fig. 5.5 shows a one-to-many mapping. It is clear that the conditional distribution $p(t|x)$ (which can be visualised by considering the density of points along a vertical slice through the data) for inputs in the range $[0.4, 0.6]$ is multi-modal, and hence cannot be represented by the uni-modal distributions corresponding to the error functions we have used earlier. This sort of difficulty often arises in *inverse problems*. We therefore need a framework for modelling a general conditional probability density.

In Chapter 3 we used Gaussian mixture models to estimate unconditional distributions. If we let the mixture model parameters $\boldsymbol{\theta}$ be functions of the input vector x then we can model distributions conditional on x. In general, the function mapping x to $\boldsymbol{\theta}(x)$ will be complicated, and we therefore use an MLP to model it. Our model now has the form

$$p(t|x) = \sum_{j=1}^{M} \alpha_j(x)\phi_j(t|x), \tag{5.31}$$

where M is the number of components, or kernels, in the mixture. The parameters $\alpha_j(x)$ are the mixing coefficients, and can be regarded as prior probabilities (conditioned on x) that the target vector t has been generated from the jth component of the mixture. This combination of a neural network that outputs the parameters of a mixture model is known as a Mixture Density

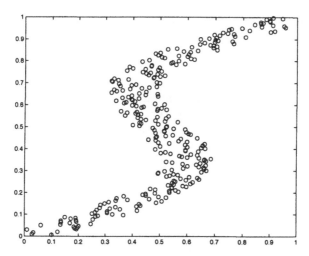

Fig. 5.5. Data drawn from a multi-valued mapping. $x = y + 0.3 \sin 2\pi y + \epsilon$, where $\epsilon \sim U(-0.1, 0.1)$.

Network (MDN). It is closely related to the mixture of experts model (Jacobs *et al.*, 1991). The rest of this section is devoted to a brief explanation of the theory of MDNs and their implementation in NETLAB.

5.7.1 Model Structure

Various choices for the kernel function in (5.31) are possible, but we shall restrict attention to Gaussian functions with spherical covariance structure of the form

$$\phi_j(t|x) = \frac{1}{(2\pi)^{c/2}\sigma_j^c(x)} \exp\left\{-\frac{\|t - \mu_j(x)\|^2}{2\sigma_j^2(x)}\right\}, \tag{5.32}$$

where the vector $\mu_j(x)$ represents the *centre* of the jth kernel and c is the dimension of the target space. There are a total of $M(c+2)$ parameters in the mixture model, and hence the same number of neural network outputs: M mixing coefficients; M centres, each of dimension c; and M covariance values. This compares with a total of c outputs for a network used with a sum-of-squares error function.

Clearly, other choices for the kernel functions in (5.31) are possible (for example, Gaussians with diagonal or even full covariance matrices could be used). In addition, it is possible to make only some of the parameters in (5.31) determined by the network: for example, kernel functions with fixed centres and variances can be used in conjunction with mixing coefficients that do depend on the input x. These possibilities have not been implemented in NETLAB, but the function mdn that sets up the MDN data structure has an argument **type** which is currently ignored, but could be used to distinguish different types of MDN.

The obvious way to represent the parameters is to use an array of **gmm** data structures: one for each input pattern. This was the method used in the first implementation, but it turned out to be prohibitively inefficient for training the network, when many computations of the data likelihood and its gradient are needed. Instead, **mdnmixes**, a specialised data structure which is optimised for speed of access, is used; this was introduced by David Evans. The parameter vector for the nth pattern is defined by:

$$
[\underbrace{\alpha_{1,n}, \alpha_{2,n}, \ldots, \alpha_{j,n}, \ldots, \alpha_{M,n},}_{M \text{ mixing coefficients}}
$$

$$
\underbrace{\mu_{11,n}, \mu_{12,n}, \ldots, \mu_{1c,n},}_{1^{st} \text{ kernel centre}} \ldots, \underbrace{\mu_{j1,n}, \mu_{j2,n}, \ldots, \mu_{jc,n},}_{j^{th} \text{ kernel centre}} \ldots,
$$

$$
\underbrace{\mu_{M1,n}, \mu_{M2,n}, \ldots, \mu_{Mc,n},}_{M^{th} \text{ kernel centre}} \underbrace{\sigma_{1,n}^2, \sigma_{2,n}^2, \ldots, \sigma_{j,n}^2, \ldots, \sigma_{M,n}^2]}_{M \text{ widths}} \quad (5.33)
$$

The structure **mdnmixes** has three sub-matrices $\boldsymbol{P}^\alpha$, $\boldsymbol{P}^\mu$, and $\boldsymbol{P}^\sigma$ containing the mixing coefficients, centres, and variances of each kernel respectively. Each row corresponds to a training pattern:

$$
\mathbf{P}^\alpha = \overbrace{\begin{bmatrix} \alpha_{1,1} & \alpha_{2,1} & \cdots & \alpha_{M,1} \\ \alpha_{1,2} & \alpha_{2,2} & \cdots & \alpha_{M,2} \\ \vdots & \vdots & \vdots & \vdots \\ \alpha_{1,n} & \alpha_{2,n} & \cdots & \alpha_{M,n} \\ \vdots & \vdots & \vdots & \vdots \\ \alpha_{1,N} & \alpha_{2,N} & \cdots & \alpha_{M,N} \end{bmatrix}}^{\text{dimension} M} \quad (5.34)
$$

$$
\mathbf{P}^\mu = \overbrace{\begin{bmatrix} \mu_{11,1} & \mu_{12,1} & \cdots & \mu_{1c,1} & \cdots & \mu_{M1,1} & \mu_{M2,1} & \cdots & \mu_{Mc,1} \\ \mu_{11,2} & \mu_{12,2} & \cdots & \mu_{1c,2} & \cdots & \mu_{M1,2} & \mu_{M2,2} & \cdots & \mu_{Mc,2} \\ \vdots & \vdots & \vdots & \vdots & \vdots & \vdots & \vdots & \vdots & \vdots \\ \mu_{11,n} & \mu_{12,n} & \cdots & \mu_{1c,n} & \cdots & \mu_{M1,n} & \mu_{M2,n} & \cdots & \mu_{Mc,n} \\ \vdots & \vdots & \vdots & \vdots & \vdots & \vdots & \vdots & \vdots & \vdots \\ \mu_{11,N} & \mu_{12,N} & \cdots & \mu_{1c,N} & \cdots & \mu_{M1,N} & \mu_{M2,N} & \cdots & \mu_{Mc,N} \end{bmatrix}}^{\text{dimension} Mc} \quad (5.35)
$$

$$\mathbf{P}^\sigma = \overset{\overset{\text{dimension}\,M}{\overbrace{\hphantom{\sigma_{1,1}^2 \quad \sigma_{2,1}^2 \quad \cdots \quad \sigma_{M,1}^2}}}}{\begin{bmatrix} \sigma_{1,1}^2 & \sigma_{2,1}^2 & \cdots & \sigma_{M,1}^2 \\ \sigma_{1,2}^2 & \sigma_{2,2}^2 & \cdots & \sigma_{M,2}^2 \\ \vdots & \vdots & \vdots & \vdots \\ \sigma_{1,n}^2 & \sigma_{2,n}^2 & \cdots & \sigma_{M,n}^2 \\ \vdots & \vdots & \vdots & \vdots \\ \sigma_{1,N}^2 & \sigma_{2,N}^2 & \cdots & \sigma_{M,N}^2 \end{bmatrix}} \tag{5.36}$$

The matrices $\mathbf{P}^\alpha$, $\mathbf{P}^\mu$ and $\mathbf{P}^\sigma$ correspond to the fields mixcoeffs, centres and covars respectively in the NETLAB data structure mdnmixes. The complete definition of the data structure is given in Table 5.2. The information

Table 5.2. Fields in the mdnmixes data structure.

type	Type (always 'mdnmixes')
ncentres	Number of kernels M
dim_target	Dimension of target space c
nparams	Number of parameters in model
mix_coeffs	Mixture coefficients α
centres	Kernel centres μ
covars	Kernel covariances σ^2

contained in this data structure is equivalent to that contained in an array of gmm structures. A utility function mdn2gmm converts from the mdnmixes data structure to an array of gmm data structures.

```
1  function gmmmixes = mdn2gmm(mdnmixes)
2
3  nmixes = size(mdnmixes.centres, 1);
4  tempmix= gmm(mdnmixes.dim_target, mdnmixes.ncentres, 'spherical');
5  f = fieldnames(tempmix);
6  gmmmixes = cell(size(f, 1), 1, nmixes);
7  gmmmixes = cell2struct(gmmmixes, f,1);
8
9  for i = 1:nmixes
10    centres=reshape(mdnmixes.centres(i,:), mdnmixes.dim_target, ...
11      mdnmixes.ncentres)';
12    gmmmixes(i) = gmmunpak(tempmix, [mdnmixes.mixcoeffs(i,:),...
13      centres(:)', mdnmixes.covars(i,:)]);
14  end
```

The array is allocated in lines 3–7. The tempmix variable is created solely in order to determine the fields in a gmm data structure: this protects this function against any changes to the latter structure. A cell array of the right dimensions is created and then converted into an array of structures. Each data structure in turn is filled with the correct parameters by lines 9–14. This construction shows up the disadvantage of this representation: accessing each data structure has to be done through a loop, which is always very inefficient in MATLAB. However, the gmm data structures can be useful in circumstances where the loop over the patterns has to be done only once, such as plotting the conditional density function for a given pattern. This is because more functions (such as gmmpost) have been defined for this data structure.

5.7.2 Network Creation and Initialisation

The creation and initialisation of the mdn data structure is basically a combination of the relevant functions for an mlp and an mdnmixes structure. The interface is the same as that for mlp with the addition of an argument for the target dimension and another (mix_type, currently ignored) for the type of mixture model.

```
1   net = mdn(nin, nhidden, ncentres, dim_target, mix_type, ...
2           prior, beta)
3
4   net.type = 'mdn';
5   mdnmixes.type = 'mdnmixes';
6   mdnmixes.ncentres = ncentres;
7   mdnmixes.dim_target = dim_target;
8   mdnmixes.nparams = ncentres + ncentres*dim_target + ncentres;
9   mdnmixes.mixcoeffs = [];
10  mdnmixes.centres = [];
11  mdnmixes.covars = [];
12  nout = mdnmixes.nparams;
13
14  if (nargin == 5)
15    mlpnet = mlp(nin, nhidden, nout, 'linear');
16  elseif (nargin == 6)
17    mlpnet = mlp(nin, nhidden, nout, 'linear', prior);
18  elseif (nargin == 7)
19    mlpnet = mlp(nin, nhidden, nout, 'linear', prior, beta);
20  end
21  net.mdnmixes = mdnmixes;
22  net.mlp = mlpnet;
23  net.nin = nin;
24  net.nout = dim_target;
25  net.nwts = mlpnet.nwts;
```

The mdnmixes data structure is set up in lines 5–11. The nparams field is computed (line 8) on the basis of spherical covariances. Note that the parameters in mdnmixes are all set to the empty matrix. This is because they can only be given meaningful values when inputs are propagated through the network.

The number of network outputs is set to be equal to the number of mixture model parameters (line 12). The MLP data structure mlpnet is constructed in lines 14–20. The MLP outputs are linear because different transformations are necessary for different outputs, and this is controlled by the function mdnfwd.

Finally, the complete data structure is put together. Note that the field net.nout is set (line 24) to the dimension of the target space rather than the number of network outputs. This is so that when this field is tested by the consist function to ensure that it matches the number of columns in the target data, the correct value is used.

Although the call to mlp in the function mdn randomly initialises the weights of the network, a much better initialisation can be achieved by taking into account the (unconditional) distribution of the target data. Experiments have shown that this significantly reduces both the training time and the probability that the network gets caught in a poor local minimum. The procedure we adopt is to set the output biases in the MLP so that the mixture model coefficients match those of an unconditional Gaussian mixture model fitted to the target data. There is no need to run the EM algorithm: simply initialising a Gaussian mixture model using K-means is quite adequate. The other second-layer weights are randomly initialised and add small fluctuations to break the symmetry. The function mdninit is called with the following syntax, where the prior is passed directly to mlpinit to initialise randomly the MLP weights.

```
net = mdninit(net, prior, t, options);
```

The matrix t denotes the target data and the options vector is used to control the fitting of the Gaussian mixture model. These last two arguments are optional: if they are omitted then the network data structure is returned with the weights set to the values computed by mlpinit. Otherwise, a Gaussian mixture model with spherical covariances is constructed for the target data t and initialised in the function gmminit using the K-means algorithm:

```
1   function net = mdninit(net, prior, t, options)
2
3   net.mlp = mlpinit(net.mlp, prior);
4
5   if nargin > 2
6     temp_mix = gmm(net.mdnmixes.dim_target, ...
7                    net.mdnmixes.ncentres, 'spherical');
8     temp_mix = gmminit(temp_mix, t, options);
9     net.mlp.b2(1:ncentres) = temp_mix.priors;
10    end_centres = ncentres*(dim_target+1);
11    net.mlp.b2(ncentres+1:end_centres) = ...
12          reshape(temp_mix.centres', 1, ncentres*dim_target);
13    net.mlp.b2((end_centres+1):net.mlp.nout) = log(temp_mix.covars);
14  end
```

The initialisation of the output bias weights depends on the type of mixture model parameters they correspond to.

- The first ncentres bias weights correspond to the mixing coefficients (line 9).

- The next `ncentres*dim_target` weights correspond to the kernel centres. Because of their ordering, the gmm centres have to be transposed and re-shaped (lines 10–12).
- Finally, since the kernel variances are computed by applying an exponential function to the network outputs, we must take the logarithm of the gmm covariances to find the correct biases (line 13).

The function `mdnpak` constructs a single weight row vector from the weights stored in the mdn data structure. This is achieved simply by a call to `mlppak` weight manipulation

```
w = mlppak(net.mlp);
```

since all the adjustable weights are stored in the MLP data structure `net.mlp`. Similarly, the function `mdnunpak(net, w)`, which carries out the reverse of this process, calls `mlpunpak` on the weight row vector `w`:

```
net.mlp = mlpunpak(net.mlp, w);
```

5.7.3 Forward Propagation

There are two parts to forward propagation in MDNs. First, the activations of the hidden and output units must be computed. Then the outputs of the MLP must be converted into Gaussian mixture model parameters, with one set of parameters for each pattern. These mixture model parameters are contained in an `mdnmixes` data structure as described in Section 5.7.2. Thus the interface to the function `mdnfwd`

```
[mixparams, y, z, a] = mdnfwd(net, x)
```

is the same as that for `mlpfwd` with the addition of the `mixparams` return value to contain the mixture model parameters. The remaining return values y, z, and a are all optional.

```
1  function [mixparams, y, z, a] = mdnfwd(net, x)
2
3  mlpnet = net.mlp;
4  mixes = net.mdnmixes;
5  ncentres = mixes.ncentres;        % Number of mixture components
6  dim_target = mixes.dim_target;    % Dimension of targets
7  nparams = mixes.nparams;          % Number of mixture parameters
8
9  % Propagate forwards through MLP
10 [y, z, a] = mlpfwd(mlpnet, x);
11
12 mixcoeff  = [1:1:ncentres];
13 centres   = [ncentres+1:1:(ncentres*(1+dim_target))];
14 variances = [(ncentres*(1+dim_target)+1):1:nparams];
15
16 % Convert output values into mixture model parameters
17 maxcut = log(realmax) - log(ncentres);
18 % Ensure that exp(y) > 0
```

```
19  mincut = log(realmin);
20  temp = min(y(:,1:ncentres), maxcut);
21  temp = max(temp, mincut);
22  temp = exp(temp);
23  mixpriors = temp./(sum(temp, 2)*ones(1,ncentres));
24  mixcentres =  y(:,(ncentres+1):ncentres*(1+dim_target));
25  mixwidths = exp(y(:,(ncentres*(1+dim_target)+1):nparams));
26
27  % Now build up all the mixture model weight vectors
28  ndata = size(x, 1);
29  mixparams.type        = mixes.type;
30  mixparams.ncentres    = mixes.ncentres;
31  mixparams.dim_target  = mixes.dim_target;
32  mixparams.nparams     = mixes.nparams;
33  mixparams.mixcoeffs   = mixpriors;
34  mixparams.centres     = mixcentres;
35  mixparams.covars      = mixwidths;
```

After giving local names to certain parameters of the net for convenience, the activations of the MLP component are computed in line 10. The positions of the different types of mixture model parameters in the matrix of outputs are then calculated by lines 12–14. Then the mixture parameters themselves are computed. The mixture coefficients are found by applying the softmax function (lines 17–23, compare glmfwd), the centres are simply copies of the corresponding network outputs (line 24), and the variances are found by applying the exponential function (line 25). This information is then stored in the mixparams data structure and returned.

5.7.4 Conditional Probabilities

The functions mdnprob and mdnpost are provided in order to work with the conditional distribution $p(t|x)$ (for example, to find its modes or to compute the error gradient). The function mdnpost computes the conditional probability responsibility for each Gaussian component ϕ_j for $j = 1, \ldots, M$, while mdnprob computes the conditional probability density. These functions are equivalent to gmmpost and gmmprob respectively, but work with an mdnmixes data structure rather than a gmm data structure, for reasons of efficiency.

```
1   function [prob,a] = mdnprob(mixparams, t)
2
3   dim_target = mixparams.dim_target;
4   ntarget    = size(t, 1);
5
6   dist2 = mdndist2(mixparams, t);
7
8   variance = 2.*mixparams.covars;
9   normal   = ((2.*pi).*mixparams.covars).^(dim_target./2);
10  a = exp(-(dist2./variance))./normal;
11
12  % Accumulate negative log likelihood of targets
13  prob = mixparams.mixcoeffs.*a;
```

The computation requires the squared distance between the targets and the centres of the Gaussian to be computed. For each centre for each pattern we require

$$d_{j,n} = \|t_n - \mu_j(x_n)\|^2. \tag{5.37}$$

This is computed by line 6, where the function mdndist2 corresponds to dist2 for the gmm functions. The 'activation' matrix

$$
\mathbf{A} =
\overbrace{
\begin{bmatrix}
a_{1,1} & a_{2,1} & \cdots & a_{M,1} \\
a_{1,2} & a_{2,2} & \cdots & a_{M,2} \\
\vdots & \vdots & \vdots & \vdots \\
a_{1,n} & a_{2,n} & \cdots & a_{M,n} \\
\vdots & \vdots & \vdots & \vdots \\
a_{1,N} & a_{2,N} & \cdots & a_{M,N}
\end{bmatrix}
}^{\text{dimension} M}
\tag{5.38}
$$

with entries

$$a_{j,n} = \phi_j(t_n|x_n) = -\frac{1}{(2\pi\sigma_{j,n}^2)^{\frac{c}{2}}} \exp\left\{\frac{-d_{j,n}}{2\sigma_{j,n}^2}\right\} \tag{5.39}$$

is computed by lines 8–10, which are identical to the code used in gmmactiv for the spherical Gaussian case. The probabilities of each Gaussian are then computed by multiplying each activation by the corresponding mixing coefficient (line 13):

$$
\mathbf{Pr} =
\overbrace{
\begin{bmatrix}
\alpha_{1,1}a_{1,1} & \alpha_{2,1}a_{2,1} & \cdots & \alpha_{M,1}a_{M,1} \\
\alpha_{1,2}a_{1,2} & \alpha_{2,2}a_{2,2} & \cdots & \alpha_{M,2}a_{M,2} \\
\vdots & \vdots & \vdots & \vdots \\
\alpha_{1,n}a_{1,n} & \alpha_{2,n}a_{2,n} & \cdots & \alpha_{M,n}a_{M,n} \\
\vdots & \vdots & \vdots & \vdots \\
\alpha_{1,N}a_{1,N} & \alpha_{2,N}a_{2,N} & \cdots & \alpha_{M,N}a_{M,N}
\end{bmatrix}
}^{\text{dimension} M}
\tag{5.40}
$$

The posterior probability of each kernel is defined by

$$\pi_j = \frac{\alpha_j\phi_j}{\sum_{l=1}^m \alpha_l\phi_l}. \tag{5.41}$$

The function mdnpost implements this calculation.

```
1  function [post, a] = mdnpost(mixparams, t)
2
3  [prob a] = mdnprob(mixparams, t);
4
```

```
5  s = sum(prob, 2);
6  % Set any zeros to one before dividing
7  s = s + (s==0);
8  post = prob./(s*ones(1, mixparams.ncentres));
```

The Gaussian density values (activations) ϕ_j are computed in line 3. Note that the last line of mdnprob is unnecessary and adds a small inefficiency to mdnpost. However, in most circumstances, mdnpost will only be called once for the entire dataset, so this will not have a significant impact on computational speed. The numerator in (5.41) is computed in line 5. To avoid division by zero, which could occur only if a target point was a long way from any kernel centre, line 7 replaces any zeros in s by ones. A zero in s can only occur if all the kernel densities are zero, in which case dividing by any non-zero number will give zero posterior probabilities[1]. Finally, we compute the posteriors by dividing the kernel densities by s.

The function mdndist2 calculates the distance between targets and centres for the specialised mdnmixes structure. For each centre for the nth pattern we need the value:

$$\mathbf{d}_{j,n} = \|t_n - \boldsymbol{\mu}_j(x_n)\|^2. \tag{5.42}$$

To compute the distance the following calculation is performed for the centre of each Gaussian for each pattern:

$$\begin{pmatrix} t_{1,n} \\ t_{2,n} \\ \vdots \\ t_{c,n} \end{pmatrix} - \begin{pmatrix} \mu_{j1,n} \\ \mu_{j2,n} \\ \vdots \\ \mu_{jc,n} \end{pmatrix}. \tag{5.43}$$

This can be computed with a single matrix operation as follows:

$$\mathbf{D} = \overbrace{\begin{bmatrix} t_{1,1} & t_{2,1} & \cdots & t_{c,1} & \cdots & t_{1,1} & t_{2,1} & \cdots & t_{c,1} \\ t_{1,2} & t_{2,2} & \cdots & t_{c,2} & \cdots & t_{1,2} & t_{2,2} & \cdots & t_{c,2} \\ \vdots & \vdots & \vdots & \vdots & \vdots & \vdots & \vdots & \vdots & \vdots \\ t_{1,n} & t_{2,n} & \cdots & t_{c,n} & \cdots & t_{1,n} & t_{2,n} & \cdots & t_{c,n} \\ \vdots & \vdots & \vdots & \vdots & \vdots & \vdots & \vdots & \vdots & \vdots \\ t_{1,N} & t_{2,N} & \cdots & t_{c,N} & \cdots & t_{1,N} & t_{2,N} & \cdots & t_{c,N} \end{bmatrix}}^{\text{dimension}Mc} - \mathbf{P}^{\mu}, \tag{5.44}$$

which can be written out in full

---

[1] In this pathological case, the sum of the posteriors will not be 1.

$$
\mathbf{D} =
\overbrace{
\begin{bmatrix}
t_{1,1} & t_{2,1} & \cdots & t_{c,1} & \cdots & t_{1,1} & t_{2,1} & \cdots & t_{c,1} \\
t_{1,2} & t_{2,2} & \cdots & t_{c,2} & \cdots & t_{1,2} & t_{2,2} & \cdots & t_{c,2} \\
\vdots & \vdots & \vdots & \vdots & \vdots & \vdots & \vdots & \vdots & \vdots \\
t_{1,n} & t_{2,n} & \cdots & t_{c,n} & \cdots & t_{1,n} & t_{2,n} & \cdots & t_{c,n} \\
\vdots & \vdots & \vdots & \vdots & \vdots & \vdots & \vdots & \vdots & \vdots \\
t_{1,N} & t_{2,N} & \cdots & t_{c,N} & \cdots & t_{1,N} & t_{2,N} & \cdots & t_{c,N}
\end{bmatrix}
}^{\text{dimension} Mc}
$$

$$
-
\overbrace{
\begin{bmatrix}
\mu_{11,1} & \mu_{12,1} & \cdots & \mu_{1c,1} & \cdots & \mu_{M1,1} & \mu_{M2,1} & \cdots & \mu_{Mc,1} \\
\mu_{11,2} & \mu_{12,2} & \cdots & \mu_{1c,2} & \cdots & \mu_{M1,2} & \mu_{M2,2} & \cdots & \mu_{Mc,2} \\
\vdots & \vdots & \vdots & \vdots & \vdots & \vdots & \vdots & \vdots & \vdots \\
\mu_{11,n} & \mu_{12,n} & \cdots & \mu_{1c,n} & \cdots & \mu_{M1,n} & \mu_{M2,n} & \cdots & \mu_{Mc,n} \\
\vdots & \vdots & \vdots & \vdots & \vdots & \vdots & \vdots & \vdots & \vdots \\
\mu_{11,N} & \mu_{12,N} & \cdots & \mu_{1c,N} & \cdots & \mu_{M1,N} & \mu_{M2,N} & \cdots & \mu_{Mc,N}
\end{bmatrix}
}^{\text{dimension} Mc}
\tag{5.45}
$$

Inspection of equation (5.45) reveals that the target data is repeated once for each centre, and so by re-shaping the target matrix the distances can be computed as matrix operations within MATLAB.

```
1  function n2 = mdndist2(mixparams, t)
2
3  ncentres   = mixparams.ncentres;
4  dim_target = mixparams.dim_target;
5  ntarget    = size(t, 1);
6
7  t = kron(ones(1, ncentres), t);
8
9  diff2 = (t - mixparams.centres).^2;
10 diff2 = reshape(diff2', dim_target, (ntarget*ncentres))';
11 n2 = sum(diff2, 2);
12 n2 = reshape(n2, ncentres, ntarget)';
```

Line 7 reshapes the t vector into the form required in equation (5.45). So, for example, if the target vector is the matrix

```
1 2 3
4 5 6
7 8 9
```

and there are four centres, then this is augmented to

```
1 2 3 1 2 3 1 2 3 1 2 3
4 5 6 4 5 6 4 5 6 4 5 6
7 8 9 7 8 9 7 8 9 7 8 9
```

The rest of the function calculates the distance between each centre and the corresponding target pattern.

5.7.5 Error and Gradient Calculation

The Error Function

The error function for an MDN is the negative log likelihood of the training set. This is defined as

$$E = \sum_{n=1}^{N} -\ln\left\{ \sum_{j=1}^{m} \alpha_j(\mathbf{x}_n)\phi_j(\mathbf{t}_n|\mathbf{x}_n) \right\}. \tag{5.46}$$

The function mdnerr, which implements equation (5.46), has three main steps.

```
1  function e = mdnerr(net, x, t)
2
3  mixparams = mdnfwd(net, x);
4  probs     = mdnprob(mixparams, t);
5  e         = sum( -log(max(eps, sum(probs, 2))));
```

First, we propagate forwards through the network and calculate the mixture model coefficients for each pattern (line 3), then the likelihoods for each mixture model component are computed (line 4), and finally the negative log likelihood is accumulated (line 5). Because some of the mixture model centres may be a long way from particular targets, the likelihood terms may be very small. To prevent any numerical difficulties (such as log not being computable), the likelihood is thresholded from below using eps.

The Error Gradient

The error gradient can be evaluated with the standard back-propagation procedure once we have obtained expressions for the derivatives of the error with respect to the outputs of the network. The error gradient with respect to the mixing coefficients is given by

$$\frac{\partial E_n}{\partial z_j^{\alpha}} = \alpha_j - \pi_j, \tag{5.47}$$

where π_j is the posterior probability of the jth kernel. This can simply be computed as

$$\frac{\partial E_n}{\partial z^{\alpha}} = \Delta^{\alpha} = \mathbf{P}^{\alpha} - \mathbf{\Pi}. \tag{5.48}$$

The error gradient with respect to the kernel centres is given by

$$\frac{\partial E_n}{\partial z_{jk}^{\mu}} = \pi_j \left\{ \frac{\mu_{jk} - t_k}{\sigma_j^2} \right\}. \tag{5.49}$$

This is computed with the matrix

$$\overbrace{\hspace{9cm}}^{\text{dimension}Mc}$$

$$
\begin{bmatrix}
\pi_{1,1}\left\{\dfrac{\mu_{11,1}-t_{1,1}}{\sigma^2_{1,1}}\right\} & \cdots & \pi_{M,1}\left\{\dfrac{\mu_{M1,1}-t_{1,1}}{\sigma^2_{M,1}}\right\} & \cdots & \pi_{M,1}\left\{\dfrac{\mu_{Mc,1}-t_{c,1}}{\sigma^2_{M,1}}\right\} \\[2mm]
\pi_{1,2}\left\{\dfrac{\mu_{11,2}-t_{1,2}}{\sigma^2_{1,2}}\right\} & \cdots & \pi_{M,2}\left\{\dfrac{\mu_{M1,2}-t_{1,2}}{\sigma^2_{M,2}}\right\} & \cdots & \pi_{M,2}\left\{\dfrac{\mu_{Mc,2}-t_{c,2}}{\sigma^2_{M,2}}\right\} \\[2mm]
\vdots & \vdots & \vdots & \vdots & \vdots \\[2mm]
\pi_{1,n}\left\{\dfrac{\mu_{11,n}-t_{1,n}}{\sigma^2_{1,n}}\right\} & \cdots & \pi_{M,n}\left\{\dfrac{\mu_{M2,n}-t_{2,n}}{\sigma^2_{M,n}}\right\} & \cdots & \pi_{M,n}\left\{\dfrac{\mu_{Mc,n}-t_{c,n}}{\sigma^2_{M,n}}\right\} \\[2mm]
\vdots & \vdots & \vdots & \vdots & \vdots \\[2mm]
\pi_{1,N}\left\{\dfrac{\mu_{11,N}-t_{1,N}}{\sigma^2_{1,N}}\right\} & \cdots & \pi_{M,N}\left\{\dfrac{\mu_{M2,N}-t_{2,N}}{\sigma^2_{M,N}}\right\} & \cdots & \pi_{M,N}\left\{\dfrac{\mu_{Mc,N}-t_{c,N}}{\sigma^2_{M,N}}\right\}
\end{bmatrix}
$$

The gradient with respect to the kernel variances is given by

$$
\frac{\partial E_n}{\partial z_j^{\sigma}} = -\frac{\pi_{j,n}}{2}\left\{\frac{\|t_n - \mu_j(x_n)\|^2}{\sigma^2_{j,n}} - c\right\}. \tag{5.50}
$$

The matrix form of this computation is

$$
\frac{\partial E_n}{\partial z_j^{\sigma}} = \Delta^{\sigma} = \frac{\Pi}{2}\left\{D./P^{\sigma} - C\right\}, \tag{5.51}
$$

where D is a matrix of squared distances between kernel centres and target vectors and C is a matrix of dimension npatterns x ncentres with each element taking the value c, the dimension of the target space.

The NETLAB function mdngrad performs these computations.

```
1   function g = mdngrad(net, x, t)
2
3   [mixparams, y, z] = mdnfwd(net, x);
4
5   % Compute gradients at MLP outputs: put the answer in deltas
6   ncentres = net.mdnmixes.ncentres;
7   dim_target = net.mdnmixes.dim_target;
8   nmixparams = net.mdnmixes.nparams;
9   ntarget = size(t, 1);
10  deltas = zeros(ntarget, net.mlp.nout);
11  e = ones(ncentres, 1);
12  f = ones(1, dim_target);
13
14  post = mdnpost(mixparams, t);
15
16  deltas(:,1:ncentres) = mixparams.mixcoeffs - post;
17
18  long_t     = kron(ones(1, ncentres), t);
19  centre_err = mixparams.centres - long_t;
20
21  long_post = kron(ones(dim_target, 1), post);
22  long_post = reshape(long_post, ntarget, (ncentres*dim_target));
```

```
23
24   var = mixparams.covars;
25   var = kron(ones(dim_target, 1), var);
26   var = reshape(var, ntarget, (ncentres*dim_target));
27
28   % Compute centre deltas
29   deltas(:, (ncentres+1):(ncentres*(1+dim_target))) = ...
30                         (centre_err.*long_post)./var;
31
32   % Compute variance deltas
33   dist2 = mdndist2(mixparams, t);
34   c     = dim_target*ones(ntarget, ncentres);
35   deltas(:, (ncentres*(1+dim_target)+1):nmixparams) = ...
36                         post.*((dist2./mixparams.covars)-c)./(-2);
37
38   g = mlpbkp(net.mlp, x, z, deltas);
```

The inputs are propagated through the network to set the mixture model coefficients, and the posterior probabilities are calculated (lines 3 and 14). The matrix deltas is used to contain the output error gradients. The first ncentres columns contain the mixture coefficient derivatives, as given by (5.48), line 16. The next Mc columns contain the centre derivatives. Following (5.49) we must augment and reshape the target, posterior and variance matrices. The matrix long_t contains M copies of the target matrix t as columns (line 18). This is the same process as was required in the function mdndist2. The matrix long_post copies each posterior probability c times for each kernel. Lines 21–22 carry out the necessary computation. For example, if post is given by

```
0.1 0.2 0.7
0.3 0.4 0.3
```

and the dimension of the target space c is 2, then the matrix long_post has the value

```
0.1 0.1 0.2 0.2 0.7 0.7
0.3 0.3 0.4 0.4 0.3 0.3
```

The matrix var is the mixture covariance matrix transformed in the same way as the posterior matrix (lines 24–26). The computation of the centre derivatives is now straightforward (line 29–30). The variance derivatives occupy the last M columns of the deltas matrix. Their computation (lines 33–36) follows easily from (5.51). The final step of the computation is to back-propagate the errors through the MLP component of the network. This is accomplished in line 38.

5.7.6 Demonstration Program

To illustrate the use of Mixture Density Networks, the demonstration script demmdn1 uses data generated from a simple one-to-many mapping with one input and one target variable. This allows us to plot the full conditional distribution and show its fit to the data, and compare this with the poor fit given by an MLP trained with a least squares approach.

1. The generating function is defined by

$$x = t + 0.3\sin(2\pi t) + \epsilon, \tag{5.52}$$

where ϵ is a random variable with a $U(-0.1, 0.1)$ distribution. As usual, x denotes the input variable and t is the target variable. Note that x is a proper function of t: this data models applications where the 'forward' problem (mapping t to x) is a single-valued mapping while the 'inverse' problem (mapping x to t) is multi-valued. For $x \in [0.35, 0.65]$ the function has three branches (see Fig. 5.5).

The data is generated and plotted with the lines.

```
1  ndata = 300;              % Number of data points.
2  noise = 0.2;              % Noise standard deviation.
3  t = [0:1/(ndata - 1):1]';
4  x = t + 0.3*sin(2*pi*t) + noise*rand(ndata, 1) - noise/2;
5  p1 = plot(x, t, 'ob');
```

2. The Mixture Density Network is created and initialised:

```
6  nin = 1;            % Number of inputs.
7  nhidden = 5;        % Number of hidden units.
8  ncentres = 3;       % Number of mixture components.
9  dim_target = 1;     % Dimension of target space
10 mdntype = '0';      % Reserved for future use
11 alpha = 100;        % Inverse variance for weight initialisation
12 net = mdn(nin, nhidden, ncentres, dim_target, mdntype);
```

In contrast with the initialisation of the MLP, we must also specify the number of mixture components. This is is set to 3 as we know that the function to be modelled has at most three branches. The centres and variances of the mixture model (as determined by the output biases) are initialised using ten iterations of the K-means algorithm.

```
13 init_options = zeros(1, 18);
14 init_options(1) = -1;   % Suppress all messages
15 init_options(14) = 10;  % 10 iterations of K means in gmminit
16 net = mdninit(net, alpha, t, init_options);
```

3. Training of the network takes place in the usual way. We set up an options vector to control the process

```
17 options = foptions;
18 options(1) = 1;         % Display error values.
19 options(14) = 200;      % Number of training cycles.
```

and then the network is trained using the scaled conjugate gradients algorithm netopt

```
20 [net, options] = netopt(net, options, x, t, 'scg');
```

For comparison purposes, we also train an MLP on the same data with the quasi-Newton algorithm for 80 iterations.

```
21  mlp_nhidden = 8;
22  net2 = mlp(nin, mlp_nhidden, dim_target, 'linear');
23  options(14) = 80;
24  [net2, options] = netopt(net2, options, x, t, 'quasinew');
```

4. The next stage is to plot the MDN predictions and compare them with the function underlying the data. If we used the mean of the conditional distribution represented by the MDN then this would give a poor fit in the multi-branched region of the mapping. Instead we use the mode of the conditional distribution: we compute this as the centre corresponding to the kernel with the largest mixing coefficient. For simplicity this is computed in a loop, and stored in a variable y.

```
25  mixes = mdn2gmm(mdnfwd(net, plotvals));
26  for i = 1:length(plotvals)
27    [m, j] = max(mixes(i).priors);
28    y(i) = mixes(i).centres(j,:);
29  end
```

The MDN prediction is then plotted on the same graph with the underlying function and the MLP prediction (see Fig. 5.6):

```
29  yplot = t+0.3*sin(2*pi*t);
30  p2 = plot(yplot, t, '--y');
31  p3 = plot(plotvals, y, '*r');
32  p4 = plot(plotvals, mlpfwd(net2, plotvals), 'g');
```

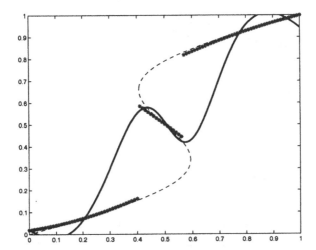

Fig. 5.6. Comparison of MDN conditional mode (*stars*), MLP regression (*solid line*), and data generator (*dashed line*).

To gain more insight into the nature of the conditional density modelled by the MDN, the full demonstration program plots graphs of the mixture model coefficients as functions of the input variable x. Finally, a contour plot of the conditional density shows that the multi-branched nature of the underlying function has been captured by the MDN (see Fig. 5.7).

```
33  i = 0:0.01:1.0;  j = 0:0.01:1.0;
34  [I, J] = meshgrid(i,j);
35  I = I(:);  J = J(:);
36  Z = zeros(length(i), length(j));
37  for k = 1:length(i);
38    Z(:,k) = gmmprob(mixes(k), j');
39  end
40  v = [2 2.5 3 3.5 5:3:18];
41  contour(i, j, Z, v)
```

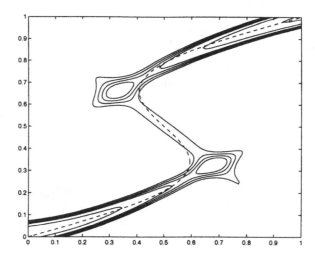

Fig. 5.7. Contour plot of conditional density modelled by MDN with data generator (*dashed line*).

5.8 Worked Example: Adding Direct Connections

In many applications it is useful to extend the simple two-layer MLP to allow connections directly from the inputs to the output layer. This is because these connections can model linear relationships between inputs and outputs, leaving the hidden units to model the non-linear residual. This often allows the use of significantly smaller networks, with the usual advantages of faster training times and smaller training data requirements.

For the basic training of MLPs in a maximum likelihood framework, as discussed in this chapter, very few modifications are required to the NETLAB software to include direct connections; just five program files need to be changed. (These should be compared with the original versions given earlier in this chapter.)

In mlp.m, the line that calculates the number of weights must be changed to

```
7   net.nwts = (nin + 1)*nhidden + (nhidden + 1 + nin)*nout;
```

to take account of the additional nin*nout weights in the direct connections. These weights should be randomly initialised after line 29 using the following MATLAB instruction:

```
30   net.wd = randn(nin, nout)/sqrt(nin + 1);
```

which uses the matrix net.wd to store the direct connection weights. The inclusion of an additional weight matrix entails modifications to the routines that convert between the two views of the network weights. The key line in mlppak must be changed to

```
w = [net.w1(:)', net.b1, net.w2(:)', net.b2, net.wd(:)'];
```

where we have added the new weights at the end of the packed weight vector w. The corresponding modification to mlpunpak occurs at the end of the function, and takes the last nin*nout elements of the weight vector and reshapes them into net.wd:

```
18   mark5 = mark4 + nin*nout;
19   net.wd = reshape(w(mark4 + 1: mark5), nin, nout);
```

The check on the size of the weight vector in lines 2–4 of mlpunpak is still valid, due to the change made to net.nwts in the function mlp.

The only line in the forward propagation function mlpfwd that needs modification is the one which computes the output activations. Equation (5.4) is modified so that the output activations $a_k^{(2)}$ are computed by

$$a_k^{(2)} = \sum_{j=1}^{M} w_{kj}^{(2)} z_j + b_k^{(2)} + \sum_{l=1}^{d} w_{kl}^{(d)} x_l \qquad k = 1, \ldots, c, \quad l = 1, \ldots, d, \quad (5.53)$$

where c is the number of outputs, d is the number of inputs, and $w_{kl}^{(d)}$ are the elements of the direct connection weight matrix. The corresponding forward propagation code in mlpfwd is:

```
5   a = z*net.w2 + ones(ndata, 1)*net.b2 + x*net.wd;
```

which adds a linear combination of the inputs to the standard linear combination of hidden unit activations. With this modification, the calculation of the error in mlperr is correct as it stands. The last change needed is to the error back-propagation. First, we must calculate the error gradient with respect to the direct connections by differentiating equation (5.53) with respect to $w_{kl}^{(d)}$:

$$\frac{\partial E}{\partial w_{kl}^{(d)}} = \sum_{n=1}^{N} \delta_k^{(2)n} x_l^n \tag{5.54}$$

which is implemented by a new line in mlpbkp:

```
6  gwd = x'*deltas;
```

This new component of the gradient must be added to the gradient vector, in the same position as in mlppak. The revised function is

```
1  function g = mlpbkp(net, x, z, deltas)
2
3  % Evaluate second-layer gradients.
4  gw2 = z'*deltas;
5  gb2 = sum(deltas, 1);
6  gwd = x'*deltas;
7
8  % Now do the backpropagation.
9  delhid = deltas*net.w2';
10 delhid = delhid.*(1.0 - z.*z);
11
12 % Finally, evaluate the first-layer gradients.
13 gw1 = x'*delhid;
14 gb1 = sum(delhid, 1);
15
16 g = [gw1(:)', gb1, gw2(:)', gb2, gwd];
```

After such significant changes to a model, it is always a good idea to check that the model error and gradient functions are consistent using the gradchek utility.

```
1  % Test script for modified MLP
2  randn('state', 1729);
3  x = randn(10, 1); t = randn(10, 1);
4  net = mlp(1, 3, 1, 'linear');
5  w = mlppak(net);
6  gradchek(w, 'neterr', 'netgrad', net, x, t);
```

You should obtain output similar to the following, where the important point is that the delta column contains values that are zero (to the standard four decimal place precision of MATLAB).

Checking gradient ...

analytic	diffs	delta
-1.6414	-1.6414	0.0000
-1.3505	-1.3505	0.0000
1.8233	1.8233	0.0000
-5.7202	-5.7202	0.0000
6.2884	6.2884	0.0000
5.7500	5.7500	0.0000
12.2485	12.2485	0.0000
-8.9647	-8.9647	0.0000
-8.0019	-8.0019	0.0000

```
-17.3421   -17.3421    0.0000
  3.5654     3.5654    0.0000
```

The changes to other `mlp` functions needed for other derivative calculations are set as Exercise 5.6.

Exercises

5.1 ($\star$) Write a demonstration program for a classification problem with more than two classes. It should be based on `demmlp2` with the following modifications:

1. Generate data from more than a Gaussian mixture model with more than three components. Make sure that at least one class corresponds to more than one component so that the decision boundary is non-linear.
2. The target data should have a one-of-n encoding rather than a 0–1 encoding.
3. The output activation function of the MLP should be a softmax.

5.2 ($\star\star$) Compare the speed of back-propagation with using numerical approximations for calculating the error gradient. You should use both central differences and single-sided differences. If ϵ_i denotes a vector with the same length as the weight vector that is zero except in the ith position, where it has the value ϵ, then the central difference formula is

$$\frac{\partial E}{\partial w_i} \approx \frac{E(\boldsymbol{w} + \epsilon_i) - E(\boldsymbol{w} - \epsilon_i)}{2|\epsilon|} \tag{5.55}$$

and the formula for single-sided difference is

$$\frac{\partial E}{\partial w_i} \approx \frac{E(\boldsymbol{w} + \epsilon_i) - E(\boldsymbol{w})}{|\epsilon|}. \tag{5.56}$$

Also compare the results for different step sizes in the difference algorithms.

5.3 ($\star\star$) The Jacobian matrix $\boldsymbol{J}$ has elements given by the derivatives of the network outputs with respect to the input values, so that

$$J_{ki} \equiv \frac{\partial y_k}{\partial x_i}. \tag{5.57}$$

This can be compared with the function `mlpderiv`, which computes the derivatives of the network activations with respect to the weights

$$J_{ijk} \equiv \frac{\partial a_k^i}{\partial w_j^i}. \tag{5.58}$$

For a two-layer feed-forward network with linear output units, the elements of the Jacobian matrix can be computed using

$$J_{ki} = \sum_{j=1}^{M} w_{kj}(1 - z_j^2)w_{ji}, \qquad (5.59)$$

where we have assumed a tanh hidden unit activation function. Verify (5.59) starting from (5.1), (5.2), (5.3) and (5.4). Write a MATLAB function to evaluate the Jacobian matrix. This function should have the definition J = mlpjacob(w, np, x) where w is the weight vector, np is the vector of network parameters, and x is an input vector. The matrix J should have dimension nout × nin where nout is the number of outputs and nin is the number of inputs. Test your function by evaluating the Jacobian matrix for random weights and random choices of x by comparison against the Jacobian evaluated using central differences of the form

$$\frac{\partial y_k}{\partial x_i} = \frac{y_k(x_i + \epsilon) - y_k(x_i - \epsilon)}{2\epsilon} + \mathcal{O}(\epsilon^2). \qquad (5.60)$$

5.4 (⋆⋆) Compare the accuracy and efficiency of the full Hessian calculation mlphess with a diagonal approximation (Becker and Le Cun, 1989; Le Cun *et al.*, 1990) defined by

$$\frac{\partial^2 E}{\partial w_{ji}^2} = \sum_n \frac{\partial^2 E}{\partial a_j^2} z_i^2 \qquad (5.61)$$

$$\frac{\partial^2 E^n}{\partial a_j^2} = g'(a_j)^2 \sum_k w_{kj}^2 \frac{\partial^2 E^n}{\partial a_k^2} + g''(a_j) \sum_k w_{kj} \frac{\partial E^n}{\partial a_k}, \qquad (5.62)$$

where E^n denotes the error on the nth pattern. Use (5.61) and (5.62) to implement a back-propagation procedure to calculate the diagonal approximation.

5.5 (⋆⋆) Compare the accuracy and efficiency of the full Hessian calculation mlphess with an outer product approximation defined by

$$\frac{\partial^2 E}{\partial w_{ji} \partial w_{lk}} = \sum_n \frac{\partial y^n}{\partial w_{ji}} \frac{\partial y^n}{\partial w_{lk}}, \qquad (5.63)$$

for a sum-of-squares error function and a single output. Extend the approximation to the case of multiple outputs. This approximation should only be valid on a dataset with the same statistical properties as the dataset the network was trained on (see Bishop, 1995, Section 4.10.2). Test the truth of this assertion.

5.6 (⋆⋆) Complete the implementation of the MLP network with direct connections from input to output.

  1. The function mlpderiv needs no modification, since the key computations use the functions mlpfwd and mlpbkp.

2. To compute the Hessian correctly, changes are needed in the function mlphdotv. Apply the $\mathcal{R}\{\cdot\}$-operator to equation (5.53) to derive a new $\mathcal{R}$-forward propagation equation in place of equation (5.23) and modify the corresponding line to mlphdotv. Apply the $\mathcal{R}\{\cdot\}$-operator to equation (5.54) to derive a new $\mathcal{R}$-backward propagation equation for the direct connection weights and add a corresponding line to mlphdotv to compute a contribution hwd. Add this matrix to the Hessian vector in the final line of the function. Check that your implementation is correct using the hesschek utility.

3. The function mlpprior needs modifications in a similar style to mlp and mlppak, but is best left until Chapter 9, on Bayesian methods and Automatic Relevance Determination, has been studied.

4. The visualisation function mlphint can be simply modified to display the additional weights in a third figure, whose handle h3 should be included as an additional return value.

5.7 (⋆⋆⋆) Extend the two-layer MLP network in NETLAB so that an arbitrary number of hidden layers are possible. The changes required are analogous to those needed for direct connections, but more complicated. As all the hidden layers apart from the first and final layer are treated in the same way, a sensible method for storing these layers is as a cell array of matrices.

5.8 (⋆⋆) Verify empirically that an MLP network with a sum-of-squares error function that is trained on target data with a 1-of-c encoding satisfies the constraint that its outputs sum to one. (Compare with problem 6.10.)

5.9 (⋆) Compare the initialisation algorithm in mdninit with random initialisation by considering its effect on the time taken for subsequent training to converge and the proportion of poor local minima reached.

5.10 (⋆⋆) It has been observed empirically that an MDN is less likely to overfit than an MLP when trained on the same dataset. Construct a suitable one-dimensional problem and test the truth of this assertion.

5.11 (⋆⋆⋆) Implement an MDN where the kernels have fixed means and variances and the mixing coefficients are the only adjustable parameters. Compared with the standard MDN, this model has fewer parameters for a given number of kernels. On the other hand, more kernels are needed to cover the target space since the means are fixed; this implies that the model is only viable for one or two-dimensional target space.

Use the mixtype field in the MDN data structure to distinguish the two types of MDN. The error and gradient functions should be quite straightforward to implement; the former is the same as mdnerr and the latter is a simplification of mdngrad. However, more care needs to be taken with the network initialisation to ensure that the means and variances of the kernels are set to sensible values. The best way to do this is to use gmmem so that the kernels model the unconditional density of the targets.

6. Radial Basis Functions

The radial basis function (RBF) network is the main practical alternative to the multi-layer perceptron for non-linear modelling. Instead of units that compute a non-linear function of the scalar product of the input vector and a weight vector, the activation of the hidden units in an RBF network is given by a non-linear function of the distance between the input vector and a weight vector.

One attraction of RBF networks is that there is a two-stage training procedure which is considerably faster than the methods used to train multi-layer perceptrons. In the first stage, the parameters of the basis functions are set so that they model the unconditional data density. The second stage of training determines the weights in the output layer, and this is a quadratic optimisation problem, which can be solved efficiently using methods from linear algebra. A further attraction of this approach to training RBF networks is that it is possible to assign an interpretation to the hidden units and also to determine the intrinsic degrees of freedom of the network. In certain circumstances, the network complexity can be matched to the data complexity to provide a simple way of determining the optimal size of the network. These ideas are developed in the worked examples at the end of the chapter.

The speed of training RBF networks also makes them attractive for use as a component in more complex models. The Generative Topographic Mapping (GTM) contains a non-linear map that must be retrained at each iteration of the EM algorithm used to train the GTM. If an MLP were used, the training times would be prohibitive, but because each iteration with an RBF network requires a single matrix inversion, the algorithm is tractable.

The standard NETLAB implementation of the RBF network also includes support for a Bayesian treatment of regularisation, so some of the functions below are also analysed in Chapter 9. The Neuroscale error function is applicable when the RBF network is used for topographic mapping; this is discussed in Section 7.4. All the functions discussed in this chapter are listed in Table 6.1.

Table 6.1. Functions in this chapter.

Radial Basis Function Networks	
demrbf1	Demonstration of RBF regression
rbf	Create a radial basis function network
rbfbkp	Back-propagation of error gradient
rbfderiv	Evaluate derivatives of network outputs with respect to weights
rbferr	Evaluate error function
rbffwd	Forward propagation
rbfgrad	Evaluate the error gradient
rbfhess	Evaluate the Hessian matrix
rbfjacob	Evaluate derivatives of network outputs with respect to inputs
rbfpak	Combine weights and biases into one parameter vector
rbfsetbf	Set basis functions from data
rbfsetfw	Set width of basis functions from data
rbftrain	Two-stage training of RBF network
rbfunpak	Separate parameter vector into weight and bias matrices

6.1 The RBF Network

In this section we discuss the basic theory of RBF networks and their implementation in NETLAB.

6.1.1 Theory

We shall write the radial basis function network mapping in the following form:

$$y_k(x) = \sum_{j=1}^{M} w_{kj} \phi_j(x) + w_{k0},$$

(6.1)

where the ϕ_j are the basis functions, and the w_{kj} are the output layer weights. It is often convenient to absorb the bias weights into the summation by including an extra basis function ϕ_0 whose activation is the constant value 1

$$y_k(x) = \sum_{j=0}^{M} w_{kj} \phi_j(x).$$

(6.2)

For a large class of basis functions, RBF networks are universal approximators (Hartman *et al.*, 1990; Park and Sandberg, 1993). Radial basis function networks can be linked with a number of other modelling techniques: function approximation, noisy interpolation, and kernel regression (see Bishop, 1995, Chapter 5). A common theme of all these viewpoints is that the sum of the basis functions $\sum_{j=0}^{M} \phi_j$ should form a representation of the unconditional probability density of the input data. We shall see later how this can be used to develop efficient training algorithms for RBF networks, but first we use it to motivate the choice of basis function. Let us suppose that we are solving a classification problem with c classes. We use a set of M density functions, labelled by an index j, to represent the class-conditional probability densities:

$$p(\boldsymbol{x}|\mathcal{C}_k) = \sum_{j=1}^{M} p(\boldsymbol{x}|j)P(j|\mathcal{C}_k), \qquad k = 1, \ldots, c. \tag{6.3}$$

To find the unconditional data density, we sum (6.3) over all classes

$$p(\boldsymbol{x}) = \sum_{k=1}^{c} p(\boldsymbol{x}|\mathcal{C}_k)P(\mathcal{C}_k) \tag{6.4}$$

$$= \sum_{j=1}^{M} p(\boldsymbol{x}|j)P(j), \tag{6.5}$$

where

$$P(j) = \sum_{k=1}^{c} P(j|\mathcal{C}_k)P(\mathcal{C}_k). \tag{6.6}$$

Then we can compute the posterior probabilities of class membership by substituting (6.3) and (6.5) into Bayes' theorem to obtain

$$P(\mathcal{C}_k|\boldsymbol{x}) = \sum_{j=1}^{M} w_{kj}\phi_j(\boldsymbol{x}), \tag{6.7}$$

where the basis functions ϕ_j are given by

$$\phi_j(\boldsymbol{x}) = \frac{p(\boldsymbol{x}|j)P(j)}{\sum_{j'=1}^{M} p(\boldsymbol{x}|j')P(j')} \tag{6.8}$$

$$= P(j|\boldsymbol{x}) \tag{6.9}$$

and the second layer weights are given by

$$w_{kj} = \frac{P(j|\mathcal{C}_k)P(\mathcal{C}_k)}{P(j)} \tag{6.10}$$

$$= P(\mathcal{C}_k|j). \tag{6.11}$$

To ensure that the network as a whole approximates probabilities, we can use positive definite normalised basis functions which are themselves density functions: in this case, we have a mixture model formalisation. One obvious choice for the basis functions is therefore a Gaussian. However, there is a drawback to this choice: the resulting density estimator is necessarily biased for a finite set of samples. If we allow non-negative basis functions, then the asymptotic convergence of the bias (as the number of samples n tends to infinity) is faster than if we insist on positive definite basis functions (Rosenblatt, 1956; Shapiro, 1969; Yamato, 1972). The NETLAB implementation of radial basis function networks therefore includes a choice of three different basis functions, written as a function of the *radial distance* $r = \|x - \mu_j\|$:

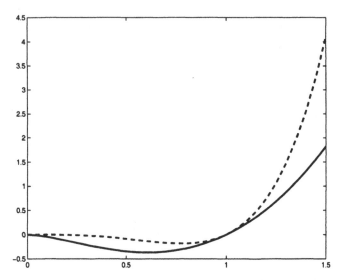

Fig. 6.1. Non-local basis functions. Thin plate spline (*solid line*) and $r^4 \log r$ (*dashed line*).

Gaussian This is left unnormalised, $\exp(-r^2/\sigma^2)$, as the output weights can provide any scaling required.

Thin plate spline The thin plate spline function $r^2 \log(r)$ is derived from the theory of function interpolation. Note that it is an unbounded function that takes on negative values for $0 < r < 1$. It is an easy exercise in calculus to show that

$$\lim_{r \to 0} r^2 \log(r) = 0. \tag{6.12}$$

$r^4 \log r$ This is also an unbounded function that takes on negative values for $0 < r < 1$. It is easy to show that

$$\lim_{r \to 0} r^4 \log(r) = 0. \tag{6.13}$$

When MLPs are applied to classification tasks, it is common practice to use logistic or softmax output activation functions and the corresponding cross-entropy error function cross-entropy error function so as to ensure that the outputs sum to one and all lie in the interval $[0, 1]$. This does not add significantly to the time taken to train an MLP since even with linear outputs, general purpose optimisation routines must be used.

However, an RBF network with logistic or softmax outputs no longer has a quadratic error surface for the output layer. If general purpose optimisation algorithms are used, much of the speed advantage over MLPs is lost. For this reason, the NETLAB implementation of RBF networks only offers linear outputs, but see also Exercise 6.11.

6.1.2 NETLAB Implementation

The following three sub-sections describe the NETLAB implementation of the basic network functions: network creation, weight manipulation, and forward propagation.

Network Creation and Initialisation

An RBF network is created using the NETLAB function rbf, which has the syntax

```
net = rbf(nin, nhidden, nout, func);
```

where func is a string specifying the basis function. The possible choices are 'gaussian', 'tps' (for thin plate spline, and 'r4logr'. In order to specify the network architecture, the user must provide values for the number of inputs, the number of hidden units, and the number of output units. The function rbf returns the network data structure net, which has the following fields:

```
type      % string describing network type: always 'rbf'
nin       % number of inputs
nhidden   % number of hidden units
nout      % number of outputs
nwts      % total number of weights and biases
actfn     % string describing the hidden unit basis function
c         % hidden unit centres
wi        % hidden unit widths
w2        % second-layer weight matrix
b2        % second-layer bias vector
```

The matrices have the following dimensions: c is nhidden $\times$ nin; wi is 1 $\times$ nhidden; w2 is nhidden $\times$ nout; b2 is 1 $\times$ nout.

```
1   function net = rbf(nin, nhidden, nout, rbfunc, outfunc, ...
2     prior, beta)
3   net.type = 'rbf';
4   net.nin = nin;
5   net.nhidden = nhidden;
6   net.nout = nout;
7
8   actfns = {'gaussian', 'tps', 'r4logr'};
9   if (strcmp(rbfunc, actfns)) == 0
10     error('Undefined activation function.')
11   else
12     net.actfn = rbfunc;
13   end
14   outfns = {'linear', 'neuroscale'};
15   if nargin <= 4
16     net.outfn = outfns{1};
17   elseif (strcmp(outfunc, outfns) == 0)
18     error('Undefined output function.')
19   else
20     net.outfn = outfunc;
21   end
22
23   net.nwts = nin*nhidden + (nhidden + 1)*nout;
24   if strcmp(rbfunc, 'gaussian')
25     % Extra weights for width parameters
26     net.nwts = net.nwts + nhidden;
27   end
28
29   if nargin > 5
30     if isstruct(prior)
31       net.alpha = prior.alpha;
32       net.index = prior.index;
33     elseif size(prior) == [1 1]
34       net.alpha = prior;
35     else
36       error('prior must be a scalar or a structure');
37     end
38   end
39
40   w = randn(1, net.nwts);
41   net = rbfunpak(net, w);
42
43   if strcmp(rbfunc, 'gaussian')
44     net.wi = ones(1, nhidden);
45   end
46   if strcmp(net.outfn, 'neuroscale')
47     net.mask = rbfprior(rbfunc, nin, nhidden, nout);
48   end
```

The RBF model is also used for visualisation with a non-linear output function specified with the argument outfunc: this is discussed further in Section 7.4.

The type and size of the network are stored in the data structure in lines 3–6. To ensure that the user does not specify an unsupported basis function, lines 8–13 test that the string passed in rbfunc matches one of the allowed values.

The parameters of a NETLAB RBF network consist of a centre row vector c(j,:) and width wi(j) for each function, hidden layer to output weights w2 and biases b2. Only the Gaussian basis function requires a width. The total number of weights in the model is computed by lines 23–7. Lines 29–38 are concerned with initialising a Bayesian prior for the network: more details can be found in Section 9.2.2.

The weights are initialised by random selection from a zero mean, unit variance isotropic Gaussian (line 40), while the width parameters are set to 1 (lines 43–45). The easiest way to initialise the weights is to 'unpack' a weight vector into the network data structure using the NETLAB function rbfunpak, as in line 41. As usual, the seed for the weight initialisation can be set to the value s by calling

```
randn('state', s);
```

before invoking rbf.

Manipulating Weights

By defining separate matrices and vectors for the parameters of the RBF network, it is possible to write the code for RBF algorithms in a particularly simple way. As with the MLP, however, we sometimes wish to treat all the parameters in the network in a single block. The function rbfpak, with calling syntax

```
w = rbfpak(net);
```

packs all the parameters in the network net into a single weight vector w. The key line is

```
w = [net.c(:)', net.wi, net.w2(:)', net.b2];
```

Here the : operator takes a matrix and converts it to a column vector by concatenating successive columns. Thus net.c(:) consists of a column vector of length nin × nhidden, and net.c(:)' is the corresponding row vector. The function

```
net = rbfunpak(net, w)
```

performs the inverse operation to rbfpak.

```
1  function net = rbfunpak(net, w)
2
3  if net.nwts ~= length(w)
4    error('Invalid length of weight vector')
5  end
6
7  nin     = net.nin;
```

```
 8  nhidden = net.nhidden;
 9  nout    = net.nout;
10
11  mark1 = nin*nhidden;
12  net.c = reshape(w(1:mark1), nhidden, nin);
13  if strcmp(net.actfn, 'gaussian')
14    mark2 = mark1 + nhidden;
15    net.wi = reshape(w(mark1+1:mark2), 1, nhidden);
16  else
17    mark2 = mark1;
18    net.wi = [];
19  end
20  mark3 = mark2 + nhidden*nout;
21  net.w2 = reshape(w(mark2+1:mark3), nhidden, nout);
22  mark4 = mark3 + nout;
23  net.b2 = reshape(w(mark3+1:mark4), 1, nout);
```

After checking that the weight vector w has the correct size for the specified network data structure (lines 3–5), the component weight matrices are extracted from w in lines 11–23. The width field is set to the empty matrix for non-Gaussian basis functions (line 18).

Forward Propagation

As for the MLP forward propagation function mlpfwd, we consider a dataset of input vectors x_n with components x_{ni} where $n = 1, \ldots, N$. In NETLAB the number of data points is denoted ndata, and the input vectors form the rows of a matrix x of dimensions ndata × nin. The function rbffwd has the following syntax:

```
y = rbffwd(net, x);
```

The output matrix y has dimensions ndata × nout. The function rbffwd has additional optional return arguments of the form

```
[y, z, n2] = rbffwd(net, x);
```

where z is a matrix of size ndata*nhidden containing the hidden unit values corresponding to $\phi_j(x)$ in (6.1) and n2 is a matrix of size ndata*nhidden containing the squared distances between the hidden unit centres and the data points. These additional arguments are used when we compute the error gradient in rbfgrad.

```
 1  function [a, z, n2] = rbffwd(net, x)
 2
 3  [ndata, data_dim] = size(x);
 4  n2 = dist2(x, net.c);
 5
 6  switch net.actfn
 7    case 'gaussian'        % Gaussian
 8      % Calculate width factors: net.wi contains squared widths
 9      wi2 = ones(ndata, 1) * (2 .* net.wi);
10      % Now compute the activations
```

```
11        z = exp(-(n2./wi2));
12     case 'tps'                % Thin plate spline
13        z = n2.*log(n2+(n2==0));
14     case 'r4logr'        % r^4 log r
15        z = n2.*n2.*log(n2+(n2==0));
16     otherwise
17        error('Unknown activation function in rbffwd')
18     end
19     a = z*net.w2 + ones(ndata, 1)*net.b2;
```

The calculation starts by finding the squared Euclidean distance between the centres and the data points (line 4). The basis function activations are then calculated using a method which depends on the nature of the function.

Gaussian The values in n2 are scaled by the widths wi, which represent the variances of the basis function before applying the exponential function (lines 7–11). Line 7 creates a matrix of dimension ndata*nhidden where each value in the jth column contains the width for the jth basis function.

Thin plate spline We actually calculate $r^2 \log r^2$ (line 13), since this is equal to $2r^2 \log r$ and the constant multiple can be absorbed into the output weights. Hence there is no need to incur the extra computational cost of taking the square root of n2. If $r = 0$, then we use (6.12) to compute the basis function. The expression

log(n2+(n2==0))

has the property that it equals log(n2) unless n2 is zero, when it equals zero (see Section 1.1.1). This ensures that z has the correct value and there are no arithmetical exceptions caused by taking the log of zero.

$r^4 \log r$ This is calculated in line 15. The value computed is equal to $r^2 \log r^2$, where again we absorb the factor of 2 into the output weights. For $r = 0$ we follow (6.13), and can use the same expression to calculate log(n2) as in the thin plate spline case.

Finally the network outputs are calculated as in (6.1)

6.2 Special Purpose Training Algorithms

One of the main advantages of RBF networks, as compared with the MLP, is that it is possible to choose good (though possibly not optimal) parameters for the hidden units without having to perform a full non-linear optimisation of all the network parameters. Recall that the sum of the basis functions $\sum_{j=0}^{M} \phi_j$ represents the unconditional density of the input data. Therefore we can use an unsupervised learning procedure for choosing the basis function parameters, and a supervised method for optimising the output layer weights.

6.2.1 Basis Function Optimisation

The aim of this part of the RBF network training algorithm is to choose the basis function centres c_j and, where appropriate, widths wi_j (for Gaussian basis functions). Note that the data used for this part need not be labelled with its target value. The simplest procedure, which is surprisingly successful in practice, is simply to choose a subset of the data points at random and use these as the basis function centres c_j.

A more sophisticated approach is to *cluster* the data into an appropriate number of clusters, and then to use the cluster centres for the c_j. As the aim is to model the data density with a linear combination of basis functions, an obvious approach is to treat the basis functions as a mixture model and to use the EM algorithm to find the parameters. Note, however, that practical experience has shown that setting the widths of the basis functions equal to the variances of the corresponding mixture model tends to give poor results because the widths are too small and there is insufficient overlap between the basis functions.

The NETLAB function rbfsetbf sets the basis function parameters from an input dataset x. As usual with training algorithms, it takes an options vector in order to control its operation. The options vector is passed straight to gmmem for controlling the EM algorithm used for the Gaussian mixture model. The only option specific to this function is options(7) which is used when setting the basis function widths in rbfsetfw.

The main interface for users to the RBF network training algorithm is the function rbftrain, but there are some occasions when it may be useful to call rbfsetbf directly. It is separate from rbftrain because it is called directly when initialising the RBF component of the Generative Topographic Mapping (see Section 7.3.2).

```
1  function net = rbfsetbf(net, options, x)
2
3  % Create a spherical Gaussian mixture model
4  mix = gmm(net.nin, net.nhidden, 'spherical');
5
6  % Just use a small number of k means iterations
7  kmoptions = zeros(1, 18);
8  kmoptions(1) = -1;  % Turn off warnings
9  kmoptions(14) = 5;
10 mix = gmminit(mix, x, kmoptions);
11
12 [mix, options] = gmmem(mix, x, options);
13
14 % Now set the RBF centres from the mixture model centres
15 net.c = mix.centres;
16
17 % options(7) gives scale of function widths
18 net = rbfsetfw(net, options(7));
```

To carry out the data clustering, we create a *local* Gaussian mixture model mix with spherical covariance structure in line 4. This model has the same number of inputs as the RBF network and the same number of centres as the RBF network has hidden units. The mixture model is initialised in the usual way by a call to gmminit (line 10); since it is not important to get a very close fit to the data density, only five iterations of K-means are used. The mixture model is trained using EM (line 12) and the centres are then transferred to the RBF network (line 15), which is simply achieved because both models use the same representation. The function rbfsetfw is then called.

```
1   function net = rbfsetfw(net, scale)
2
3   if strcmp(net.actfn, 'gaussian')
4      cdist = dist2(net.c, net.c);
5      if scale > 0.0
6         cdist = cdist + realmax*eye(net.nhidden);
7         widths = scale*mean(min(cdist));
8      else
9         widths = max(max(cdist));
10     end
11     net.wi = widths * ones(size(net.wi));
12  end
```

This function only has any work to do if the basis functions are Gaussian. It first calculates the inter-centre distance matrix (line 4). If the function is called with a single argument (representing the network), it sets the basis function variances to be the largest squared distance between centres (line 9). If a second argument is passed, this represents the *scale* applied. The minimum distance from each centre to its neighbour is calculated: the zeros down the diagonal of cdist are replaced by realmax (the largest magnitude real number in MATLAB) so that the result is computed for distinct centres (line 6). The mean of this is calculated and scaled (line 7). Finally, all the basis function widths are set to the same value in line 11.

6.2.2 Output Weight Optimisation

We can write (6.2) in matrix form as

$$y(x) = \phi W, \tag{6.14}$$

where $W = (w_{kj})$ is the output layer weight matrix and $\phi = (\phi(j))$ is the matrix of hidden unit activations. Suppose that we have a data set X: then we can extend (6.14) and write

$$Y(X) = \Phi W, \tag{6.15}$$

where Φ is the *design* matrix. We use a sum-of-squares error function given by

$$E = \frac{1}{2} \sum_n \sum_k \{y_k(x^n) - t_k^n\}^2. \tag{6.16}$$

Since this error function is quadratic in the weights, its minimum can be found using the pseudo-inverse of the design matrix as discussed in Chapter 4:

$$W = \Phi^\dagger T \tag{6.17}$$

Computing the pseudo-inverse of a matrix is a relatively fast procedure compared with a full non-linear optimisation of a two-layer network. This expression of the weights in terms of the design matrix and target values also has theoretical benefits: it gives us an interpretation of RBF networks as smoothing splines; we can give a localised interpretation of the non-local thin plate spline and $r^4 \log r$ basis functions; and we can also define and calculate the number of degrees of freedom of an RBF network (see Section 6.6). If a different choice of error function is made that is no longer quadratic in the weights, then we can no longer use such efficient methods for determining the output layer weights. This question is addressed in Exercise 6.11.

6.2.3 NETLAB Implementation

The NETLAB implementation of the two-stage training algorithm is contained in the function rbftrain. To call this function, the user must pass the network net, input data x and target data t as arguments. The algorithm is controlled by an options vector in the same way as the general purpose optimisation functions.

```
net = rbftrain(net, options, x, t)
```

In this version of the function call, the same options vector is used for RBF network training and for the function rbfsetbf. It is also possible to pass an options *matrix* which has two rows, the second of which is passed to rbfsetbf and the first of which is used to train the output layer weights (lines 3–8 below).

```
1  function [net, options] = rbftrain(net, options, x, t)
2
3  if size(options, 1) == 2
4    setbfoptions = options(2, :);
5    options = options(1, :);
6  else
7    setbfoptions = options;
8  end
9
10 % Set the basis functions to model the input data density
11 net = rbfsetbf(net, setbfoptions, x);
12
13 % Compute the design (or activations) matrix
14 [y, act] = rbffwd(net, x);
15 ndata = size(x, 1);
```

```
16
17  switch net.outfn
18  case 'linear'
19    Phi = [act ones(ndata, 1)];
20    if ~isfield(net, 'alpha')
21      % Solve for the weights and biases using left matrix divide
22      temp = pinv(Phi)*t;
23    elseif size(net.alpha == [1 1])
24      % Use normal form equation
25      hessian = Phi'*Phi + net.alpha*eye(net.nin+1);
26      temp = pinv(hessian)*(Phi'*t);
27    else
28      error('Only scalar alpha allowed');
29    end
30    net.w2 = temp(1:net.nhidden, :);
31    net.b2 = temp(net.nhidden+1, :);
32  case 'neuroscale'
33    % Neuroscale code omitted here
34  otherwise
35    error(['Unknown output function ', net.outfn]);
36  end
```

The basis function parameters are set with a call to `rbfsetbf` using the appropriate `options` vector (line 11). The second stage of the RBF network training algorithm is to compute the output weights. Following (6.17) we calculate the activations matrix `act` (line 14). Because the bias is not included in the matrix `act`, we add a column of ones to this matrix to form the design matrix Φ (line 19) and then compute the pseudo-inverse of the result and multiply this by the targets `t` (line 22). The pseudo-inverse is used as this is more robust to ill-conditioned design matrices than using the MATLAB right divide operator. If weight decay is used (i.e. `net.alpha` is a scalar) then a slightly different method of solution is appropriate; this follows (4.44) with the design matrix Φ replacing the input data X. The output weight and bias matrices are then extracted from `temp` (lines 30–31).

6.3 Error and Error Gradient Calculation

As an alternative to the two-step training procedure described in Section 6.2, it is possible to use standard non-linear optimisation algorithms to determine all the parameters in the network with the `netopt` function in an analogous way to the MLP. For this purpose, NETLAB provides functions to compute the error and error gradient for a pattern set. Setting the basis function parameters by supervised learning is typically much more computationally intensive than the unsupervised methods used in the two-step training procedure. While in theory the supervised procedure should lead to lower error values, in practice it makes little difference at significantly greater computational cost. The error function is the usual sum-of-squares:

$$E = \frac{1}{2} \sum_{n=1}^{N} \sum_{k=1}^{c} \{y_k(x_n; w) - t_{nk}\}^2. \tag{6.18}$$

The NETLAB function rbferr computes this error function.

```
1  function [e, edata, eprior] = rbferr(net, x, t)
2
3  switch net.outfn
4  case 'linear'
5    y = rbffwd(net, x);
6    edata = 0.5*sum(sum((y - t).^2));
7  case 'neuroscale'
8    % Neuroscale code omitted
9  otherwise
10    error(['Unknown output function ', net.outfn]);
11  end
12
13  % Compute Bayesian regularised error
14  [e, edata, eprior] = errbayes(net, edata);
```

The output matrix y is computed in line 5, and (6.18) is calculated in line 6. Line 14 modifies the error function to include regularisation terms, and will be discussed further in Chapter 9.

The first step in evaluating the error derivatives is to perform a forward propagation for the complete dataset in order to evaluate the squared radial distances $r^2 = \|x - \mu_j\|^2$, the activations z_j^n of the hidden units and the activations y_k^n of the output units for each pattern n in the data set. The partial derivative of the error with respect to y_k^n is the same for all hidden unit activation functions

$$\frac{\partial E^n}{\partial y_k} = y_k^n - t_k^n. \tag{6.19}$$

As in the case of MLP networks, it is convenient to label these values as

$$\delta_k^n = y_k^n - t_k^n. \tag{6.20}$$

The partial derivatives with respect to the output layer weights are the same as for the MLP:

$$\frac{\partial E}{\partial w_{kj}^{(2)}} = \sum_{n=1}^{N} \delta_k^n z_j^n, \tag{6.21}$$

while the derivatives for the output-unit biases are given by

$$\frac{\partial E}{\partial b_k^{(2)}} = \sum_{n=1}^{N} \delta_k^n. \tag{6.22}$$

When it comes to the derivatives of the error function with respect to the basis function parameters, we must consider each type separately. It is convenient to define the derivatives with respect to the hidden unit activations

$$\delta_j^n = \sum_{k=1}^{c} w_{kj}^{(2)} \delta_k^n.$$

(6.23)

The next step depends on the basis function type.

Gaussian The derivatives with respect to the components μ_{ji} of the jth centre μ_j are given by

$$\frac{\partial E}{\partial \mu_{ji}} = \sum_{n} \delta_j^n \exp\left(-\frac{\|x^n - \mu_j\|^2}{2\sigma_j^2}\right) \frac{(x_i^n - \mu_{ji})}{\sigma_j^2},$$

(6.24)

while the derivatives with respect to the standard deviation σ_j of the jth centre are

$$\frac{\partial E}{\partial \sigma_j} = \sum_{n} \delta_j^n \exp\left(-\frac{\|x^n - \mu_j\|^2}{2\sigma_j^2}\right) \frac{\|x^n - \mu_j\|^2}{\sigma_j^3}.$$

(6.25)

Since the NETLAB data structure contains σ^2, not σ, we apply the chain rule to obtain the derivative we need

$$\frac{\partial E}{\partial (\sigma^2)} = \frac{\partial E}{\partial \sigma} \frac{d\sigma}{d(\sigma^2)} = \frac{\partial E}{\partial \sigma} \frac{1}{2\sigma}.$$

(6.26)

Thin plate spline To calculate the error derivatives with respect to the hidden unit centres, we first compute the derivative of the activation function with respect to r. Recall that for efficiency, the activation function we actually use is

$$f(r) = r^2 \log r^2 = 2r^2 \log r,$$

(6.27)

so

$$\frac{df}{dr} = 2\left(\frac{r^2}{r} + 2r \log r\right) = 2r(1 + \log r^2)$$

(6.28)

and

$$\frac{df}{dr^2} = \frac{df}{dr} \frac{dr}{dr^2} = \frac{1}{2r} 2r(1 + \log r^2)$$

(6.29)

$$= 1 + \log r^2.$$

(6.30)

Using the fact that

$$\frac{\partial r^2}{\partial \mu} = 2\|x - \mu\|,$$

(6.31)

the derivatives of the error function with respect to the basis function centres can be calculated easily with the chain rule:

$$\frac{\partial E}{\partial \mu_{ji}} = 2 \sum_n \delta_j^n (1 + \log r_n^2)(x_i^n - \mu_{ji}). \tag{6.32}$$

The thin plate spline activation function has no width parameters.
$r^4 \log r$ The activation function computed in rbffwd is given by $g(r) = r^4 \log r^2$, so the relevant derivative is

$$\frac{dg}{dr^2} = \frac{1}{2r}\frac{dg}{dr} = \frac{1}{2r} 2(r^3 + 4r^3 \log r) \tag{6.33}$$

$$= r^2 (1 + 2\log r^2). \tag{6.34}$$

It follows that the derivatives of the error function with respect to the hidden unit centres are

$$\frac{\partial E}{\partial \mu_{ji}} = 2 \sum_n \delta_j^n r_n^2 (1 + \log r_n^2)(x_i^n - \mu_{ji}). \tag{6.35}$$

Again, there are no width parameters for this activation function.

The NETLAB function rbfgrad implements the error gradient computation.

```
1   function [g, gdata, gprior] = rbfgrad(net, x, t)
2
3   ndata = size(x, 1);
4   [y, z, n2] = rbffwd(net, x);
5
6   switch net.outfn
7   case 'linear'
8     delout = y - t;
9     gdata = rbfbkp(net, x, z, n2, delout);
10    [g, gdata, gprior] = gbayes(net, gdata);
11  case 'neuroscale'
12    % Neuroscale code omitted
13  otherwise
14    error(['Unknown output function ', net.outfn]);
15  end
```

The first step in evaluating the error derivatives is to perform a forward propagation (line 4), where y represents the network outputs, z the hidden unit activations, and n2 the squared radial distance r^2. Because the back-propagation of error signals is common to several functions requiring gradient calculations, this is encapsulated in the NETLAB function rbfbkp. Line 10 modifies the error gradient to include regularisation terms, and will be discussed further in Chapter 9.

The NETLAB implementation of rbfbkp runs as follows.

```
1   function g = rbfbkp(net, x, z, n2, deltas)
2
3   % Evaluate second-layer gradients.
4   gw2 = z'*deltas;
5   gb2 = sum(deltas);
6
7   % Evaluate hidden unit gradients
8   delhid = deltas*net.w2';
9
10  gc = zeros(net.nhidden, net.nin);
11  ndata = size(x, 1);
12  t1 = ones(ndata, 1);
13  t2 = ones(1, net.nin);
14  % Switch on activation function type
15  switch net.actfn
16  case 'gaussian' % Gaussian
17    delhid = (delhid.*z);
18    % A loop seems essential, so use the shortest index vector
19    if (net.nin < net.nhidden)
20      for i = 1:net.nin
21  '      gc(:,i) = (sum(((x(:,i)*ones(1, net.nhidden)) - ...
22          (ones(ndata, 1)*(net.c(:,i)'))).*delhid, 1)./net.wi)';
23      end
24    else
25      for i = 1:net.nhidden
26        gc(i,:) = sum((x - (t1*(net.c(i,:)))./net.wi(i)).* ...
27          (delhid(:,i)*t2), 1);
28      end
29    end
30    gwi = sum((n2.*delhid)./(2.*(ones(ndata, 1)*(net.wi.^2))), 1);
31  case 'tps'       % Thin plate spline activation function
32    delhid = delhid.*(1+log(n2+(n2==0)));
33    for i = 1:net.nhidden
34      gc(i,:) = sum(2.*((t1*(net.c(i,:))-x)).*(delhid(:,i)*t2), 1);
35    end
36    % widths are not adjustable in this model
37    gwi = [];
38  case 'r4logr' % r^4 log r activation function
39    delhid = delhid.*(n2.*(1+2.*log(n2+(n2==0))));
40    for i = 1:net.nhidden
41      gc(i,:) = sum(2.*((t1*(net.c(i,:))-x)).*(delhid(:,i)*t2), 1);
42    end
43    % widths are not adjustable in this model
44    gwi = [];
45  otherwise
46    error('Unknown activation function in rbfgrad')
47  end
48
49  g = [gc(:)', gwi, gw2(:)', gb2];
```

The output layer weight derivatives are computed in lines 4–5 following (6.21) and (6.22). Equation (6.23) is used to compute the gradients with respect to the hidden unit activations (line 8). Because it is not possible to implement the gradient calculations completely with matrix operations, a loop is used instead, and so the matrix of gradients with respect to the basis function centres gc is pre-allocated in line 10.

The first two terms in (6.24) are computed in line 17. Because a loop is required to complete the calculation, the remainder of the calculation is organised in one of two ways, depending on working through the input units (19–23) or the hidden units (24–29) is more efficient. Finally, line 30 implements (6.26).

For the thin plate spline activation, line 32 computes the first two terms in (6.32), while the loop in lines 33–35 finishes the calculation. Similarly, for the $r^4 \log r$ activation function, line 39 computes the first two terms in (6.35) and lines 40–42 complete the calculation. Line 49 combines the different gradient matrices to obtain a single gradient vector, so that each component of g contains the derivative of E with respect to the corresponding component of the weight vector w. The ordering of the weights is the same as that used in rbfpak.

6.4 Evaluating Other Derivatives

The error gradient is needed for training RBF networks using non-linear optimisation algorithms. In other situations, for example Bayesian methods or where an RBF network forms part of a composite model, different derivatives are useful. In this section we consider the derivatives of the output with respect to the weights (rbfderiv), the derivatives of the output with respect to the inputs (rbfjacob), and the second derivatives of the error with respect to the weights (rbfhess).

6.4.1 Output Derivatives

The function rbfderiv is used to compute the derivatives of the network output activations with respect to the weights and biases

$$\frac{\partial a^{(2)}}{\partial w_{ji}}. \tag{6.36}$$

These derivatives are required in Section 9.5 to evaluate error bars on network predictions in a Bayesian framework. As the notation indicates, since a is a vector, the result of this calculation when applied to a dataset is a three-dimensional array. The implementation is similar to that in mlpderiv; the output 'errors' are

$$\frac{\partial y_k}{\partial y_j} = \delta_{kj} \tag{6.37}$$

and these are then back-propagated through the network.

```
1   function g = rbfderiv(net, x)
2
3   if ~strcmp(net.outfn, 'linear')
4     error('Function only implemented for linear outputs')
5   end
6
7   [y, z, n2] = rbffwd(net, x);
8   ndata = size(x, 1);
9
10  g = zeros(ndata, net.nwts, net.nout);
11  for k = 1 : net.nout
12    delta = zeros(1, net.nout);
13    delta(1, k) = 1;
14    for n = 1 : ndata
15      g(n, :, k) = rbfbkp(net, x(n, :), z(n, :), n2(n, :),...
16        delta);
17    end
18  end
```

The first stage of the computation is to perform a forward propagation for the complete data set using rbffwd (line 7). The result is stored in a three-dimensional array g which is pre-sized (for efficiency) in line 10. The matrix g(:, :, k) is the gradient for output k. The output errors are set to the Kronecker delta in lines 12–13. The gradient for each data point is then computed by lines 15–16.

6.4.2 Network Jacobian

The Jacobian matrix of the derivative of the network output with respect to the network inputs

$$J_{ki} = \frac{\partial y_k}{\partial x_i}\bigg|_{x} \tag{6.38}$$

is used in the Generative Topographic Mapping to compute 'magnification factors' (see Section 7.3.5). The result of this computation for a dataset is a three-dimensional array.

The Jacobian can be evaluated at a single input vector using a back-propagation procedure that is similar to that used for evaluating $\partial E/\partial w_i$. We start by applying the chain rule:

$$J_{ki} = \frac{\partial y_k}{\partial x_i} = \sum_{j=1}^{M} \frac{\partial y_k}{\partial \phi_j} \frac{\partial \phi_j}{\partial x_i}$$

$$= \sum_{j=1}^{M} w_{kj} \frac{\partial \phi_j}{\partial x_i}, \tag{6.39}$$

where w_{kj} runs over all the second-layer weights. The biases are not included in this sum since they are not affected by the input vectors. The remaining computation of the derivative is done on a case by case basis. Since

$$\phi_j(x) = \phi(\|x - \mu_j\|^2) = \phi(r_j^2), \tag{6.40}$$

it is convenient to use the following identity:

$$\Psi_{ji} = \frac{\partial \phi_j}{\partial x_i} = \frac{\partial \phi_j}{\partial r_j^2} \frac{\partial \left(r_j^2\right)}{\partial x_i} = \frac{\partial \phi_j}{\partial \left(r_j^2\right)} \left(2(x_i - \mu_{ji})\right). \tag{6.41}$$

The derivative $\partial \phi_j / (r_j^2)$ is easily found:

Gaussian

$$\frac{\partial \phi_j}{\partial \left(r_j^2\right)} = -\frac{1}{2\sigma^2} \exp\left(-\frac{\|x - \mu_j\|^2}{2\sigma_j^2}\right) = -\frac{1}{2\sigma^2}\phi_j(r_j^2). \tag{6.42}$$

Thin plate spline Recall that we actually calculate $r^2 \log r^2$ in the NETLAB implementation.

$$\frac{\partial \phi_j}{\partial \left(r_j^2\right)} = 1 + \log r^2. \tag{6.43}$$

$r^4 \log r$ Recall that we actually calculate $r^4 \log r^2$ in the NETLAB implementation

$$\frac{\partial \phi_j}{\partial \left(r_j^2\right)} = r^2 + 2r^2 \log r^2. \tag{6.44}$$

These equations are all that is required to implement rbfjacob.

```
1  function jac = rbfjacob(net, x)
2
3  if ~strcmp(net.outfn, 'linear')
4    error('Function only implemented for linear outputs')
5  end
6
7  [y, z, n2] = rbffwd(net, x);
8
9  ndata = size(x, 1);
10 jac = zeros(ndata, net.nin, net.nout);
11 Psi = zeros(net.nin, net.nhidden);
12 % Calculate derivative of activations wrt n2
13 switch net.actfn
14 case 'gaussian'
15   dz = -z./(ones(ndata, 1)*net.wi);
16 case 'tps'
17   dz = 2*(1 + log(n2+(n2==0)));
18 case 'r4logr'
19   dz = 2*(n2.*(1+2.*log(n2+(n2==0))));
```

```
20  otherwise
21    error(['Unknown activation function ', net.actfn]);
22  end
23
24  % Ignore biases as they cannot affect Jacobian
25  for n = 1:ndata
26    Psi = (ones(net.nin, 1)*dz(n, :)).* ...
27      (x(n, :)'*ones(1, net.nhidden) - net.c');
28    % Now compute the Jacobian
29    jac(n, :, :) = Psi * net.w2;
30  end
```

For simplicity, the function is implemented only for linear outputs. It starts with a forward propagation through the network (line 7). The three-dimensional array jac that stores the result of the calculation is pre-allocated in line 10 for efficiency. The matrix Psi, which contains $\partial \phi_j / \partial x_i$ for each input pattern x^n, is pre-allocated in line 11. The derivative $2\partial \phi_j / \partial (r_j^2)$ is computed according to (6.42) in line 15, (6.43) in line 17, and (6.44) in line 19.

Lines 25–30 then complete the computation for each pattern in turn. The matrix Psi is computed in lines 26–27 in accordance with (6.41), and J_{ki} is found by (6.39) in line 29.

6.4.3 Network Hessian

The computation of the Hessian matrix for an RBF network is considerably more complicated than for an MLP or GLM. This is because each type of weight plays a very different role in the overall function of the network. However, the Hessian is mainly used in a Bayesian treatment of learning, which uses the two-stage training algorithm so that the output layer weights are the only adjustable parameters. For this reason, the implementation in NETLAB is restricted to consider just those weights.

Just as with mlphess, the data-dependent and Bayesian (i.e. regularisation) component of the Hessian are computed separately.

```
1   function [h, hdata] = rbfhess(net, x, t, hdata)
2
3   if nargin == 3
4     % Data term in Hessian needs to be computed
5     [a, z] = rbffwd(net, x);
6     hdata = datahess(net, z, t);
7   end
8
9   % Add in effect of regularisation
10  [h, hdata] = hbayes(net, hdata);
11
12  % Sub-function to compute data part of Hessian
13  function hdata = datahess(net, z, t)
14
15  % Only implemented for output layer Hessian
16  if (isfield(net, 'mask') & ~any(net.mask(...
```

```
17            1:(net.nwts - net.nout*(net.nhidden+1)))))
18    hdata = zeros(net.nwts);
19    ndata = size(z, 1);
20    out_hess = [z ones(ndata, 1)]'*[z ones(ndata, 1)];
21    for j = 1:net.nout
22      hdata = rearrange_hess(net, j, out_hess, hdata);
23    end
24  else
25    error('Output layer Hessian only.');
26  end
27  return
28
29  % Sub-function to rearrange Hessian matrix
30  function hdata = rearrange_hess(net, j, out_hess, hdata)
31
32  % Because all the biases come after all the input weights,
33  % we have to rearrange the blocks that make up network Hessian.
34  % This function assumes that we are on the jth output and that
35  % all outputs are independent.
36
37  % Start of bias weights block
38  bb_start = net.nwts - net.nout + 1;
39  % Start of weight block for jth output
40  ob_start = net.nwts - net.nout*(net.nhidden+1) + ...
41    (j-1)*net.nhidden + 1;
42  % End of weight block for jth output
43  ob_end = ob_start + net.nhidden - 1;
44  % Index of bias weight
45  b_index = bb_start+(j-1);
46  % Put input weight block in right place
47  hdata(ob_start:ob_end, ob_start:ob_end) = ...
48    out_hess(1:net.nhidden, 1:net.nhidden);
49  % Put second derivative of bias weight in right place
50  hdata(b_index, b_index) = out_hess(net.nhidden+1, net.nhidden+1);
51  % Put cross terms (input weight v bias weight) in right place
52  hdata(b_index, ob_start:ob_end) = out_hess(net.nhidden+1, ...
53    1:net.nhidden);
54  hdata(ob_start:ob_end, b_index) = out_hess(1:net.nhidden, ...
55    net.nhidden+1);
56
57  return
```

The sub-function **datahess** computes the data component of the Hessian matrix. Lines 16–17 test that all but the output layer weights are masked out (i.e. the **mask** vector is set to zero); see Section 9.2.4. The Hessian matrix for linear outputs is given by

$$H = \Phi^T \Phi, \tag{6.45}$$

where Φ denotes the design matrix (including the bias term). This is computed in line 20. However, because of the ordering of the weights (all the biases come after the weights from the hidden units), H must be rearranged. This is done by a sub-function **rearrange_hess**, which is identical to the function of the same name in glmhess. Unfortunately, in MATLAB sub-functions cannot be called from outside their own file, so the code has to be repeated here.

6.5 Demonstration Program

The demonstration program demrbf1 shows how the NETLAB RBF network implementation can be used for regression. It illustrates this by using all three activation functions on the same problem. The process can be divided into four stages:

1. loading the training data;
2. creating and initialising the network;
3. training the network;
4. loading the test data and making predictions.

We now look at the details of each stage for the same example problem as used in demmlp1.

1. The data set used in demrbf1 is the standard noisy sine wave:

```
1   rand('state', 42);
2   randn('state', 42);
3   ndata = 20;          % Number of data points.
4   noise = 0.2;         % Noise standard deviation.
5   x = (linspace(0, 1, ndata))';
6   t = sin(2*pi*x) + noise*randn(ndata, 1);
7   mu = mean(x);
8   sigma = std(x);
9   tr_in = (x - mu)./(sigma);
```

Note how the input data is normalised to have zero mean and unit variance (lines 7–9). This improves the performance of the non-local basis functions.

2. The network data structure net is then created by a call to rbf:

```
10   nin = 1;                      % Number of inputs.
11   nhidden = 7;                  % Number of hidden units.
12   nout = 1;                     % Number of outputs.
13   net = rbf(nin, nhidden, nout, 'gaussian');
```

This network has Gaussian basis functions.

3. To train the network, the options vector is set up and the function rbftrain is called:

```
15   options = foptions;
16   options(1) = 1;      % Display error values.
17   options(14) = 10;    % Number of iterations of EM.
18   net = rbftrain(net, options, tr_in, t);
```

We then create a second RBF network net2 with thin plate spline activation functions:

```
15  net2 = rbf(nin, nhidden, nout, 'tps');
```

Rather than call `rbftrain` again, we simply reuse the centres from the trained network `net`. The output weights are then found using the pseudo-inverse of the design matrix for `net2` (lines 22–24); compare lines 22 and 30–31 of `rbftrain`.

```
20  net2.c = net.c;
21  [y, act2] = rbffwd(net2, x);
22  temp = pinv([act ones(ndata, 1)]) * t;
23  net2.w2 = temp(1:nhidden, :);
24  net2.b2 = temp(nhidden+1, :);
```

`demrbf1` repeats this procedure for the network `net3` with $r^4 \log r$ basis functions.

4. The final task is to plot the function encapsulated by all three trained networks. This is performed using `rbffwd` to compute the network outputs y, y2 and y3 at a regular grid of values contained in the matrix `plotvals`:

```
25  plotvals = [x(1):0.01:x(end)]';
26  inputvals = (plotvals-mu)./sigma;
27  y = rbffwd(net, inputvals);
28  y2 = rbffwd(net2, inputvals);
29  y3 = rbffwd(net3, inputvals);
```

The resulting graph is shown in Fig. 6.2.

6.6 Worked Examples: Linear Smoothing

In this section we show how a different view of the RBF network, which uses results from linear smoothing theory, gives insight into how non-local basis functions (such as the thin plate spline) can give useful results. The framework of *dual* basis functions also allows us to derive practical methods for determining the optimal network complexity.

6.6.1 Dual Basis Functions

It is perhaps slightly surprising that non-positive and non-local basis functions should be good for density estimation. One way to explain this is to consider the dual function space, also known as the equivalent *smoothing kernels*. We start by considering again (6.2):

$$y_k(x) = \sum_{j=0}^{M} w_{kj} \phi_j(x).$$ (6.46)

In this representation, the basis functions ϕ_j are usually similar (except for $\phi_0 \equiv 1$ as the bias) and the task is to estimate the weights w_{kj}. If the network

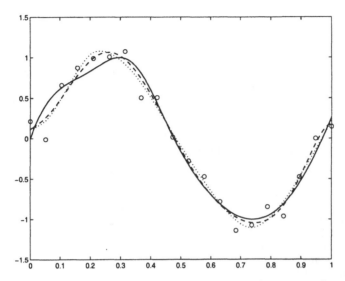

Fig. 6.2. Demonstration of RBF regression. Gaussian (*dashed line*), thin plate spline (*dotted line*), $r^4 \log r$ (*solid line*). Corresponding training set errors are 0.14586, 0.14092 and 0.26191.

weights are estimated using a least squares criterion, then the optimum weight matrix W is given by (6.17):

$$W^T = \Phi^\dagger T, \tag{6.47}$$

where Φ is the design matrix and T is the matrix of targets calculated for the whole training dataset. The key step is to rewrite (6.46) using (6.47).

$$y_k(x) = \sum_{j=0}^{M} \phi_j(x) \sum_{l=1}^{N} \Phi_{jl}^\dagger T_{lk}$$

$$= \sum_{l=1}^{N} \left[\sum_{j=0}^{M} \phi(x) \Phi_{jl}^\dagger \right] T_{lk} \qquad \text{rearranging the order of summation}$$

$$= \sum_{l=1}^{N} \Psi_l(x) T_{lk}. \tag{6.48}$$

In this alternative view, the RBF output is again a linear combination of functions. However, the 'weights' T_{lk} are now given by the training targets and the *dual* basis functions Ψ are data-dependent:

$$\Psi(x) = \sum_{j=0}^{M} \phi_j(x)\Phi_{jl}^{\dagger}. \tag{6.49}$$

Note also that there are N dual basis functions. This shows that an RBF network can be regarded as a *linear smoother* on the target values.

In most cases the dual basis functions are localised around the data point that they correspond to, which explains how the network output can be localised, at least in the region of the training data. The following MATLAB script graphically illustrates this point.

```
1   % DUAL  Demonstration of dual basis functions
2   randn('state', 42);
3   rand('state', 42);
4   ndata = 50;              % Number of data points.
5   noise = 0.1;            % Noise standard deviation.
6   x = (linspace(0, 1, ndata))';
7   t = sin(2*pi*x) + noise*randn(ndata, 1);
8   mu = mean(x);
9   sigma = std(x);
10  tr_in = (x-mu)./sigma;
11
12  nin = 1;               % Number of inputs.
13  nhidden = 6;           % Number of hidden units.
14  nout = 1;              % Number of outputs.
15
16  net = rbf(nin, nhidden, nout, 'r4logr');
17  options = foptions;
18  options(1) = 1;        % Display EM training
19  options(14) = 5;       % number of iterations of EM
20  net = rbftrain(net, options, tr_in, t);
21
22  plotvals = [-0.1:0.01:1.1]';
23  inputvals = (plotvals-mu)./sigma;
24  [y_plot, act_plot] = rbffwd(net, inputvals);
25  phi_plot = [act_plot, ones(size(inputvals))];
26
27  % Compute dual basis functions
28  [y, act] = rbffwd(net, tr_in);
29  Phi = [act ones(ndata, 1)];
30  PhiDag = pinv(Phi);
31  dual_plot = phi_plot*PhiDag;
32
33  % Now plot three of them on one graph
34  fh2 = figure;
35  plot(plotvals, dual_plot(:, 1), '-r', 'LineWidth', 2);
36  hold on
37  a = axis; % Get current axis limits
38  l1 = line([x(1) x(1)], [a(3) a(4)]);
39  plot(plotvals, dual_plot(:, 20), '-.k', 'LineWidth', 2);
40  l2 = line([x(20) x(20)], [a(3) a(4)]);
41  plot(plotvals, dual_plot(:, 48), '--g', 'LineWidth', 2);
42  l3 = line([x(48) x(48)], [a(3) a(4)]);
```

In this demonstration, 50 points from the noisy sine curve are generated and normalised in the usual way (lines 2–10). In lines 12–20, an RBF network with $r^4 \log r$ basis functions is created and trained using rbftrain. The vector of test points, plotvals is created and then the trained network is used to make predictions y_plot and corresponding activations act_plot (lines 22–24). The design matrix at these test points, phi_plot, is computed by adding a column of ones to the activation matrix (line 25).

Lines 28–31 compute the values of the dual basis functions at the test points according to (6.49), using the training set design matrix Phi, its pseudo-inverse PhiDag, and the test set design matrix phi_plot. Each column of the matrix dual_plot represents a different dual basis function (so there are the same number of columns as training data points), and in the last section of code three of them are plotted with a vertical line representing the position of the corresponding training data point.

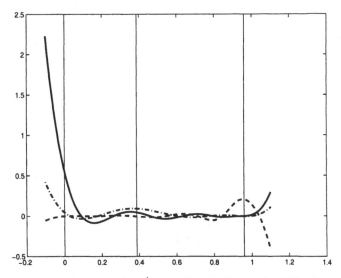

Fig. 6.3. Dual basis functions for $r^4 \log r$. Plotted for 1st (*solid line*), 20th (*dash-dotted line*) and 48th (*dashed line*) points in the dataset. The x-coordinate of the data points are given by the vertical lines from left to right.

Figure 6.3 shows the dual basis functions generated by this script. It is clear that the dual basis functions show localised damped oscillations in the training data range $[0, 1]$, while outside that region they grow rapidly. Figure 6.4 shows the corresponding plot for thin plate spline basis functions.

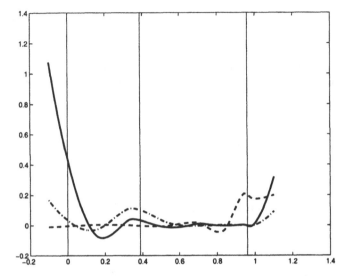

Fig. 6.4. Dual basis functions for thin plate spline. Plotted for 1st (*solid line*), 20th (*dash-dotted line*) and 48th (*dashed line*) points in the dataset. The x-coordinate of the data points are given by the vertical lines from left to right.

6.6.2 Characterising Network Complexity

We can put the linear smooth view of RBF networks to practical use. In a Bayesian context, if there are Gaussian priors on the weights and data, then the posterior covariance of y is $\Psi \sigma^2$ (see Silverman (1985) and Section 10.1.1). The number of degrees of freedom of the model is given by $\operatorname{tr} \Psi$, which can be easily calculated as the sum of the eigenvalues of the smoother matrix.

The number of degrees of freedom can be viewed as the complexity of the model, and this can now be linked with the RBF network (Lowe, 1998). The smooth matrix Ψ is equal to $\Phi\Phi^\dagger$ as shown in (6.49). Consider now the singular value decomposition of the design matrix

$$\Phi = U \Sigma V^T. \tag{6.50}$$

Since the pseudo-inverse is given by $V \widetilde{\Sigma}^{-1} U^T$, it follows that $\Psi := \Phi\Phi^\dagger = UU^T$ which is an idempotent projection matrix with the property $\Psi^2 = \Psi$. This implies that all its eigenvalues are 0 or 1. Hence the number of unit eigenvalues is the same as the rank of U which is equal to the rank of Φ (see Fig. 6.5(a)). Hence, we can use the rank of Φ to compute the number of degrees of freedom of an RBF network.

Unfortunately in real problems, due to data noise, Ψ is of full rank whatever the true complexity of the model. However, we can estimate the rank in a more robust fashion by considering the singular spectrum of Φ. It is well known (Broomhead and King, 1986) that isotropic (i.e. spherical) additive

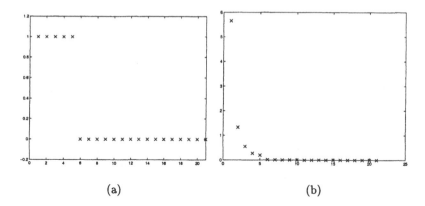

(a)   (b)

Fig. 6.5. Estimating RBF complexity on the sine data with a noise standard deviation of 0.25. (a) Using the eigenvalue spectrum of P computed by pinv with a tolerance of 0.1. (b) Using the singular spectrum of Φ.

Gaussian noise affects the singular spectrum by raising all the values by an amount related to the noise standard deviation. Heuristically, we should inspect the singular spectrum for 'kinks' or sudden drops (the *scree test*) which may indicate the separation between signal and noise; see Fig. 6.5(b) for an example. Multiple sources of noise will give rise to multiple kinks. The index at which this occurs is the number of degrees of freedom in the RBF network.

The complete procedure is:

1. Train an RBF network with a relatively large number of hidden units.
2. Compute the singular spectrum of the design matrix and decompose it into signal and noise segments. The index of this discontinuity gives the true number of degrees of freedom for the model.
3. This can be checked by inspecting the eigenvalues of the smooth matrix.
4. The number of basis functions should be reduced to one less than the number of degrees of freedom found in the previous two steps (to allow for the output bias term). The network can then be retrained.

The following simple function implements this procedure on the noisy sine data. The user can specify the activation function (the default is $r^4 \log r$) and the number of training data points (the default is 30); see lines 4–9. (The details of the plotting have been omitted for clarity.)

```
1  function [net, net2] = rbfcomp(act_fun, ndata)
2  % RBFCOMP Demonstrate complexity of RBF model
3
4  if nargin < 2
5    ndata = 30;
6    if nargin < 1
```

```
 7       act_fun = 'r4logr';
 8     end
 9   end
10
11   randn('state', 42);
12   rand('state', 42);
13   noise = 0.25;            % Noise standard deviation.
14   x = (linspace(0, 1, ndata))';
15   t = sin(2*pi*x) + noise*randn(ndata, 1);
16
17   nin = 1;                         % Number of inputs.
18   nhidden = 20;                    % Number of hidden units.
19   nout = 1;                        % Number of outputs.
20   net = rbf(nin, nhidden, nout, act_fun);
21   options = foptions;
22   options(1) = 1;           % Display EM training
23   options(14) = 5;          % number of iterations of EM
24   net = rbftrain(net, options, x, t);
25
26   plotvals = [-0.1:0.01:1.1]';
27   [y_plot, phi_plot] = rbffwd(net, plotvals);
28   % Plot RBF predictions (omitted)
29
30   % Compute singular values of design matrix
31   [y, act] = rbffwd(net, x);
32   Phi = [act, ones(ndata, 1)];
33
34   S = svd(Phi);
35   % Plot singular values of design matrix (omitted)
36
37   tol = input('Enter pseudo-inverse tolerance (0 for none) ');
38   if (logical(tol))
39     Phidag = pinv(Phi, tol);
40   else
41     Phidag = pinv(Phi);
42   end
43   Psi = Phi*Phidag;
44   % Sort eigenalues into descending order
45   evalues = -sort(-eig(Psi));
46   % Plot eigenvalues of Psi (omitted)
47
48   nh = input('Enter new number of hidden units to train: ')
49   nhidden = nh;
50
51   net2 = rbf(nin, nhidden, nout, act_fun);
52   net2 = rbftrain(net2, options, x, t);
53   y2_plot = rbffwd(net2, plotvals);
54
55   % Plot predictions of reduced complexity RBF (omitted)
```

Much of this code should be familiar to you by now (the input data normalisation has been omitted for simplicity). The network is trained initially
with 20 hidden units, and the regression fit to the underlying function is

computed in lines 26–27. The training set design matrix is computed in lines 31–32 and its singular value decomposition computed (line 34) and plotted in a second figure. As a comparison, the dual basis Ψ and its eigenspectrum are calculated in lines 43–45 and plotted in a third figure. These two plots are Figs. 6.5(a) and 6.5(b). These plots show that there are five singular values

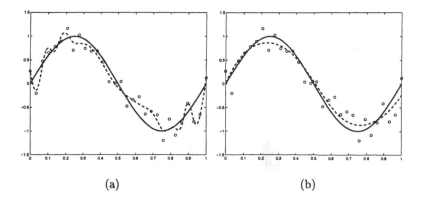

(a)   (b)

Fig. 6.6. Reduction in overfitting in RBF networks. **(a)** RBF trained with 20 hidden units. **(b)** RBF trained with four hidden units.

significantly different from zero. The user can now input a reduced number of hidden units after inspecting these two plots, and the network is then re-trained. Figure 6.6 shows the RBF network predictions before and after the reduction in the number of hidden units. It is clear that the network with 20 hidden units overfits the training data, while that with four hidden units will generalise significantly better.

Exercises

6.1 ($\star$) Write a function rbfsetow to compute output layer weights for an RBF network based on rbftrain. This can be used to replace lines 21–24 in the version of demrbf1 given in this chapter.

6.2 ($\star\star$) Using rbfsetow from Exercise 6.1, write a new version of rbftrain that sets the centres by random sampling from the training data points. Evaluate the effect on training time and accuracy compared with the standard rbftrain.

6.3 ($\star\star$) Using rbfsetow from Exercise 6.1, write a new version of rbftrain that sets the centres by random sampling from the training data points followed by K-means clustering. Evaluate the effect on training time and accuracy compared with Exercise 6.2.

6.4 ($\star$) RBF networks can be trained using `netopt` together with `rbferr` and `rbfgrad`. Using the noisy sine wave and other datasets, compare the efficiency, training and generalisation error of this approach with `rbftrain`.

6.5 ($\star\star$) Evaluate weight decay as a regularisation mechanism for RBF network training using the `alpha` parameter in the network data structure. Use cross-validation to determine the optimal value of α: train models for a range of different values of α and evaluate their performance on a validation dataset that is distinct from the training and test sets. The optimal value of α is that which gives lowest validation set error.

6.6 ($\star$) Try the effect of using different basis function widths in `rbfsetfw` during network training for Gaussian basis functions. For what range of values does the parameter significantly affect the results?

6.7 ($\star$) Write a test script containing a suitable call to the NETLAB function `gradchek` to test empirically that the implementation of `rbfjacob` is correct.

6.8 ($\star\star$) Implement a new basis function `'cubic'` defined by r^3 and compare its performance with the existing basis functions. You should check that the network gradients are correctly computed using `gradchek` and `hesschek`. Generate plots of the dual basis functions to demonstrate that they are bounded and localised.

6.9 ($\star\star$) Develop an RBF network with direct (linear) input to output connections. You may find the worked example of direct connections for the MLP useful (see Section 5.8).

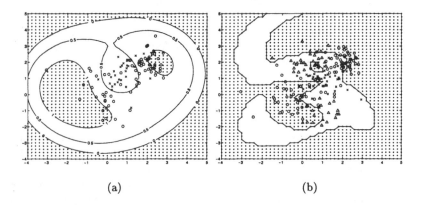

(a)   (b)

Fig. 6.7. Linear output RBF applied to classification problem. (a) Two-class problem. Contours at 0, 0.5 and 1.0. Non-probabilistic predictions (*dotted region*). (b) Three-class problem. Non-probabilistic predictions (*dotted region*).

6.10 (⋆⋆) A standard RBF network with linear outputs applied to a classification problem is guaranteed to generate outputs that sum to 1, even though not all the outputs need lie between 0 and 1. Generate some simple two-dimensional data and write a short test script that demonstrates the truth of this statement (see Fig. 6.7).

6.11 (⋆⋆) If an RBF network has non-linear output functions, then it is no longer possible to use a pseudo-inverse to compute the output layer weights of the network. However there is a special purpose algorithm that trains such models faster than a general non-linear optimiser. Once the basis function parameters are fixed, the mapping from hidden units to outputs is the same as a GLM, so iterated re-weighted least squares can be used to train the output layer weights (Nabney, 1999). Develop an RBF with logistic and softmax outputs that is trained using IRLS (see **glmtrain**) and compare the training times and generalisation performance with a similar network trained using SCG or quasi-Newton.

6.12 (⋆) Carry out the dual basis functions calculation and plotting for a simple one-dimensional input on a dataset with a bimodal input density.

6.13 (⋆⋆) Extend the **dual** script to a training dataset where the input data is not uniformly distributed. Show that the dual basis functions are more tightly localised in regions of higher data density.

6.14 (⋆) Develop a function to compute the degrees of freedom (dof.) of an RBF network. Using the noisy sine wave example, investigate the dependence of the number of dof. on the data noise level and the tolerance chosen in the pseudo-inverse calculation. Also experiment with real-world datasets where the true noise level is unknown: how easy is it to decide the correct cut-off point in the singular value spectrum?

6.15 (⋆⋆) Edit the **rbfcomp** function so that the user can set the basis function widths for Gaussian activation functions. The network should be trained in three phases: train the centres using **rbfsetbf**; reset the widths directly in the data structure; train the output weights (using **rbfsetow** if you have written it, or by copying the relevant code from **rbftrain** if you haven't). Experiment with the effect of the basis function width on the number of degrees of freedom of the trained RBF. What happens as the width is reduced towards zero?

6.16 (⋆⋆⋆) In Chapter 5 the MDN model was introduced to model general conditional density functions. Using this as a model, develop an MDN variant of the RBF that uses a Gaussian mixture model for its output layer. Compare the results and training times of the RBF-MDN with the MLP-MDN.

7. Visualisation and Latent Variable Models

Data visualisation is an important means of extracting useful information from large quantities of raw data. The human eye and brain together make a formidable pattern detection tool, but for them to work the data must be represented in a low-dimensional space, usually of two dimensions. Even quite simple relationships can seem very obscure when the data is presented in tabular form, but are often very easy to see by visual inspection.

This chapter collects together a number of visualisation techniques implemented in NETLAB, both linear and non-linear:

- Principal Component Analysis (PCA), a classical linear projection method;
- Probabilistic Principal Component Analysis (PPCA) and mixtures of PPCA, a latent variable formulation of PCA that provides a density model;
- Generative Topographic Mapping (GTM), a non-linear latent variable model;
- Neuroscale, a non-linear topographic (i.e. distance preserving) projection that uses an RBF network.

Which method to use on a particular application will depend on whether a density model is required, and what prior information is available about how the data is distributed.

PPCA and GTM are density models; in fact both are Gaussian mixture models with certain constraints. In PPCA, each Gaussian has a covariance matrix which is diagonal along q *axes* and has a single variance parameter to describe all other variance in each component. This is a good model for data that is piecewise linear. In GTM, the centre of each Gaussian is constrained to lie on a smooth manifold of low dimension (usually 1 or 2) but all Gaussians have a common spherical covariance.

Classical PCA and Neuroscale are projection methods for mapping data to a lower dimensional space. PCA does this with a linear transformation that preserves as much data variance as possible. As well as being useful in its own right, as a fast and simple method it is commonly used as a component in other training algorithms or for initialising models (e.g. GTM). Neuroscale is non-linear, but is fast to train on datasets of medium size. Large datasets need to be sub-sampled, since the matrix of inter-point distances required for training is $N \times N$, and will exhaust computer memory for large N.

To complement these techniques, the worked example is an implementation of canonical variates, a linear projection technique like PCA that is used with classified data and that maximises the inter-class separation of the projected data.

The principal functions described in this chapter are listed in Table 7.1. In the case of the Gaussian mixture model and the RBF network, this chap-

Table 7.1. Functions in this chapter.

	Visualisation
demgmm5	Demonstration of mixtures of PPCA
demgtm1	Demonstration of EM training of GTM
demgtm2	Demonstration of visualisation with GTM
demns1	Demonstration of Neuroscale
gmm	Create mixtures of PPCA
gmmactiv	Compute the activations of mixture of PPCA
gmmem	EM training algorithm for mixture of PPCA
gmminit	Initialise mixture of PPCA from data
gmmpost	Compute class posterior probabilities of a mixture of PPCA
gmmprob	Compute data probability for a mixture of PPCA
gmmsamp	Sample from a mixture of PPCA
gtm	Create a GTM
gtmem	EM training algorithm for GTM
gtmfwd	Forward propagation through GTM
gtminit	Initialise GTM from data
gtmlmean	Compute posterior mean for GTM
gtmlmode	Compute posterior mode for GTM
gtmmag	Magnification factors for GTM
gtmpost	Compute class posterior probabilities for GTM
gtmprob	Compute data probability for GTM
pca	Principal Component Analysis
rbf	Create a radial basis function network
rbferr	Evaluate error function
rbffwd	Forward propagation
rbfgrad	Evaluate error gradient
rbftrain	Shadow targets training of RBF network

ter focuses on the features relevant to mixtures of PPCA and Neuroscale respectively. For full details of these models, see Chapters 3 and 6.

7.1 Principal Component Analysis

Principal Component Analysis (PCA) is the most commonly used feature extraction and visualisation technique in practice. There are two reasons for its popularity: it is fast and easy to compute, and it retains maximal information (in the sense of retained variance of projected data) amongst all linear projections.

7.1.1 Theory

Suppose that we are trying to map a dataset of vectors x^n for $n = 1, \ldots, N$ in $V = \mathbb{R}^d$ to vectors z^n in $U = \mathbb{R}^M$, a subspace of V. For visualisation, $M = 2$ so that the vectors z^n can be shown in a scatter plot. We can choose an orthonormal basis $u_1, \ldots, u_M$ for U and extend this to an orthonormal basis $u_1, \ldots, u_d$ for V; see App. A. The orthonormality property implies that

$$u_i^T u_j = \delta_{ij}, \tag{7.1}$$

where δ_{ij} is the Kronecker delta. A vector x can be represented by the vector $(x_1, \ldots, x_d)$, or equivalently:

$$x = \sum_{i=1}^{M} x_i u_i + \sum_{i=M+1}^{d} x_i u_i. \tag{7.2}$$

Now suppose that we project to the M-dimensional space spanned by the first M vectors:

$$z = \sum_{i=1}^{M} x_i u_i + \sum_{i=M+1}^{d} b_i u_i, \tag{7.3}$$

where the b_i are constants. We choose the coefficients b_i and vectors u_i so that the projected vectors z^n best approximate x^n. The quality of the approximation is measured by the *residual* (or *reconstruction*) sum of squares error between the two vectors:

$$
\begin{aligned}
E &= \frac{1}{2} \sum_{n=1}^{N} \|x^n - z^n\|^2 \\[2mm]
&= \frac{1}{2} \sum_{n=1}^{N} \sum_{i=M+1}^{d} \sum_{j=M+1}^{d} (x_i^n - b_i)(x_j^n - b_j) u_i^T u_j \\[2mm]
&= \frac{1}{2} \sum_{n=1}^{N} \sum_{i=M+1}^{d} (x_i^n - b_i)^2 \quad \text{since the } u_i \text{ are orthonormal.}
\end{aligned}
\tag{7.4}
$$

Setting the derivative of E with respect to b_i to zero, we obtain

$$b_i = \frac{1}{N} \sum_{n=1}^{N} x_i^n, \tag{7.5}$$

which is the ith coordinate of the mean vector $\bar{x}$ with respect to the coordinate system $u_1, \ldots, u_d$. This is equal to $u_i^T \bar{x}$. It follows that the error term in (7.4) can be written (after reordering the summations) as

$$E = \frac{1}{2} \sum_{i=M+1}^{d} \sum_{n=1}^{N} \left\{ u_i^T (x^n - \bar{x})^T \right\} \left\{ (x^n - \bar{x}) u_i \right\}$$

$$= \frac{1}{2} \sum_{i=M+1}^{d} u_i^T \Sigma u_i, \tag{7.6}$$

where Σ is the covariance matrix of the data. Using Lagrange multipliers, it can be shown that the stationary points of E with respect to the vectors u_i occur at the eigenvectors of Σ, so that $\Sigma u_i = \lambda_i u_i$. Substituting such vectors into (7.6), we find that the residual error is given by

$$E = \frac{1}{2} \sum_{i=M+1}^{d} \lambda_i. \tag{7.7}$$

Since Σ is symmetric, it has a full set of d eigenvectors, and these can be chosen to be orthonormal as required. Furthermore, as it is a covariance matrix, it is positive semi-definite, so each $\lambda_i \geq 0$. Hence the minimal error E is achieved by choosing the $d - M$ smallest eigenvalues in (7.7), and we project data onto the space spanned by the eigenvectors corresponding to the largest M eigenvalues. These eigenvectors are called the first M *principal components*.

It is usual to list the principal components in descending order of eigenvalues; so the first principal component corresponds to the largest eigenvalue and has the largest variance of any linear combination of the original variables. There is no general technique for deciding how many principal components should be used to represent the data adequately (though a Bayesian approach has been proposed for probabilistic PCA: see Section 7.2), but a useful heuristic is to plot the singular values (or their logarithm) to see if there is a point at which the values level off, or to choose a fraction (often 0.90 or 0.95) of the variance to be retained by computing

$$\frac{\sum_{i=1}^{M} \lambda_i}{\sum_{i=1}^{d} \lambda_i}. \tag{7.8}$$

7.1.2 NETLAB Implementation

The NETLAB function pca (also discussed in Section 1.1.4) implements PCA:

```
1  function [PCcoeff, PCvec] = pca(data, N)
2
```

```
 3  if nargin == 1
 4     N = size(data, 2);
 5  end
 6
 7  if nargout == 1
 8     evals_only = logical(1);
 9  else
10     evals_only = logical(0);
11  end
12
13  % Find the sorted eigenvalues of the data covariance matrix
14  if evals_only
15     PCcoeff = eigdec(cov(data), N);
16  else
17     [PCcoeff, PCvec] = eigdec(cov(data), N);
18  end
```

The function returns the first N principal values and (optionally) the principal components as well (this is tested in lines 7–11). It is worth differentiating the two cases since calculating both eigenvectors and eigenvalues is much more computationally expensive than eigenvalues alone. In lines 15 and 17, the eigenvalues and eigenvectors of Σ are computed in order of descending magnitude of λ_i by the NETLAB function eigdec.

```
 1  function [evals, evec] = eigdec(x, N)
 2
 3  if nargout == 1
 4     evals_only = logical(1);
 5  else
 6     evals_only = logical(0);
 7  end
 8
 9  % Find the eigenvalues of the data covariance matrix
10  if evals_only
11     % Use eig as always more efficient than eigs here
12     temp_evals = eig(x);
13  else
14     % Use eig unless fraction of eigenvalues required is tiny
15     if (N/size(x, 2)) > 0.04
16        [temp_evec, temp_evals] = eig(x);
17     else
18        options.disp = 0;
19        [temp_evec, temp_evals] = eigs(x, N, 'LM', options);
20     end
21     temp_evals = diag(temp_evals);
22  end
23
24  [evals perm] = sort(-temp_evals);
25  evals = -evals(1:N);
26  if ~evals_only
27     if evals == temp_evals(1:N)
28        % Originals were in order
29        evec = temp_evec(:, 1:N);
```

```
30        return
31    else
32        % Need to reorder the eigenvectors
33        for i=1:N
34            evec(:,i) = temp_evec(:,perm(i));
35        end
36    end
37 end
```

This function uses the MATLAB function `eig` (line 16) to compute the eigen-values (and optionally the eigenvectors) of the matrix x. However, if only a small fraction of the principal components are required, it is more efficient to use the MATLAB function `eigs` (line 19) to compute just the largest few eigenvalues. A fraction of 0.04 seems to be the empirical threshold that makes the use of `eigs` worthwhile. Both functions usually return the eigenvalues in descending order, but to make absolutely sure, the eigenvalues are sorted in lines 30–32, and the same reordering is applied to the eigenvectors in lines 33–44.

7.1.3 Examples

In this section we show how PCA can be applied to a selection of datasets. The first is a synthetic dataset that models gamma radiation measurements taken from a pipeline used to transport a mixture of oil, water and gas. There are twelve measurements (two wavelengths at six different positions) to use as inputs and two real-valued outputs (the fraction of oil and the fraction of water) which are the regression targets. An alternative task is to predict the configuration of the flow. In this example we consider three possible configu-rations: stratified (with water, oil and gas in horizontal layers), annular (with the liquids arranged in concentric cylinders along the pipe) and homogeneous (when there is no separation of the liquids).

Figure 7.1 shows the eigenvalues from the PCA decomposition of this data. They show a smooth decay with no abrupt breaks in the curve, which indicates that there is no obvious separation between meaningful informa-tion and noise. The cumulative plot shows that six principal components are needed to explain 95% of the variance in the data. To visualise the data, we project it onto the first two principal components after first subtracting the data mean. The following code fragment is useful for this:

```
[pcvals, pcvecs] = pca(data);
mu = mean(data);
projdata = (data - ones(size(data, 1), 1)*mu)*pcvecs(:, 1:2);
```

The resulting graph is shown in Fig. 7.2. Note how the class denoted by crosses is scattered in five distinct clusters, while the other two classes are more tightly grouped. Although this linear map shows reasonably good class separation, the cross and circle classes do overlap.

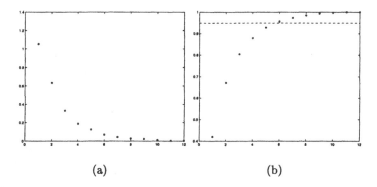

(a)   (b)

Fig. 7.1. Demonstration of PCA on pipeline data. (a) Eigenvalues arranged in decreasing magnitude. (b) Cumulative sum of the eigenvalues, expressed as a fraction of the whole sum. Threshold of 0.95 (*dashed line*).

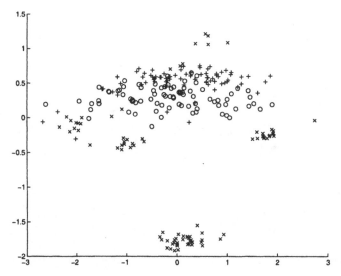

Fig. 7.2. Projection of pipeline data using PCA. Three classes are shown: (*plus signs*), (*crosses*) and (*circles*).

The second illustrative example uses images of handwritten digits from the MNIST database Each digit is represented as an 8 bit gray level matrix of dimension 28×28. They have been rotated and scaled to have similar orientations and sizes. Figure 7.3 shows one example from each class. In Fig. 7.4 we illustrate the first 10 principal component vectors extracted from the class of 5s. Remember that these show 'directions' of large variation away from the class mean. The images are displayed so that mid-grey represents

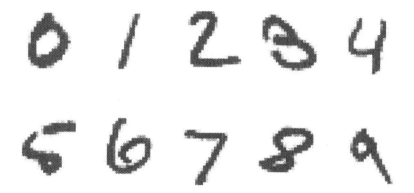

Fig. 7.3. Representative images from digit database.

a value of zero (i.e. no change), black is a large positive value and white is a large negative value. To understand how well a reduced number of principal

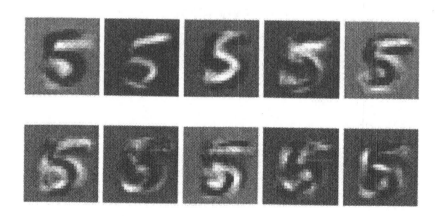

Fig. 7.4. First 10 principal components for the 5 class.

components represents the data, we can plot the eigenvalues, as in the pipeline example. Another method is to look at the reconstruction error obtained with different number of principal components. To compute this we first project the data, and then multiply the resulting coefficients by the corresponding principal components.

```
[pcvals, pcvecs] = pca(data);
mu = mean(data);
```

```
projdata = (data - ones(size(data, 1), 1)*mu)*pcvecs(:, 1:num_pcs);
recondata = projdata*(pcvecs(:, 1:num_pcs))' + mu;
```

Figure 7.5 shows a '5' and the reconstruction error with different numbers of principal components. In the last of these, the near uniform grey picture shows that there is little reconstruction error left, which is to be expected when 60 principal components are used for a dataset containing 100 patterns.

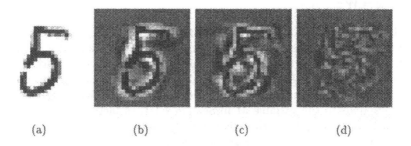

(a)   (b)   (c)   (d)

Fig. 7.5. PCA reconstruction error. (a) Original image and reconstruction errors with (b) 10, (c) 30 and (d) 60 principal components.

7.2 Probabilistic Principal Component Analysis

The motivation for the definition of PCA given in Section 7.1 is in terms of minimising the squared reconstruction error

$$E = \frac{1}{2} \sum_{n=1}^{N} \|x^n - z^n\|^2 \tag{7.9}$$

between the projected and original vectors. The disadvantage of this approach is that it does not define a *generative* model: there is no density model $p(x|z)$ or, to put it another way, there is no principled interpretation of the error function E. This was the motivation for developing probabilistic PCA, known as PPCA (Tipping and Bishop, 1999). A density model offers several advantages:

- The definition of a likelihood allows us to compare this model with other density models in a quantitative way.
- If PPCA is used to model class-conditional densities, then posterior probabilities of class membership may be calculated (as in Section 3.7.1, where this method was used with a mixture of Gaussians).

- A single PPCA model may be extended to a mixture of PPCA models.
- Bayesian inference methods may be applied if a suitable prior is chosen.

7.2.1 Probabilistic PCA

Classical PCA is made into a density model by using a latent variable approach, derived from standard factor analysis, in which the data x is generated by a linear combination of a number of hidden variables z

$$x = Wz + \mu + \epsilon, \tag{7.10}$$

where z has a zero mean, unit isotropic variance, Gaussian distribution $N(0, I)$, μ is a constant (whose maximum likelihood estimator is the data mean), and ϵ is an x-independent noise process. The latent variable space has dimension q, which is usually chosen to be less than the data dimension d so that the model is a more economical description of the data; this corresponds to the variable M in Section 7.1.1. In factor analysis, the noise model is $\epsilon \sim N(0, \Psi)$, with Ψ diagonal. The model for x is then also normal $N(\mu, L)$, with $L = WW^T + \Psi$. Since Ψ is diagonal, the observed variables x are conditionally independent given the values of the latent variables z. Thus all conditional dependence is captured in the latent distribution over z, while ϵ represents the independent noise. Unlike PCA, there is no analytic solution for W and Ψ, so an iterative algorithm (such as a variant of EM) must be used to commpute them.

The change needed to make this into a probabilistic model for PCA is very small. In the PCA model, there is a systematic component in the data plus an independent error term for each variable with common variance. This is captured by assuming a noise model with an isotropic variance $\Psi = \sigma^2 I$. The probability model for PPCA can now be written as a combination of the conditional distribution

$$p(x|z) = \frac{1}{(2\pi\sigma^2)^{d/2}} \exp\left\{ -\frac{\|x - Wz - \mu\|^2}{2\sigma^2} \right\} \tag{7.11}$$

and the latent variable distribution

$$p(z) = \frac{1}{(2\pi)^{q/2}} \exp\left\{ -\frac{z^T z}{2} \right\}. \tag{7.12}$$

By integrating out the latent variables z, we obtain the *marginal* distribution of the observed data, which is also Gaussian:

$$x \sim N(\mu, C), \tag{7.13}$$

where $C = WW^T + \sigma^2 I$. Thus this model represents the data as a 'pancake' consisting of a (lower dimensional) linear subspace surrounded by equal noise in all directions.

To fit this model to data, we use the log-likelihood as an error measure

$$\mathcal{L} = \sum_{n=1}^{N} \log p(\boldsymbol{x}_n) = -\frac{N}{2}\{d\log(2\pi) + \log|\boldsymbol{C}| + \mathrm{tr}(\boldsymbol{C}^{-1}\boldsymbol{S})\}, \qquad (7.14)$$

where

$$\boldsymbol{S} = \frac{1}{N}\sum_{n=1}^{N}(\boldsymbol{x}_n - \boldsymbol{\mu})(\boldsymbol{x}_n - \boldsymbol{\mu})^T \qquad (7.15)$$

is the sample covariance matrix of the observed data, provided that $\boldsymbol{\mu}$ is set to its maximum likelihood estimate, which is the sample mean. Estimates of $\boldsymbol{W}$ and σ^2 can be obtained by an iterative maximisation of $\mathcal{L}$ using an EM algorithm similar to that used for factor analysis. However, it is also possible to find an analytic solution for the maximum likelihood estimate:

$$\boldsymbol{W}_{ML} = \boldsymbol{U}_q(\boldsymbol{\Lambda}_q - \sigma^2\boldsymbol{I})^{1/2}\boldsymbol{R}, \qquad (7.16)$$

where the q column vectors in the $d \times q$ matrix $\boldsymbol{U}_q$ are the principal q eigenvectors of $\boldsymbol{S}$, with corresponding eigenvalues $\lambda_1, \dots, \lambda_q$ in the $q \times q$ diagonal matrix $\boldsymbol{\Lambda}_q$, and $\boldsymbol{R}$ is an arbitrary $q \times q$ orthogonal (rotation) matrix. Other combinations of eigenvectors correspond to saddlepoints of the likelihood function. Thus the latent space is a projection of the original space onto the principal subspace of the data. The effect of the matrix $\boldsymbol{R}$ is simply to choose different orthogonal axes for the principal subspace.

If we use the maximum likelihood solution for $\boldsymbol{W}$, then the maximum likelihood estimator for σ^2 is given by

$$\sigma^2_{ML} = \frac{1}{d-q}\sum_{j=q+1}^{d}\lambda_j, \qquad (7.17)$$

which can be interpreted as the variance lost in the projection to the latent space, averaged over the dimensions left out. Because the rotation matrix $\boldsymbol{R}$ is arbitrary, if we compute $\boldsymbol{W}_{ML}$ by an eigendecomposition of $\boldsymbol{S}$ (which is typically much more computationally efficient than using the EM algorithm), then we may as well assume that $\boldsymbol{R}$ is the identity.

We can also take a probabilistic view of projecting the observed data onto the latent space by using the *posterior* distribution of the latent variables z given the observed data x. By a standard manipulation using Bayes' theorem and a Gaussian integral, we obtain the distribution

$$p(z|x) \sim N(\boldsymbol{M}^{-1}\boldsymbol{W}^T(\boldsymbol{x} - \boldsymbol{\mu}), \sigma^2\boldsymbol{M}^{-1}), \qquad (7.18)$$

where the $q \times q$ matrix $\boldsymbol{M} = \boldsymbol{W}^T\boldsymbol{W} + \sigma^2\boldsymbol{I}$. It is usually more convenient to map x to a single point in latent space rather than a complete distribution. This can be done by considering the mean of the posterior distribution

$M^{-1}W^T(x - \mu)$. When $\sigma^2 \to 0$, $M^{-1} \to (W^T W)^{-1}$ and (7.18) represents an orthogonal projection equivalent to standard PCA. In practice, with $\sigma^2 > 0$, the latent projection becomes skewed towards the origin. Because of this, the reconstruction $W_{ML}\langle z_n|x_n\rangle + \mu$ is not an orthogonal projection of x_n and does not minimise the squared reconstruction error as in PCA (7.4). This is shown clearly in Fig. 7.6 where PPCA has been applied to two-dimensional data. The one-dimensional principal subspace is the same as that found by PCA, but the reconstructed data points are pulled towards the data mean at $(1, 1)$ instead of being projected perpendicularly to the line.

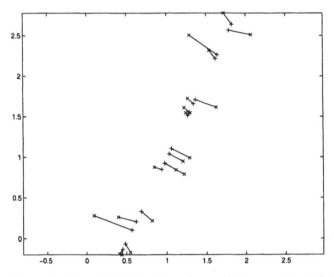

Fig. 7.6. Demonstration of PPCA. Data (*crosses*) is reconstructed in a one-dimensional PPCA subspace (*plus signs*). Lines join each point with its reconstruction and are clearly not orthogonal to the subspace.

7.2.2 PPCA Implementation

The NETLAB implementation of PPCA is based on a data covariance matrix eigendecomposition, since this is more efficient than the more general EM latent variable algorithm. This is important, since ppca is used as a component in the EM algorithm for mixtures of PPCA in Section 7.2.4.

The function ppca returns three values: var, which represents the noise parameter σ^2; U, whose columns span the PPCA subspace of the data space; and lambda, a vector containing the first q eigenvalues. It is assumed that the data x is a covariance matrix, with data weighted by responsibility when this function is used to train mixtures of PPCA models.

```
1   function [var, U, lambda] = ppca(x, ppca_dim)
2
3   [ndata, data_dim] = size(x);
4   [l Utemp] = eigdec(x, data_dim);
5   % Zero any negative eigenvalues (caused by rounding)
6   l(l<0) = 0;
7   % Compute sigma squared values for all possible q
8   s2_temp = cumsum(l(end:-1:1))./[1:data_dim]';
9   % If necessary, reduce the value of q so that var is at least
10  % eps * largest eigenvalue
11  q_temp = min([ppca_dim; data_dim-min(find(s2_temp/l(1) > eps))]);
12  if q_temp ~= ppca_dim
13    warning('Bad conditioning: q for %d is %d\n', ppca_dim, q_temp);
14    if q_temp == 0
15      % All the latent dimensions have disappeared, so we are
16      % just left with the noise model
17      var = l(1)/data_dim;
18      lambda = var*ones(1, ppca_dim);
19    end
20    lambda(q_temp+1:ppca_dim) = var;
21  end
22  if q_temp
23    U = Utemp(:, 1:ppca_dim);
24    var = mean(l(q_temp+1:end));
25    lambda(1:q_temp) = l(1:q_temp);
26  end
```

For robustness, we make sure in lines 8–11 that σ^2 is at least eps times the largest eigenvalue; this ensures the covariance matrix of the PPCA model will be reasonable to compute with numerically. If this is not the case (the branch in line 12), the calculation continues with a reduced value of q, and a warning message is output.

7.2.3 Mixture of PPCA

Because PCA only defines a linear projection of data, it is a rather limited technique. One way around this is to use a global non-linear method, such as the Generative Topographic Mapping or Neuroscale model discussed later in this chapter. An alternative approach is to model a complex non-linear structure by a collection of local linear models. The attraction of this is that each model is simpler to understand and usually easier to fit. The mixture of PPCA model is appropriate when the data is approximately piece-wise linear (see Fig. 7.7).

To fit a collection of linear models requires two steps: first, a partition of the data into regions; second, fitting models by estimating the principal components within each region. The question of how to combine these two steps is not trivial, since the partition depends on the data model and the principal components depend on the data partition. Several heuristic schemes using classical PCA have been proposed (Khambatla and Leen, 1994; Hinton

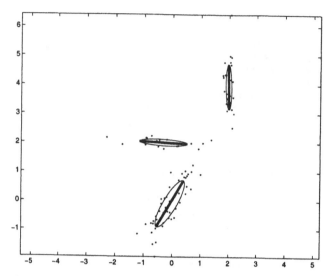

Fig. 7.7. Mixture of PPCA model. Sampled data (*dots*) and three component mixture model with principal components (*thick line*) and one standard deviation error bars (*thin line*).

et al., 1997), but there have always been difficulties in applying them in practice and parameters that had to be set heuristically.

A major advantage of developing a probabilistic model for PCA is that we can formalise the idea of a collection of models as a mixture of PPCA. The fact that the PPCA is a Gaussian model makes it clear that it is possible to train such a model in a maximum likelihood framework using an EM algorithm. This gives us a principled way of tackling the two steps, which correspond to the E-step and the M-step respectively.

The log-likelihood of the dataset is given by

$$\mathcal{L} = \sum_{n=1}^{n} \ln \sum_{j=1}^{M} \pi_j p(x_n|j), \tag{7.19}$$

where each $p(x_n|j)$ is a PPCA model and π_j is the mixing coefficient. Each component is associated with a mean vector μ_j, projection matrix W_j and noise model σ_j^2.

The EM algorithm for this model has a very similar form to that for other Gaussian mixture models (see Section 3.3). In the E-step, we compute the *responsibility* R_{nj} of component j for generating data point x_n:

$$R_{nj} = P(j|x_n) = \frac{p(x_n|j)\pi_j}{p(x_n)}. \tag{7.20}$$

In the M-step we re-estimate the parameters of each component. The equations for the means and mixing coefficients are identical to those for other Gaussian mixture models: (3.30) and (3.31).

$$\pi_j^{(m+1)} = \frac{1}{N} \sum_{n=1}^{N} P^{(m)}(j|x_n), \qquad (7.21)$$

$$\mu_j^{(m+1)} = \frac{\sum_{n=1}^{N} P^{(m)}(j|s_n)x_n}{\sum_{n=1}^{N} P^{(m)}(j|x_n)}. \qquad (7.22)$$

To re-estimate the covariance structure, we apply PPCA to S_j, the covariance matrix computed for data weighted by the responsibility of the jth component:

$$S_j = \frac{1}{\pi_j^{(m+1)} N} \sum_{n=1}^{N} P^{(m)}(j|x_n)(x_n - \mu_j^{(m+1)})(x_n - \mu_j^{(m+1)})^T. \qquad (7.23)$$

7.2.4 Mixture of PPCA Implementation

The mixture of PPCA model is implemented in NETLAB as a type of the Gaussian mixture model, where the covariance structure is given by ppca. In this section we will review the relevant functions (all with a gmm prefix), focusing on just those aspects relevant for mixtures of PPCA. The NETLAB implementation is relatively simple in that it constrains all the mixture components to have the same dimension (i.e. number of principal components). It would be reasonably straightforward, if a bit tedious in detail, to allow different dimensions for each model.

The model construction function gmm takes an additional argument, which specifies the dimension of the PPCA subspaces.

```
1   function mix = gmm(dim, ncentres, covar_type, ppca_dim)
2
3   % Other initialisation as before
4   % Make default dimension of PPCA subspaces one.
5   if strcmp(covar_type, 'ppca')
6     if nargin < 4
7       ppca_dim = 1;
8     end
9     if ppca_dim > dim
10      error('Dimension of PPCA subspaces must be less than data.')
11    end
12    mix.ppca_dim = ppca_dim;
13  end
14  % Initialise priors and centres as before
15  % Initialise all the variances to unity
16  switch mix.covar_type
17
```

```
18  % Other cases as before
19  case 'ppca'
20    % This is the off-subspace noise: make it smaller than
21    % lambdas
22    mix.covars = 0.1*ones(1, mix.ncentres);
23    % Also set aside storage for principal components and
24    % associated variances
25    init_space = eye(mix.nin);
26    init_space = init_space(:, 1:mix.ppca_dim);
27    init_space(mix.ppca_dim+1:mix.nin, :) = ...
28      ones(mix.nin - mix.ppca_dim, mix.ppca_dim);
29    mix.U = repmat(init_space , [1 1 mix.ncentres]);
30    mix.lambda = ones(mix.ncentres, mix.ppca_dim);
31    % Take account of additional parameters
32    mix.nwts = mix.ncentres + mix.ncentres*mix.nin + ...
33      mix.ncentres + mix.ncentres*mix.ppca_dim + ...
34      mix.ncentres*mix.nin*mix.ppca_dim;
35  end
```

Compared with the usual Gaussian mixture model data structure there are some additional parameters required to define the PPCA subspaces and covariance function. U is a three-dimensional array, with each of the mix.ncentres entries being a $d \times q$-dimensional matrix, the columns of which span the PPCA subspace. The $c \times q$ matrix lambda contains, in each row, the eigenvalues for the corresponding PPCA subspace. The spherical noise σ^2 for each component is stored in the corresponding entry of mix.covars. The matrices in U are initialised to the first q columns of a $d \times d$ identity matrix with ones in the remaining rows (lines 25–29), all the lambda values are set to 1 (line 30) and all the σ^2 values are set to 0.1 (lines 22) so that they are smaller than the lambda values. These extra fields in the data structure lead to the obvious additions to gmmpak and gmmunpak, but they are quite clear in the software.

Model initialisation is relatively straightforward: we use K-means to cluster the data as for the other Gaussian mixture models, and then use PPCA on the covariance matrix of the data points closest to each cluster centre.

```
1  function mix = gmminit(mix, x, options)
2
3  perm = randperm(ndata);
4  perm = perm(1:mix.ncentres);
5  % Assign first ncentres (permuted) data points as centres
6  mix.centres = x(perm, :); options(5) = 0;
7  [mix.centres, options, post] = kmeans(mix.centres, x, options);
8  % Set priors depending on number of points in each cluster
9  cluster_sizes = max(sum(post, 1), 1);  % Make sure no zero priors
10 mix.priors = cluster_sizes/sum(cluster_sizes); % Normalise priors
11
12 switch mix.covar_type
13 case 'ppca'  % Other cases as before
14   for j = 1:mix.ncentres
15     c = x(find(post(:,j)),:);
```

```
16      diffs = c - (ones(size(c, 1), 1) * mix.centres(j, :));
17      [tempcovars, tempU, templambda] = ...
18         ppca((diffs'*diffs)/size(c, 1), mix.ppca_dim);
19      if length(templambda) ~= mix.ppca_dim
20         error('Unable to extract enough components');
21      else
22        mix.covars(j) = tempcovars;
23        mix.U(:, :, j) = tempU;
24        mix.lambda(j, :) = templambda;
25      end
26    end
27  end
```

To compute likelihoods with this model, it is necessary to add some code to gmmactiv that calculates the correct Gaussian activation:

```
1  function a = gmmactiv(mix, x)
2
3  switch mix.covar_type
4  case 'ppca'   % Other cases as before
5    log_normal = mix.nin*log(2*pi);
6    d2 = zeros(ndata, mix.ncentres);
7    logZ = zeros(1, mix.ncentres);
8    for j = 1:mix.ncentres
9      k = 1 - mix.covars(j)./mix.lambda(j, :);
10     logZ(j) = log_normal + mix.nin*log(mix.covars(j)) - ...
11       sum(log(1 - k));
12     diffs = x - ones(ndata, 1)*mix.centres(j, :);
13     proj = diffs*mix.U(:, :, j);
14     d2(:, j) = (sum(diffs.*diffs, 2) - ...
15       sum((proj.*(ones(ndata, 1)*k)).*proj, 2)) / ...
16         mix.covars(j);
17   end
18   a = exp(-0.5*(d2 + ones(ndata, 1)*logZ));
19 end
```

Tipping and Bishop (1999) discuss how to carry out this computation most efficiently. The covariance matrix C for each PPCA component is given by

$$WW^T + \sigma^2 I \tag{7.24}$$

but, because we calculate the PCA space using an eigendecomposition,

$$W = U_q(\Lambda_q - \sigma^2 I)^{1/2}. \tag{7.25}$$

Using the matrix identity

$$(WW^T + \sigma^2 I)^{-1} = \{I - W(W^T W + \sigma^2 I)^{-1} W^T\}/\sigma^2, \tag{7.26}$$

and (7.25), we find that

$$C^{-1} = \frac{1}{\sigma^2}\{I - U_q(\Lambda_q - \sigma^2 I)\Lambda_q^{-1} U_q^T\}, \tag{7.27}$$

and so

$$p(x) \propto \exp\left\{ -\frac{1}{2\sigma^2}(x - \mu)^T[I - U_q K U_q^T](x - \mu) \right\}, \tag{7.28}$$

where $K = \text{diag}(k_1, k_2, \ldots, k_q)$ with $k_j = 1 - \sigma^2/\lambda_j$ (line 9). Apart from the factor of $1/2$, (7.28) is calculated in lines 12–16. With this representation, we do not need to explicitly calculate any matrix inverse, which is a great saving of computational effort.

Similarly, it can be shown that

$$\log|WW^T + \sigma^2 I| = (d - q)\log\sigma^2 + \sum_{j=1}^{q}\log\lambda_j$$

$$= d\log(\sigma)^2 - \sum_{j=1}^{q}\log(1 - k_j), \tag{7.29}$$

and this is used to calculate the (log) normalisation term logZ (lines 10–11). With these modifications to gmmactiv, no further changes are needed to gmmpost and gmmprob.

We also use the identity (7.25) when sampling from a mixture of PPCA in the function gmmsamp

```
1   case 'ppca'
2     covar = mix.covars(j) * eye(mix.nin) + ...
3       mix.U(:, :, j)*(diag(mix.lambda(j, :)) - ...
4       diag(mix.covars(j))) * (mix.U(:, :, j)'));
```

where the calculation of the covariance matrix is equivalent to the identity

$$WW^T + \sigma^2 I = U_q(\Lambda_q - \sigma^2 I)U_q^T + \sigma^2 I. \tag{7.30}$$

Finally, we must consider the implementation of the EM training algorithm. Just as for gmminit, this is relatively straightforward given the rest of the NETLAB toolbox. The E step is based on gmmpost, so is unchanged, while the M step requires the computation of a new covariance matrix for each component, which is accomplished using ppca (lines 5–6) applied to the responsibility-weighted covariance matrix (lines 3–4). Lines 8–12 simply check whether any of the off-manifold noise values are smaller than the value MIN_COVAR and resets them if this is the case. This is to prevent the covariance matrix collapsing to a singularity.

```
1    case 'ppca'
2      for j = 1:mix.ncentres
3        diffs = x - (ones(ndata, 1) * mix.centres(j,:));
4        diffs = diffs.*(sqrt(post(:,j))*ones(1, mix.nin));
5        [mix.covars(j), mix.U(:,:,j), mix.lambda(j,:)] = ...
6          ppca((diffs'*diffs)/new_pr(j), mix.ppca_dim);
7      end
8      if check_covars
9        if mix.covars(j) < MIN_COVAR
10         mix.covars(j) = init_covars(j);
```

11		end
12	end	
13	end	

7.3 Generative Topographic Mapping

We have already seen how a latent variable approach provides a generative model for PCA. However, a single low-dimensional linear space is not a realistic model for many real datasets. The aim of the Generative Topographic Mapping (GTM) is to allow a non-linear transformation from latent space to data space but still make the model computationally tractable. In this approach, the data is modelled by a mixture of Gaussians, in which the centres of the Gaussians are constrained to lie on a lower dimensional manifold. The *topographic* nature of the mapping comes about because the kernel centres in the data space preserve the structure of the latent space. By careful selection of the form of the non-linear mapping (using an RBF network), it is possible to train the model using a generalisation of the EM algorithm.

One of the motivations for developing this model was to provide a principled alternative to the self-organising map (SOM) algorithm (Kohonen, 1982) in which a set of data vectors x_n $(n = 1, \ldots, N)$ in a d-dimensional data space is summarised by a set of reference vectors organised on a lower dimensional sheet: the sheet is generally two-dimensional so that the map can be visualised. This algorithm has been successfully used in many applications, but suffers from a number of drawbacks:

1. the absence of a cost function;
2. no general proof of convergence;
3. the lack of a theoretical basis for choosing training algorithm parameters, such as learning rate and neighbourhood function;
4. the lack of a density model.

These problems arise due to the heuristic nature of the SOM algorithm. GTM overcomes most of these problems; the only drawback is that it is more complicated to program.

7.3.1 The GTM Model

Model Definition

We shall represent the data $x = (x_1, \ldots, x_d)$ in a d-dimensional space using a q-dimensional latent variable space $z = (z_1, \ldots, z_q)$. The two spaces are linked by a function $y(z; W)$ which maps z to $y(z; W)$ and is parameterised with the matrix W. This maps the latent space to a q-dimensional manifold S embedded in $\mathbb{R}^d$. We shall use an RBF network for this mapping, and W represents the adjustable network weights. For this model to be useful, we will usually need $q < d$: in fact, as we will see, GTM is most practical when $q = 1$ or 2.

If we define a probability density $p(z)$ on the latent space, this will induce a density $p(y|W)$ in the data space. Since $q < d$, this density will be zero away from the manifold S. This is an unrealistic constraint, since we cannot reasonably expect the data to lie *exactly* on a q-dimensional manifold. Hence we add a noise model for x. For real-valued data, it is convenient and appropriate to use a spherical Gaussian with variance σ^2 (in the original article (Bishop *et al.*, 1996) the variable β is used for the *inverse* variance), so that the data density conditional on the latent variables is given by

$$p(x|z, W, \sigma) = \frac{1}{(2\pi\sigma^2)^{d/2}} \exp\left\{-\frac{\|y(z; W) - x\|^2}{2\sigma^2}\right\}. \tag{7.31}$$

The density in data space is then obtained by integrating out the latent variables:

$$p(x|W, \sigma) = \int p(x|z, W, \sigma)p(z) \, dz. \tag{7.32}$$

However, for a general model $y(z; W)$, this integral is analytically intractable. We have seen that if $p(z)$ is Gaussian and y is a linear function of W, then the integral can be computed (7.13). Here we take a different approach. Let the density $p(z)$ be given by a sum of delta functions centred on *nodes* $z_1, \ldots, z_M$ in latent space:

$$p(z) = \frac{1}{M} \sum_{j=1}^{M} \delta(z - z_j). \tag{7.33}$$

If the nodes are uniformly spread in latent space, this is an approximation to a uniform distribution. Equation (7.32) is now tractable, and becomes a simple sum of M Gaussians:

$$p(x|W, \sigma) = \frac{1}{M} \sum_{j=1}^{M} p(x|z_j, W, \sigma). \tag{7.34}$$

This is a mixture model where all the kernels have the same mixing coefficient $1/M$ and variance σ^2, and the jth centre is given by $y(z_j; W)$. It is a *constrained* mixture model because the centres are not independent but are related by the mapping y. If this mapping is smooth, then the centres will necessarily be topographically related in the sense that two points z_a and z_b which are close in latent space will be mapped to points $y(z_a; W)$ and $y(z_b; W)$ which are close in data space (see Fig. 7.8).

The log likelihood for a dataset x_n, $n = 1, \ldots, N$ is given by

$$\mathcal{L}(W, \sigma) = \sum_{n=1}^{N} \ln\left\{\frac{1}{M} \sum_{j=1}^{M} p(x_n|z_j, W, \sigma)\right\}. \tag{7.35}$$

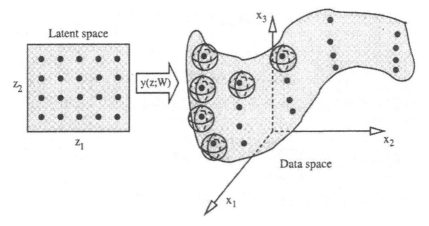

Fig. 7.8. GTM mapping and manifold.

This opens the way to determining the parameters W and σ using maximum likelihood.

The EM Algorithm

If $y(z; W)$ is a differentiable function of W then we can compute the partial derivatives $\partial \mathcal{L} / \partial w_{ij}$ and $\partial \mathcal{L} / \partial \sigma$ and use standard non-linear optimisation methods to find the model parameters. However, because the model consists of a mixture of Gaussians, it is possible to use a generalised EM algorithm to train the model. By choosing an RBF for $y(z; W)$ the M-step is not too computationally demanding to be performed several times and the algorithm is then a practical proposition.

We shall write

$$y(z; W) = W \phi(z), \tag{7.36}$$

where $\phi(z)$ are K fixed basis functions $\phi_i(z)$, and W is a $d \times K$ matrix. Because the latent space usually has dimension 2 or less, the curse of dimensionality for RBF networks does not arise. The parameters of the basis functions can be fixed to model the density of latent space: this has been chosen to be (approximately) uniform, so the RBF centres can be uniformly spread with widths chosen appropriately.

The E-step of the algorithm is the same as that for the Gaussian mixture model, which is not surprising since GTM is a constrained mixture of Gaussians. We need to calculate the posterior probability, or responsibility, of each component j for each data point x_n.

$$R_{jn}^{(m)}(\boldsymbol{W}^{(m)}, \sigma^{(m)}) = P^{(m)}(j|\boldsymbol{x}_n, \boldsymbol{W}^{(m)}, \sigma^{(m)})$$

$$= \frac{p(\boldsymbol{x}_n|\boldsymbol{z}_j, \boldsymbol{W}^{(m)}, \sigma^{(m)})}{\sum_{j'=1}^{M} p(\boldsymbol{x}_n|\boldsymbol{z}_{j'}, \boldsymbol{W}^{(m)}, \sigma^{(m)})}. \tag{7.37}$$

The M-step consists of maximising the expectation of the complete-data log likelihood

$$\langle \mathcal{L}_{\text{comp}}(\boldsymbol{W}, \sigma) \rangle = \sum_{n=1}^{N} \sum_{j=1}^{M} R_{jn}^{(m)}(\boldsymbol{W}^{(m)}, \sigma^{(m)}) \ln\{p(\boldsymbol{x}_n|\boldsymbol{z}_j, \boldsymbol{W}, \sigma)\}, \tag{7.38}$$

which gives the following equation for $\boldsymbol{W}$:

$$\sum_{n=1}^{N} \sum_{j=1}^{M} R_{jn}^{(m)}(\boldsymbol{W}^{(m)}, \sigma^{(m)})\{\boldsymbol{W}^{(m+1)}\phi(\boldsymbol{z}_j) - \boldsymbol{x}_n\}\phi^T(\boldsymbol{z}_j) = 0. \tag{7.39}$$

This can be written in matrix form as

$$\boldsymbol{\Phi}^T \boldsymbol{G}^{(m)} \boldsymbol{\Phi}(\boldsymbol{W}^{(m+1)})^T = \boldsymbol{\Phi}^T \boldsymbol{R}^{(m)} \boldsymbol{X}, \tag{7.40}$$

where $\boldsymbol{\Phi}$ is the $M \times K$ RBF design matrix with elements $\Phi_{ji} = \phi_i(\boldsymbol{z}_j)$, $\boldsymbol{X}$ is the $N \times d$ data matrix, $\boldsymbol{R}$ is an $M \times N$ responsibility matrix with elements R_{jn}, and $\boldsymbol{G}$ is an $M \times M$ diagonal matrix with elements

$$G_{jj} = \sum_{n=1}^{N} R_{jn}(\boldsymbol{W}, \sigma). \tag{7.41}$$

It is straightforward to solve (7.40) using standard techniques from linear algebra, providing some care is taken over ill-conditioning. Because the matrix $\boldsymbol{\Phi}$ is constant, it need only be computed at the first iteration.

Maximising (7.37) with respect to σ gives the following re-estimation formula

$$(\sigma^{(m+1)})^2 = \frac{1}{Nd} \sum_{n=1}^{N} \sum_{j=1}^{M} R_{jn}(\boldsymbol{W}^{(m)}, \sigma^{(m)}) \|\boldsymbol{W}^{(m+1)}\phi(\boldsymbol{z}_j) - \boldsymbol{x}_n\|^2. \tag{7.42}$$

This can be compared with (3.32), which is the re-estimation formula for a Gaussian mixture model with spherical covariance structure. In (7.42) we also compute the new variance as the average squared distance from the data to the new component centres $(\boldsymbol{W}^{(m+1)}\phi(\boldsymbol{z}_j))$ weighted by the old responsibilities. Because of the constrained centres of the Gaussian components and the single noise model variance σ^2, it is very rare for the estimate of σ^2 to collapse towards zero, and so it is not necessary to use heuristics to prevent this from happening, unlike the Gaussian mixture model case (see gmmmem).

As with the standard EM algorithm, it can be shown that the data likelihood increases at each step of the algorithm until a local maximum is reached. In practice we minimise the negative log likelihood for consistency with other algorithms.

If the RBF has a large number of degrees of freedom, it is possible that the map $y(z; W)$ is overly complex and the manifold may exhibit high curvature. One way to prevent this is to add a weight decay regularisation term $\lambda \sum_{i=1}^{K} \sum_{k=1}^{d} w_{ik}^2$ to the error function. This leads to a small modification to the M-step (7.40) to give

$$(\boldsymbol{\Phi}^T \boldsymbol{G}^{(m)} \boldsymbol{\Phi} + \lambda \boldsymbol{I})(\boldsymbol{W}^{(m+1)})^T = \boldsymbol{\Phi}^T \boldsymbol{R}^{(m)} \boldsymbol{X}. \tag{7.43}$$

Application to Visualisation

To use GTM for visualisation, it is necessary to map data points x_n to corresponding points in latent space. As with PPCA, we do this by using Bayes' theorem to compute the posterior density $p(z|x_n)$. With our choice of prior distribution (7.33), this is given by a sum of delta functions centred at the lattice points z_j with weights given by the responsibilities R_{jn}. However, in order to visualise a whole dataset in a single plot, we need to find a statistic to summarise this distribution. One convenient statistic to use is the mean:

$$\langle z|x_n, W, \sigma \rangle = \sum_{j=1}^{M} R_{jn} z_j. \tag{7.44}$$

However, because the map is non-linear, the posterior distribution can be multi-modal, in which case the mean may be a misleading summary. An alternative choice is the posterior mode, given by

$$j_{\max} = \arg \max_{j} R_{jn}. \tag{7.45}$$

Practical Considerations

Although the EM training algorithm for GTM does not require any arbitrary choice or adjustment of parameters, there are still some aspects of the model architecture that do have to be selected by hand. These are the number and type of the basis functions in the RBF and the number and distribution of the latent space sample points.

The RBF basis function parameters control the complexity, or smoothness, of the map from latent space to data space. For example, if Gaussian basis functions are used, then the ratio of their standard deviation σ_y to the spacing of the basis functions s affects the curvature of the manifold in data space.

By contrast, increasing the number of latent space sample points z_i can only improve the data model. If there are too few sample points compared to the number of basis functions, then the Gaussian components in data space become relatively independent and there is effectively no manifold. The sample points provide an approximation to the integral over the latent space in (7.32) and this approximation is improved by increasing the sample density. The only drawback to a high latent space sample density is the increased computational cost.

All mixture models are highly susceptible to local minima in the error surface, and good initialisation is very important to obtain useful results. The properties that we need for the initial parameters are that they should be fast to compute and yet reasonably close to the optimal solution. The requirement for speed suggests using a linear method: the approach we take is to use a q-dimensional linear subspace as the initial manifold, and this can be found easily using PCA. Then we determine $\boldsymbol{W}$ by minimising the error

$$E = \frac{1}{2} \sum_{j=1}^{M} \|\boldsymbol{W}\phi(\boldsymbol{z}_j) - \boldsymbol{U}\boldsymbol{z}_j\|^2 \tag{7.46}$$

where the columns of $\boldsymbol{U}$ are the relevant eigenvectors of the data covariance matrix. E represents the squared error between the projections of the latent points into data space by the GTM model and PCA. The initial value of σ^2 is set heuristically to a relatively large value to prevent premature convergence of the main EM algorithm.

7.3.2 Model Creation and Initialisation

The description of GTM has made it clear that the model consists of an RBF non-linearly mapping a latent space density to a mixture of Gaussians in data space. This can be achieved by combining the NETLAB RBF and GMM functions with very little loss of computational efficiency and very compact programs.

The GTM model is created using the function gtm. The data structure it returns contains the following fields:

```
type        % 'gtm'
nin         % dimension of data space
dimlatent   % dimension of latent space
rbfnet      % RBF network data structure
gmmnet      % GMM data structure
X           % sample of latent points
```

The user specifies the latent space dimension q, the number of latent points M, the data space dimension d, the number and type of the RBF functions and (optionally) the weight decay prior:

```
1  function net = gtm(dim_latent, nlatent, dim_data, ncentres, ...
2                     rbfunc, prior)
3
4  net.type = 'gtm';
```

```
5    % Input to functions is data
6    net.nin = dim_data;
7    net.dim_latent = dim_latent;
8    % Default is no regularisation
9    if nargin == 5
10     prior = 0.0;
11   end
12   % Only allow scalar prior
13   if isstruct(prior) | size(prior) ~= [1 1]
14     error('Prior must be a scalar');
15   end
16   % Create RBF network
17   net.rbfnet = rbf(dim_latent, ncentres, dim_data, rbfunc, ...
18                    'linear', prior);
19   % Mask all but output weights
20   net.rbfnet.mask=rbfprior(rbfunc, dim_latent, ncentres, dim_data);
21   % Create field for GMM output model
22   net.gmmnet = gmm(dim_data, nlatent, 'spherical');
23   % Create empty latent data sample
24   net.X = [];
```

Line 20 masks all but the output weights: this is because the basis function parameters are considered to be fixed and any gradients needed should only be calculated for the output layer weights of the RBF. When the GTM model is run, the inputs are always data points, and hence the number of model inputs nin is set to the data space dimension for checking by the consist function. The latent data sample is just the empty matrix at this stage (line 24): it is constructed in gtminit.

7.3.3 Computing Probabilities

To compute probabilities with the GTM model it is first necessary to determine the parameters of the output Gaussian mixture model. This is done with the function gtmfwd, which passes the latent data sample net.X to the RBF network net.rbfnet. The outputs of this network become the centres of the GMM net.gmmnet.

```
1    function mix = gtmfwd(net)
2
3    net.gmmnet.centres = rbffwd(net.rbfnet, net.X);
4    mix = net.gmmnet;
```

The mixture model returned by this function can then be used to compute probabilities in the data space. Two functions that are used frequently in the GTM software are gtmprob, which computes $p(x|z, W, \sigma)$, and gtmpost, which computes the responsibilities $p(i|x, W, \sigma)$. The implementation of both functions is very simple given the rest of the NETLAB toolbox.

```
1    function prob = gtmprob(net, data)
2
3    net.gmmnet.centres = rbffwd(net.rbfnet, net.X);
4    prob = gmmprob(net.gmmnet, data);
```

gtmpost also returns the GMM activations since this is used in gtmem.

```
1  function [post, a] = gtmpost(net, data)
2
3  net.gmmnet.centres = rbffwd(net.rbfnet, net.X);
4  [post, a] = gmmpost(net.gmmnet, data);
```

The other two GTM functions in this category are used to compute summary statistics for the latent space posterior distribution $p(z|x, W, \sigma)$. These play an important role in visualising data with a trained GTM.

The function gtmlmean computes the posterior mean. Line 4 implements (7.44).

```
1  function means = gtmlmean(net, data)
2
3  R = gtmpost(net, data);
4  means = R*net.X;
```

The function gtmlmode computes the posterior mode. Line 5 computes the index of the component with the maximal responsibility, and line 6 extracts the corresponding latent data point, as in (7.45).

```
1  function modes = gtmlmode(net, data)
2
3  R = gtmpost(net, data);
4  % Mode is maximum responsibility
5  [max_resp, max_index] = max(R, [], 2);
6  modes = net.X(max_index, :);
```

7.3.4 EM Algorithm

Just as with the training algorithm for the Gaussian mixture model, we divide the training algorithm for GTM into two separate phases: initialisation and the EM algorithm.

Initialisation The function gtminit performs two tasks: selecting the latent space sample z_i and initialising the RBF network weights. The options argument is used to control the RBF initialisation, while samp_type selects the type of initialisation used for the latent space:

Regular A regular rectangular grid inside the hypercube $[-1, 1]^q$.
Uniform A uniform random sample inside the hypercube $[-1, 1]^q$.
Gaussian A Gaussian random sample with spherical covariance 0.25. Most points lie inside the hypercube $[-1, 1]^q$.

A regular grid with l points to a side in $\mathbb{R}^q$ contains l^q points. This is a prohibitively large number if $q > 2$, so lines 44–46 exclude this possibility. If the latent sample is regular, a regular grid is also used for the RBF centres, and two additional arguments are passed to specify the dimensions of these grids. For example, the line

```
net = gtminit(net, options, data, 'regular', [10 8], [5 4]);
```

specifies a regular 10×8 grid for the latent data sample and a 5×4 grid for the RBF centres: this is for a two-dimensional latent space.

If the latent sample is random, then no additional arguments are needed, as the RBF centres are determined from the data using rbfsetbf.

```
1  function net = gtminit(net, options, data, samp_type, varargin)
2
3  % Check type of sample
4  stypes = {'regular', 'uniform', 'gaussian'};
5  if (strcmp(samp_type, stypes)) == 0
6    error('Undefined sample type.')
7  end
8
9  if net.dim_latent > size(data, 2)
10   error('Latent dimension must be no greater than data dimension')
11 end
12 nlatent = net.gmmnet.ncentres;
13 nhidden = net.rbfnet.nhidden;
14
15 % Create latent data sample and set RBF centres
16 switch samp_type
17 case 'regular'
18   if nargin ~= 6
19     error('Regular type must specify latent and RBF shapes');
20   end
21   l_samp_size = varargin{1};
22   rbf_samp_size = varargin{2};
23   if round(l_samp_size) ~= l_samp_size
24     error('Latent sample spec must contain integers')
25   end
26   % Check existence and size of rbf specification
27   if any(size(rbf_samp_size) ~= [1 net.dim_latent]) | ...
28       prod(rbf_samp_size) ~= nhidden
29     error('Incorrect specification of RBF centres')
30   end
31   % Check dimension and type of latent data specification
32   if any(size(l_samp_size) ~= [1 net.dim_latent]) | ...
33       prod(l_samp_size) ~= nlatent
34     error('Incorrect dimension of latent sample spec.')
35   end
36   if net.dim_latent == 1
37     net.X = [-1:2/(l_samp_size-1):1]';
38     net.rbfnet.c = [-1:2/(rbf_samp_size-1):1]';
39     net.rbfnet = rbfsetfw(net.rbfnet, options(7));
40   elseif net.dim_latent == 2
41     net.X = gtm_rctg(l_samp_size);
42     net.rbfnet.c = gtm_rctg(rbf_samp_size);
43     net.rbfnet = rbfsetfw(net.rbfnet, options(7));
44   else
45     error('For regular sample, input dimension must be 1 or 2.')
46   end
47
```

```
48   case {'uniform', 'gaussian'}
49     if strcmp(samp_type, 'uniform')
50       net.X = 2 * (rand(nlatent, net.dim_latent) - 0.5);
51     else
52       net.X = randn(nlatent, net.dim_latent)/2;
53     end
54     net.rbfnet = rbfsetbf(net.rbfnet, options, net.X);
55   otherwise
56     % Shouldn't get here
57     error('Invalid sample type');
58   end
59
60   % Latent data sample and basis function parameters chosen.
61   % Now set output weights
62   [PCcoeff, PCvec] = pca(data);
63   % Scale PCs by eigenvalues
64   A = PCvec(:, 1:net.dim_latent)*...
65           diag(sqrt(PCcoeff(1:net.dim_latent)));
66   [temp, Phi] = rbffwd(net.rbfnet, net.X);
67   normX = (net.X - ones(size(net.X))*diag(mean(net.X)))* ...
68           diag(1./std(net.X));
69   net.rbfnet.w2 = Phi \ (normX*A');
70   % Bias is mean of target data
71   net.rbfnet.b2 = mean(data);
72
73   net.gmmnet.centres = rbffwd(net.rbfnet, net.X);
74   d = dist2(net.gmmnet.centres, net.gmmnet.centres) + ...
75     diag(ones(net.gmmnet.ncentres, 1)*realmax);
76   sigma = mean(min(d))/2;
77
78   % Now set covariance to min of this and next largest eigenvalue
79   if net.dim_latent < size(data, 2)
80     sigma = min(sigma, PCcoeff(net.dim_latent+1));
81   end
82   net.gmmnet.covars = sigma*ones(1, net.gmmnet.ncentres);
83
84   % Sub-function to create the sample data in 2d
85   function sample = gtm_rctg(samp_size)
86
87   xDim = samp_size(1);
88   yDim = samp_size(2);
89   % Produce a grid with the right number of rows and columns
90   [X, Y] = meshgrid([0:1:(xDim-1)], [(yDim-1):-1:0]);
91
92   sample = [X(:), Y(:)];
93   maxXY= max(sample);
94   sample(:,1) = 2*(sample(:,1) - maxXY(1)/2)./maxXY(1);
95   sample(:,2) = 2*(sample(:,2) - maxXY(2)/2)./maxXY(2);
96   return;
```

Lines 17–46 are concerned with setting up a regular latent data sample and RBF network. The dimensions of the grids are specified as scalars or two-dimensional vectors to match the latent space dimension in varargin{1} and `varargin{2}` (the first and second optional arguments) respectively. The arguments are checked to make sure that they contain integers (lines 23–25) and that the number of points they specify (given by the product of the number of points in each dimension) is equal to the number of latent sample points `net.gmmnet.ncentres` (lines 26–30) and the number of RBF hidden units `net.rbfnet.nhidden` (lines 31–35) respectively.

A one-dimensional regular grid is easily constructed with MATLAB's sequence notation (lines 37–38). It just remains to set the widths of the RBF network basis functions (line 39). The two-dimensional grids are constructed by the sub-function `gtm_rctg` (lines 85–96). In line 90, the grid is constructed by taking the `meshgrid` of two sequences. The matrix this produces is changed to a set of (x, y) coordinates in line 92, and this is then linearly shifted to $[-1, 1]^2$ by lines 93–95.

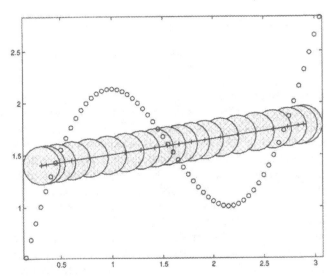

Fig. 7.9. GTM initialisation. Data (*circles*) is drawn from a non-linear function, representing a one-dimensional manifold in $\mathbb{R}^2$. A one-dimensional GTM has been initialised. The mixture centres (*crosses*) lie along the first principal component of the data. Contours at two standard deviations (*large circles*) are shown around each centre.

The uniform and Gaussian random latent samples are less complicated. A random sample of the correct size is drawn for the latent sample (lines 50 and 52 respectively), and then the standard RBF hidden unit initialisation that models the density of the latent data (which is the RBF input) is applied (line 54).

The aim of the initialisation of the RBF output weights is to map the latent space to the q-dimensional principal component subspace of the data.

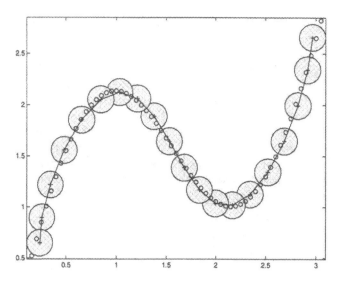

Fig. 7.10. Trained GTM model. Details as in Fig. 7.9.

This subspace is computed in lines 62–65. It is necessary to scale the principal components by the corresponding eigenvalues (or variances), since PCA returns orthonormal vectors. Line 66 calculates $\boldsymbol{\Phi}$, the design matrix of the RBF excluding the bias. The latent data is then normalised to zero mean and unit variance, normX, (lines 67–68) and projected onto the principal component subspace, normX*A' as in (7.46). These points are treated as the initial target of the RBF, whose output weights are computed with a least squares solver in line 69. The optimal bias weight is known to be the unconditional mean of the target data (line 71).

The initial value of σ^2, the variable sigma, is set to the minimum of the $(d+1)$st eigenvalue and half the average squared distance between Gaussian mixture centres (lines 74–82). The GMM centres are set to their correct values by forward propagating through the RBF in line 73.

The effect of this initialisation algorithm is shown in Fig. 7.9 (based on demgtm1), where a one-dimensional GTM, containing 20 latent data points and an RBF with five basis functions, has been initialised using data drawn from a non-linear one-dimensional manifold in $\mathbb{R}^2$. Note how the principal direction has been captured, the cluster centres are well spaced along the line, and the initial variance is a reasonable value. With such a good initial state for the model, it requires only 15 iterations of EM to reach the model shown in Fig. 7.10.

EM Algorithm

The function gtmem carries out the EM algorithm for a GTM model.

```
1   function [net, options, errlog] = gtmem(net, t, options)
2
3   % Calculate quantities that remain constant during training
4   [ndata, tdim] = size(t);
5   ND = ndata*tdim;
6   [net.gmmnet.centres, Phi] = rbffwd(net.rbfnet, net.X);
7   Phi = [Phi ones(size(net.X, 1), 1)];
8   PhiT = Phi';
9   [K, Mplus1] = size(Phi);
10
11  A = zeros(Mplus1, Mplus1);
12  cholDcmp = zeros(Mplus1, Mplus1);
13  % Use a sparse representation for the weight regularising matrix.
14  if (net.rbfnet.alpha > 0)
15    Alpha = net.rbfnet.alpha*speye(Mplus1);
16    Alpha(Mplus1, Mplus1) = 0;
17  end
18
19  for n = 1:niters
20    % Calculate responsibilities
21    [R, act] = gtmpost(net, t);
22    % Calculate error value if needed
23    if (display | store | test)
24      prob = act*(net.gmmnet.priors)';
25      % Error value is negative log likelihood of data
26      e = - sum(log(max(prob, eps)));
27      if store
28        errlog(n) = e;
29      end
30      if display > 0
31        fprintf(1, 'Cycle %4d  Error %11.6f\n', n, e);
32      end
33      if test
34        if (n > 1 & abs(e - eold) < options(3))
35          options(8) = e;
36        return;
37        else
38          eold = e;
39        end
40      end
41    end
42    if (net.rbfnet.alpha > 0)
43      A = full(PhiT*spdiags(sum(R)', 0, K, K)*Phi + ...
44          (Alpha.*net.gmmnet.covars(1)));
45    else
46      A = full(PhiT*spdiags(sum(R)', 0, K, K)*Phi);
47    end
48    [cholDcmp singular] = chol(A);
49    if (singular)
50      if (display)
51        fprintf(1, ...
52      'Warning: M-Step matrix singular in gtmem, using pinv.\n');
53      end
```

```
54     W = pinv(A)*(PhiT*(R'*t));
55     else
56       W = cholDcmp \ (cholDcmp' \ (PhiT*(R'*t)));
57     end
58     % Put new weights into network
59     net.rbfnet.w2 = W(1:net.rbfnet.nhidden, :);
60     net.rbfnet.b2 = W(net.rbfnet.nhidden+1, :);
61
62     d = dist2(t, Phi*W);
63     net.gmmnet.covars = ones(1, net.gmmnet.ncentres)*...
64                         (sum(sum(d.*R))/ND);
65   end
66   options(8) = -sum(log(gtmprob(net, t)));
67   if (display >= 0)
68     disp('Warning: Max. number of iterations has been exceeded');
69   end
```

The structure of this implementation is similar to that for **gmmem**, with just some minor differences in the details of the E- and M-steps. After the initial housekeeping (omitted here for clarity), line 6 propagates the latent data through the RBF to set the GTM centres. In line 7 the design matrix Φ is computed, including the bias term, and PhiT is set to Φ^T in line 8. If the weight decay parameter net.rbfnet.alpha is set, then the regularisation matrix Alpha is set to αI for the hidden units (no regularisation is applied to the bias unit). A sparse representation of Alpha is used (lines 15–16) to save memory.

The main loop starts in line 19. The E-step consists of a call to gtmpost (line 21). The matrix A is the matrix that must be inverted to update the mixture centres. Line 46 computes $\Phi^T G\Phi$, which is correct for the case of no weight decay (see (7.40)), while lines 43–44 compute $\Phi^T G\Phi + \alpha I$, which is appropriate for $\alpha > 0$ (7.43). A sparse representation of G normally executes faster and saves memory.

A is a symmetric matrix which should be positive definite, so it is worth trying a fast Cholesky decomposition to calculate W (lines 48 and 56). If the Cholesky decomposition fails (probably because rounding errors mean that A is numerically not positive definite), we have to use the pseudo-inverse (line 54). Note that (PhiT*(R*t)) is computed right-to-left, which is the most efficient order, since R and t are normally larger than PhiT. The RBF output layer and bias weights are extracted from W in lines 59–60. Finally, following (7.42), the variance is updated in lines 62–64. Note that all the variances are set to the same value.

7.3.5 Magnification Factors

GTM is a powerful visualisation tool but there are some aspects of data structure that it does not show clearly in its standard form. In particular, even if the data consists of well-separated clusters of points, the latent space representation will be much closer to a uniform distribution; see Fig. 7.13(a).

It is easy to see why this should be so if we consider the Gaussian mixture model on the GTM manifold. The EM algorithm will attempt to place the mixture components in regions of high data density and will move the components away from regions of low data density. It can do this because the non-linear map from latent space to data space enables the manifold to stretch across regions of low data density. This stretching (or magnification) can be measured using techniques of differential geometry, and plotting the magnification factors in latent space allows the user to see separation between clusters.

Consider a rectangular Cartesian set of coordinates z_i for $i = 1, \ldots, q$ in the latent space. Under the smoothly differentiable RBF mapping, these are transformed to a set of q curvilinear coordinates ζ^i on the q-dimensional manifold $\mathcal{M}$. To determine the magnification factor, we need to work out the change in a small volume dV in latent space[1] mapped to a small volume dV' on $\mathcal{M}$. The volume dV is infinitesimal, so we shall consider a hypercuboid at a point p in latent space (a square for $q = 2$) whose sides are aligned with the latent variable axes. This is mapped, up to first order, to a d-dimensional parallelepiped (a parallelogram for $q = 2$) at a point $p' = y(p; W)$ in the data space whose sides are given by the tangent vectors to the curvilinear coordinates ζ_i at p', i.e. $(\partial y/\partial z_i)dz_i$.

We denote by J the $q \times d$ Jacobian matrix of the map $y(z; W)$:

$$J = (J_{kl}) = \frac{\partial y_k}{\partial z_l}. \tag{7.47}$$

The volume of a d-dimensional parallelepiped is equal to the determinant of the vectors along its sides expressed with respect to a d-dimensional basis. However, the sides of dV' are given by the q rows of J in a d-dimensional space. Let V_P denote the vector space spanned by the rows of J; we can find an orthogonal basis $\mathcal{B}$ for this space by the Gram-Schmidt process. Let the $d \times q$ matrix M contain this basis as its columns, and compute

$$\hat{J} = JM. \tag{7.48}$$

Since M is a projection matrix, it follows that the rows of $\hat{J}$ are the same vectors as the rows of J but expressed with respect to the basis $\mathcal{B}$. Hence the volume dV' is equal to $\det \hat{J}$, which can be computed since $\hat{J}$ is a square $q \times q$ matrix.

However, we can avoid having to find the matrix M by the following observation:

$$\hat{J}\hat{J}^T = JMM^T J^T = JJ^T. \tag{7.49}$$

Then by (7.49) and the properties of determinants,

---

[1] We are mainly interested in the case $q = 2$, when we can replace 'volume' by 'area'.

$$(\det(\widehat{\boldsymbol{J}}))^2 = \det(\widehat{\boldsymbol{J}}) \det(\widehat{\boldsymbol{J}}) = \det(\widehat{\boldsymbol{J}}) \det(\widehat{\boldsymbol{J}}^T)$$

$$= \det(\widehat{\boldsymbol{J}}\widehat{\boldsymbol{J}}^T) = \det(\boldsymbol{J}\boldsymbol{J}^T). \tag{7.50}$$

But

$$\boldsymbol{J} = \boldsymbol{\psi}\boldsymbol{W}, \tag{7.51}$$

where $\boldsymbol{\psi}$ has elements $\psi_{ji} = \partial\phi_j/\partial z^i$. Hence the magnification factors are given by

$$\frac{dV'}{dV} = \det{}^{1/2}\left(\boldsymbol{\psi}\boldsymbol{W}^T\boldsymbol{W}\boldsymbol{\psi}^T\right), \tag{7.52}$$

which are calculated by the function gtmmag.

```
1   function mags = gtmmag(net, latent_data)
2
3   Jacs = rbfjacob(net.rbfnet, latent_data);
4   nlatent = size(latent_data, 1);
5   mags = zeros(nlatent, 1);
6   temp = zeros(net.rbfnet.nin, net.rbfnet.nout);
7   for m = 1:nlatent
8     temp = squeeze(Jacs(m, :, :));  % Turn into a 2d matrix
9     mags(m) = sqrt(det(temp*temp'));
10  end
```

In line 3, the function rbfjacob computes the Jacobian $\boldsymbol{W}\boldsymbol{\psi}$ of the RBF network for each latent data pattern. Each row of the 3d array Jacs contains the corresponding Jacobian. In line 8 the mth row of this matrix is converted into the nin × nout Jacobian matrix for the mth latent sample, and the magnification factor is then computed as in (7.52). The loop introduces inefficiency, but magnification factors need only be computed once for the trained model, and the overhead is relatively small compared to computing the determinant in line 9.

It is usual to compute the magnification factor at the latent points net.X, since a regular grid of values can be displayed as an image. However, the function works with any set of latent points.

7.3.6 Demonstration Programs

There are two demonstrations of GTM in NETLAB; one illustrates the EM algorithm while the other shows the use of magnification factors.

EM Algorithm

In this demonstration, a one-dimensional latent space (i.e. a curved line) is embedded non-linearly in a two-dimensional data space. This makes it convenient to plot the effect of EM training on the GTM manifold and noise model.

```
1   data_min = 0.15;
2   data_max = 3.05;
3   T = [data_min:0.05:data_max]';
4   T = [T (T + 1.25*sin(2*T))];
5   plot(T(:,1), T(:,2), 'ro');
6   hold on;
7   axis([data_min-0.05 data_max+0.05 data_min-0.05 data_max+0.05]);
8   % Generate a unit circle figure, to be used for plotting
9   src = [0:(2*pi)/(20-1):2*pi]';
10  unitC = [sin(src) cos(src)];
11
12  num_latent_points = 20;
13  num_rbf_centres = 5;
14  net = gtm(1, num_latent_points, 2, num_rbf_centres, 'gaussian');
15
16  options = zeros(1, 18);
17  options(7) = 1;
18  net = gtminit(net, options, T, 'regular', num_latent_points, ...
19     num_rbf_centres);
20
21  mix = gtmfwd(net);
22  plot(mix.centres(:,1),  mix.centres(:,2), 'g');
23  plot(mix.centres(:,1),  mix.centres(:,2), 'g+');
24  for i=1:num_latent_points
25    c = 2*unitC*sqrt(mix.covars(1))+[ones(20,1)*mix.centres(i,1) ...
26        ones(num_latent_points,1)*mix.centres(i,2)];
27    fill(c(:,1), c(:,2), [0.8 1 0.8]);
28  end
29  plot(T(:,1), T(:,2), 'ro');
30  axis([data_min-0.05 data_max+0.05 data_min-0.05 data_max+0.05]);
31  drawnow;
32  title('Initial configuration');
33  disp(' ')
34
35  figure(fh1);
36  % Train the GTM and plot it as training proceeds
37  options = foptions;
38  options(1) = -1;  % Turn off all warning messages
39  options(14) = 1;
40  for j = 1:15
41    [net, options] = gtmem(net, T, options);
42    hold off;
43    mix = gtmfwd(net);
44    plot(mix.centres(:,1),  mix.centres(:,2), 'g');
45    hold on;
46    for i=1:20
47      c = 2*unitC*sqrt(mix.covars(1)) + ...
48          [ones(20,1)*mix.centres(i,1) ones(20,1)*mix.centres(i,2)];
49      fill(c(:,1), c(:,2), [0.8 1.0 0.8]);
50    end
51    plot(T(:,1), T(:,2), 'ro');
52    plot(mix.centres(:,1),  mix.centres(:,2), 'g+');
53    plot(mix.centres(:,1),  mix.centres(:,2), 'g');
```

```
54    axis([0 3.5 0 3.5]);
55    title(['After ', int2str(j),' iterations of training.']);
56    drawnow;
57  end
```

The data is generated (line 4) as a parametric curve $(T, T + 1.25 \sin(2T))$ for $T \in [0.15, 3.05]$. The GTM is created (line 13) with a one-dimensional latent space, a five hidden unit Gaussian RBF, and 20 latent data points (so there are 20 components in the output Gaussian mixture model). In lines 16–19 the model is initialised with a regular grid using the dataset T. To plot the initial manifold in data space, we first extract the constrained Gaussian mixture model with a call to gtmfwd (line 21). In lines 22–23, the centres are plotted with a line joining them: this line represents the (one-dimensional) manifold. It is nearly a straight line, since the initial parameters are based on a PCA projection of the data. In lines 24–28, the circles that are plotted represent two standard deviations around each centre.

The loop in lines 40–57 performs 15 cycles of the EM training algorithm, one on each iteration. This does not adversely affect the training process, since the EM algorithm does not build any approximation of the error surface (unlike non-linear optimisers such as the quasi-Newton algorithm). In normal practice, there is no reason not to run the algorithm for all the iterations in a single function call, but the purpose of this script is to demonstrate how the manifold converges to the data generator. Line 41 carries out the model training, while the remaining code in the loop updates the plot of the manifold and noise model.

Visualisation with Magnification Factors

The demonstration program demgtm2 shows how the GTM model can be used to visualise and understand high-dimensional data.

```
1   % Create data
2   ndata = 300
3   data_dim = 4;
4   latent_dim = 2;
5   mix = gmm(data_dim, 2, 'spherical');
6   mix.centres = [1 1 1 1; 0 0 0 0];
7   mix.priors = [0.5 0.5];
8   mix.covars = [0.2 0.2];
9   [data, labels] = gmmsamp(mix, ndata);
10
11  % Create and initialise GTM model
12  latent_shape = [15 15];  % Shape of latent space
13  nlatent = prod(latent_shape);  % Number of latent points
14  num_rbf_centres = 16;
15  net = gtm(latent_dim, nlatent, data_dim, num_rbf_centres, ...
16      'gaussian', 0.1);
17
18  options = foptions;
```

```
19  options(1) = -1;
20  options(7) = 1;    % Set width factor of RBF
21  net = gtminit(net, options, data, 'regular', latent_shape, [4 4]);
22
23  options = foptions;  options(14) = 30;  options(1) = 1;
24  [net, options] = gtmem(net, data, options);
25
26  % Plot posterior summary statistics
27  means = gtmlmean(net, data);
28  modes = gtmlmode(net, data);
29
30  PointSize = 12;  ClassSymbol1 = 'r.';  ClassSymbol2 = 'b.';
31  fh1 = figure;
32  hold on;
33  title('Visualisation in latent space')
34  plot(means((labels==1),1), means(labels==1,2), ...
35    ClassSymbol1, 'MarkerSize', PointSize)
36  plot(means((labels>1),1),means(labels>1,2),...
37    ClassSymbol2, 'MarkerSize', PointSize)
38  ClassSymbol1 = 'ro';  ClassSymbol2 = 'bo';
39  plot(modes(labels==1,1), modes(labels==1,2), ClassSymbol1)
40  plot(modes(labels>1,1),modes(labels>1,2), ClassSymbol2)
41
42  % Join up means and modes
43  for n = 1:ndata
44    plot([means(n,1); modes(n,1)], [means(n,2); modes(n,2)], 'g-')
45  end
46
47  fh3 = figure;
48  mags = gtmmag(net, net.X);
49  % Reshape into grid form
50  Mags = reshape(mags, fliplr(latent_shape));
51  imagesc(net.X(:, 1), net.X(:,2), Mags);
52  hold on
53  title('Dataset visualisation with magnification factors')
54  set(gca,'YDir','normal')
55  colormap(hot);
56  colorbar
57  hold on; % Else the magnification plot disappears
58  plot(means(labels==1,1), means(labels==1,2), ...
59    ClassSymbol1, 'MarkerSize', PointSize)
60  plot(means(labels>1,1), means(labels>1,2), ...
61    ClassSymbol2, 'MarkerSize', PointSize)
```

Lines 1–9 create a data set in $\mathbb{R}^4$ which is sampled from two separated Gaussians. The next section of software sets up the GTM with a 15×15 regular grid of latent points (lines 12–16), initialises the model from the training data (lines 18–21), and trains it with 30 iterations of EM (lines 23–24). At this point, the model is ready for use in visualisation.

The first plot shows the basic visualisation of the data in latent space. In lines 27–28 the posterior means and modes are computed for each data point. They are then plotted on a single graph with colour coding of red for class 1 and blue for class 2: the means in lines 30–37 and the modes in lines 38–40. If the posterior distribution is unimodal and symmetric (or reasonably close to being so), then the mean and mode will be close together. If the posterior distribution is more complicated, perhaps because the manifold is twisted or highly curved in the region of a given data point, then the two may be more separated. To make this clearer, lines 43–45 join the mean and mode for each point by a line. A modified version of this plot is shown in Fig. 7.11. The

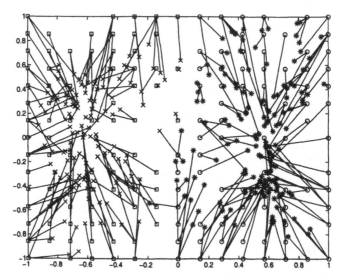

Fig. 7.11. Summary of posterior distribution in latent space of two-dimensional GTM. Means (*star* for class 1 and *cross* for class 2) and modes (*circle* for class 1 and *plus* for class 2) for each data point are joined by a line.

points with large distances between mean and mode are typically located where the manifold has curved round on itself, giving rise to a point with a significant level of responsibility at widely separated parts of latent space. This is illustrated by Fig. 7.12.

While this plot does display the data, it doesn't show the clustering in it. For this we need to superimpose the magnification factors on the latent space visualisation. Line 48 computes the magnification factors, and line 50 reshapes them into a grid with the same dimensions as the latent space points. (The call to the MATLAB function `fliplr` is necessary because of the way that `imagesc` indexes rows and columns.) Line 51 plots the magnification factors as an image, and the rest of the code superimposes a plot of the posterior means, colour coded as before. The `hot` colourmap is an effective way of displaying the magnification factors; areas of large stretching are bright on the map. (For the purposes of printing the map, the inverse of the `gray` colourmap has been used, so that areas of large stretching are dark and areas

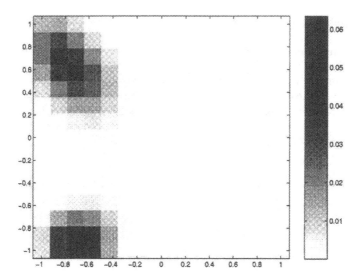

Fig. 7.12. Responsibility (posterior) plot for a single data point. The colourmap is chosen so that black indicates areas of high probability.

of high compression are white.) In the example shown in Fig. 7.13, there is a vertical area with large magnification that clearly divides the two classes of data and makes the clustering apparent. The clustering is not so obvious on the plot without magnification factors.

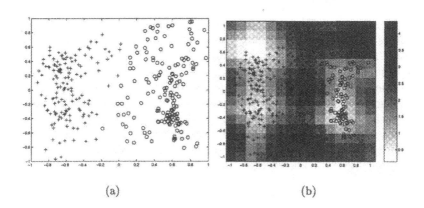

(a)   (b)

Fig. 7.13. GTM visualisation. Data is drawn from two classes, (*circles*) and (*squares*) respectively. (**a**) Without magnification factors. (**b**) With magnification factors: stretching increases with darkness.

7.4 Topographic Projection

7.4.1 Neuroscale Algorithm

A quite different approach to visualisation is based not on a density model, but instead on the concept of data *topography*. This is assumed to be captured by the inter-point distances, usually measured with a Euclidean metric:

$$d_{ij}^* = \|x_i - x_j\|. \tag{7.53}$$

Each data point $x_i \in \mathbb{R}^d$ is projected (by some function yet to be defined) to a point $y_i \in \mathbb{R}^q$. The distance between points y_i and y_j is denoted by d_{ij}, and the quality of the projection is measured by the *Sammon stress metric*:

$$E_{\text{sam}} = \sum_{i=1}^{N} \sum_{j>i}^{N} (d_{ij} - d_{ij}^*)^2. \tag{7.54}$$

The smaller the stress, the more closely the distances between the y_i match the distances in the original data space between the x_i, and hence the better preserved is the data structure in the projected space used for visualisation.

Note that there is no necessity for using the Euclidean metric to measure the distances (or 'dissimilarities') between data points. Instead, other norms can be used, for example the l_p norms

$$\|x_i - x_j\|_p = \left(\sum_{k=1}^{d} |x_{ik} - x_{jk}|^p \right)^{1/p}, \tag{7.55}$$

where the Euclidean metric is equivalent to $p = 2$. However, if the main purpose of the projection is to visualise the data, it is worth remembering that our visual system is highly tuned to discriminating patterns based on Euclidean distances, and so it makes most sense for the metric in the projection space to be Euclidean. If the metrics in the two spaces are not the same, it may be hard to interpret the results since spurious structure may be visible simply because of the properties of the metric (Hughes, 1999).

One useful change can be made to the distance measure if some additional dissimilarity information is known about the data. For example, if each data point x_i belongs to a known class C_i, a dissimilarity measure s_{ij} can be defined by

$$s_{ij} = \begin{cases} 0 & \text{if } i = j \\ 1 & \text{if } i \neq j. \end{cases} \tag{7.56}$$

This can then be incorporated into the distance measure:

$$\delta_{ij} = (1 - \alpha)d_{ij}^* + \alpha s_{ij}, \tag{7.57}$$

where the parameter $\alpha \in [0,1]$ controls the degree of supervisory information in the mapping. When $\alpha = 0$, this is the original definition (7.53), while if $\alpha = 1$, there is no distance information and points will be projected using only the class information. Intermediate values of α allow the points to be projected so as to retain the distance structure with extra separation from the classes. This can help to expose inconsistencies such as incorrectly labelled data.

In Sammon's original paper (Sammon, 1969), there was no mapping defined between $\mathbb{R}^d$ and $\mathbb{R}^q$. Instead, the points y_i, for $i = 1, \ldots, n$ were treated as variables in an optimisation problem, with E_{sam} used as the objective function. In this approach, the mapping is defined simply by the lookup table of ordered pairs (x_i, y_i). This has a number of disadvantages:

1. The number of parameters in the optimisation problem grows linearly with the size of the dataset.
2. The mapping is defined only for the original data points x_i.
3. The only way to compute the mapping for a new point x^* is to add it to the dataset and reoptimise the stress measure (though most of the y_i can be started at their earlier values to cut down on some of the computational cost).
4. As the mapping does not generalise, it is impossible to take a sub-sample of the training data to train the map more efficiently.

To get round these difficulties, the Neuroscale model was introduced in (Lowe and Tipping, 1996). This model defines a nonlinear map $\mathbb{R}^d \to \mathbb{R}^q$ using a neural network (an RBF, since a particularly efficient training algorithm is available).

Unfortunately, both the original Sammon mapping and Neuroscale suffer from the fact that the computational demands grow with the square of the number of data points. This is simply because there are $N(N-1)/2$ distances included in the sum for E_{sam}. The simplest approach to training the model is simply to compute the partial derivatives of $E = E_{\text{sam}}$ with respect to the network weights, and then to use a non-linear optimisation algorithm to find the optimal weights.

Using the chain rule, we write

$$\frac{\partial E}{\partial w_{kr}} = \sum_{i}^{N} \frac{\partial E}{\partial y_i} \frac{\partial y_i}{\partial w_{kr}}. \tag{7.58}$$

By differentiating (7.54), it is easy to see that

$$\frac{\partial E}{\partial y_i} = -2 \sum_{j \neq i} \left(\frac{d_{ij}^* - d_{ij}}{d_{ij}} \right) (y_i - y_j), \tag{7.59}$$

while, for an RBF network, the gradient of y_i with respect to the output network weights is given by the same equation as for the sum-of-squares error

$$\frac{\partial y_i}{\partial w_{kr}} = \delta_{ir} z_k, \tag{7.60}$$

where z_k is the output of the kth hidden unit, and δ_{ir} is the Kronecker delta. Assuming that the hidden unit centres and widths are chosen to model the input data distribution as in the usual two-stage training process for supervised problems, these derivatives are all that is needed to train an RBF network to perform a topographic projection.

One advantage of using RBF networks in supervised regression problems with a sum-of-squares error function is that the output layer weights can be trained very efficiently with a single pass matrix pseudo-inverse computation. This advantage is lost here, since the error function contains quartic terms. However, Tipping and Lowe (1997) showed that there is a training algorithm that is more efficient than using a general non-linear optimiser. This algorithm, called *shadow targets*, makes use of the special form of the error function and the linear dependence of the network output on the output layer weights. It is based on a model trust region approach, analogous to that used in the scaled conjugate gradient algorithm in Section 2.6.

We write the output of the network in matrix form as

$$Y = \Phi W, \tag{7.61}$$

where Φ is the matrix of hidden unit activations including bias terms. (We assume that the hidden unit parameters have been already determined.)

$$\Phi = \begin{bmatrix} \phi_0(x_1) & \phi_1(x_1) & \phi_2(x_1) & \cdots & \phi_M(x_1) \\ \phi_0(x_2) & \phi_1(x_2) & \phi_2(x_2) & \cdots & \phi_M(x_2) \\ \cdots & \cdots & \cdots & \cdots & \cdots \\ \phi_0(x_N) & \phi_1(x_N) & \phi_2(x_N) & \cdots & \phi_M(x_N) \end{bmatrix}. \tag{7.62}$$

Then we can express (7.58) (for output dimension r) in the form

$$\nabla E = \Phi^T e_r, \tag{7.63}$$

where

$$\nabla E = \left(\frac{\partial E}{\partial w_{1r}}, \frac{\partial E}{\partial w_{2r}}, \ldots, \frac{\partial E}{\partial w_{Mr}} \right)^T, \tag{7.64}$$

and

$$e_r = \left(\frac{\partial E}{\partial y_{1r}}, \frac{\partial E}{\partial y_{2r}}, \ldots, \frac{\partial E}{\partial y_{Mr}} \right)^T. \tag{7.65}$$

Equation (7.63) is simply an expression of the chain rule for a model whose output is linear in its weights. In a least-squares problem, with error

$$E = \frac{1}{2} \sum_{i=1}^{N} \| y_i - t_i \|, \tag{7.66}$$

where t_i represents an explicit target value, the same equation is valid but with

$$\frac{\partial E}{\partial y_i} = (y_i - t_i). \tag{7.67}$$

The key idea of the shadow targets algorithm is to use (7.67) to estimate *hypothetical* targets $\hat{t}_i$.

$$\hat{t}_i = y_i - \frac{\partial E}{\partial y_i}$$

$$= y_i + 2 \sum_{j \neq i} \left(\frac{d_{ij} - d_{ij}^*}{d_{ij}} \right) (y_i - y_j), \tag{7.68}$$

the last step following from (7.59). The vectors $\hat{t}_i$ represent (or shadow) the exact targets for the network that would lead to an identical expression for the weight derivatives in the RBF in the least squares regression problem. For a fixed set of targets, the least squares problem can be solved directly:

$$W = \Phi^\dagger \hat{T}. \tag{7.69}$$

Of course, for our problem the estimated targets $\hat{t}_i$ are not fixed, since $\partial E/\partial y_i$ depends on the network weights. A logical approach is to iterate this procedure, re-estimating the shadow targets at each step. However, in the early stages of training, the targets estimated by (7.68) may be poor, and hence the weights given by (7.69) may increase the error. It is therefore more practical to trust the approximation given by (7.68) to a limited extent and to increase our trust only when E_{sam} decreases. This is achieved by introducing an additional parameter η and estimating the targets by

$$\hat{t}_i = y_i - \eta \frac{\partial E}{\partial y_i}. \tag{7.70}$$

It is clear that η should be restricted to the range $(0, 1)$.

The full shadow targets algorithm consists of the following steps:

1. Initialise the weights W to small random values.
2. Initialise η to some small positive value.
3. Calculate $\Phi^\dagger$.
4. Use (7.70) to compute estimated targets $\hat{t}_i$.
5. Solve for the weights $W = \Phi^\dagger \hat{T}$.
6. Calculate E_{sam} and compare with previous value.
   a) If E_{sam} has increased, set $\eta = \eta \times k_{\text{down}}$. Restore previous values of W.
   b) If E_{sam} has decreased, set $\eta = \eta \times k_{\text{up}}$.
7. If convergence has not been achieved, return to Step 4.

Note that one of the most computationally expensive parts of this algorithm, the calculation of the pseudo-inverse $\Phi^\dagger$, need only be done once. The algorithm is robust to changes in k_{down} and k_{up}: in practice the values 0.1 and 1.2 have worked well. It has been shown that the stationary points of this algorithm are the same as gradient-based optimisation algorithms, but that it tends to produce models with better generalisation (Tipping, 1996).

7.4.2 Neuroscale Implementation

The NETLAB implementation of the Neuroscale model is a variant on the RBF. The model data structure is constructed with the command: rbf

```
net = rbf(nin, nhidden, nout, rbfunc, 'neuroscale');
```

where the first four arguments have the same meaning as Section 6.1.2. The additions needed in the function rbf follow:

```
1 if strcmp(net.outfn, 'neuroscale')
2   net.mask = rbfprior(rbfunc, nin, nhidden, nout);
3 end
```

If the output function is set to neuroscale, then a mask is created (line 2) that ensures that only the output layer weights are adjustable. The use of masks will be discussed in more detail in Chapter 9. For now, it is only necessary to note that it is a vector whose length is equal to the number of weights and whose entries are 0 or 1. Any weight corresponding to a 0 is not adjusted during training.

The calculation of E_{sam} in rbferr is performed with the following code fragment.

```
1 switch net.outfn
2 case 'neuroscale'
3   y = rbffwd(net, x);
4   y_dist = sqrt(dist2(y, y));
5   % Take t as target distance matrix
6   edata = 0.5.*(sum(sum((t-y_dist).^2)));
7 end
```

Note that the consistency check in this and rbfgrad does *not* include the dimension of the target matrix t. For these functions, t is interpreted as the target distance matrix d_{ij}, so has dimension $N \times N$ rather than $N \times$ nout which is appropriate for supervised learning, and that the consist function checks for.

The error gradient is computed in rbfgrad. The implementation is more complex than might have been expected: this is because it uses vectorised operations instead of a loop. It is particularly important since the gradient calculation is the most computationally expensive part of training and scales $\mathcal{O}(N^2)$.

```
1 ndata = size(x, 1);
2 [y, z, n2] = rbffwd(net, x);
```

```
3   switch net.outfn
4   case 'neuroscale'
5      % Compute the error gradient with respect to outputs
6      y_dist = sqrt(dist2(y, y));
7      D = (t - y_dist)./(y_dist+diag(ones(ndata, 1)));
8      temp = y';
9      gradient = -2.*sum(kron(D, ones(1, net.nout)) .* ...
10         (repmat(y, 1, ndata) - repmat((temp(:))', ndata, 1)), 1);
11     gradient = (reshape(gradient, net.nout, ndata))';
12     % Compute error gradient with respect to output weights
13     g = rbfbkp(net, x, z, n2, gradient);
14  end
```

Lines 5–11 compute the matrix $\partial E/\partial y_i$. The matrix D contains the terms

$$\frac{d_{ij}^* - d_{ij}}{d_{ij}}. \qquad (7.71)$$

The matrix y_dist is zero on the diagonal, since it contains the Euclidean distances between the points y_i. Thus (y_dist+diag(ones(ndata, 1))) is the same as y_dist except that it has a diagonal of ones. This prevents division by zero in line 7. The matrix D has entries $(d_{ij} - d_{ij}^*)/d_{ij}$ as given in (7.68). This is multiplied by $(y_i - y_j)$ and summed over all $i \neq j$. For concreteness, suppose that ndata=3 and net.nout=2. Then D is a 3×3 matrix and the Kronecker product in line 9 generates a matrix

```
[D(:, 1) D(:, 1) D(:, 2) D(:, 2) D(:, 3) D(:, 3)]
```

The row vector temp(:)' contains the elements of y row by row.

```
[y(1, 1) y(1, 2) y(2, 1) y(2, 2) y(3, 1) y(3, 2)]
```

or in vector form

```
[y(1, :) y(2, :) y(3, :)]
```

The call to repmat for temp generates the following matrix

```
[y(1, :) y(2, :) y(3, :);
 y(1, :) y(2, :) y(3, :);
 y(1, :) y(2, :) y(3, :)]
```

while the call to repmat for y generates

```
[y(1, :) y(1, :) y(1, :);
 y(2, :) y(2, :) y(2, :);
 y(3, :) y(3, :) y(3, :)]
```

Hence the difference between these two matrices is a block matrix whose ijth entry is the vector difference between y_i and y_j, as required. The final call to rbfbkp computes the gradient with respect to the weights.

The two functions rbferr and rbfgrad can be combined with any non-linear optimiser in the usual way to train a Neuroscale model. However, it is much more efficient to use the shadow targets algorithm, and this is implemented in rbftrain. The first part of the function sets the hidden unit parameters to model the input data density and is shared with the standard regression training algorithm. The function is controlled by an `options` vector, and the available entries (1, 2, 3, 8, and 14) have their usual meaning: see Section 2.1. The additional option, defined by `options(6)` determines whether the output weights are initialised using PCA. If it is set to 1, then the data x is projected using PCA and the output layer found using a least squares fit (lines 1–10).

```
1   if net.outfn == 'neuroscale' & options(6)
2     % Initialise output layer weights by projecting data with PCA
3     mu = mean(x);
4     [pcvals, pcvecs] = pca(x, net.nout);
5     xproj = (x - ones(ndata, 1)*mu)*pcvecs;
6     % Now use projected data as targets to compute output weights
7     temp = pinv([act ones(ndata, 1)]) * xproj;
8     net.w2 = temp(1:net.nhidden, :);
9     net.b2 = temp(net.nhidden+1, :);
10  end
11
12    [y, act] = rbffwd(net, x);
13    if nargin < 4
14      % If optional input distances not passed in, then use
15      % Euclidean distance
16      x_dist = sqrt(dist2(x, x));
17    else
18      x_dist = t;
19    end
20    Phi = [act, ones(ndata, 1)];
21    PhiDag = pinv(Phi);
22    y_dist = sqrt(dist2(y, y));
23
24    wold = netpak(net);
25    errold = 0.5*(sum(sum((x_dist - y_dist).^2)));
26
27    eta = 0.1;    % Initial value for eta
28    k_up = 1.2;
29    k_down = 0.1;
30    success = 1;  % Force initial gradient calculation
31
32    for j = 1:options(14)
33      if success
34        % Negative error gradient with respect to network outputs
35        D = (x_dist - y_dist)./(y_dist+diag(ones(ndata, 1)));
36        temp = y';
37        neg_gradient = 2.*sum(kron(D, ones(1, net.nout)) .* ...
38          (repmat(y, 1, ndata) - repmat((temp(:))', ndata, 1)), 1);
39        neg_gradient = (reshape(neg_gradient, net.nout, ndata))';
40      end
41      % Compute the shadow targets
42      t = y - eta*neg_gradient;
43      % Solve for the weights and biases
44      temp = PhiDag * t;
45      net.w2 = temp(1:net.nhidden, :);
46      net.b2 = temp(net.nhidden+1, :);
```

```
47
48       % Do housekeeping and test for convergence
49       ynew = rbffwd(net, x);
50       y_distnew = sqrt(dist2(ynew, ynew));
51       err = 0.5.*(sum(sum((x_dist-y_distnew).^2)));
52       if err > errold
53         success = 0;
54         % Restore previous weights
55         net = netunpak(net, wold);
56         err = errold;
57         eta = eta * k_down;
58       else
59         success = 1;
60         eta = eta * k_up;
61         errold = err;
62         y = ynew;
63         y_dist = y_distnew;
64         if test & j > 1
65           w = netpak(net);
66           if (max(abs(w - wold)) < options(2) & ...
67                 abs(err-errold) < options(3))
68             options(8) = err;
69             return;
70           end
71         end
72         wold = netpak(net);
73       end
74       if options(1)
75         fprintf(1, 'Cycle %4d Error %11.6f\n', j, err)
76       end
77       if nargout >= 3
78         errlog(j) = err;
79       end
80     end
81     options(8) = errold;
82     if (options(1) >= 0)
83       disp('Warning: Max. number of iterations has been exceeded');
84     end
```

Lines 13–19 select the distance metric d_{ij}^* to be used. If a matrix of inter-point distances is passed to the function (as the variable t), then it is used. This matrix can be prepared by the user to incorporate extra information as in (7.57). If no matrix is passed, then the standard Euclidean metric is computed for x.

The remainder of the fragment carries out the shadow targets algorithm.

1. Weight initialisation was carried out in rbf when the network was constructed or using PCA in lines 1–10.
2. η is initialised in line 27.
3. $\Phi^\dagger$ is computed in lines 20–21. Note that the main loop starts on line 32.
4. The shadow targets are calculated on lines 42. The error gradient $\partial E/\partial y_i$ is only calculated in lines 33–40 if the weights have changed since the

previous iteration of the loop. This is copied from rbfgrad, since it was not worth making a function in its own right.

5. The new weights are found using the pre-computed pseudo-inverse in lines 44–46.

6. The new error is calculated in lines 49–51.

   a) Increased E_{sam} is dealt with in lines 52–57. Note that the weights are restored to their previous values and η is decreased. There is no need to recompute $\partial E/\partial y_i$ in this case.

   b) Decreased E_{sam} is dealt with in lines 58–72.

7. The final section of code is the usual housekeeping for iterative optimisation algorithms: testing for convergence, displaying and storing error values, and testing for loop termination.

7.4.3 Demonstration of Neuroscale

The demonstration program demns1 shows how easy it is to use Neuroscale for visualisation.

```
1   % Generate the data
2   input_dim = 4;
3   output_dim = 2;
4   mix = gmm(input_dim, 2, 'spherical');
5   mix.centres = [1 1 1 1; 0 0 0 0];
6   mix.priors = [0.5 0.5];
7   mix.covars = [0.1 0.1];
8   ndata = 60;
9   [data, labels] = gmmsamp(mix, ndata);
10
11  ncentres = 10;
12  net = rbf(input_dim, ncentres, output_dim, 'tps', 'neuroscale');
13
14  % First row controls shadow targets, second row controls rbfsetbf
15  options(1, :) = foptions;
16  options(2, :) = foptions;
17  options(1, 1) = 1;
18  options(1, 2) = 1e-2;
19  options(1, 3) = 1e-2;
20  options(1, 6) = 1;    % Switch on PCA initialisation
21  options(1, 14) = 60;
22  options(2, 1) = -1;    % Switch off all warnings
23  options(2, 5) = 1;
24  options(2, 14) = 10;
25  net2 = rbftrain(net, options, data);
26
27  % Plot the result
28  y = rbffwd(net2, data);
29  ClassSymbol1 = 'r.';
30  ClassSymbol2 = 'b.';
31  PointSize = 12;
32  fh1 = figure;
33  hold on;
```

```
34   plot(y((labels==1),1),y(labels==1,2),ClassSymbol1, ...
35        'MarkerSize', PointSize)
36   plot(y((labels>1),1),y(labels>1,2),ClassSymbol2, ...
37        'MarkerSize', PointSize)
38   % Plot test data on same axes
39   [test_data, test_labels] = gmmsamp(mix, 100);
40   ytest = rbffwd(net2, test_data);
41   ClassSymbol1 = 'ro';
42   ClassSymbol2 = 'bo';
43   PointSize = 6;
44   hold on
45   plot(ytest((test_labels==1),1),ytest(test_labels==1,2), ...
46     ClassSymbol1, 'MarkerSize', PointSize)
47   plot(ytest((test_labels>1),1),ytest(test_labels>1,2),...
48     ClassSymbol2, 'MarkerSize', PointSize)
49   hold on
50   legend('Class 1', 'Class 2', 'Test Class 1', 'Test Class 2')
```

In lines 1–9 a sample of data from two Gaussians is generated in $\mathbb{R}^4$ (compare the data used in demgtm2; see Section 7.3.6). The two Gaussians are well separated in data space, so a successful visualisation method should show this separation clearly. The Neuroscale model is created in lines 11–12: the RBF has 10 centres with thin plate spline activation functions and a two-dimensional output space. The model is trained in lines 14–25: most of the work goes into setting up the options. The algorithm has a two row options vector (uniquely in NETLAB). The first row specifies a maximum of 60 iterations of the shadow targets algorithm, and a convergence criterion of 10^{-2}. The second row controls the adjustment of the parameters of the basis functions: 10 iterations of EM are used and the variances are reset if they collapse (options(2, 5)). After the model is trained by a call to rbftrain it is ready for use.

Data is projected by forward propagation through the RBF, as in line 28. Lines 29–37 plot the projections of the training data points, colour coded red for class 1 and blue for class 2. These points are clearly separated, but the question remains; does this relationship generalise to new data? To test this, an independent dataset is generated from the original Gaussian mixture model (line 39), projected (line 40) and then plotted on the same axes with the same colour coding but different symbols (lines 41–50). The results of this projection (modified for printing) are shown in Fig. 7.14. The separation of the two classes into distinct clusters holds just as well for the test data as for the training data, showing that the model is generalising successfully.

7.5 Worked Example: Canonical Variates

Consider again the setup for PCA. We have a dataset of vectors x^n for $n = 1, \ldots, N$ in $V = \mathbb{R}^d$ which we want to map to vectors z^n in $U = \mathbb{R}^M$, a subspace of V. We can choose an orthonormal basis $u_1, \ldots, u_M$ for U and

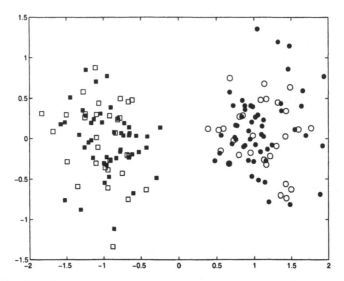

Fig. 7.14. Visualisation with Neuroscale. Training data from class 1 (*open circles*) and class 2 (*open squares*) is projected by a Neuroscale model. The test data (*filled circles* and *filled squares*) clusters in a similar way.

extend this to an orthonormal basis $\boldsymbol{u}_1, \ldots, \boldsymbol{u}_d$ for $\boldsymbol{V}$. A vector $\boldsymbol{x}$ can be represented by the vector $(x_1, \ldots, x_d)$, or equivalently:

$$x = \sum_{i=1}^{M} x_i u_i + \sum_{i=M+1}^{d} x_i u_i. \tag{7.72}$$

Now suppose that we have additional information in the form of a class label $t = t_c^n$ for each vector, where t_c^n is an indicator variable:

$$t_{ij}^n = \begin{cases} 1 & \text{if } \boldsymbol{x}^n \in \mathcal{C}_c \\ 0 & \text{otherwise.} \end{cases} \tag{7.73}$$

We would like to use this information to improve the visualisation plot we obtain with PCA by showing greater class separation; this will also improve the results of any classifier we build using the features.

The method of *canonical variates* provides the optimal linear discrimination between classes with a linear projection of the data. It does this by taking account of the scatter of data within each class and across classes. Let Σ denote the covariance matrix. Then the covariance matrix of class c, Σ_c can be written

$$\Sigma_c = \frac{1}{N_c} \sum_{n=1}^{N} t_c^n (\boldsymbol{x}^n - \boldsymbol{\mu}_c)(\boldsymbol{x}^n - \boldsymbol{\mu}_c)^T, \tag{7.74}$$

where $\boldsymbol{\mu}_c$ is the cth class mean, and N_c is the number of examples in the cth class. The within-class scatter matrix $\boldsymbol{S}_W$ is a weighted sum of the class covariance matrices

$$S_W = \sum_{c=1}^{C} \frac{N_c}{N} \boldsymbol{\Sigma}_c. \tag{7.75}$$

The between-class scatter matrix $\boldsymbol{S}_B$ is the weighted covariance of the class means:

$$S_B = \sum_{c=1}^{C} \frac{N_c}{N} (\boldsymbol{\mu}_c - \boldsymbol{\mu})(\boldsymbol{\mu}_c - \boldsymbol{\mu})^T \tag{7.76}$$

$$= \boldsymbol{\Sigma} - \boldsymbol{S}_W, \tag{7.77}$$

where $\boldsymbol{\mu}$ is the mean of the data. The criterion used to optimise the choice of the projection vectors $\boldsymbol{u}_i$ is to maximise the ratio of the between-class scatter to the within-class scatter:

$$\frac{\boldsymbol{u}^T \boldsymbol{S}_B \boldsymbol{u}}{\boldsymbol{u}^T \boldsymbol{S}_W \boldsymbol{u}} \tag{7.78}$$

which generalises (7.6), the error criterion used in PCA. Webb (1999) discusses several other possible generalisations of PCA to labelled data. The vectors $\boldsymbol{u}$ that maximise (7.78) can be shown to be *generalised* eigenvectors of $\boldsymbol{S}_B$ and $\boldsymbol{S}_W$, that is solutions of the equation

$$S_B \boldsymbol{u} = \lambda S_W \boldsymbol{u}, \tag{7.79}$$

where the generalised eigenvalues λ can be used to rank the canonical variates.

The function canvar computes the canonical variates for a dataset x and targets t, which should be represented in a 1-of-c encoding. The optional third argument defines the number of canonical variates required. Note that it is not possible to find more than $c - 1$ variates because of the dependency between $\boldsymbol{S}_B$ and $\boldsymbol{S}_W$ (7.77).

```
1  function [cvals, cvecs] = canvar(x, t, N)
2
3  nclasses = size(t, 2);
4  [ndata, nin] = size(x);
5  if nargin < 3
6    N = min(nclasses - 1, nin);
7  end
8
9  if N ~= round(N) | N < 1 | N > nin | N >= nclasses
10   error('No. of canonical variates must be integer, >0, < dim');
11 end
12
13 % Find in-class scatter matrix
```

```
14  S_W = zeros(nin, nin);
15  N_c = zeros(1, nclasses);
16  for c = 1:nclasses
17    N_c(c) = sum((t(:, c) == 1), 1);
18    if (N_c(c) > 1)
19      S_W = S_W + ((N_c(c)-1)/ndata) * cov(x(find(t(:, c)==1), :));
20    end
21  end
22  % Between class covariance matrix
23  Sigma = cov(x, 1);   % Ensure normalisation by ndata
24  S_B = Sigma - S_W;
25  % Now compute canonical variates using generalised eigenvalues
26  [temp_cvecs, temp_cvals] = eig(S_B, S_W);
27  % Sort values and vectors into descending order
28  Tc = diag(temp_cvals);
29  [cvals perm] = sort(-Tc);
30  cvals = -cvals(1:N);
31  if cvals == Tc(1:N)
32    % Originals were in order
33    cvecs = temp_cvecs(:, 1:N);
34    return
35  else
36    % Need to reorder the eigenvectors
37    for i=1:N
38      cvecs(:,i) = temp_cvecs(:,perm(i));
39    end
40  end
```

After the housekeeping, the scatter matrices are computed: Σ in line 21; S_W according to (7.75) in lines 14–21; and S_B according to (7.77) in line 24. The expression

```
x(find(t(:, c)==1), :)
```

extracts those rows of x corresponding to target vectors with a 1 in the cth column. The generalised eigenvector problem is solved in line 26, and then the eigenvalues and eigenvectors are sorted into decreasing order using the same method as the NETLAB function eigdec.

Figure 7.15 shows the result of applying both canonical variates and PCA to the same dataset. Data was generated from two classes in $\mathbb{R}^2$ so that the within-class scatter in the y-direction was much greater than the between-class scatter in the x-direction. The first principal component is in the y-direction (the line of greatest data variance, ignoring the labels) while the first (and only) canonical variate is in the x-direction. Data projected onto the canonical variate can be almost perfectly separated by class, while the principal component provides no class separation at all. This figure also illustrates the fact that the canonical variates computed by canvar are *not* normalised by default; they are, however, still orthogonal.

Figure 7.16 shows the visualisation results achieved on the oil pipeline dataset using the first two canonical variates. This should be compared with Fig. 7.2, which shows much less separation of the three classes.

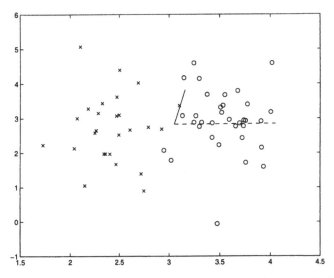

Fig. 7.15. Demonstration of canonical variates. The two classes are indicated by circles and crosses respectively. The canonical variate (*dashed line*) and first principal component (*solid line*) are clearly contrasted.

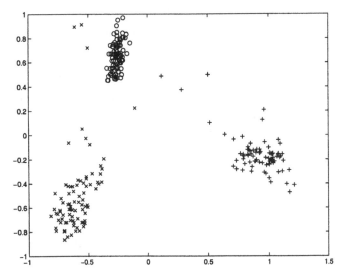

Fig. 7.16. Projection of pipeline data using canonical variates. Three classes are shown: (*plus signs*), (*crosses*) and (*circles*).

Exercises

7.1 (⋆⋆) Generate some data from the surface of a hemisphere in $\mathbb{R}^2$ with some additive Gaussian noise. Fit a mixture of PPCA to this dataset and visualise the results by creating a three-dimensional graph of the principal component subspace for each mixture component.

7.2 ($\star\star\star$) In place of an eigendecomposition of the covariance matrix, the parameters in PPCA can be found using an EM algorithm, which may be more efficient when the data lies in a high-dimensional space. The algorithm proposed in Tipping and Bishop (1997) is a generalised EM algorithm that works in two stages.

1. Calculate the responsibility R_{nj} of mixture component j for data point x_n (as in (7.20)):

$$R_{nj} = P(j|x_n) = \frac{p(x_n|j)\pi_j}{p(x_n)}. \tag{7.80}$$

The M-step computes new mixing coefficients and mean vectors using the same equations as the NETLAB implementation (7.21) and (7.22):

$$\pi_j^{(m+1)} = \frac{1}{N}\sum_{n=1}^{N} P^{(m)}(j|x_n), \tag{7.81}$$

$$\mu_j^{(m+1)} = \frac{\sum_{n=1}^{N} P^{(m)}(j|x_n)x_n}{\sum_{n=1}^{N} P^{(m)}(j|x_n)}. \tag{7.82}$$

2. To re-estimate the matrix W and the covariance structure, we use the covariance matrix of the data weighted by the responsibility of the jth component:

$$S_j = \frac{1}{\pi_j^{(m+1)}N}\sum_{n=1}^{N} P^{(m)}(j|x_n)(x_n-\mu_j^{(m+1)})(x_n-\mu_j^{(m+1)})^T, \tag{7.83}$$

and the matrix $M_j = (\sigma_j^{(m)})^2 I + (W^{(m)})_j^T W_j^{(m)}$ in the update equations

$$W_j^{(m+1)} = S_j W_j^{(m)}\left(\pi_j^{(m+1)}(\sigma_j^{(m)})^2 I\right.$$

$$\left. + M_j^{-1}(W_j^{(m)})^T S_j W_j^{(m)}\right)^{-1} \tag{7.84}$$

$$(\sigma_j^{(m+1)})^2 = \frac{\mathrm{tr}\left[S_j - S_j W_j^{(m)} M_j^{-1}\left(W_j^{(m+1)}\right)^T\right]}{\pi_j^{(m+1)}d}. \tag{7.85}$$

Implement this algorithm and compare it with the NETLAB implementation on datasets in 2, 10 and 50 dimensions. You should consider speed of convergence, susceptibility to local optima in training and generalisation performance (assessed using likelihood on a test set).

7.3 ($\star\star$) Extend the EM algorithm for PPCA in Exercise 7.2 to deal with missing data. The equations in Exercise 3.2 are relevant here, but with the covariance structure relevant to PPCA replacing the full covariance matrix.

7.4 ($\star\star$) The classical factor analysis model for data has the form

$$x = Wz + \mu + \epsilon, \tag{7.86}$$

where z has a zero mean unit isotropic Gaussian distribution $N(0, I)$, μ is a constant (whose maximum likelihood estimator is the data mean), and ϵ is an x-independent noise process. The noise model is $\epsilon \sim N(0, \Psi)$, with Ψ diagonal. The model for x is then also normal $N(\mu, C)$, with $C = \Psi + WW^T$. The log likelihood of the data is

$$\mathcal{L} = -\frac{Nd}{2}\ln(2\pi) - \frac{N}{2}\ln|C| - \frac{N}{2}\mathrm{tr}\left[C^{-1}S\right], \tag{7.87}$$

where S is the sample covariance matrix of the observed data x.
The posterior distribution of the latent variables is given by

$$p(z|x) \sim N(Vx, P), \tag{7.88}$$

where

$$V = W^T C^{-1} \quad \text{and} \quad P = I - W^T C^{-1} W. \tag{7.89}$$

Use this equation to derive and implement an EM algorithm for factor analysis. To project data onto the latent variable space, use the posterior mean (cf. GTM).

7.5 ($\star\star\star$) Extend the implementation of factor analysis in problem 7.4 to a mixture of factor analysers using a similar structure to mixtures of PPCA.

7.6 ($\star\star\star$) Multi-layer neural networks can be used for non-linear dimensionality reduction. Create an MLP with d inputs, $M < d$ hidden units and d outputs (with linear activation functions). Train the network on a dataset where the targets and inputs are the same. This network forms an *auto-associative* mapping, and the hidden unit activations can be used as a reduced-dimensionality feature set. It was shown by Bourlard and Kamp (1988) that such a network projects the data onto the same M-dimensional subspace as PCA, though the vectors need not be orthogonal or of unit length.

Verify experimentally that this is true by forming the projection of a dataset onto matrices A and B using an auto-associative network and PCA respectively. Then compute ran $A \cap$ ran B using the following algorithm (see Golub and van Loan, 1996, Section 12.4.4).

1. Using the MATLAB function qr, compute the QR factorisations:

$$A = Q_A R_A \qquad Q_A^T Q_A = I$$

$$B = Q_B R_B \qquad Q_B^T Q_B = I. \tag{7.90}$$

2. Set $C = Q_A^T Q_B$.
3. Compute the SVD of C so that

$$C = Y \operatorname{diag}(\cos \theta_k) Z^T. \tag{7.91}$$

4. Define the index s, which is the effective rank of ran $A \cap$ ran B, by

$$1 = \cos(\theta_1) = \cdots = \cos(\theta_s) > \cos(\theta_{s+1}). \tag{7.92}$$

Because floating point arithmetic is used, the equalities will have to allow a certain tolerance.

5. Find $\operatorname{ran}(A) \cap \operatorname{ran}(B)$ as

$$\operatorname{span}\{u_1, \ldots, u_s\} = \operatorname{span}\{v_1, \ldots, v_s\} \tag{7.93}$$

where u_i are the columns of $Q_A Y$ and v_i are the columns of $Q_B Z$.

7.7 ($\star\star\star$) An auto-associative network can perform non-linear principal component analysis if there are more than two layers of weights. A suitable structure is a four layer $d - H - M - H - d$ network with non-linear activations in the first and third hidden layers (though the activations in the second hidden layer can be linear). It is best to choose $d > H > M$. Implement such a network as an extension of the NETLAB MLP. To provide the functions needed to train the model you will need to modify mlp, mlppak, mlpunpak, mlpfwd and mlpbkp. Evaluate the results of applying this network, and compare it with both PCA and Neuroscale. You should compare the probability of finding local minima in training, training efficiency, and reconstruction error.

7.8 ($\star\star$) Evaluate the differences between the GTM with the SOM when applied to high-dimensional data lying around a two-dimensional manifold. You should compare quantitative factors, such as the computational effort required to train the models, sensitivity to initial conditions and training parameters, and qualitative factors, such as the quality of the visualisation maps provided by the trained models.

7.9 ($\star\star$) Extend the GTM model to allow each centre its own spherical covariance model. You will need to revisit (7.42) and modify the corresponding section of gtmem. Apply the new model to data that lies close to a one-dimensional manifold in $\mathbb{R}^2$ (see demgtm1, for example) where the noise around the manifold is location dependent. Evaluate the fit of your model (using test set likelihood and a visual inspection of the fit) and compare the results with standard GTM.

7.10 ($\star\star\star$) Write functions `gtmerr` and `gtmgrad` to compute the error function E and the gradient of E with respect to the adjustable weights in the RBF network. Using these functions, train GTMs using general non-linear optimisation algorithms and compare the results and performance with `gtmem`.

7.11 ($\star\star\star$) Extend the GTM model to discrete data using a sigmoid or softmax noise model. There is no covariance model. Modify the M-step of the EM algorithm to use IRLS to update the RBF weights (compare Exercise 6.11 in Chapter 6).

7.12 ($\star$) Compare the training time and final error for a Neuroscale model with and without PCA initialisation.

7.13 ($\star\star$) Compare the efficiency of training a Neuroscale model with shadow targets and non-linear optimisation algorithms such as `quasinew` and `scg`. You should consider both flops and the time taken. Your comparison should look at the dependence on the number of data points and the dimension of the data space.

7.14 ($\star\star$) Use `gmmsamp` to generate some synthetic data from a mixture of Gaussians and label each point with the component it was generated from. Use this to investigate the effect of class information in the distance measure (7.57) on the visualisation results. Vary α from 0 to 1 in a number of steps and plot the results.

7.15 ($\star\star$) Write an implementation of the Sammon mapping. Given some training data, it should compute a set of mapped points that minimise the stress metric given in (7.54) using the gradients computed by (7.59). By writing appropriate error and gradient functions (much of which can be derived from the Neuroscale portion of `rbftrain`) it should be possible to use a standard NETLAB non-linear optimisation function to compute the Sammon mapping for a given dataset. Use your implementation to project the dataset used in `demns1` and compare the results with Neuroscale.

7.16 ($\star\star$) It has been observed that a topographic mapping of high-dimensional randomly distributed data gives rise to an illusory structure to the visualised data (Klock and Buhmann, 1997). Generate datasets containing 1000 points from a uniform random distribution in $\mathbb{R}^5$, $\mathbb{R}^{10}$ and $\mathbb{R}^{30}$. Train a Neuroscale model with two outputs on each dataset in turn, plotting the projected data. Show that as the dimension of the data grows, a ring-like structure can be seen in the visualisation space.

8. Sampling

As will be seen in Chapter 9, integration plays a key role in the Bayesian approach to pattern analysis. The integrals of interest are over the weight space w, and hence are high dimensional. For non-linear models, the integrals are not usually analytically tractable, but standard methods of numerical integration, which are very accurate, only apply to low-dimensional spaces. Monte Carlo integration is a less accurate method of performing integrals that does generalise to higher dimensional spaces, provided that a sample of points can be drawn from the function of interest.

This chapter discusses how sampling can be used in Monte Carlo methods, and then describes gradually more sophisticated methods of sampling, culminating in Markov Chain methods (the Metropolis–Hastings algorithm and hybrid Monte Carlo (HMC)) that are applicable to practical inference problems for neural networks. In fact, as Brooks (1998) points out, it is often possible to mix different sampling techniques in a single method (for example, by splitting the vector into distinct components and using different algorithms in each component), so it is useful to know about a range of techniques so that the most appropriate one can be used for each component.

The NETLAB implementations of these algorithms have a similar interface to the optimisation algorithms: this enables them to be used in neural network training in a familiar way. The worked example implements a simple convergence diagnostic statistic and demonstrates how it can be used to detect whether Markov chains have converged to the target distribution.

All the functions discussed in this chapter are listed in Table 8.1.

Table 8.1. Functions in this chapter.

Sampling	
demmet1	Demonstration of Metropolis–Hastings sampling
demhmc1	Demonstration of HMC with bimodal Gaussian
gsamp	Sample from a Gaussian distribution
hmc	Hybrid Monte Carlo sampling algorithm
metrop	Metropolis–Hastings sampling algorithm

8.1 Monte Carlo Integration

Consider an integral, typical of those that arise in Bayesian inference, of the form

$$E(f(w)) = \int_{\mathbb{R}^m} f(w)p(w) \, dw, \tag{8.1}$$

where there are m weights in the vector w. For example, to compute the expected mean prediction of a neural network model $f(x; w)$ given some training data $\mathcal{D}$, we need to calculate

$$E(f(x; w)|\mathcal{D}) = \int_{\mathbb{R}^m} f(x; w)p(w|\mathcal{D}) \, dw. \tag{8.2}$$

For a non-linear model, such as a neural network, m will typically be in the range 10–100, and the integral is impossible to evaluate analytically (i.e. in closed form).

If $m = 1$, then there are many techniques available from 'classical' numerical analysis, such as the Newton–Cotes formulae (Kincaid and Cheney, 1996), based on the principle of approximating the integrand on sub-intervals by a function that is simple to integrate (such as a polynomial) and then adding up the results of integrating the approximating function on each sub-interval. These techniques can be very accurate with comparatively few function evaluations and, for smooth functions, reliable error estimates can also be calculated.

Integrals like (8.1) are intrinsically hard when the dimension is greater than 1 for two reasons:

- the curse of dimensionality; the number of points at which the functions p and f need to be evaluated goes up exponentially with the dimension of the space;
- it is impossible to evaluate the integral over the whole of $\mathbb{R}^m$ in practice; we must concentrate on regions where the integrand is significantly different from zero.

These problems mean that extending the one-dimensional approach much beyond $\mathbb{R}^2$ is not feasible.

An alternative is to use stochastic sampling methods, known as Monte Carlo integration. These are suitable if high accuracy (for example, more than four significant figures) is not required. If the integrand has local strong peaks at known locations, then it is best to divide and conquer, by breaking the integral up into a distinct region around each peak. While Monte Carlo methods do make it feasible to tackle high-dimensional integrals, they do not give a quick result. For a reasonably reliable answer it may be necessary to generate tens or hundreds of thousands of points, and computation times in the order of days are not uncommon.

Integration is used throughout probability and statistics to evaluate probabilities and expectations. With Monte Carlo integration, we reverse the process and use expectations to calculate integrals. If X is a continuous random variable with density function $p(x)$ such that for some region V

$$\int_V p(x) \, dx = 1, \tag{8.3}$$

then

$$E\left[f(x)\right] = \langle f \rangle_X = \int_V f(x)p(x) \, dx. \tag{8.4}$$

We can approximate $\langle f \rangle$ by sampling independent points $x_1, \ldots, x_N$ from the distribution $p(x)$ and then computing the sample mean

$$\langle f \rangle \approx \sum_{n=1}^{N} \frac{f(x_n)}{N}. \tag{8.5}$$

We obtain a *statistical* error estimate by considering the variance of this statistic. If the x_n are independent samples, the variance is

$$\frac{\langle f^2 \rangle - \langle f \rangle^2}{N}, \tag{8.6}$$

so we can write

$$\int_V f(x)p(x) \, dx = \langle f \rangle \pm \sqrt{\frac{\langle f^2 \rangle - \langle f \rangle^2}{N}}, \tag{8.7}$$

which represents one standard deviation around the expected value of the statistic.

The main problem with this simple approach is that the error decreases with order $N^{-1/2}$, which is rather slow. (By comparison, the error of a simple one-dimensional algorithm such as the extended trapezium rule decreases as N^{-2}.)

8.2 Basic Sampling

To use Monte Carlo integration effectively, it is necessary to be able to sample from a wide range of probability density functions. For example, in (8.2) we shall sample from $p(w|y)$. In this section, we discuss a number of simple sampling methods suitable for low-dimensional distributions.

8.2.1 Random Number Generators

A basic building block in most sampling methods is being able to sample from a uniform distribution $U(0, 1)$. Most computer-based random number generators are, in fact, not random at all. They are deterministic algorithms that generate sequences of numbers which have the same properties as a sequence of values generated from a random variable. For this reason, the algorithms are often called *pseudo-random number generators* because they generate sequences which cannot be distinguished from true random samples by a certain set of statistical tests. The properties that are considered depend on the application, but typically we require that the values have close to the correct distribution, and that they are uncorrelated over a range of sampling intervals. To use the values as coordinates in a higher dimensional space, we also require that the vectors created fill the space pseudo-randomly, and not lie on regular lower dimensional subspaces.

Most practical random number generators are based on a linear congruential algorithm

$$I_{j+1} \equiv aI_j + c \pmod{n} \tag{8.8}$$

with a, c, and n positive integers. This generates integer values I_j in the range $[1, n)$. If these are divided by n, we obtain a generator that has a uniform distribution on the interval $(0, 1)$. If the values of a, c, and n are properly chosen, then the period of the generator, i.e. the number of distinct values it generates before repetition, is n.

This algorithm is very fast to compute and simple to program, which explains its popularity. The drawback of such generators is that successive calls are serially correlated (i.e. the sequence has non-trivial autocorrelation). If k random numbers at a time are used as points in the hypercube $[0, 1]^k$, then they will tend to lie on $(k - 1)$-dimensional hyperplanes.

The values generated by the algorithm are entirely determined by the first values I_1, known as the 'seed'. When carrying out experiments based on random samples you should always save the seed that was used so that they are repeatable. It is very irritating to get interesting results in an experiment and then never be able to obtain them again.

The uniform random number generator in MATLAB is called **rand**. This is a combination of congruential random generators of a similar type to that described in this section and is formed so that it has a period of more than 2^{1492}, adequate for the most demanding Monte Carlo integrals. Instead of a seed, it has a 'state' vector with 35 components which can be saved and reused:

```
1  s = rand('state'); % Save 35 dimensional vector
2  % Now draw lots of samples
3  a = rand(1000, 10);
4  rand('state', s); % Reset state
5  % Can now draw identical samples, so b = a
6  b = rand(1000, 10);
```

To control the initial state, it is easier to use the function call

`rand('state', j); % Choose an integer j`

which puts the generator into its jth state. Initialisation of this type can be found at the start of every demonstration program in NETLAB.

8.2.2 Transformation Methods

There are many distributions other than the uniform that we need to sample from. The basic idea for the simplest cases is to use a uniform generator and *transform* its output.

The density of $y(x)$ is given by the Jacobian

$$p(y) = p(x) \left| \frac{\mathrm{d}x}{\mathrm{d}y} \right|. \tag{8.9}$$

For example, if $y(x) = -\log(x)$ and x has a uniform distribution, then

$$p(y)\,\mathrm{d}y = 1. \left| \frac{\mathrm{d}x}{\mathrm{d}y} \right| \mathrm{d}y = e^{-y}\,\mathrm{d}y \tag{8.10}$$

and y/λ has density $\lambda e^{-\lambda y}$, which is an exponential distribution with parameter λ. The transformation method works by finding a function $y(x)$ such that

$$\frac{\mathrm{d}x}{\mathrm{d}y} = p(y) \tag{8.11}$$

is the distribution of interest. Let

$$F(y) = \int_\infty^y p_y(\tau)\,\mathrm{d}\tau. \tag{8.12}$$

Then $y(x) = F^{-1}(x)$. So this method can be applied only if F^{-1}, can be computed. Unfortunately, there are not many interesting distributions for which this is true. For example, the cumulative distribution function for a Gaussian random variable, given by

$$F(y) = \int_{-\infty}^y \frac{1}{2\pi} \exp\left[\frac{-\tau^2}{2} \right] \mathrm{d}\tau, \tag{8.13}$$

must be found numerically, since there is no analytic form for F. Hence the inverse function F^{-1} would also have to be found numerically and so the transformation method is impractical for a Gaussian distribution.

Fortunately, there is a simple method of sampling from a Gaussian distribution using a uniform random number generator. Let x_1 and x_2 be $U(0,1)$ random variables and set

$$y_1 = \sqrt{-2\log x_1} \cos 2\pi x_2 \qquad y_2 = \sqrt{-2\log x_1} \sin 2\pi x_2, \qquad (8.14)$$

or, equivalently,

$$x_1 = \exp\left[\frac{-1}{2}(y_1^2 + y_2^2)\right] \qquad x_2 = \frac{1}{2\pi}\arctan\frac{y_2}{y_1}. \qquad (8.15)$$

Then the Jacobian of the transformation is given by

$$\frac{\partial(x_1, x_2)}{\partial(y_1, y_2)} = -\left[\frac{1}{\sqrt{2\pi}}e^{-y_1^2/2}\right]\left[\frac{1}{\sqrt{2\pi}}e^{-y_2^2/2}\right], \qquad (8.16)$$

which implies that y_1 and y_2 are independent normal $N(0,1)$ distributions.

The MATLAB function randn implements a sampler from $N(0,1)$. Like rand, it has a state and can be initialised in a similar way. All that is required to convert a sample from $N(0,1)$ into a sample from $N(\mu, \sigma^2)$ is to add the mean μ and multiply by the standard deviation σ:

```
% Create a 10x1 sample from N(1, 4)
sigma = 2;
mu = 1;
x = randn(10, 1)*sigma + mu;
```

This can be generalised to a multi-dimensional Gaussian in $\mathbb{R}^d$ with covariance matrix Σ. Since Σ is symmetric and positive definite, it has an eigendecomposition $\Sigma u_k = \lambda_k u_k$ with an orthonormal basis of eigenvectors u_k for $k = 1, \ldots, d$. If X is a random variable with distribution $N(\mu, \Sigma)$, then $X - \mu$ is Gaussian with zero mean and covariance matrix

$$\Lambda = \text{diag}(\lambda_1, \ldots, \lambda_d) \qquad (8.17)$$

with respect to the basis $\{u_1, \ldots, u_d\}$. This means that it is the product of d uncorrelated one-dimensional Gaussian distributions with covariances $\lambda_1, \ldots, \lambda_d$, and we can apply the one-dimensional sampling approach to each. This is implemented in the NETLAB function gsamp.

```
1  function x = gsamp(mu, covar, nsamp)
2
3  d = size(covar, 1);
4  mu = reshape(mu, 1, d);   % Ensure that mu is a row vector
5
6  [evec, eval] = eig(covar);
7  coeffs = randn(nsamp, d)*sqrt(eval);
8  x = ones(nsamp, 1)*mu + coeffs*evec';
```

Line 7 generates a matrix coeffs which is a sample from $N(0, \Lambda)$, and line 8 transforms this to have mean μ and align the covariance matrix along the eigenvectors.

An alternative approach to sampling from a multivariate Gaussian is to invert the covariance matrix and then use a Cholesky decomposition: this is discussed in Section 10.2.1 where samples are generated from a Gaussian Process. The NETLAB function gmmsamp uses gsamp to sample from a Gaussian mixture model (see Section 3.1.2).

8.2.3 Rejection Sampling

Suppose that we are trying to sample from a random variable with density function $p(x)$ which can be evaluated, and that we have a function $f(x)$ which has the following properties:

$$f(x) \geq p(x) \quad \forall x \tag{8.18}$$

$$f(x) = Ah(x) \tag{8.19}$$

for some known (positive) constant A and density function h, so f has finite area. We suppose that random samples *can* be generated from h. Then to generate samples from p we use the following procedure:

1. Generate a value x from h.
2. Generate a value u from $U(0,1)$.
3. If $p(x)/f(x) \geq u$ then accept the sample x. Otherwise reject it.
4. Repeat from 1 until sufficiently many samples have been generated.

A simple geometric argument shows that this procedure generates samples from p. The probability density of sampling from any point x is given by $h(x)p(x)/h(x) = p(x)$, since the probability of accepting the sample in step 3 is $p(x)/Ah(x)$ and all the rejected samples are ignored. On average, about A samples from h are required for every sample from p.

It is easy to see that the better the match between p and f, the more samples will be accepted. Unfortunately, for neural networks and other models with many parameters, rejection sampling is not very effective. This is because it becomes harder to find a good dominating function f with reasonably small A because of the curse of dimensionality.

8.2.4 Importance Sampling

Equation (8.7) suggests that reducing the variance of the integrand at the sample points reduces the error in Monte Carlo integration; ideally, the integrand would be constant. Suppose that $f(x) = p(x) \cdot h(x)$ with $p(x) \geq 0$ and $h(x)$ 'near constant'. Then

$$\int_V f(x) \, dx = \int_V \left(\frac{f(x)}{p(x)} \right) p(x) \, dx = \int_V h(x)p(x) \, dx. \tag{8.20}$$

If we choose p to be a probability density function, called the *importance distribution*, then we can integrate f by averaging h with respect to p rather than averaging f from a uniform sample.

By the fundamental error formula for Monte Carlo integration in (8.7), we have

$$\int_V f(x)\,\mathrm{d}x = \int_V \frac{f(x)}{p(x)}p(x)\,\mathrm{d}V \approx \left\langle \frac{f}{p} \right\rangle \pm \sqrt{\frac{\left\langle \frac{f^2}{p^2} \right\rangle - \left\langle \frac{f}{p} \right\rangle^2}{N}}. \qquad (8.21)$$

To reduce the size of the error bars, we want $f(x)/p(x)$ as near constant as possible.

Of course, to make this method practical, we must choose p so that it is possible to sample from the underlying random variable. However, it is still the case that the better the match between the importance distribution and $|f|$, the lower the error in the Monte Carlo integral. Unfortunately, for many high-dimensional models such as neural networks, the distributions of interest are very narrowly peaked and correlated, while simple choices of the importance distribution tend to be rather broad and have spherical covariance. This means that importance sampling is usually not very effective for the integrals we are concerned with.

8.3 Markov Chain Sampling

The basic principle of Markov chain sampling is that each sample $x^{(n+1)}$ is generated from the previous sample $x^{(n)}$ by taking a step determined by a stochastic transition kernel $T(x^{(n+1)}|x^{(n)})$. We shall assume that the chain is *homogeneous*, which means that the kernel is fixed for all times t.

The Monte Carlo integration method still gives an unbiased estimate of (8.1) even when the $x^{(n)}$ are dependent, so long as the dependence is not too great. The effect of dependencies on the accuracy of a Monte Carlo estimate can be quantified in terms of the autocorrelations in the sequence $f(x^{(n)})$. If f has finite variance, then we know that the variance of the estimate of (8.1) is given by $\mathrm{var}[f]/N$ if the samples are independent. For large N and dependent samples, the variance is $\mathrm{var}[f]/(N/\tau)$, where

$$\tau = 1 + 2 \sum_{s=1}^{\infty} \rho(s), \qquad (8.22)$$

and $\rho(s)$ is the autocorrelation of $f(x^{(n)})$ at lag s (Neal, 1996). For MCMC methods, autocorrelations are usually positive, which increases the variance and thus increases the number of samples required to achieve a specified accuracy.

As it stands, it is unclear how the transition kernel T should be chosen to ensure that the random steps eventually sample from the distribution $\pi(x)$ we want. In the next section we discuss the fundamental properties of these Markov chains and how distributions of interest can arise in the limit of long sequences of samples. To avoid having to tangle with the complexities of measure theory, we mainly concentrate on discrete rather than continuous sample spaces to motivate the approach.

8.3.1 Markov Chain Fundamentals

Consider a set of random variables $X(n)$ for $n \in \mathbb{N}$. This process is Markov if

$$P(X(n_i) \leq x | X(n_1), \ldots, X(n_{i-1})) = P(X(n_i) \leq x | X(n_{i-1})), \qquad (8.23)$$

for all x and $n_1 < n_2 < \cdots < n_i$. This means that the state of the process at time n_i given values at times $n_1 < n_2 < \cdots < n_{i-1}$ depends only on the last value $X(n_{i-1})$.

If X is discrete (with the outcomes labelled by the integers) then we define the transition matrix $\boldsymbol{P} = (p_{ij})$ of probabilities:

$$p_{ij} = P(X(n+1) = j | X(n) = i). \qquad (8.24)$$

All entries in $\boldsymbol{P}$ lie between 0 and 1, and each row sums to 1. A state i is said to be *persistent* if

$$P(X(n) = i \text{ for some } n \geq 1 | X(1) = i) = 1 \qquad (8.25)$$

(i.e. eventual return to the state is certain). A persistent state is *non-null* if the expected return time μ_i is finite. A state is said to be *ergodic* if it is persistent, non-null and aperiodic (which means that the highest common factor of the return times is 1). An irreducible chain has a *stationary* distribution $\boldsymbol{\pi} = \boldsymbol{\pi P}$ if and only if all states are non-null persistent: in that case $\pi_i = \mu_i^{-1}$ where μ_i is the expected time to return to state i, from which we can see that the stationary distribution is unique. The chain will always converge to this distribution, though the length of time it takes to converge depends on the starting point; just as with optimisation, it pays to take some trouble over initialisation. When using MCMC it is normal to throw away the first part of the chain (known as the *burn in period*) so that samples are taken only from the stationary distribution. However, for most Markov chains there are no convergence tests that are both rigorous and practical, and we usually have to rely on more empirical methods.

For a finite sample space, the definition of the stationary distribution shows that it can be calculated as the eigenvector of $\boldsymbol{P}$ corresponding to an eigenvalue of 1. As an example, consider a two-state Markov chain with transition matrix

$$\boldsymbol{P} = \begin{pmatrix} \frac{1}{2} & \frac{1}{2} \\ \frac{1}{4} & \frac{3}{4} \end{pmatrix}. \qquad (8.26)$$

It is easy to check that this matrix has an eigenvector $\boldsymbol{\pi} = (1/3, 2/3)^T$ with eigenvalue 1. Thus the stationary distribution of this Markov chain is to spend $1/3$ of the time in state 1 and $2/3$ of the time in state 2. Figure 8.1 shows a

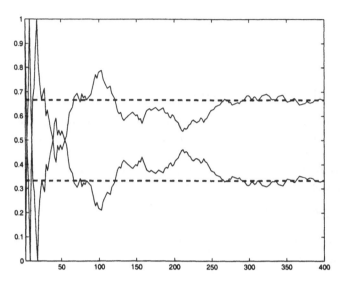

Fig. 8.1. Simulation from Markov chain with transition matrix P defined in (8.26). 400 samples were generated. The graph shows $P(1)$ and $P(2)$ averaged over the second half of the samples from $n = 2, \ldots, 400$. True values from the stationary distribution (1/3 and 2/3) are shown by dashed lines.

simulation from this Markov chain: after 400 iterations it has converged close to the stationary distribution.

Suppose that $\{X(n) : -\infty < n < \infty\}$ is an ergodic Markov chain with transition kernel P and stationary distribution π and also each $X(n)$ has distribution π for all $n \in (-\infty, \infty)$. Let $Y(n)$ denote the reversed chain $Y(n) = X(-n)$: we say that W is *time-reversible* if the transition matrices of X and Y are the same. It is easy to show (Grimmett and Stirzaker, 1992) that X is time-reversible if and only if

$$\pi_i p_{ij} = \pi_j p_{ji} \qquad \text{for all } i, j. \tag{8.27}$$

In this case, rather than solve the eigenproblem for the transition matrix P, it is sufficient to find a vector π that satisfies (8.27) and the usual conditions for a probability vector:

$$0 \leq \pi_i \leq 1 \qquad \text{and} \qquad \sum_i \pi_i = 1. \tag{8.28}$$

Of course, a discrete Markov chain is of relatively little use for sampling: if a distribution is defined on a finite space, it is very easy to sample from directly. However, this approach can be generalised to continuous spaces with suitable changes.

We define a Markov chain on a continuous space by the initial distribution for the first state, $x^{(1)}$, and a *transition density* $T(x^{(n+1)}|x^{(n)})$, which replaces the transition matrix. The definitions of recurrence, aperiodicity etc. can all be extended to the continuous case.

A density function π is the *stationary* (or *invariant*) distribution of the chain if

$$\pi(x') = \int T(x'|x)\pi(x) \, dx. \tag{8.29}$$

This property is implied by the stronger condition of *detailed balance* (which is the analogue of time-reversibility, (8.27)):

$$T(x'|x)\pi(x) = T(x|x')\pi(x'). \tag{8.30}$$

It is straightforward to prove that detailed balance implies that π is a stationary distribution for the Markov chain.

$$\int T(x'|x)\pi(x) \, dx = \int T(x|x')\pi(x') \, dx \tag{8.31}$$

$$= \pi(x') \int T(x|x') \, dx \tag{8.32}$$

$$= \pi(x'), \tag{8.33}$$

where (8.31) uses (8.30), (8.32) uses the fact that $\pi(x')$ is independent of the integrating variable x, and (8.33) follows since $T(x|x')$ is a density function for x and so integrates to 1. A chain satisfying detailed balance is said to be *reversible*.

Our aim is to define a Markov chain which has the distribution that we want to sample from as its stationary distribution, and is such that we can generate samples easily from the chain. For this it is important to be able to sample easily from the transition distribution T. Phrased like this, the problem seems hopeless: even if we could find such a Markov chain, it would seem likely that it would have to be very carefully tailored to the properties of the particular distribution $\pi(x)$. However, it is a remarkable fact that there are several general purpose methods for constructing Markov chains with a given stationary distribution. To construct such a chain we can combine several different transition kernels, since as long as each such transition leaves π invariant, the result of applying these transitions, either in a deterministic sequence or selected at random, will also leave π invariant. The next three sections describe three methods for constructing Markov chains with a prescribed stationary distribution.

8.3.2 Gibbs Sampling

This is the simplest MCMC sampling method. It is applicable when sampling from $\pi(x)$ directly is impossible, but it is possible to generate samples from the *conditional* distribution (under π) of one component of $x \in \mathbb{R}^m$ given values for all the other components. (This involves sampling from a one-dimensional distribution, and may in its turn require importance or rejection sampling to be used.) Given $x^{(n)}$, we generate $x^{(n+1)}$ using the following m steps:

- Sample $w_1^{(n+1)}$ from the conditional distribution of w_1 given $w_2^{(n)}, w_3^{(n)}$, $\ldots, w_m^{(n)}$.
- Sample $w_2^{(n+1)}$ from the conditional distribution of w_2 given $w_1^{(n+1)}, w_3^{(n)}$, $\ldots, w_m^{(n)}$.

    $\ldots$

- Sample $w_j^{(n+1)}$ from the conditional distribution of w_j given $w_1^{(n+1)}, \ldots$, $w_{j-1}^{(n)}, w_{j+1}^{(n+1)}, \ldots, w_m^{(n)}$.

    $\ldots$

- Sample $w_m^{(n+1)}$ from the conditional distribution of w_n given $w_1^{(n+1)}, \ldots$, $w_{n-1}^{(n)}$.

Note that the new value for w_j is used immediately when considering the conditional distribution for w_{j+1}.

This transition distribution leaves the desired distribution $\pi(x)$ invariant if all the steps making up each transition also leave π invariant. Since step j leaves w_k unchanged for $k \neq j$, the desired marginal distribution for these components is certainly invariant. Furthermore, the sample of x_j is taken from the correct conditional distribution. Together, these two properties ensure that if we started with a sample from the desired distribution, then the joint distribution of all the x_j after all m of the above steps must also be the desired distribution.

Whether this sampler is useful for Bayesian inference depends on whether it is reasonably easy to define and sample from the posterior distribution of one parameter conditional on the values of all the rest. For many statistical models this is the case. However, for neural networks, the posterior conditional distributions are extremely complex, and so Gibbs sampling cannot be used directly. However, it is often an appropriate way to sample hyperparameters, particularly when we assume that their distribution factorises.

Because Gibbs sampling depends on the form of the conditional densities of the form $\pi(x_1|x_2, \ldots, x_m)$ it is not easy to write a general purpose sampling algorithm using this approach. To do so requires a whole language to manipulate densities to be available and is outside the scope of NETLAB. The BUGS software toolkit (Thomas *et al.*, 1992) provides such a framework to support Gibbs sampling for a range of statistical models.

8.3.3 Metropolis–Hastings Algorithm

Theory

In the Markov chain defined by the Metropolis–Hastings algorithm, a new state $x^{(n+1)}$ is generated from the old state $x^{(n)}$ by first (stochastically) generating a *candidate state* from a *proposal distribution*, and then deciding whether or not to accept the candidate state. If it is accepted, then $x^{(n+1)}$ is made equal to the candidate state, otherwise the new state is the same as the previous state. The details of this process are as follows:

1. Generate the candidate state x^* with density given by the proposal distribution $S(x^*|x^{(n)})$. Note that the proposal distribution typically depends on the old state; for example, it may be a Gaussian centred on $x^{(n)}$.
2. If $\pi(x^*) \geq \pi(x^{(n)})$, then accept the candidate state. If $\pi(x^*) < \pi(x^{(n)})$, then accept the candidate state with probability $\pi(x^*)/\pi(x^{(n)})$.
3. If the candidate state is accepted, let $x^{(n+1)} = x^*$. If the candidate state is rejected, let $x^{(n+1)} = x^{(n)}$.

In this version of the algorithm, the proposal distribution must satisfy a symmetry condition

$$S(x'|x) = S(x|x'). \tag{8.34}$$

Often we will define an 'energy' or 'cost' function E as the negative log likelihood, so $p(x) \propto \exp(-E(x))$. Then the test for acceptance can be rephrased as always accepting candidate states with lower energy, but only accepting candidate states of higher energy with probability $\exp(-(E(x^*) - E(x^{(n)})))$.

For non-symmetric proposal distributions, detailed balance can be maintained by modifying the acceptance criterion 2 in the list above to give the *Metropolis–Hastings* algorithm (Hastings, 1970).

a If $E(x^{(n+1)}) < E(x^{(n)})$ then accept $x^{(n+1)}$.
b If $E(x^{(n+1)}) > E(x^{(n)})$ then accept $x^{(n+1)}$ with probability

$$\exp\left\{E(x^{(n)}) - E(x^{(n+1)}))\right\} \frac{S(x^{(n)}, x^{(n+1)})}{S(x^{(n+1)}, x^{(n)})}. \tag{8.35}$$

To show that these transitions leave π invariant, we first need to work out the transition density function. This density function is singular, since there is a non-zero point probability mass that the new state will be the same as the old state. Luckily the detailed balance condition (8.30) need only be verified for transitions that change the state. For $x' \neq x$, the transition density for the Metropolis–Hastings algorithm is given by

$$T(x'|x) = S(x'|x) \min\left(1, \frac{\pi(x')}{\pi(x)}\right). \tag{8.36}$$

Then detailed balance can be verified as follows:

$$T(x'|x)\pi(x) = S(x'|x) \min\left(1, \frac{\pi(x')}{\pi(x)}\right)\pi(x)$$

$$= S(x'|x) \min(\pi(x), \pi(x'))$$

$$= S(x|x') \min(\pi(x'), \pi(x)) \quad \text{by symmetry of } S$$

$$= S(x|x') \min\left(1, \frac{\pi(x)}{\pi(x')}\right)\pi(x')$$

$$= T(x|x')\pi(x').$$

Although π is guaranteed to be invariant, we must check if the chain is ergodic. This depends on the details of π and on the S.

There are many possible proposal distributions that can be used. One simple choice is a Gaussian distribution centred on $x^{(n)}$, with standard deviation chosen so that the probability of the candidate state being accepted is reasonably high (which usually means that the standard deviation should not be too large). A very low acceptance rate means that states are often repeated, leading to high values of the autocorrelation. However, although a small standard deviation will usually improve the acceptance rate, it also leads to a high degree of dependence between successive states, since many steps are needed to move a substantial distance. This problem is made worse by the fact that these movements take the form of a random walk, rather than a systematic exploration of the distribution. (Note that the proposal distribution does not depend on π.) If there are strong correlations in the distribution that we wish to sample from (and there commonly are for neural networks) then 'most' random steps will try to climb the side of the valley walls. Thus, although the Metropolis–Hastings algorithm is feasible for small neural networks, it breaks down for networks of more reasonable size.

Implementation

The Metropolis–Hastings algorithm is implemented in NETLAB by the function metrop, whose interface is similar to that used by the optimisers, using an options vector to control its operation. In addition, it is possible to set and save the state of the sampler in a similar way to the MATLAB functions rand and randn.

The program fragment

```
s = metrop('state');
```

returns a state structure that contains the state of the two random number generators rand and randn that uniquely define the state of the Metropolis–

Hastings sampler. These states are contained in fields s.randstate and s.randnstate. The sub-function get_state stores the information.

The program fragment

```
metrop('state', s);
```

resets the state to s. If s is an integer, then it is passed to rand and randn. This is useful to set the initial state of the sampler. If s is a structure returned by a call to metrop then the generator is reset to exactly the same state. This is performed by the sub-function set_state.

To generate samples from the function, an error (energy) function (such as neterr), an initial state x and an options vector are needed. An error gradient function is not required and the argument gradf is ignored. It is only included to make the interface the same as other samplers (such as hmc) and the optimisation functions.

```
 1  function [samples, energies, diagn] = metrop(f, x, options, ...
 2                                      gradf, varargin)
 3  if nargin <= 2
 4    if ~strcmp(f, 'state')
 5      error('Unknown argument to metrop');
 6    end
 7    switch nargin
 8      case 1
 9        % Return state of sampler
10        samples = get_state(f);    % Function defined below
11        return;
12      case 2
13        % Set the state of the sampler
14        set_state(f, x);           % Function defined below
15        return;
16    end
17  end
18
19  display = options(1);
20  if options(14) > 0
21    nsamples = options(14);
22  else
23    nsamples = 100;
24  end
25  if options(15) >= 0
26    nomit = options(15);
27  else
28    nomit = 0;
29  end
30  if options(18) > 0.0
31    std_dev = sqrt(options(18));
32  else
33    std_dev = 1.0;   % default
34  end
35  nparams = length(x);
36
37  % Set up string for evaluating potential function.
```

```
38  f = fcnchk(f, length(varargin));
39
40  samples = zeros(nsamples, nparams); % Matrix of returned samples.
41  if nargout >= 2
42    en_save = 1;
43    energies = zeros(nsamples, 1);
44  else
45    en_save = 0;
46  end
47  if nargout >= 3
48    diagnostics = 1;
49    diagn_pos = zeros(nsamples, nparams);
50    diagn_acc = zeros(nsamples, 1);
51  else
52    diagnostics = 0;
53  end
54
55  % Main loop.
56  k = - nomit + 1;
57  Eold = feval(f, x, varargin{:});      % Evaluate initial energy.
58  nreject = 0;                          % Count of rejected states.
59  while k <= nsamples
60
61    xold = x;
62    % Sample a new point from the proposal distribution
63    x = xold + randn(1, nparams)*std_dev;
64
65    % Now apply Metropolis algorithm.
66    Enew = feval(f, x, varargin{:});      % Evaluate new energy.
67    a = exp(Eold - Enew);                 % Acceptance threshold.
68    if (diagnostics & k > 0)
69      diagn_pos(k,:) = x;
70      diagn_acc(k,:) = a;
71    end
72    if (display > 1)
73      fprintf(1, 'New position is\n');
74      disp(x);
75    end
76
77    if a > rand(1)         % Accept the new state.
78      Eold = Enew;
79      if (display > 0)
80        fprintf(1, 'Finished step %4d  Threshold: %g\n', k, a);
81      end
82    else                   % Reject the new state
83      if k > 0
84        nreject = nreject + 1;
85      end
86      x = xold;    % Reset position
87      if (display > 0)
88        fprintf(1, ' Sample rejected %4d. Threshold: %g\n', k, a);
89      end
90    end
```

```
91    if k > 0
92      samples(k,:) = x;                    % Store sample.
93      if en_save
94        energies(k) = Eold;                % Store energy.
95      end
96    end
97    k = k + 1;
98  end
99
100 if (display > 0)
101   fprintf(1, '\nFraction of samples rejected:  %g\n', ...
102           nreject/(nsamples));
103 end
104
105 if diagnostics
106   diagn.pos = diagn_pos;
107   diagn.acc = diagn_acc;
108 end
109
110 % Return complete state of the sampler.
111 function state = get_state(f)
112
113 state.randstate = rand('state');
114 state.randnstate = randn('state');
115 return
116
117 % Set state of sampler, either from full state, or an integer
118 function set_state(f, x)
119
120 if isnumeric(x)
121   rand('state', x);
122   randn('state', x);
123 else
124   if ~isstruct(x)
125     error('Second argument to metrop must be number or ...
126       state structure');
127   end
128   if (~isfield(x, 'randstate') | ~isfield(x, 'randnstate'))
129     error('Second argument to metrop must contain correct fields')
130   end
131   rand('state', x.randstate);
132   randn('state', x.randnstate);
133 end
134 return
```

After some housekeeping at the start of the function, the important options are acted on. The number of states in the burn in period is contained in options(15) (lines 25–29). The variance of the proposal distribution is contained in options(18) (lines 30–34); the distribution is taken to be Gaussian with spherical covariance, which assumes that all variables have the same scale (see Exercise 8.8).

The first return value is the matrix of states from the Markov chain (ignoring the burn in period). Lines 41–46 test whether the energies of these states should also be returned as a second value, while lines 47–53 test whether further diagnostic information is required:

- `diagn.pos` contains each state of the chain, whether or not it is accepted.
- `diagn.acc` contains the acceptance threshold $\exp(-(E(x^*) - E(x^{(n)})))$ for each state of the chain.

The loop counter variable k is then initialised in line 56 to `options(15)` – 1 so that when it reaches the value `options(14)`, sampling is complete, including the burn in.

The main sampling loop starts at line 59. A new sample point is generated from the proposal distribution on line 63. Lines 66–67 calculate the acceptance threshold probability a. This is compared with a single sample from $U(0, 1)$ on line 77: thus the new point is accepted with probability a. In lines 78–81 the chain is updated for a new accepted state, while lines 83–89 do the same thing for a rejected state; the state variable x is returned to its old value, and the number of rejected states is incremented provided burn in is finished.

8.3.4 Hybrid Monte Carlo

This algorithm combines the Metropolis–Hastings algorithm with sampling techniques based on dynamical simulation. This allows us to incorporate gradient information from π, the distribution of interest, which is used to bias the directions in which we move. This information can be calculated relatively easily for neural networks using error back-propagation. The original algorithm is due to Duane et al. (1987), and our treatment follows that of Neal (1996).

Reformulation of the Problem

In order to incorporate gradient information into our sampling procedure, it turns out to be useful to reformulate the problem as one of analytical mechanics, which is a way of analysing arbitrary mechanical systems in terms of a single function, the *Hamiltonian*. We sample from the *canonical* (or *Boltzmann*) distribution for the state of a hypothetical physical system defined in terms of a given energy function (which corresponds to the negative log likelihood of the data).

We consider the variable $x \in \mathbb{R}^m$ as denoting a position vector for the corresponding physical system so that it represents the positions of all the particles. The probability density for this variable under the canonical distribution is defined by

$$\pi(x) \propto \exp(-E(x)),$$

(8.37)

where $E(x)$ represents the 'potential energy' of the particles. Any probability density that is nowhere zero can be put in this form by defining

$$E(x) = -\log \pi(x) - \log Z, \tag{8.38}$$

for any convenient value Z. This means that we can use an un-normalised likelihood in the hybrid Monte Carlo algorithm since Z does not have to be the normalisation constant. This is very important, since the normalisation constant is often unknown, and computing it involves integrating the likelihood function.

To model the dynamics of the system, we create a 'momentum' variable p, which also has m real-valued components p_i. The canonical distribution over the space of x and p together is defined to be

$$p(x, p) \propto \exp(-H(x, p)), \tag{8.39}$$

where $H(x, p) = E(x) + K(p)$ is the Hamiltonian function giving the total energy of the system. Here $K(p)$ is the 'kinetic energy', which can be computed from the momentum by the usual formula from mechanics (think of momentum of a particle as Mv and its kinetic energy as $Mv^2/2$):

$$K(p) = \sum_{i=1}^{m} \frac{p_i^2}{2M_i}, \tag{8.40}$$

where M_i is the 'mass' associated with the ith component. Adjustment of these masses can improve sampling efficiency, but we shall assume that they are all one in the basic algorithm. Giving them distinct values is equivalent to choosing different step sizes for each component.

In the distribution defined in (8.39), x and p are independent, and the marginal distribution of x is the same as that in (8.37). We shall generate samples by defining a Markov chain that converges to the canonical distribution $p(x, p)$ and then simply ignore the values of p and generate samples using x. Although it might appear that we have made the problem more complex by doubling the dimensionality of the space from which we must sample, in fact this is more than compensated by the avoidance of random walk behaviour. In particular, the dynamics of the system are influenced by the gradient of the potential energy (i.e. the gradient of the log-likelihood), which means that exploration of the sample space is more focused on regions of higher likelihood than with completely stochastic transition kernels such as the Metropolis–Hastings algorithm.

Stochastic Dynamics

In the stochastic dynamics method, sampling from $p(x, p)$ is performed in two parts: sampling from the values of x and p at a fixed total energy $H(x, p)$, and sampling states with different values of H.

Sampling at a fixed value of H is done by simulating the dynamics of the system, in which the state evolves in a fictitious continuous 'time', t, according to the dynamical equations

$$\frac{\mathrm{d}x_i}{\mathrm{d}t} = +\frac{\partial H}{\partial p_i} = \frac{p_i}{M_i} \tag{8.41}$$

$$\frac{\mathrm{d}p_i}{\mathrm{d}t} = -\frac{\partial H}{\partial x_i} = -\frac{\partial E}{\partial x_i}. \tag{8.42}$$

In order to use this approach, we must be able to compute the partial derivatives of E with respect to the components x_i. For a statistical model, this amounts to computing the derivative of the log likelihood with respect to the parameters. Once the simulation is complete, we obtain a new position variable x and momentum p.

There are three crucial properties of Hamiltonian dynamics that we make use of:

1. H is constant as x and p vary:

$$\frac{\mathrm{d}H}{\mathrm{d}t} = \sum_i \left[\frac{\partial H}{\partial x_i} \frac{\mathrm{d}x_i}{\mathrm{d}t} + \frac{\partial H}{\partial p_i} \frac{\mathrm{d}p_i}{\mathrm{d}t} \right] = \sum_i \left[\frac{\partial H}{\partial x_i} \frac{\partial H}{\partial p_i} - \frac{\partial H}{\partial p_i} \frac{\partial H}{\partial x_i} \right] = 0. \tag{8.43}$$

2. Hamiltonian dynamics are volume preserving. If the points in some region, of volume V, follow a trajectory according to the dynamical equations, we find that the region where these points finish also has volume V.

3. The dynamics are time-reversible. After following the dynamics forwards for t time units, we can recover the original state by following the dynamics backward in time for t.

These properties imply that the distribution of x and p is invariant with respect to (deterministic) transitions that consist of following a trajectory for a certain period of time using Hamiltonian dynamics. The probability that the system is in some region after the transition is the same as the probability that we started in the corresponding region (of equal volume) found by reversing the dynamics.

By taking enough samples from this simulation, we will eventually explore the whole space with a given value of H. Such transitions are not sufficient to produce an ergodic Markov chain, since the value of H does not change. In order to correct this, we alternate deterministic dynamical transitions and stochastic Gibbs sampling updates of the momentum p. Since x and p are independent, the conditional distribution of p is the same as the marginal distribution. Thus p may be updated by drawing a new value with probability density proportional to $\exp(-K(p))$. For the quadratic kinetic energy function of (8.40), this is easy since the p_i have independent Gaussian distributions. Updates of p will usually change the total energy H, and thus the whole space can be explored.

In practice, the dynamics cannot be simulated exactly, as they are based on differential equations, but are approximated using time steps of finite size using a very simple approach similar to Euler's method for solving differential equations. In the *leapfrog* method, approximations $\hat{x}$ and $\hat{p}$ to the true position and momentum are updated as follows:

$$\hat{p}_i\left(t + \frac{\epsilon}{2}\right) = \hat{p}_i(t) - \frac{\epsilon}{2}\frac{\partial E}{\partial x_i}(\hat{x}(t)) \tag{8.44}$$

$$\hat{x}_i(t + \epsilon) = \hat{x}_i(t) + \epsilon\frac{\hat{p}_i(t + \frac{\epsilon}{2})}{M_i} \tag{8.45}$$

$$\hat{p}_i(t + \epsilon) = \hat{p}_i\left(t + \frac{\epsilon}{2}\right) - \frac{\epsilon}{2}\frac{\partial E}{\partial x_i}(\hat{x}(t + \epsilon)). \tag{8.46}$$

This iteration consists of a half step for the $\hat{p}_i$, a full step for the $\hat{x}_i$ and another half step for the $\hat{p}_i$. To model the dynamics, we choose a value of ϵ (the time step size) that is sufficiently small and then we apply the updates defined by (8.44)–(8.46) for L iterations. In this procedure, the last half step for $\hat{p}_i$ in one iteration is immediately followed by the first half step for $\hat{p}_i$ in the next iteration. Inspecting the equations carefully, we see that, except for the very first and last half steps, these half steps can be merged into full steps starting at $t + m\epsilon + \epsilon/2$, which 'leapfrog' over the steps for $\hat{w}_i$ starting at $t + \epsilon$. This is illustrated in Fig. 8.2.

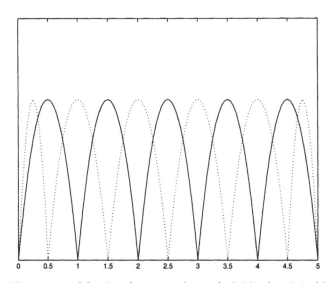

Fig. 8.2. Illustration of five leapfrog steps for $\hat{w}_i$ (*solid line*) and $\hat{p}_i$ (*dotted line*).

In this discretisation of the dynamics, phase space volume is preserved and the dynamics can be reversed (properties 2 and 3 above), but the value of H is no longer guaranteed to remain constant, because of the truncation error introduced by approximating the derivatives over each time interval of length ϵ with a constant value. Because of this, the sample has a systematic error which goes to zero only when $\epsilon \to 0$.

Hybrid Monte Carlo Algorithm

In the hybrid Monte Carlo (HMC) algorithm of Duane *et al.* (1987), the systematic error of the stochastic dynamics method is eliminated by merging it with the Metropolis algorithm. As before, stochastic transitions use Gibbs sampling to update the momentum values. The dynamical transitions of HMC are similar to those for the stochastic dynamics method, but with two changes:

1. A random decision is made for each transition whether to simulate the dynamics forward or backward in time.
2. The point reached at the end of the dynamics is only a *candidate* for a new state, to be accepted or rejected based on the change in total energy H just as in the Metropolis–Hastings algorithm. If the dynamics were simulated precisely, then H would be constant and the new point would always be accepted. Because of the discretisation, H will probably change, and therefore some moves may be rejected: these rejections exactly eliminate the bias introduced by the non-zero step size in the dynamical simulation.

Once the step size ϵ and number of iterations L are fixed, a dynamical transition consists of the following steps:

1. Randomly choose a direction $\lambda \in \{-1, +1\}$ with equal probability for the trajectory, where $+1$ represents a forward trajectory. Both directions are equally likely.
2. Starting from the current state $(x, p) = (\hat{x}(0), \hat{p}(0))$, carry out L leapfrog iterations with a step size of $\lambda\epsilon$, resulting in the candidate state $(\hat{x}(\lambda\epsilon L), \hat{p}(\lambda\epsilon L)) = (x^*, p^*)$.
3. Accept the candidate state with probability

$$\min(1, \exp(-(H(x^*, p^*) - H(x, p)))). \qquad (8.47)$$

If the candidate state is rejected, then the new state will be the old state (x, p).

The preservation of phase space volume by the dynamics, together with the random choice of λ ensures that the proposal of candidate moves is symmetric, as required for the Metropolis–Hastings sampler. The values for ϵ and L may be chosen at random from some fixed distribution. To avoid periodic

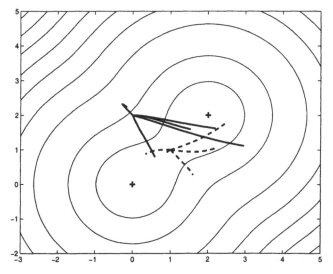

Fig. 8.3. HMC dynamical simulation. Target distribution is a mixture of spherical Gaussians with two centres (*plus signs*) and log probability contours (*thin lines*). Dynamical transitions are shown with five different random initial momenta starting from $(0,2)$ (*thick solid line*) and $(1,1)$ (*thick dashed line*).

return to regions that will interfere with ergodicity, it is usual to randomly perturb the step length ϵ by a small amount, but periodicity is rarely a problem in practice for continuous state spaces.

It is best to use trajectories that result in relatively large changes in x. This reduces the correlation between successive samples and avoids the random walk effects that would result from resampling the momentum too frequently; it is precisely this effect that we are trying to avoid by using gradient information and dynamic simulation. A single step taken with random initial momenta is similar to a single step in the Metropolis–Hastings algorithm. Trajectories should be long enough so that they typically lead to states distant from their starting point, but no longer. Shorter trajectories lead to random walk behaviour, while longer trajectories would wastefully curve back on themselves. Fig. 8.3 shows how the trajectories move to regions of high probability: if the initial momentum moves 'uphill', then the path will curve back downhill. One way to achieve long trajectories is to increase the number of steps L. Although this can increase the accumulated error in H, in practice the value of H oscillates in a random walk along the trajectory (because there is usually no systematic value for the approximation error in (8.44), (8.45) and (8.46)), and the acceptance rate is almost independent of L. The penalty for increasing L is that we have to take more steps between each sample, and each step requires the calculation of an error gradient at a new point in sample space. For a neural network, each error gradient computation requires a forward and backward pass over the entire dataset, which is the same as a single iteration of an optimisation algorithm.

An alternative to increasing L and still achieve long trajectories is to make ϵ bigger. For step sizes greater than a certain critical value, the leapfrog discretisation becomes unstable (just as it does for Euler's method (Kincaid and Cheney, 1996)) and the error in H can become very large. In this case the acceptance rate drops to an unacceptable value. The optimal strategy is to select a step size just below the point of instability.

Another way to avoid increasing L (and thus evaluating the gradient many times per sample) and yet avoid random walk behaviour is to allow the motion to *persist*. Instead of choosing a random momentum variable p at the end of every trajectory, the new momentum is a weighted sum of the old value and a random component, as proposed by Horowitz (1991). This means that if states are accepted, then motion on the next dynamic simulation will tend to be in a similar direction. This helps move towards modes of the distribution. However, some care is needed to preserve the canonical distribution π; Neal (1996) describes the following algorithm:

1. The momentum update is given by

$$p_i' = \alpha p_i + \sqrt{1 - \alpha_i^2} n_i, \qquad (8.48)$$

   where n_i is sampled from a Gaussian random variable with zero mean and variance M_i. The parameter α determines the degree of persistence and must lie between 0 and 1. The closer α is to 1, the more persistent the motion.

2. Perform a dynamical transition using L leapfrog steps in a forward direction (i.e. set $\lambda = 1$) to a state $(\hat{x}, \hat{p})$.

3. Negate the momentum variables to produce a candidate state $(x^*, p^*) = (\hat{x}, -\hat{p})$. Accept this state with probability

$$\min(1, \exp(-(H(x^*, p^*) - H(x, p)))). \qquad (8.49)$$

4. Negate the momentum variables whether or not the candidate state is accepted.

The negation of momentum in both steps 3 and 4 is essential to ensure that the canonical distribution is invariant for the chain. Note that if the candidate state is rejected, then the new direction will reverse (or at least will have a strong reverse component from momentum). Thus many rejected states will lead to many trajectory reversals and a return to random walk behaviour. It is therefore important to have a high acceptance rate: this may be achieved by using a shorter trajectory than for 'vanilla' hybrid Monte Carlo.

Hybrid Monte Carlo Implementation

The NETLAB function hmc implements the hybrid Monte Carlo algorithm both with and without momentum persistence. As with the Metropolis–

Hastings implementation `metrop`, it is possible to set and save the state of the sampler, allowing complete reproducibility of experiments. In this case the state contains not only the state of the MATLAB functions `rand` and `randn` but also the momentum vector p, which is required if persistence is used. This is saved in the global variable `HMC_MOM` after each call to `hmc` (line 166), so that it can be accessed by the sub-function `get_state`.

```
1   function [samples, energies, diagn] = hmc(f, x, options, gradf,...
2                                           varargin)
3   % Global variable to store state of momentum variables.
4   % Set by set_state. Used to initialise variable if set.
5   global HMC_MOM
6   if nargin <= 2
7     if ~strcmp(f, 'state')
8       error('Unknown argument to hmc');
9     end
10    switch nargin
11      case 1
12        samples = get_state(f);
13        return;
14      case 2
15        set_state(f, x);
16        return;
17    end
18  end
19
20  display = options(1);
21  if (round(options(5) == 1))
22    persistence = 1;
23    % Set alpha to lie in [0, 1)
24    alpha = max(0, options(17));
25    alpha = min(1, alpha);
26    salpha = sqrt(1-alpha*alpha);
27  else
28    persistence = 0;
29  end
30  L = max(1, options(7)); % At least one step in leap-frogging
31  if options(14) > 0
32    nsamples = options(14);
33  else
34    nsamples = 100;        % Default
35  end
36  if options(15) >= 0
37    nomit = options(15);
38  else
39    nomit = 0;
40  end
41  if options(18) > 0
42    step_size = options(18);        % Step size.
43  else
44    step_size = 1/L;        % Default
45  end
46  x = x(:)';                % Force x to be a row vector
```

```
47  nparams = length(x);
48
49  % Set up strings for evaluating function and its gradient.
50  f = fcnchk(f, length(varargin));
51  gradf = fcnchk(gradf, length(varargin));
52
53  % Check the gradient evaluation.
54  if (options(9))
55    % Check gradients
56    feval('gradchek', x, f, gradf, varargin{:});
57  end
58
59  samples = zeros(nsamples, nparams);
60  if nargout >= 2
61    en_save = 1;
62    energies = zeros(nsamples, 1);
63  else
64    en_save = 0;
65  end
66  if nargout >= 3
67    diagnostics = 1;
68    diagn_pos = zeros(nsamples, nparams);
69    diagn_mom = zeros(nsamples, nparams);
70    diagn_acc = zeros(nsamples, 1);
71  else
72    diagnostics = 0;
73  end
74
75  n = - nomit + 1;
76  Eold = feval(f, x, varargin{:});  % Evaluate initial energy.
77  nreject = 0;
78  if (~persistence | isempty(HMC_MOM))
79    p = randn(1, nparams);  % Initialise momenta at random
80  else
81    p = HMC_MOM;                   % Initialise momenta from stored state
82  end
83  lambda = 1;
84
85  while n <= nsamples
86
87    xold = x;                 % Store starting position.
88    pold = p;                 % Store starting momenta
89    Hold = Eold + 0.5*(p*p'); % Recompute H as momenta have changed
90
91    if ~persistence
92      % Choose a direction at random
93      if (rand < 0.5)
94        lambda = -1;
95      else
96        lambda = 1;
97      end
98    end
99    % Perturb step length.
```

```
100     epsilon = lambda*step_size*(1.0 + 0.1*randn(1));
101
102     % First half-step of leapfrog.
103     p = p - 0.5*epsilon*feval(gradf, x, varargin{:});
104     x = x + epsilon*p;
105
106     % Full leapfrog steps.
107     for m = 1 : L - 1
108       p = p - epsilon*feval(gradf, x, varargin{:});
109       x = x + epsilon*p;
110     end
111
112     % Final half-step of leapfrog.
113     p = p - 0.5*epsilon*feval(gradf, x, varargin{:});
114
115     % Now apply Metropolis algorithm.
116     Enew = feval(f, x, varargin{:});        % Evaluate new energy.
117     p = -p;                                 % Negate momentum
118     Hnew = Enew + 0.5*p*p';                 % Evaluate new H.
119     a = exp(Hold - Hnew);                   % Acceptance threshold.
120     if (diagnostics & n > 0)
121       diagn_pos(n,:) = x;
122       diagn_mom(n,:) = p;
123       diagn_acc(n,:) = a;
124     end
125     if (display > 1)
126       fprintf(1, 'New position is\n');
127       disp(x);
128     end
129
130     if a > rand(1)                          % Accept the new state.
131       Eold = Enew;                          % Update energy
132       if (display > 0)
133         fprintf(1, 'Finished step %4d  Threshold: %g\n', n, a);
134       end
135     else                                    % Reject the new state.
136       if n > 0
137         nreject = nreject + 1;
138       end
139       x = xold;                             % Reset position
140       p = pold;                             % Reset momenta
141       if (display > 0)
142         fprintf(1, ' Sample rejected %4d. Threshold: %g\n', n, a);
143       end
144     end
145     if n > 0
146       samples(n,:) = x;                     % Store sample.
147       if en_save
148         energies(n) = Eold;                 % Store energy.
149       end
150     end
151
152     % Set momenta for next iteration
```

```
153    if persistence
154      p = -p;
155      % Adjust momenta by a small random amount.
156      p = alpha.*p + salpha.*randn(1, nparams);
157    . else
158      p = randn(1, nparams);        % Replace all momenta.
159    end
160
161    n = n + 1;
162  end
163
164  if (display > 0)
165    fprintf(1, '\nFraction of samples rejected:  %g\n', ...
166      nreject/(nsamples));
167  end
168  if diagnostics
169    diagn.pos = diagn_pos;
170    diagn.mom = diagn_mom;
171    diagn.acc = diagn_acc;
172  end
173  % Store final momentum value in global to retrieve it later
174  HMC_MOM = p;
175  return
176
177  % Return complete state of sampler (including momentum)
178  function state = get_state(f)
179
180  global HMC_MOM
181  state.randstate = rand('state');
182  state.randnstate = randn('state');
183  state.mom = HMC_MOM;
184  return
185
186  % Set complete state of sampler (including momentum) or
187  % just set randn and rand with integer argument.
188  function set_state(f, x)
189
190  global HMC_MOM
191  if isnumeric(x)
192    rand('state', x);
193    randn('state', x);
194    HMC_MOM = [];
195  else
196    if ~isstruct(x)
197      error('Second argument must be number or state structure');
198    end
199    if (~isfield(x, 'randstate') | ~isfield(x, 'randnstate') ...
200        | ~isfield(x, 'mom'))
201      error('Second argument to hmc must contain correct fields')
202    end
203    rand('state', x.randstate);
204    randn('state', x.randnstate);
205    HMC_MOM = x.mom;
```

```
206  end
207  return
```

The first block of code (lines 6–18) is concerned with initialising and resetting the state of the sampler, and works in similar fashion to metrop. In lines 21–26, options(5) is checked to see if persistence is being used: if it is, the parameter α is taken from options(17), and the variable salpha is set to $\sqrt{1 - \alpha^2}$. L, the number of leapfrog steps, is taken from options(7) (line 30), and the burn in period from options(15) (lines 36–40). The step size ϵ is read from options(18), or set to $1/L$ by default. The last of the initial housekeeping is to check the function string (lines 50–51) and to check the gradient numerically (lines 54–57) just as in the optimisation routines.

The main loop counter is initialised taking account of the burn in period on line 75, and the initial energy computed on line 76. The momentum variable p is initialised in lines 78–82; this is random unless the global variable HMC_MOM has been set by a previous call to set_state.

At the start of the main loop the position vector x and the momentum vector p are saved in case the candidate state is rejected. Since the momentum changes at every iteration (except for the degenerate case of persistence with $\alpha = 1$), the Hamiltonian Hold is recalculated (line 89). In lines 91–100 the step for this iteration is chosen, incorporating a random choice of direction (lambda; see step 1 of the dynamical simulation algorithm) and a random perturbation of the step size. Lines 103–104 implement the first half leapfrog step, lines 107–110 the $L - 1$ full leapfrog steps, and line 113 the final half step. This sequence generates the new state pair x and p.

Because H may not be preserved by the discretised dynamics, we now apply the Metropolis–Hastings test. The new energy Enew ($E(x^*)$) is evaluated (line 116) and the momentum negated, as required in step 3 of the persistence algorithm. This makes no difference to the new value of H (line 118), since that involves p only through a weighted sum of p_i^2, and doesn't affect the next iteration of the standard algorithm, since that replaces the momentum variable completely. However, it is necessary for the persistence method. Lines 119 and 130–144 apply the Metropolis–Hastings test to decide whether or not to accept the candidate state. The final part of the loop calculates the momentum variable to be used in the next iteration; with persistence (lines 154–156) or without (line 158).

8.4 Demonstration Programs

In this section we shall describe just two of the demonstration programs of Markov Chain sampling; applications to Bayesian inference are discussed in Chapter 9.

8.4.1 Metropolis–Hastings Sampling

In this demonstration, the Metropolis–Hastings algorithm is used to sample from a two-dimensional Gaussian distribution. Of course, the NETLAB function gsamp can be used to sample much more efficiently from such a distribution, but this toy example is used to show that Markov Chain sampling does converge to a reasonable sample from the intended distribution. The following function is a simplified version of demmet1.

```
1   function demmet1(plot_wait)
2
3   if nargin == 0 | plot_wait < 0
4     plot_wait = 0;        % No wait if not specified or incorrect
5   end
6   dim = 2;                % Data dimension
7   ncentres = 1;           % Number of centres in mixture model
8
9   seed = 42;              % Seed for random weight initialization.
10  randn('state', seed);
11  rand('state', seed);
12
13  % Set up mixture model to sample from
14  mix = gmm(dim, ncentres, 'spherical');
15  mix.centres(1, :) = [0 0];
16  x = [0 4]; % Start vector
17
18  % Set up vector of options for hybrid Monte Carlo.
19  nsamples = 150;         % Number of retained samples.
20
21  options = foptions;     % Default options vector.
22  options(1) = 0;         % Switch off diagnostics.
23  options(14) = nsamples; % Number of Monte Carlo samples returned.
24  options(18) = 0.1;
25  [samples, energies] = metrop('dempot', x, options, '', mix);
26
27  fh1 = figure;
28  g1end = floor(nsamples/4);
29
30  for n = 1:nsamples
31    if n < g1end
32      Marker = 'k.';
33      p1 = plot(samples(n,1), samples(n,2), Marker, ...
34        'EraseMode', 'none', 'MarkerSise', 12);
35      if n == 1
36        axis([-3 5 -2 5])
37      end
38    else
39      Marker = 'r.';
40      p2 = plot(samples(n,1), samples(n,2), Marker, ...
41        'EraseMode', 'none', 'MarkerSize', 12);
42    end
43    hold on
44    drawnow;  % Force drawing immediately
```

```
45    pause(plot_wait);
46    end
```

This program shows how easy it is to use the sampling functions in NET-LAB. After the initial housekeeping (lines 1–11), a Gaussian mixture model is created (lines 14–15) with one centre at $(0,0)$ and variance of 1. This is the target distribution. The starting point for the Markov Chain is $(0,4)$ (line 16); this is chosen in order to show how the chain explores the state space. 150 samples are generated (line 19).

Just five lines are needed to generate the samples: lines 21–24 set up the options vector (line 24 sets the variance of the proposal distribution to 0.1); line 25 creates the sample. The function dempot computes the energy function $E = -\log p(x)$ under the Gaussian mixture model:

```
1    function e = dempot(x, mix)
2    e = -log(gmmprob(mix, x));
```

The remainder of the program creates a scatter plot of the sample: the first quarter in black (lines 32–37) and the remainder in red (lines 38–42). This plot shows the path of the chain in sample space and demonstrates that the chain converges after the first quarter of the sample. Figure 8.4 illustrates this process; the first quarter of the sample is from the burn in period, while the other groups of samples are clustered around the mean of the target distribution.

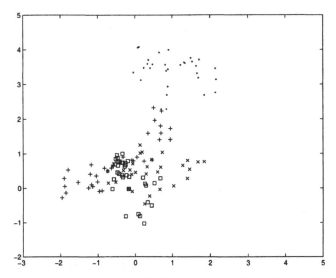

Fig. 8.4. Demonstration of Metropolis–Hastings algorithm. Target distribution is $N(0,1)$. Samples are shown in groups: first quarter (*dots*), second quarter (*plus signs*), third quarter (*crosses*), fourth quarter (*squares*).

8.4.2 Hybrid Monte Carlo Sampling

The first demonstration program for HMC, demhmc1, samples from a two-dimensional mixture of two Gaussians.

```
 1  dim = 2;                 % Data dimension
 2  ncentres = 2;            % Number of centres in mixture model
 3
 4  seed = 42;               % Seed for random weight initialisation
 5  randn('state', seed);
 6  rand('state', seed);
 7
 8  % Set up mixture model to sample from
 9  mix = gmm(dim, ncentres, 'spherical');
10  mix.centres(1, :) = [0 0];
11  mix.centres(2, :) = [2 2];
12  x = [0 1];  % Start vector
13
14  % Set up vector of options for hybrid Monte Carlo.
15  nsamples = 160;          % Number of retained samples.
16
17  options = foptions;      % Default options vector.
18  options(1) = 1;          % Switch on diagnostics.
19  options(5) = 1;          % Use persistence.
20  options(7) = 50;         % Number of steps in trajectory.
21  options(14) = nsamples;  % Number of HMC samples returned.
22  options(15) = 30;        % Number of burn in samples.
23  options(18) = 0.02;      % Size of leapfrog steps.
24  [samples, energies] = hmc('dempot', x, options, 'demgpot', mix);
25
26  fh1 = figure;
27  % Plot data in 4 groups
28  ngroups = 4;
29  g1end = floor(nsamples/ngroups);
30  g2end = floor(2*nsamples/ngroups);
31  g3end = floor(3*nsamples/ngroups);
32  p1 = plot(samples(1:g1end,1), samples(1:g1end,2), 'k.', ...
33          'MarkerSize', 12); hold on;
34  lstrings = char(['Samples 1-' int2str(g1end)], ...
35    ['Samples ' int2str(g1end+1) '-' int2str(g2end)], ...
36    ['Samples ' int2str(g2end+1) '-' int2str(g3end)], ...
37    ['Samples ' int2str(g3end+1) '-' int2str(nsamples)]);
38  p2 = plot(samples(g1end+1:g2end,1), samples(g1end+1:g2end,2), ...
39    'r.', 'MarkerSize', 12);
40  p3 = plot(samples(g2end+1:g3end,1), samples(g2end+1:g3end,2), ...
41    'g.', 'MarkerSize', 12);
42  p4 = plot(samples(g3end+1:nsamples,1), ...
43    samples(g3end+1:nsamples,2), 'b.', 'MarkerSize', 12);
44  legend([p1 p2 p3 p4], lstrings, 2);
45
46  % Fit a mixture model to the sample
47  newmix = gmm(dim, ncentres, 'spherical');
48  options = foptions;
49  options(1) = -1;         % Switch off all diagnostics
```

```
50  options(14) = 5;          % Just 5 iterations of k-means in init.
51  % Initialise the model parameters from the samples
52  newmix = gmminit(newmix, samples, options);
53
54  % Set up vector of options for EM trainer
55  options = zeros(1, 18);
56  options(1)  = 1;                 % Prints out error values.
57  options(14) = 15;                % Max. Number of iterations.
58  [newmix, options, errlog] = gmmem(newmix, samples, options);
```

This program is similar to demmet1, but the target distribution is harder to sample from since it is multi-modal. After the housekeeping (lines 1–6), a two-component mixture model is created (lines 9–11) with mixing coefficients of 0.5, spherical covariance equal to 1, and means $(0,0)$ and $(2,2)$ respectively.

Table 8.2. Results of HMC demonstration. Parameters of target distribution and mixture model fitted to samples.

	Priors	Centres		Variances
Target Distribution				
Component 1	0.5000	0.0000	0.0000	1.0000
Component 2	0.5000	2.0000	2.0000	1.0000
Fitted Distribution				
Component 1	0.4376	−0.0114	0.0401	1.2240
Component 2	0.5624	2.0974	1.9659	0.8256

The starting point for the Markov chain is $(0,1)$, halfway between the means of the two components (line 12). The options vector for hmc is initialised in lines 17–23. We need to allow the trajectories to be long enough to move from one mode to the other. The sampling is done in line 24 with a call to hmc. The remainder of the script assesses the quality of the sample: visually using a scatterplot with each quarter of the sample coloured differently in lines (26–44); and quantitatively by fitting a mixture of two Gaussians to the sample and comparing the parameters with those of the model mix that defines the target distribution. The results of this comparison are contained in Table 8.2, which shows that after a 50 sample burn in period, the samples are a good representation of the target distribution, though more samples are needed to estimate the variance better. The visual plot (see Fig. 8.5), shows that the samples are well mixed over time.

In addition to the energy function $E = -\log p(x)$ required by metrop, HMC also needs the gradient of E with respect to the position vector x. This is provided by the function demgpot.

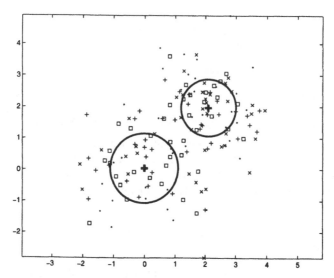

Fig. 8.5. Demonstration of the hybrid Monte Carlo algorithm. Target distribution is a mixture of two Gaussians (see Table 8.2 for parameters). Samples are shown in groups: first quarter (*dots*), second quarter (*plus*), third quarter (*cross*), fourth quarter (*square*). Fitted mixture of two Gaussians is shown with centres (*solid crosses*) and one standard deviation contours (*large circles*).

```
1   function g = demgpot(x, mix)
2   % Computes the potential gradient
3   temp = (ones(mix.ncentres,1)*x)-mix.centres;
4   temp = temp.*(gmmactiv(mix,x)'*ones(1, mix.nin));
5   % Assume spherical covariance structure
6   if ~strcmp(mix.covar_type, 'spherical')
7     error('Spherical covariance only.')
8   end
9   temp = temp./(mix.covars'*ones(1, mix.nin));
10  temp = temp.*(mix.priors'*ones(1, mix.nin));
11  g = sum(temp, 1)/gmmprob(mix, x);
```

As this function is used only for demonstrations, it has been implemented only for a spherical covariance structure. The energy function E is given by

$$E = -\log p(\boldsymbol{x}) = -\log \sum_{j=1}^{M} P(j) \frac{1}{(2\pi\sigma_j^2)^{d/2}} \exp\left\{-\frac{\|\boldsymbol{x} - \boldsymbol{\mu}_j\|^2}{2\sigma_j^2}\right\}. \quad (8.50)$$

A simple application of the chain rule shows that

$$\frac{\partial E}{\partial x_i} = -\frac{1}{p(\boldsymbol{x})} \sum_{j=1}^{M} P(j) \frac{|x_i - (\boldsymbol{\mu}_j)_i|}{\sigma_j^2} \frac{1}{(2\pi\sigma_j^2)^{d/2}} \exp\left\{-\frac{\|\boldsymbol{x} - \boldsymbol{\mu}_j\|^2}{2\sigma_j^2}\right\}. \quad (8.51)$$

Line 3 of demgpot computes a ncentres x nin matrix where the jth row is the difference between x and the jth mixture centre $\boldsymbol{x} - \boldsymbol{\mu}_j$. Line 4 multiplies the ith column of this matrix by the activation of the ith component of the mixture model, equal to

$$\frac{1}{(2\pi\sigma_j^2)^{d/2}} \exp\left\{ -\frac{\|x - \mu_j\|^2}{2\sigma_j^2} \right\}. \tag{8.52}$$

Line 9 divides the jth row by σ_j^2, line 10 multiplies the jth row by $P(j)$, and line 11 sums the result and divides by $p(x)$ to complete the calculation of (8.51).

8.5 Worked Example: Convergence Diagnostics

There are several important issues that arise when using MCMC methods in practice. These include the choice and parameters of the sampler, the number of independent runs to make, and the choice of starting values. However, the issue that can cause the most serious errors is that of determining whether the Markov chain has converged to the target distribution. The difficulty is that there are no general results on the convergence rate of Markov chains, except in very special cases which are not applicable to the sorts of chains that we are using. Instead, it is necessary to perform a statistical analysis to assess in a less rigorous way whether a given chain has converged. The choice of the best convergence diagnostic is problem specific; here we describe an algorithm of Gelman and Rubin (1992) (see also Gelman (1996)) which is relatively simple to compute and has given good results in practice.

The principle of this method is that when a chain has converged it has 'forgotten' its starting point and so several sequences drawn from different starting points should be indistinguishable. A group of sequences can be overlaid on a single plot to see if they have similar properties, but a more quantitative approach is to determine if the variance *between* different sequences is of a similar size to the variance *within* each sequence. This method can be applied to any scalar function or summary statistic $\psi(x)$ of each sample, for example, a coordinate value x_i or the energy.

The first step is to generate $m \geq 2$ sequences of length $2n$, each beginning at different starting points which are overdispersed (i.e. more broadly spread) compared to the expected range of the target distribution. The burn in period is taken to be the first n samples of each sequence. We write the set of retained scalar summary values as ψ_{ij} where $i = 1, \ldots, m$ indexes the sequences and $j = 1, \ldots, n$ indexes the samples.

The next stage is to compute the standard analysis of variance (ANOVA) statistics B, the between-sequence variance, and W, the within-sequence variance:

$$B = \frac{n}{m-1} \sum_{i=1}^{m} (\overline{\psi}_{i.} - \overline{\psi}_{..})^2 \tag{8.53}$$

$$W = \frac{1}{m} \sum_{i=1}^{m} s_i^2, \quad \text{where} \quad s_i^2 = \frac{1}{n-1} \sum_{j=1}^{n} (\psi_{ij} - \overline{\psi}_{i.})^2. \tag{8.54}$$

In these equations, $\overline{\psi}_{i.}$ denotes the mean of the ith row (i.e. sequence) and $\overline{\psi}_{..}$ the mean of the means.

We then construct two estimates of the variance of ψ in the target distribution, $\text{var}(\psi)$. The first estimate is W itself: this should underestimate the $\text{var}(\psi)$ since the danger is that each sequence has not ranged over the full range of the target distribution. The second estimate,

$$\hat{V} = \frac{n-1}{n} W + \frac{1}{n} B, \tag{8.55}$$

is an estimate of $\text{var}(\psi)$ that is unbiased under stationarity (that is, the starting points were drawn from the target distribution) but is an overestimate if the starting points were overdispersed.

The convergence diagnostic statistic, known as the *estimated potential scale reduction* is given by $\sqrt{\hat{R}}$, where

$$\hat{R} = \frac{\hat{V}}{W}. \tag{8.56}$$

Rather than developing a significance test, Gelman and Rubin (1992) suggest monitoring the value of this statistic and accepting a group of sequences if it falls below 1.1 or 1.05 for all statistics of interest.

The function convcalc implements this algorithm:

```
1   function [EPSR, W, B, V] = convcalc(chains)
2
3   [m, n] = size(chains);
4
5   % Estimate B
6   psibar_i = mean(chains, 2);          % Mean of each chain
7   B = n*cov(psibar_i);
8
9   % Estimate W
10  s = chains - repmat(psibar_i, 1, n);
11  stwo_i = sum(s.*s, 2)/(n-1);
12  W = sum(stwo_i)/m;
13
14  % Estimate target variance
15  V = ((W.*(n-1))./n)+(B./n);
16  R = V/W;
17  EPSR = R.^0.5;
```

The parameter chains is assumed to contain the values ψ_{ij} for some statistic $\psi(x)$ taken from the post-burn in period. The value of B (8.53) is computed in lines 6–7; the MATLAB function cov computes the sample covariance (so divides by $m - 1$). Similarly, lines 10–12 compute s_i^2 and W following (8.54). The first return value EPSR represents $\sqrt{\hat{R}}$.

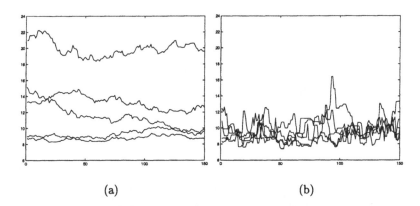

(a)   (b)

Fig. 8.6. Energies from Metropolis–Hastings sampler after burn in. Target distribution is $N(0,3)$. Proposal variance: (a) 0.01 (b) 0.8.

We can demonstrate the usefulness of this statistic by a simple experiment. The target distribution is Gaussian $N(0,3)$ in $\mathbb{R}^5$, and the summary statistics are the five coordinates $x_1, \ldots, x_5$ and the energy $-\ln p(x)$. A Metropolis–Hastings MCMC sampler was run for 300 iterations in five runs with the starting point drawn from $N(0,3)$. In the first set of runs the proposal distribution had a variance of 0.01 and in the second set the variance was 0.8.

The energies from the second half of each run are plotted in Fig. 8.6, and the value of EPSR for each statistic is given in Table 8.3. These results show that 300 samples are not nearly enough for the chain to converge with a proposal variance of 0.01, but that there is a reasonable level of confidence that the chains with proposal variance of 0.8 have converged. The one area of concern is x_3, and this suggests that lengthening the burn in period, perhaps to 600 samples in the first instance, would be worthwhile. The x_2 and x_3 coordinates from the retained samples are plotted in Fig. 8.7. These show that the spread of x_3-coordinates between the chains is greater than that for the x_2-coordinates, but only mildly so. The key steps of the demonstration program are:

1. Create the mixture model for the target distribution (lines 3–5)
2. Run metrop from nruns=5 different starting points (lines 20–26) storing the second half of each set of samples and energies (lines 28–29).

Table 8.3. Results for convergence diagnostic: proposal variance 0.01 (first run) and 0.8 (second run).

	First Run	Second Run
x_1	1.699	1.044
x_2	9.080	1.000
x_3	5.718	1.173
x_4	2.069	1.014
x_5	4.375	0.998
Energy	5.425	1.010

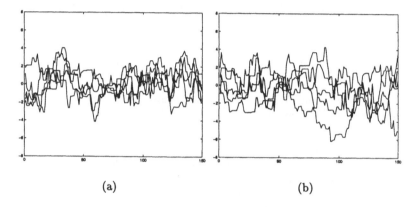

(a)   (b)

Fig. 8.7. Coordinates of retained samples from Metropolis–Hastings with proposal variance 0.8: (a) x_2 (b) x_3.

3. Present `convcalc` with a matrix containing the retained values of the summary statistics with each row representing a sequence (the coordinates in line 34 and the energies in line 37).

```
1   seeds = [1,32,234,42,332];
2
3   mix = gmm(5, 1, 'spherical');
4   mix.covars = 3;
5   mix.centres = zeros(1, 5);
6   nsamples = 300;
7   n = round(nsamples/2);        % n as in text.
8   nruns = 5;
9   dim = 5;
10  options = foptions;
11  options(1) = 0;
12  options(14) = nsamples;
```

```
13  stds  = [0.01, 0.8]; % 0.01 does not converge, 0.8 does.
14  samples = zeros(nruns, nsamples-n, dim);
15  energies = zeros(nruns, nsamples-n);
16
17  for stdidx = 1:1:2,
18    options(18) = stds(stdidx);
19    for k = 1:1:nruns,
20      seed = seeds(k);
21      randn('state', seed);
22      rand('state', seed);
23      x = randn(1,5)*3; % dispersed starting point
24
25      [run_samples, run_energies] = ...
26        metrop('dempot', x, options, '', mix);
27
28      samples(k, :, :) = run_samples(n+1:nsamples, :);
29      energies(k, :) = run_energies(n+1:nsamples)';
30    end
31
32    %%%%% Now check convergence
33    for k = 1:1:dim
34      EPSR = convcalc(samples(:, :, k));
35      fprintf(1, 'Dimension %d has EPSR %f\n', round(k), EPSR);
36    end
37    EPSR = convcalc(energies);
38    fprintf(1, 'Energies have EPSR %f\n', EPSR);
39  end
```

Exercises

8.1 ($\star$) Using (8.15), implement a Gaussian sampling algorithm just using rand. Demonstrate that it works by plotting sample histograms.

8.2 ($\star\star$) When converting a sampler from a uniform distribution into one from a normal distribution, we can avoid the relatively expensive calls to trigonometric functions at the expense of additional calls to our uniform random number generator. If we pick v_1 and v_2 uniformly inside the unit circle, then $R^2 := v_1^2 + v_2^2$ is $U(0,1)$, and the angle $2\pi x_2$ is given by the angle that (v_1, v_2) makes with the x-axis. Then

$$\cos 2\pi x_2 = \frac{v_1}{R} \quad \text{and} \quad \sin 2\pi x_2 = \frac{v_2}{R} \tag{8.57}$$

In practice we pick v_1 and v_2 by choosing points uniformly and randomly in the square $[-1, 1]^2$ and rejecting those that are outside the unit circle. The proportion of retained samples is $\pi/4$.

Implement the algorithm defined by (8.57) and compare its efficiency in flops and time with your implementation from Exercise 8.1.

8.3 ($\star$) Implement rejection sampling and test your function on a one-dimensional distribution.

8.4 (⋆ ⋆) Implement importance sampling and test your function on the beta distribution, following the steps below. The importance distribution is chosen to be a Gaussian centred at the mode with variance given by the inverse curvature at this point.

1. The density function of the beta distribution is given by

$$f(x) = \begin{cases} \frac{1}{B(a,b)}\theta^{a-1}(1-\theta)^{b-1} & \theta \in [0,1] \\ 0 & \text{otherwise.} \end{cases}$$

We shall consider only the case where a and b are positive integers. It can be shown by induction on a and b that

$$B(a,b) := \int_0^1 \theta^{a-1}(1-\theta)^{b-1}\, d\theta = \frac{(a-1)!(b-1)!}{(a+b-1)!}.$$

is the normalisation factor.

2. Show that the mean and variance of the beta distribution are given by

$$\mu = \frac{a}{a+b} \quad \text{and} \quad \sigma^2 = \frac{ab}{(a+b)^2(a+b+1)}.$$

3. Let Θ be a random variable with a beta density function $f(\theta)$. Show that the maximum value of $\log(f(\theta))$ occurs for θ equal to $\theta_0 = (a-1)/((a+b)-2)$; this is the *mode* of the distribution. Show that the second derivative of $\log f$ at θ_0 has the value

$$\kappa = \frac{-((a+b)-2)^3}{(a-1)(b-1)}.$$

4. Suppose that we have a dataset χ consisting of C samples of a Bernoulli random variable Y, $\chi = \{x_1, \ldots, x_C\}$, of which $C_1 = \sum_i x_i$ are heads (i.e. have the value 1) and $C_0 = C - C_1$ are tails (i.e. have the value 0). If we let θ denote the probability $P(Y = 1)$ then show that the likelihood of the data is given by

$$P(\chi|\theta) = \prod_{i=1}^C \theta^{x_i}(1-\theta)^{(1-x_i)}.$$

If we assume a uniform prior $p(\theta)$ on $[0, 1]$ for θ, show that the posterior distribution $p(\theta|\chi)$, which is given by

$$p(\theta|\chi) = \frac{p(\theta)\prod_{i=1}^C \theta^{x_i}(1-\theta)^{1-x_i}}{p(\chi)}.$$

is a beta distribution with $a = C_1 + 1$ and $b = C_0 + 1$. (Hint. You should not need to evaluate $p(\chi)$ as this is just a normalising constant. Instead, use the results proved in part (1).)

5. To work out the posterior probability that a new sample point x_{C+1} will be a head, you should evaluate the posterior integral

$$P(x_{C+1} = 1|\chi) = \int_0^1 P(x_{C+1} = 1|\tilde{\theta})P(\tilde{\theta}|\chi)\, d\tilde{\theta}$$

$$= \int_0^1 \tilde{\theta}\frac{(C+1)!}{C_0!\, C_1!}\tilde{\theta}^{C_1}(1-\tilde{\theta})^{C_0}\, d\tilde{\theta}$$

by Monte Carlo methods. Use importance sampling from a normal distribution $n(\tilde{\theta})$ with mean θ_0 and variance $1/|\kappa|$. You will need to ensure that you only sample from the interval $[0, 1]$: discard any points that lie outside that region giving a truncated distribution $\hat{n}$. Once you have done this, the distribution $\hat{n}$ will have to be renormalised (to ensure that it has integral one). There are (at least) two ways to do this: for the normal that you use, calculate $p(0 \le N \le 1)$ and divide your answer by this, or work out the integral of $\hat{n}$ by Monte Carlo methods at the same time as the posterior integral.

8.5 ($\star$) Experiment with sampling from a mixture of several Gaussians using metrop. As the modes move further apart, it will be necessary to increase the variance of the proposal distribution and the acceptance rate will decrease. Assess how far apart the modes have to be before the acceptance rate drops below 0.1.

8.6 ($\star$) Extend demgpot to allow diagonal and full covariance structures. Use gradchek to test the correctness of your implementation.

8.7 ($\star$) Experiment with using metrop to sample from a single correlated Gaussian with a large difference in covariance in each axis. Carry out experiments with in $\mathbb{R}^2$ and $\mathbb{R}^5$. Assess whether the sampling improves using HMC.

8.8 ($\star\star$) Extend metrop to allow a diagonal covariance matrix for the proposal distribution. Because this requires a row vector to specify the variance in each coordinate direction, it is best to replace the options vector by a cell array.

8.9 ($\star\star$) Extend metrop to allow a user-defined proposal distribution. (This could be passed as a function in place of the redundant gradf argument.) The acceptance criterion should be modified to allow for non-symmetric proposals (8.35).

8.10 ($\star\star$) Implement simulated annealing for optimisation. The function should use the standard options vector to control its operation. This stochastic optimisation algorithm uses the same procedure of trial points and acceptance thresholds as the Metropolis–Hastings algorithm, but only returns the last point visited (and optionally, also the point with the lowest error).

In detail, the acceptance probability is

$$p = \exp\left[-(E(x^{(n+1)}) - E(x^{(n)}))/T\right], \tag{8.58}$$

where T is a hypothetical temperature variable. As the algorithm progresses, T is 'annealed', that is, slowly reduced in value. For an annealing schedule, Press *et al.* (1992) suggest the following approach. Try some random steps from the starting point to determine 'typical' energy changes ΔE. Start with T_0 larger than any ΔE. After about $100m$ steps, or $10m$ successful steps, set $T_1 = 0.9T_0$ and continue in this way. This gives quite a fast reduction in T, which is exponential in form. Theory suggests that it should be of the form

$$T_i = \frac{T_0}{\ln i} \tag{8.59}$$

Implement both annealing schedules and allow the user to select them by means of the `options` vector.

Compare both variants of simulated annealing with the NETLAB optimisation algorithms on Rosenbrock's function (2.6). You should assess the achievable accuracy and the speed of convergence.

8.11 (★★) Extend the demonstration programs `demmet1` and `demhmc1` to apply the convergence diagnostic test `convcalc` to multiple runs. Are the burn in periods used in the NETLAB programs long enough for convergence?

9. Bayesian Techniques

The techniques discussed throughout the earlier chapters have used the method of maximum likelihood to fit models to data. This follows the intuitive idea that the best set of parameters are those which are most likely to have generated the dataset we see. In this approach it is recognised that the model does not generate the dataset exactly, and the differences between the two (or uncertainty in the data generated) are interpreted probabilistically using a noise model ϵ:

$$y = f(x; w) + \epsilon. \tag{9.1}$$

While this approach does take account of stochastic effects in the generation of the data, it does not take account of uncertainty in the estimation of parameters. Given ϵ, if we run the model f twice with a fixed set of parameters w and at a fixed set of input patterns $x^{(1)}$, ..., $x^{(N)}$, we would get two different datasets $\mathcal{D}_1$ and $\mathcal{D}_2$. Furthermore, the parameters w_1 learned from $\mathcal{D}_1$ using maximum likelihood will almost certainly not be equal to either the true parameters w or the parameters w_2 learned from $\mathcal{D}_2$. In particular, more complex models will usually fit the training data better but may do so by fitting the noise rather than the underlying data generator (i.e. *overfit* the training data), and will therefore give poor performance on unseen data (see Fig. 9.1). The performance on unseen data need not be well correlated with the performance on the training data, and randomly chosen initial weights can give rise to large variation in error.

In the Bayesian approach, this uncertainty about parameters estimated from data is represented by a probability distribution, and this enables us to reason with it in a unified way. However, the application of Bayesian inference to neural networks is fraught with difficulties principally because of their non-linear nature. In Chapter 10 we will see how models that were specifically designed to be amenable to Bayesian analysis are more tractable to work with.

In the Bayesian approach, we start with a *prior* probability distribution $p(w)$ which expresses our knowledge of the parameters before the data is observed. Typically this is quite a broad distribution, reflecting the fact that we only have a vague belief in a range of possible parameter values (for example, that the magnitude of the parameters should usually be less than 10, at least for normalised inputs). Once we observe the data, Bayes' theorem can be used to update our beliefs and we obtain the *posterior* probability density $p(w|\mathcal{D})$. Since some parameter values are more consistent with the data than others, the posterior distribution is concentrated on a smaller range of values than the prior distribution. With careful choice of prior, we can use the posterior distribution to evaluate the importance of each input variable for the model predictions. This process is called Automatic Relevance Determination (ARD).

There are two Bayesian approaches to neural networks which have been demonstrated to be effective in practical applications. The first of these is based on a local Gaussian approximation to the posterior distribution in weight space (known as the Laplace approximation). They are often coupled with the use of the evidence procedure to estimate optimal hyperparameters. The second class of methods is based on Monte Carlo techniques, of which the most successful is that of hybrid Monte Carlo. NETLAB provides implementations of both approaches.

In this chapter we describe in some detail how Bayesian techniques can be used in NETLAB. They are applicable to MLP, RBF and GLM networks. Gaussian processes, which are also available in NETLAB, are treated in a sufficiently different way to be worth a chapter of their own (Chapter 10).

All the functions discussed in this chapter are listed in Table 9.1.

Table 9.1. Functions in this chapter.

Bayesian Inference	
demard	Demonstration of ARD using the MLP
demev1	Demonstration of evidence procedure for MLP
demhmc2	Demonstration of HMC for MLP
demhmc3	Demonstration of HMC for MLP
demprior	Demonstration of sampling from Gaussian MLP prior
errbayes	Evaluate Bayesian error function for network
evidence	Evidence procedure for network
gbayes	Evaluate gradient of Bayesian error function for network
hbayes	Evaluate Hessian of Bayesian error function for network
mlpprior	Create Gaussian prior for MLP
nethess	Generic function to compute Hessian matrix
netpak	Generic function to combine weights in single vector
netunpak	Generic function to separate vector into weights and biases
rbfprior	Create Gaussian prior for RBF

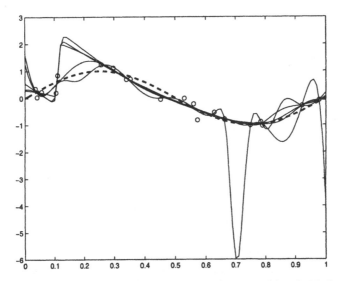

Fig. 9.1. Demonstration of overfitting with maximum likelihood. 20 data points (*circles*) taken from the noisy sine function (*dashed line*) were used to train five MLP networks (20 hidden units) with the quasi-Newton algorithm (*solid line*). Training and test errors are given in Table 9.2.

Table 9.2. Demonstration of overfitting.

Network	1	2	3	4	5
Training error	0.1714	0.2499	0.1786	0.1808	0.2396
Test error	33.3749	2.8677	· 13.2707	7.4808	3.0984

9.1 Principles of Bayesian Inference

Bayesian inference is very simple in principle. Bayes' theorem tells us that the posterior density of the parameters w given a dataset $\mathcal{D}$ is given by

$$p(w|\mathcal{D}) = \frac{p(\mathcal{D}|w)p(w)}{p(\mathcal{D})},\tag{9.2}$$

where $p(w)$ is the prior, $p(\mathcal{D}|w)$ is the dataset likelihood, and $p(\mathcal{D})$ (known as the *evidence*) is a normalisation factor that ensures that the posterior integrates to 1. It is given by an integral over the parameter space.

$$p(\mathcal{D}) = \int p(\mathcal{D}|w')p(w') \, dw'.\tag{9.3}$$

Once the posterior has been calculated, every type of inference is made by integrating over this distribution. For example, to make a prediction at a new input x^*, we need to calculate the prediction distribution

$$p(y|x^*, \mathcal{D}) = \int p(y|x^*, w)p(w|\mathcal{D}) \, dw. \qquad (9.4)$$

A point prediction uses the mean of this distribution, given by

$$E(y|x^*, \mathcal{D}) = \int y \, p(y|x^*, \mathcal{D}) \, dy, \qquad (9.5)$$

while the variance of the prediction distribution (given by a similar integral) can be used for error bars. The problem is that evaluating integrals such as (9.3) and (9.5) is very difficult because they are only analytically tractable for a small class of prior and likelihood distributions. The dimensionality of the integrals is given by the number of network parameters, so simple numerical integration algorithms break down. This is why the use of approximations to the posterior (the evidence procedure) and numerical methods for evaluating integrals (Monte Carlo methods combined with Markov Chain sampling) play such a large role in the use of Bayesian methods with neural networks.

The question remains: why should taking account of weight uncertainty reduce the problem of overfitting? To answer this, suppose that we have two different models $\mathcal{M}_1$ and $\mathcal{M}_2$ of similar type but where $\mathcal{M}_2$ has more parameters than $\mathcal{M}_1$. We can then write the posterior probability for each model, using Bayes' theorem, in the form

$$p(\mathcal{M}_i|\mathcal{D}) = \frac{p(\mathcal{D}|\mathcal{M}_i)p(\mathcal{M}_i)}{p(\mathcal{D})}. \qquad (9.6)$$

The denominator $p(\mathcal{D})$ does not depend on the model, and so can be ignored for the purposes of model comparison. If we have no reason to prefer $\mathcal{M}_1$ or $\mathcal{M}_2$, the priors $p(\mathcal{M}_i)$ should be the same, and we compare the models on the basis of $p(\mathcal{D}|\mathcal{M}_i)$. This can be written in the form (MacKay, 1992a)

$$p(\mathcal{D}|\mathcal{M}_i) = \int p(\mathcal{D}|w, \mathcal{M}_i)p(w|\mathcal{M}_i) \, dw. \qquad (9.7)$$

It is likely that the more complex model, $\mathcal{M}_2$, will fit the data better for the best choice of parameters w_{MP}, so that the peak value of the posterior $p(\mathcal{D}|w_{MP}^{(2)}, \mathcal{M}_2)$ at its mode will be greater than that of $p(\mathcal{D}|w_{MP}^{(1)}, \mathcal{M}_1)$. However, it is also likely that the more complex model is more sensitive to the exact tuning of its parameters, which means that the width of the posterior $\Delta w_{\text{posterior}}$ will be smaller for $\mathcal{M}_2$ than $\mathcal{M}_1$.

We can get an intuitive understanding of this tradeoff by supposing that the posterior is very sharply peaked so that the integral in (9.7) is approximated by

$$p(\mathcal{D}|\mathcal{M}_i) \approx p(\mathcal{D}|w_{MP}^{(i)}, \mathcal{M}_i)p(w_{MP}^{(i)}|\mathcal{M}_i)\Delta w_{\text{posterior}}^{(i)}. \qquad (9.8)$$

If we use a weight prior $p(w_{MP}^{(i)}|\mathcal{M}_i)$ that is uniform over some large region of volume Δw_{prior}, then (9.8) simplifies to

$$p(\mathcal{D}|\mathcal{M}_i) \approx p(\mathcal{D}|w_{MP}^{(i)}, \mathcal{M}_i) \left(\frac{\Delta w_{\text{posterior}}^{(i)}}{\Delta w_{\text{prior}}^{(i)}} \right). \tag{9.9}$$

The first term on the right-hand side is the likelihood of the training data evaluated at the most probable weight values, while the second term, which has value < 1 penalises the choice of weight values. This term is approximately exponential in the number of parameters, so it penalises $\mathcal{M}_2$ more than $\mathcal{M}_1$.

Rather than choosing just one from a set of models, it is more in the spirit of the Bayesian approach to make predictions by integrating over the whole of model space. With a finite number of models, this reduces to a weighted sum of the predictions of the models, where the weights are given by the probabilities $p(\mathcal{M}_i|\mathcal{D})$.

In pattern recognition applications, Bayesian methods offer a number of important practical benefits:

1. In principle, by taking account of parameter uncertainty, overfitting is not a problem.
2. Regularisation can be given a natural interpretation in the Bayesian framework. Being able to reason consistently with regularisation parameters makes it easier to find good values for them. For example, it is possible to optimise regularisation parameters as part of the training process.
3. Parameter uncertainty can be accounted for in network predictions. For regression problems, error bars, or prediction intervals, can be assigned to network predictions. For classification problems, output class probabilities are moderated to less extreme values.
4. There is a principled framework for deciding questions of model complexity.
5. The relative importance of different input variables can be determined using automatic relevance determination.

9.2 Priors for Neural Networks

We shall start detailed consideration of Bayesian methods by choosing the prior probability distribution for the weights of a neural network. This should embody our prior knowledge on the sort of mappings that are 'reasonable'. In general, we expect the underlying generator of our datasets to be smooth, and the network mapping should reflect this belief. A neural network with large weights will usually give rise to a mapping with large curvature, and so we favour small values for the network weights.

9.2.1 Theory of Priors

The requirement for small weights suggests a Gaussian prior distribution with zero mean of the form

$$p(w) = \frac{1}{Z_W(\alpha)} \exp\left(-\frac{\alpha}{2}\|w\|^2\right),$$ (9.10)

where α represents the *inverse* variance of the distribution and the normalisation constant is given by

$$Z_W(\alpha) = \left(\frac{2\pi}{\alpha}\right)^{W/2}.$$ (9.11)

Because α is a parameter for the distribution of other parameters (weights and biases), it is known as a *hyperparameter*. One of the strengths of the Bayesian formalism is that we can reason probabilistically with hyperparameters in a natural extension of inference for parameters.

Ignoring the normalisation constant, which does not depend on the weights, this prior is equivalent to a weight error term (after taking the negative log) of the form

$$\alpha E_W = \frac{\alpha}{2}\|w\|^2 = \frac{\alpha}{2}\sum_{i=1}^{W} w_i^2.$$ (9.12)

This error term *regularises* the weights by penalising overly large magnitudes. It is identical to the weight decay regulariser of Section 4.2.

It is helpful to generalise this notion to multiple hyperparameters $\alpha_1, \ldots, \alpha_g$ corresponding to groups of weights $\mathcal{W}_1, \ldots, \mathcal{W}_g$. There are two generalisations of particular interest:

1. **Consistent priors.** It can be shown (Bishop, 1995, Section 9.2.2) that a single regularisation parameter is inconsistent with linear rescaling of the input and output patterns. A prior of the form

$$p(w) \propto \exp\left(-\frac{\alpha_1}{2}\sum_{w\in\mathcal{W}_1} w^2 - \frac{\alpha_2}{2}\sum_{w\in\mathcal{W}_2} w^2\right),$$ (9.13)

   where $\mathcal{W}_1$ denotes the set of first-layer weights and $\mathcal{W}_2$ denotes the set of second-layer weights (excluding biases in both cases), makes the weights scale-invariant in layers and biases shift-invariant. This is consistent with linear rescaling provided that the regularisation parameters α_1 and α_2 are also rescaled. Because the biases are not included, they are unconstrained and this gives rise to technical difficulties when choosing hyperparameters. For this reason, it is usual to use separate priors for each layer of biases. The optimal value for the output layer bias weights are the unconditional means of the corresponding output variables, which is a good argument for normalising the target data to zero mean so that the corresponding prior has negligible effect.

2. **Automatic Relevance Determination (ARD).** Selecting relevant input variables from a large set of possibilities is a common problem in applications of pattern analysis. PCA gives a reduced set of variables, but in an unsupervised way (i.e. it doesn't take account of the input-output mapping) while canonical variates is only applicable to linear classification and has an upper bound of $c - 1$ for the number of variables created. Selecting variables based on the magnitude of their correlation with the target variable is based only on linear relationships; frequently the importance of inputs is only revealed in a non-linear mapping. What is required is a way to determine the importance of each input to a trained model.

The crudest method for doing this is to consider the magnitude of the weights fanning out from a particular input. However, this performs poorly in practice since if an input has no effect on the output, the weights leading from it can have arbitrary values. More well founded are methods for measuring weight *saliency*, based on analysis of the Hessian matrix, that are used in weight pruning algorithms such as 'optimal brain damage' (Le Cun *et al.*, 1990) and 'optimal brain surgery' (Hassibi and Stork, 1993). However, these techniques can be difficult to interpret in a quantitative way.

In the Bayesian framework, we associate a separate hyperparameter with each input variable; this represents the inverse variance of the prior distribution of the weights fanning out from that input. During Bayesian learning it is possible to modify the hyperparameters; for example, using the evidence procedure, we find their optimal value, subject to some simplifying assumptions about the network function to make the analysis tractable. Because hyperparameters represent the inverse variance of the weights, a small hyperparameter value means that large weights are allowed, and we can conclude that the corresponding input is important. A large hyperparameter value means that the weights are constrained near zero, and hence the corresponding input is less important. This still leaves the question of deciding what a 'large' hyperparameter value is (and this will depend on the measurement scale of the corresponding input; normalising inputs to zero mean and unit variance makes it easier to compare ARD hyperparameters), but it is certainly easy to decide on the relative importance of inputs. Additional hyperparameters may be used for other groups of weights in the network.

NETLAB implements both these types of prior, but the framework is sufficiently general for the user to create their own groupings of weights. For clarity of explanation, most of the theoretical descriptions in this chapter will be written in terms of a single hyperparameter α, but the implementation will be explained in full generality.

9.2.2 NETLAB Implementation of Priors

The NETLAB implementation of zero mean Gaussian priors distinguishes two cases:

1. A single hyperparameter α for all the weights in a network; it is contained in the alpha field in the network data structure.
2. Separate hyperparameters for different groups of weights. Two fields in the network structure are used:
   - alpha contains a *vector* of hyperparameters;
   - index is a matrix indicating which weights belong to each group. Each column has one element for each weight in the matrix, using the standard ordering as defined in the pak function relevant to the network type (e.g. mlppak for the MLP), and each element is 1 or 0 according to whether the weight is a member of the corresponding group or not. This format means that matrix operations can be used to compute E_W and related values.

This implementation can be used for MLP, MDN, RBF and GLM networks. The error and gradient functions for these networks automatically take account of the extra error term E_W. The second of these two implementation schemes is completely general, and can be used with any grouping of weights. To help NETLAB users, additional functions are available to define suitable hyperparameter structures for consistent priors and ARD.

When training networks, it is sometimes useful to restrict weight changes to a subgroup of weights and 'freeze' the remainder. For example, when training an RBF with a gradient based optimiser, we will still probably want to keep the hidden unit centres and widths fixed. This can be done using the field mask in the network data structure. Although its use is not restricted to a Bayesian context, its implementation is closely integrated with that of hyperparameters, and it is convenient to discuss it here.

Constructing Priors

The function mlpprior generates a data structure that specifies a zero mean Gaussian consistent prior distribution for an MLP.

```
1  function prior = mlpprior(nin, nhidden, nout, aw1, ab1, aw2, ab2)
2
3  nextra = nhidden + (nhidden + 1)*nout;
4  nwts = nin*nhidden + nextra;
5  if size(aw1) == [1,1]
6    indx = [ones(1, nin*nhidden), zeros(1, nextra)]';
7  elseif size(aw1) == [1, nin]
8    indx = kron(ones(nhidden, 1), eye(nin));
9    indx = [indx; zeros(nextra, nin)];
10 else
11   error('Parameter aw1 of invalid dimensions');
```

```
12  end
13
14  extra = zeros(nwts, 3);
15  mark1 = nin*nhidden;
16  mark2 = mark1 + nhidden;
17  extra(mark1 + 1:mark2, 1) = ones(nhidden,1);
18  mark3 = mark2 + nhidden*nout;
19  extra(mark2 + 1:mark3, 2) = ones(nhidden*nout,1);
20  mark4 = mark3 + nout;
21  extra(mark3 + 1:mark4, 3) = ones(nout,1);
22
23  indx = [indx, extra];
24
25  prior.index = indx;
26  prior.alpha = [aw1, ab1, aw2, ab2]';
```

This function differentiates between an ARD prior (if the argument aw1 is a vector) and one with a single hyperparameter for the first-layer weights. Any other form of argument aw1 is not valid for this function. The data structure prior that is returned contains an index matrix which is constructed in the local variable indx. The variable nextra is set to the number of weights and biases in the MLP excluding the first-layer weights (line 3). If the argument aw1 is a scalar, then the first column of the matrix indx is zero apart from the first nin*nhidden rows, which are one (line 5–6). If the argument aw1 is a row vector with nin entries, then it corresponds to an ARD prior, and each of the first nin columns of indx contains ones in the correct positions for the corresponding input fan-out (lines 7–9). Weights are normally stored in order of hidden unit fan-in (i.e. all the weights into hidden unit 1 are stored before those for hidden unit 2, etc.). Suppose that there are two hidden units and three inputs; the Kronecker product on line 8 generates a matrix:

$$
\begin{pmatrix}
1 & 0 & 0 \\
0 & 1 & 0 \\
0 & 0 & 1 \\
1 & 0 & 0 \\
0 & 1 & 0 \\
0 & 0 & 1
\end{pmatrix}
\tag{9.14}
$$

Line 9 generates zeros for all the other weights in the network.

Lines 14–21 create three further index columns with ones for the first-layer biases, second-layer weights and second-layer biases respectively. Line 23 puts together the input layer index matrix with that for the rest of the network, while lines 25 and 26 store the index matrix and hyperparameter vector in the prior data structure.

As well as its use in a Bayesian context, this prior can also be passed to the function mlpinit in order to control the initialisation of weights in an MLP.

```
1  function net = mlpinit(net, prior)
2
3  if isstruct(prior)
4    sig = 1./sqrt(prior.index*prior.alpha);
5    w = sig'.*randn(1, net.nwts);
6  elseif size(prior) == [1 1]
7    w = randn(1, net.nwts).*sqrt(1/prior);
8  else
9    error('prior must be a scalar or a structure');
10 end
11
12 net = mlpunpak(net, w);
```

In lines 3–5 the standard deviation of the Gaussian used to sample from is determined. If a prior data structure (such as that generated by mlpprior) is passed, then the correct hyperparameter for each weight is used because the product

```
prior.index*prior.alpha
```

picks out the entry of alpha corresponding to the columns in which a 1 appears in prior.index for each weight. (If multiple columns are one for a single row, then the sum of the corresponding hyperparameters will be used. This feature is rarely used in practice.) Because the prior is passed as an argument rather than taken from the net data structure, it is possible to separate the hyperparameters used for network training and the initial values of the weights. This is often useful, since a broad prior weight distribution is usually appropriate (corresponding to our initial ignorance of the correct weights), but initialising from this distribution gives large initial weights which often lead to difficulties with slow convergence and poor local minima in the optimisation process.

The function rbfprior facilitates the construction of a Gaussian prior for RBF networks. This function also creates a mask that selects only the output layer weights and freezes all the basis function parameters. In the usual training method, the parameters of the basis functions are set by modelling the unconditional density of the input data and fall outside the Bayesian framework. Because of this, an ARD prior is inappropriate for RBF networks.

```
1  function [mask, prior] = rbfprior(rbfunc, nin, nhidden, nout, ...
2                                    aw2, ab2)
3  nwts_layer2 = nout + (nhidden *nout);
4  switch rbfunc
5  case 'gaussian'
6    nwts_layer1 = nin*nhidden + nhidden;
7  case {'tps', 'r4logr'}
8    nwts_layer1 = nin*nhidden;
9  otherwise
10   error('Undefined activation function');
11 end
12 nwts = nwts_layer1 + nwts_layer2;
13
```

```
14  % Make a mask only for output layer
15  mask = [zeros(nwts_layer1, 1); ones(nwts_layer2, 1)];
16
17  if nargout > 1
18    % Construct prior
19    indx = zeros(nwts, 2);
20    mark2 = nwts_layer1 + (nhidden * nout);
21    indx(nwts_layer1 + 1:mark2, 1) = ones(nhidden * nout, 1);
22    indx(mark2 + 1:nwts, 2) = ones(nout, 1);
23
24    prior.index = indx;
25    prior.alpha = [aw2, ab2]';
26  end
```

Line 3 computes the number of weights and biases in the output layer. The number of first-layer weights depends on the type of the activation function, since only Gaussian functions have a width parameter (lines 4–11). The mask constructed in line 15 only selects the output layer parameters. The prior data structure is constructed in lines 17–26 in a similar way to that in mlpprior.

9.2.3 Demonstration of Gaussian Priors

A Gaussian weight prior captures our intuition that a good model has weights of small magnitude. However, given the complexity of the MLP function, it is far from clear how the prior affects the mapping. In particular, it is important to have some understanding of the relationship between the magnitude of hyperparameters for different layers and their effect on the network mapping. One way to increase this understanding is to *sample* from the prior distribution and then plot the resulting functions. The NETLAB function demprior does this for a network with a single input and single output. It is provided with a graphical user interface so that it is easy to change the values of the four hyperparameters α_{w1}, α_{b1}, α_{w2} and α_{b2} using sliders with a $\log_{10}$ scale. The following listing shows the part of the function concerned with sampling the prior and plotting the resulting MLP mappings.

```
1   function demprior(action);
2
3   % Much GUI code omitted
4
5   % Re-sample from the prior and plot graphs.
6   aw1 = 10^get(aw1slide, 'Value');
7   ab1 = 10^get(ab1slide, 'Value');
8   aw2 = 10^get(aw2slide, 'Value');
9   ab2 = 10^get(ab2slide, 'Value');
10
11  axis([-1 1 -10 10]);
12  hold on
13
14  nhidden = 12;
```

```
15  prior = mlpprior(1, nhidden, 1, aw1, ab1, aw2, ab2);
16  xvals = -1:0.005:1;
17  net = mlp(1, nhidden, 1, 'linear', prior);
18  nsample = 10;    % Number of samples from prior.
19  for i = 1:nsample
20    net = mlpinit(net, prior);
21    yvals = mlpfwd(net, xvals');
22    plot(xvals', yvals, 'y');
23  end
```

Lines 6–9 read the values of the hyperparameters from sliders in the GUI.
Lines 11–12 set up the axes for plotting: the x-scale runs from -1 to 1 and the
y-scale runs from -10 to 10. Lines 14–15 create the prior data structure for
a network with 1 input, nhidden=12 hidden units and 1 output. The function
then creates 10 sample networks from this weight prior by creating an MLP
(line 17) and then sampling the weights using a call to mlpinit with the
prior structure (line 20). To plot the resulting mapping, an evenly spaced
input vector xvals is propagated through the network with a call to mlpfwd
(line 21) and then the result is added to the graph (line 22). An illustrative
example is shown in Fig. 9.2.

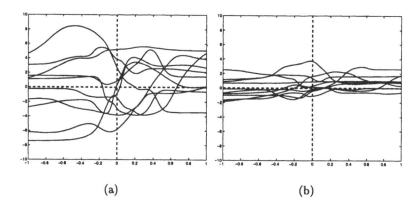

(a)   (b)

Fig. 9.2. Demonstration of Gaussian priors. Each plot shows 10 functions sampled
from a zero mean Gaussian prior for an MLP with 12 hidden units. (a) Hyperpa-
rameters $\alpha_{w1} = 0.01$, $\alpha_{b1} = 0.1$, $\alpha_{w2} = 1.0$, $\alpha_{b2} = 1.0$. (b) Hyperparameters as in
(a) but with $\alpha_{w2} = 10$. Note how the decreased variance of the output layer weights
has reduced the dynamic range of the functions.

9.2.4 Masks and Weight Manipulation

In NETLAB there are two ways to extract weights from an MLP or similar
network.

1. The function mlppak creates a single vector containing all the weights in the network.
2. The function netpak creates a single vector containing all the weights in the network not excluded by net.mask.

The netpak function is generic and can be used for any network model with a pak function. It is used by any training function that takes account of masking (such as glmtrain and rbftrain) and also in Bayesian error and gradient calculations.

```
1  function w = netpak(net)
2
3  pakstr = [net.type, 'pak'];
4  w = feval(pakstr, net);
5  % Return masked subset of weights
6  if (isfield(net, 'mask'))
7    w = w(logical(net.mask));
8  end
```

There is a corresponding generic inverse function netunpak that takes a vector of weights and replaces it in the network in just the locations selected by net.mask. It does this by extracting the current network weights fullw by a call to mlppak or equivalent (lines 11–12); calling netpak would extract just the masked weights. The masked weights are then replaced by those in w (line 14) before a call to mlppak (or equivalent) updates the net data structure.

```
1  function net = netunpak(net, w)
2
3  unpakstr = [net.type, 'unpak'];
4
5  % Check if we are being passed a masked set of weights
6  if (isfield(net, 'mask'))
7    if length(w) ~= size(find(net.mask), 1)
8      error('Weight vector length does not match mask length')
9    end
10   % Do a full pack of all current network weights
11   pakstr = [net.type, 'pak'];
12   fullw = feval(pakstr, net);
13   % Replace current weights with new ones
14   fullw(logical(net.mask)) = w;
15   w = fullw;
16 end
17
18 net = feval(unpakstr, net, w);
```

9.3 Computing Error and Gradient Functions

Once a prior has been constructed for a network and placed in the data structure, the most probable weights w_{MP} can be found by training the network as usual using netopt. This is because the error and error gradient functions, such as `mlperr` and `mlpgrad`, take account of the prior in their calculations. This is achieved using generic NETLAB functions `errbayes` and `gbayes`.

The Bayesian error term for a model is given by the negative log posterior probability $-\log p(w|\mathcal{D})$. Using Bayes' theorem (9.2) and ignoring the evidence term $p(\mathcal{D})$, which does not depend on the weights, we obtain an error function of the form

$$E = -\log p(\mathcal{D}|w) - \log p(w) = -\log p(\mathcal{D}|w) - \alpha E_W. \tag{9.15}$$

For a regression problem, we assume that the noise model for the target data is a Gaussian with zero mean and constant inverse variance β, so the likelihood of a target value t given an input vector x is given by

$$p(t|x, w) \propto \exp\left(-\frac{\beta}{2}\{y(w; w) - t\}^2\right). \tag{9.16}$$

It follows that for an i.i.d. dataset, the likelihood is

$$p(\mathcal{D}|w) = \frac{1}{Z_D(\beta)} \exp\left(-\frac{\beta}{2}\sum_{n=1}^{N}\{y(x^n; w) - t^n\}^2\right), \tag{9.17}$$

where the normalisation factor $Z_D(\beta)$ is given by

$$Z_D(\beta) = \left(\frac{2\pi}{\beta}\right)^{N/2}. \tag{9.18}$$

This means that the data component of the error function is given by the sum squared error weighted by β:

$$\beta E_D = \frac{\beta}{2}\sum_{n=1}^{N}\{y(x^n; w) - t^n\}^2. \tag{9.19}$$

Putting together (9.12) and (9.19), we derive the overall error (or misfit) function

$$E = S(w) = \beta E_D + \alpha E_W. \tag{9.20}$$

This is implemented generically in NETLAB by the function `errbayes`:

```
1  function [e, edata, eprior] = errbayes(net, edata)
2
3  % Evaluate the data contribution to the error.
4  if isfield(net, 'beta')
5    e1 = net.beta*edata;
6  else
7    e1 = edata;
8  end
```

```
9
10  % Evaluate the prior contribution to the error.
11  if isfield(net, 'alpha')
12    w = netpak(net);
13    if size(net.alpha) == [1 1]
14      eprior = 0.5*(w*w');
15      e2 = eprior*net.alpha;
16    else
17      if (isfield(net, 'mask'))
18        nindx_cols = size(net.index, 2);
19        nmask_rows = size(find(net.mask), 1);
20        index = reshape(net.index(logical(repmat(net.mask, ...
21                        1, nindx_cols))), nmask_rows, nindx_cols);
22      else
23        index = net.index;
24      end
25      eprior = 0.5*(w.^2)*index;
26      e2 = eprior*net.alpha;
27    end
28  else
29    eprior = 0;
30    e2 = 0;
31  end
32
33  e = e1 + e2;
```

This function is called at the end of mlperr and similar functions. The argument edata represents the data error E_D computed for the training dataset. The return value eprior is the prior error E_W computed for the current set of network weights. Lines 3–8 compute the βE_D contribution to the error function. In line 12 the weights of the network data structure net are extracted using netpak. Recall that this function extracts only the weights selected by the network mask. If there is a single hyperparameter α, then the prior error term is simple to calculate (lines 14–15). Otherwise we must add a contribution to E_W for each weight according to which group it belongs to. If there is no mask, we simply use the stored net.index matrix (line 23); otherwise we must remove the rows from net.index that correspond to zeros in net.mask (lines 18–21). Once this is done, it is straightforward to compute the grouped sum of squared weight values (line 25) and then sum these weighted by the appropriate hyperparameter α_i (line 26). Lines 29–30 set the prior error contribution E_W to zero if there are no hyperparameters in the net data structure, so that this function has no effect for unregularised maximum likelihood training.

The corresponding NETLAB function for computing the error gradient is gbayes. This has a very similar structure to errbayes, and is called by mlpgrad and corresponding functions.

```
1  function [g, gdata, gprior] = gbayes(net, gdata)
2
3  % Evaluate the data contribution to the gradient.
```

```
 4  if (isfield(net, 'mask'))
 5    gdata = gdata(logical(net.mask));
 6  end
 7  if isfield(net, 'beta')
 8    g1 = gdata*net.beta;
 9  else
10    g1 = gdata;
11  end
12
13  % Evaluate the prior contribution to the gradient.
14  if isfield(net, 'alpha')
15    w = netpak(net);
16    if size(net.alpha) == [1 1]
17      gprior = w;
18      g2 = net.alpha*gprior;
19    else
20      if (isfield(net, 'mask'))
21        nindx_cols = size(net.index, 2);
22        nmask_rows = size(find(net.mask), 1);
23        index = reshape(net.index(logical(repmat(net.mask, ...
24                     1, nindx_cols))), nmask_rows, nindx_cols);
25      else
26        index = net.index;
27      end
28
29      ngroups = size(net.alpha, 1);
30      gprior = index'.*(ones(ngroups, 1)*w);
31      g2 = net.alpha'*gprior;
32    end
33  else
34    gprior = 0;
35    g2 = 0;
36  end
37
38  g = g1 + g2;
```

The dataset error gradient is passed as an argument, gdata. The components of the data gradient vector that correspond to zeros in the mask are removed (line 5) and the result is then weighted by net.beta (line 8). The remainder of the function computes $\partial E_W / \partial w_i$, which is given by

$$\frac{\partial E_W}{\partial w_i} = \alpha w_i, \tag{9.21}$$

with the obvious extension to groups of weights.

The function hbayes, used for computing the Hessian of the total error function, is similar to gbayes and is called by mlphess and similar functions for other models.

```
 1  function [h, hdata] = hbayes(net, hdata)
 2
 3  if (isfield(net, 'mask'))
 4    nmask_rows = size(find(net.mask), 1);
```

```
 4    nmask_rows = size(find(net.mask), 1);
 5    hdata = reshape(hdata(logical(net.mask*(net.mask'))), ...
 6                            nmask_rows, nmask_rows);
 7    nwts = nmask_rows;
 8  else
 9    nwts = net.nwts;
10  end
11  if isfield(net, 'beta')
12    h = net.beta*hdata;
13  else
14    h = hdata;
15  end
16
17  if isfield(net, 'alpha')
18    if size(net.alpha) == [1 1]
19      h = h + net.alpha*eye(nwts);
20    else
21      if isfield(net, 'mask')
22        nindx_cols = size(net.index, 2);
23        index = reshape(net.index(logical(repmat(net.mask, ...
24            1, nindx_cols))), nmask_rows, nindx_cols);
25      else
26        index = net.index;
27      end
28      h = h + diag(index*net.alpha);
29    end
30  end
```

The dataset Hessian is passed as an argument hdata. The components of the Hessian that correspond to zeros in the mask are removed in lines 4–7 by taking the outer product of the mask vector. The contribution to the Hessian from E_W is simply αI (line 19), or the equivalent for multiple weight groups (line 28).

9.4 The Evidence Procedure

The evidence procedure is an iterative algorithm for determining optimal weights and hyperparameters. Because it does not integrate over all unknown parameters, it is not a fully Bayesian approach (because it searches for optimal hyperparameters instead of integrating them out), being equivalent to the type II maximum likelihood method (Berger, 1985). Nevertheless, it has given good results on many applications (Thodberg, 1993), and is considerably less computationally costly than fully Bayesian procedures such as Monte Carlo integration.

9.4.1 Theory

So far in this chapter we have discussed Bayesian learning in general terms and have shown how hyperparameters can be incorporated into neural network models in NETLAB, but have not yet addressed the question of how hyperparameters should be adjusted in practice to take account of training data. The correct treatment in principle is to integrate out all unknown parameters, and this applies to hyperparameters just as much as to network weights. So the posterior distribution of the network weights is given by

$$p(w|\mathcal{D}) = \iint p(w, \alpha, \beta|\mathcal{D}) \, d\alpha \, d\beta$$

$$= \iint p(w|\alpha, \beta, \mathcal{D}) p(\alpha, \beta|\mathcal{D}) \, d\alpha \, d\beta. \tag{9.22}$$

This requires us to integrate the posterior weight distribution $p(w|\alpha, \beta, \mathcal{D})$ over a space which has dimensionality equal to the number of hyperparameters, which is at least two, and usually more. This integral can be simplified and with a suitable choice of (improper) prior for the hyperparameters, $p(\alpha) = 1/\alpha$ it can even be evaluated analytically. However, the evidence approximation tends to give better results in practice, though this has been a matter for debate (MacKay, 1994; Wolpert, 1993).

The approximation that is made in the evidence procedure is that the posterior density of the hyperparameters $p(\alpha, \beta|\mathcal{D})$ is sharply peaked around α_{MP}, β_{MP}, the most probable values of the hyperparameters. This is known as the Laplace approximation. With this assumption, the integral in (9.22) reduces to

$$p(w|\mathcal{D}) \approx p(w|\alpha_{MP}, \beta_{MP}, \mathcal{D}) \iint p(\alpha, \beta|\mathcal{D}) \, d\alpha \, d\beta \tag{9.23}$$

$$\approx p(w|\alpha_{MP}, \beta_{MP}, \mathcal{D}). \tag{9.24}$$

This means that we should find the hyperparameter values that optimise the weight posterior probability and then perform all the other calculations involving $p(w|\mathcal{D})$ (such as making predictions) using the distribution with the hyperparameters fixed at those values.

To make further progress we need to perform integrals involving the weight posterior distribution $p(w|\alpha, \beta, \mathcal{D})$ and this needs another approximation. MacKay (1992c) proposed a using a spherical Gaussian distribution around a mode of the posterior. For models that are linear in their parameters, such as linear regression or RBFs with fixed basis functions, this is exact. For MLPs, the situation is more complex since there are several modes in the distribution because of the non-linear dependence of the outputs on the network weights. It is best to view this approximation as a purely local one around a particular mode w_{MP}, based on a second-order Taylor series expansion of $S(w)$:

$$S(w) \approx S(w_{MP}) + \frac{1}{2}(w - w_{MP})^T A(w - w_{MP}). \tag{9.25}$$

There is no first-order term, since it is assumed that w_{MP} is a local minimum of the error function, so $\partial S(w_{MP})/\partial w_i = 0$ for all coordinates. The matrix A is the Hessian matrix of the total error function:

$$A = \nabla\nabla S(w_{MP}) = \beta\nabla\nabla E_D(w_{MP}) + \alpha I, \qquad (9.26)$$

where $\nabla\nabla E_D(w_{MP})$ is the Hessian of the network function. Since the error function $S(w)$ is the negative log probability of the weight posterior probability, it is clear that the latter distribution is Gaussian:

$$p(w|\alpha,\beta,\mathcal{D}) = \frac{1}{Z_S^*}\exp\left(-S(w_{MP}) - \frac{1}{2}\Delta w^T A \Delta w\right), \qquad (9.27)$$

where $\Delta w = w - w_{MP}$ and Z_S^* is the normalisation constant for the approximating Gaussian, and is therefore given by

$$Z_S^*(\alpha,\beta) = \exp(-S(w_{MP}))(2\pi)^{W/2}(\det A)^{-1/2}. \qquad (9.28)$$

As well as multiple modes in the distribution caused by the non-linear network mapping, there are also many predictable modes caused by symmetries in the network. For a two-layer MLP with M hidden units, there are $2^M M!$ equivalent minima caused by changing the labelling of the hidden units or the signs of all the weights and biases fanning in and out from a given hidden unit.

The Bayesian approach to computing α_{MP} and β_{MP} is to consider the modes of their posterior distribution:

$$p(\alpha,\beta|\mathcal{D}) = \frac{p(\mathcal{D}|\alpha,\beta)p(\alpha,\beta)}{p(\mathcal{D})}. \qquad (9.29)$$

The denominator is, as always, shorthand for the integral of the numerator over the conditioned parameters (in this case, α and β). Since in the simplified view taken with the evidence procedure we need only the peaks of this density, we can ignore this term. This still leaves the choice of $p(\alpha,\beta)$, the prior over the hyperparameters (also known as the *hyperprior*). There is a wide range of possible choices for this density, but for simplicity we shall assume that $p(\alpha,\beta)$ is uniform and so it will be ignored in the subsequent analysis. (Of course, this means that the hyperprior does not have a finite integral, and is therefore an example of an *improper* prior.) This means that we shall just seek to maximise $p(\mathcal{D}|\alpha,\beta)$, which is known as the evidence for the hyperparameters, by adjusting α and β. This term is found by integrating the data likelihood over all possible weights w:

$$p(\mathcal{D}|\alpha,\beta) = \int p(\mathcal{D}|w,\alpha,\beta)p(w|\alpha,\beta)\,dw \qquad (9.30)$$

$$= \int p(\mathcal{D}|w,\alpha,\beta)p(w|\alpha)\,dw, \qquad (9.31)$$

where the second line follows since the distribution of the weights is independent of the noise variance. Using (9.12) and (9.19), we can write (9.31) in the form

$$p(\mathcal{D}|\alpha,\beta) = \frac{1}{Z_D(\beta)} \frac{1}{Z_W(\alpha)} \int \exp(-S(w)) \, dw. \tag{9.32}$$

Using (9.11), (9.18), (9.28) and (9.32), we can compute the log evidence as follows:

$$\ln p(\mathcal{D}|\alpha,\beta) = -\alpha E_W^{MP} - \beta E_D^{MP} - \frac{1}{2}\ln|A|$$

$$+ \frac{W}{2}\ln\alpha + \frac{N}{2}\ln\beta - \frac{N}{2}\ln(2\pi). \tag{9.33}$$

Unfortunately, it is not possible to optimise this expression for the log evidence with respect to α and β directly.

The first step in trying to optimise the log evidence with respect to α is to compute its partial derivative. The most difficult term is the log of the matrix determinant $|A|$. Let $\lambda_1, \ldots, \lambda_W$ be the eigenvalues of the data Hessian H. Then A has eigenvalues $\lambda_i + \alpha$, and

$$\frac{d}{d\alpha}\ln|A| = \frac{d}{d\alpha}\ln\left(\prod_{i=1}^{W}\lambda_i + \alpha\right)$$

$$= \frac{d}{d\alpha}\sum_{i=1}^{W}\ln(\lambda_i + \alpha)$$

$$= \sum_{i=1}^{W}\frac{1}{\lambda_i + \alpha} = \text{tr}(A^{-1}). \tag{9.34}$$

The reason that we cannot optimise directly for α is that for a model whose error function is not a quadratic function of the weights (i.e. a model which is not linear regression or an RBF with fixed basis functions using a sum of squares error function), the Hessian H is not constant but depends on the weights w. Since we evaluate $A = H + \alpha I$ at w_{MP}, which depends on the choice of α, the eigenvalues of H depend indirectly on α. Thus (9.34) has ignored terms in $d\lambda_i/d\alpha$ (MacKay, 1992a).

Using this approximation, the derivative of (9.33) with respect to α is

$$-E_W^{MP} - \frac{1}{2}\sum_{i=1}^{W}\frac{1}{\lambda_i + \alpha} + \frac{W}{2\alpha}. \tag{9.35}$$

Equating this to zero and rearranging gives an implicit equation for α

$$2\alpha E_W^{MP} = W - \sum_{i=1}^{W} \frac{\alpha}{\lambda_i + \alpha}. \tag{9.36}$$

The right-hand side is equal to a value γ defined as

$$\gamma = \sum_{i=1}^{W} \frac{\lambda_i}{\lambda_i + \alpha}. \tag{9.37}$$

Components of the sum for which $\lambda_i \gg \alpha$ make a contribution near to 1, while components for which $0 < \lambda_i \ll \alpha$ make a contribution near to 0. Thus we can view γ is a measure of the number of *well-determined* parameters; see Bishop (1995) Section 10.4.

We can now consider optimisation of (9.33) with respect to β. Let μ_i denote the eigenvalues of the matrix $\nabla\nabla E_D$. Since $\boldsymbol{H} = \beta\nabla\nabla E_D$, it follows that $\lambda_i = \beta\mu_i$, and so

$$\frac{d\lambda_i}{d\beta} = \mu_i = \frac{\lambda_i}{\beta}. \tag{9.38}$$

Therefore

$$\frac{d}{d\beta} \ln|\boldsymbol{A}| = \frac{d}{d\beta} \sum_{i=1}^{W} \ln(\lambda_i + \alpha) = \frac{1}{\beta} \sum_{i=1}^{W} \frac{\lambda_i}{\lambda_i + \alpha}. \tag{9.39}$$

Hence, by a derivation similar to that which led to (9.36), we find that the optimal value of β is given by

$$2\beta E_D^{MP} = N - \sum_{i=1}^{W} \frac{\lambda_i}{\lambda_i + \alpha} = N - \gamma. \tag{9.40}$$

To apply the evidence procedure, we need to convert (9.36) and (9.40) from conditions satisfied by the optimal α and β into practical estimation methods. The following algorithm describes each step of applying the evidence procedure.

1. Choose initial values for the hyperparameters α and β. Initialise the weights in the network. These weights need not be drawn from the prior distribution defined by α. If there is little prior knowledge about the weights, then α will be small and hence the initial weights, if drawn from the prior, will tend to have large magnitudes. This makes it likely that the final weights will also be large, since we use a local non-linear optimisation algorithm to find them, and thus the final solution is unlikely to be satisfactory.

2. Train the network with a suitable optimisation algorithm to minimise the misfit function $S(\boldsymbol{w})$.

3. When the network training has reached a local minimum, the Gaussian approximation can be used to compute the evidence for the hyperparameters. These can be re-estimated with the following formulae, derived from (9.36) and (9.40).

$$\alpha^{\text{new}} = \frac{\gamma}{2E_W} \tag{9.41}$$

$$\beta^{\text{new}} = \frac{N - \gamma}{2E_D}. \tag{9.42}$$

These re-estimation formulae can be iterated if desired. Note that although these formulae only apply when $S(\boldsymbol{w})$ is at a local minimum, it is possible to re-estimate the hyperparameters more frequently. However, the formulae use the eigenvalues of the Hessian matrix $\boldsymbol{A}$, so are computationally costly.

4. Repeat steps 2 and 3 until convergence.

9.4.2 NETLAB Implementation

The NETLAB function evidence performs the hyperparameter re-estimation described in step 3 above. It has been designed to work with any network whose data structure has fields for the weight prior α and for which the data Hessian can be computed. This procedure can also be used for classification models with an entropy error function. In this case, there is no noise parameter β, and only α needs to be re-estimated.

The complexity of the code compared to the description above is caused by two features:

- The desire to reduce computational effort when several re-estimation iterations are required by computing the data Hessian and its eigenvalues only once.
- The need to deal correctly with multiple hyperparameters in a general way.

The first three arguments are the network net, the input data x and the target data t. The fourth argument num, which is optional, is the number of re-estimation iterations. Its default value is 1 (lines 4–6). The return values are: the network net with modified values for the hyperparameter fields alpha and, if appropriate, beta; the final value of gamma, the number of well-determined parameters; and the final value of logev, the log of the evidence for the hyperparameters.

```
1  function [net, gamma, logev] = evidence(net, x, t, num)
2
3  ndata = size(x, 1);
4  if nargin == 3
5    num = 1;
6  end
```

```
 7
 8  % Extract weights from network
 9  pakstr = [net.type, 'pak'];
10  w = feval(pakstr, net);
11
12  % Evaluate data-dependent contribution to the Hessian matrix.
13  [h, dh] = nethess(w, net, x, t);
14  clear h;  % To save memory when Hessian is large
15  if (~isfield(net, 'beta'))
16    local_beta = 1;
17  end
18
19  [evec, evl] = eig(dh);
20  % Now set the negative eigenvalues to zero.
21  evl = evl.*(evl > 0);
22  % safe_evl is used to avoid taking log of zero
23  safe_evl = evl + eps.*(evl <= 0);
24
25  [e, edata, eprior] = neterr(w, net, x, t);
26
27  if size(net.alpha) == [1 1]
28    % Form vector of eigenvalues
29    evl = diag(evl);
30    safe_evl = diag(safe_evl);
31  else
32    ngroups = size(net.alpha, 1);
33    gams = zeros(1, ngroups);
34    logas = zeros(1, ngroups);
35    % Reconstruct data hessian with negative evalues set to zero.
36    dh = evec*evl*evec';
37  end
38
39  % Do the re-estimation.
40  for k = 1 : num
41    % Re-estimate alpha.
42    if size(net.alpha) == [1 1]
43      % Evaluate number of well-determined parameters.
44      L = evl;
45      if isfield(net, 'beta')
46        L = net.beta*L;
47      end
48      gamma = sum(L./(L + net.alpha));
49      net.alpha = 0.5*gamma/eprior;
50      % Partially evaluate log evidence
51      logev = 0.5*net.nwts*log(net.alpha);
52    else
53      hinv = inv(hbayes(net, dh));
54      for m = 1 : ngroups
55        group_nweights = sum(net.index(:, m));
56        gams(m) = group_nweights - ...
57                  net.alpha(m)*sum(diag(hinv).*net.index(:,m));
58        net.alpha(m) = real(gams(m)/(2*eprior(m)));
59        % Weight alphas by number of weights in group
```

```
60          logas(m) = 0.5*group_nweights*log(net.alpha(m));
61      end
62      gamma = sum(gams, 2);
63      logev = sum(logas);
64   end
65   % Re-estimate beta.
66   if isfield(net, 'beta')
67          net.beta = 0.5*(net.nout*ndata - gamma)/edata;
68          logev = logev+0.5*ndata*log(net.beta)-0.5*ndata*log(2*pi);
69          local_beta = net.beta;
70   end
71
72   % Evaluate new log evidence
73   e = errbayes(net, edata);
74   if size(net.alpha) == [1 1]
75      logev = logev-e-0.5*sum(log(local_beta*safe_evl+net.alpha));
76   else
77      for m = 1:ngroups
78          logev = logev-e- ...
79              0.5*sum(log(local_beta*(safe_evl*net.index(:, m))+ ...
80              net.alpha(m)));
81      end
82   end
83 end
```

Line 3 computes N, the number of data points. In lines 9–10 the network weights are extracted. Because we need to call the generic functions neterr and nethess, which take the complete set of weights, the function mlppak (or equivalent for other models) is called rather than netpak, which returns only the masked weight vector. Line 13 computes the data Hessian $\nabla\nabla E_D$ (see the later discussion of the function nethess); the regularised Hessian H is cleared in line 14 to save memory when the number of weights is large since it is not used. The eigenvalues μ_i of this matrix are computed in line 19. Because negative eigenvalues (which may occur since a minimum of the total error function $S(w)$ need not be a minimum of the data error function $E_D(w)$) invalidate the log evidence formula given by (9.33), we need to make such values zero (line 21). In addition, when computing the log evidence it is necessary to take the logarithm of the eigenvalues. To avoid singularities, a second vector safe_evl is created with non-positive eigenvalues set to eps (line 23). The function neterr is called in order to compute the value of βE_D (edata) on line 29, since this does not change inside this function. Line 31–37 set up the matrices necessary for multiple α hyperparameters and reconstruct the data Hessian H with negative eigenvalues set to zero. This is done since individual weights correspond to particular entries in A and therefore each α parameter corresponds to a sum of those entries.

The main loop starts at line 40, and is performed num times. The branch in lines 42–51 is the re-estimation for a single weight prior α; this follows closely the theoretical description in Section 9.4.1. In lines 44–47 the vector L is set to the eigenvalues $\lambda_i = \beta\mu_i$ of H. Line 48 computes γ according to

(9.37), and line 49 re-estimates α according to (9.41). Line 51 evaluates the α-dependent part of the log evidence (9.33).

Lines 52–64 form the branch for multiple α parameters. Each hyperparameter has a corresponding γ value. Here we use the $\operatorname{tr} A^{-1}$ form of the evidence derivative (9.34). In lines 54–61 we loop around each hyperparameter and its group of weights in turn. The corresponding γ_m value is computed in lines 56–57. The value W is replaced by the number of weights in the current group group_nweights, while

$$\sum_{i=1}^{W} \alpha/(\lambda_i + \alpha) \tag{9.43}$$

is replaced by

$$\alpha_m \sum_{i \in \mathcal{W}_m} (A^{-1})_{ii}, \tag{9.44}$$

where $\mathcal{W}_m$ denotes the mth group of weights defined by the mth column of net.index. The hyperparameter α_m is re-estimated using γ_m and E_W^m (line 58). The use of the MATLAB function real to take the real part of the right-hand expression is necessary because very small imaginary components can be introduced into hinv by rounding error in the matrix inversion. Line 60 computes $\ln \alpha_m$ for the mth weight group. The total number of well-determined parameters γ is the sum $\sum_m \gamma_m$ (line 62). Line 63 computes the α-dependent part of the log evidence.

The final task is to re-estimate β and add the β-dependent terms to the log evidence: this is done in the same way no matter how many weight priors are in use (lines 66–70). The log evidence is then updated for the new value of β. This involves updating the misfit error e for the new hyperparameters (line 73) and then subtracting this and $\log|A|/2$ (lines 75 and 78–80).

We complete this section with a brief description of the NETLAB function nethess:

```
1  function [h, varargout] = nethess(w, net, x, t, varargin)
2
3  hess_str = [net.type, 'hess'];
4  net = netunpak(net, w);
5
6  [s{1:nargout}] = feval(hess_str, net, x, t, varargin{:});
7  h = s{1};
8  for i = 2:nargout
9    varargout{i-1} = s{i};
10  end
```

This function calls the appropriate network-specific function (e.g. mlphess) for the network passed as an argument. Note that its use in evidence assumes that there are two calling sequences for the network specific function (using mlphess as an example):

```
[h, dh] = mlphess(net, x, t);
```

which computes computes $\nabla\nabla E_D$ and hence derives the total Hessian A and the data component H. The alternative calling sequence

```
h = mlphess(net, x, t, dh);
```

recomputes A using the matrix H that is passed as the argument dh. This is usually much more efficient than the first form if H does not need to be recomputed.

9.5 Predictions and Error Bars

Once we have trained a network to find the most probable weights w_{MP} and estimated the optimal hyperparameters α and β we are ready to make predictions. Using the Gaussian approximation to the posterior weight distribution given by (9.27) we can compute the distribution of output values for an input pattern x

$$p(t|x, \mathcal{D}) = \int p(t|x, w)p(w|\mathcal{D})\, dw. \tag{9.45}$$

The distribution $p(t|x, w)$ is simply the model for the distribution of the noise on the target for a given weight vector w. The computation of (9.45) depends on the form of this noise model, and we shall consider regression and classification models separately.

9.5.1 Predictions for Regression

With a sum of squares error function (corresponding to a Gaussian noise model) and a Gaussian approximation to the posterior weight distribution, the integral we want to compute has the form

$$p(t|x, \mathcal{D}) \propto \int \exp\left(-\frac{\beta}{2}\{t - y(x; w)\}^2\right) \exp\left(-\frac{1}{2}\Delta w^T A \Delta w\right)\, dw. \tag{9.46}$$

This is still intractable for non-linear network functions $y(x; w)$. However, if the training set is reasonably large, the weight posterior will be locally sharply peaked about its mode, and we can approximate the network output y by its linearisation around w_{MP}:

$$y(x; w) = y(x; w_{MP}) + g^T \Delta w, \tag{9.47}$$

where g denotes the gradient of y with respect to the weights w evaluated at w_{MP}. The integral can now be evaluated to give a Gaussian distribution with mean $y(x; w_{MP})$, the standard prediction for the most probable weights, and variance

$$\sigma^2 = \frac{1}{\beta} + g^T A^{-1} g. \tag{9.48}$$

This variance has contributions both from the output noise model $(1/\beta)$ and from the posterior distribution in the weights.

This predictive distribution allows us to provide error bars for the network output instead of just a single answer. The size of the error bar varies approximately with the inverse data density (Williams *et al.*, 1995), so that the error bars are broader in regions where the training data density is low. This corresponds with our intuition that the weight posterior should be broader (i.e. more uncertain) in regions where there is little information from the data.

9.5.2 Predictions for Classification

For classification problems a Gaussian noise model is not appropriate, and instead we use a cross-entropy (for two-class problems) or entropy (for 1-of-c problems) error function for the MLP and GLM (see Section 4.1). We shall consider the likelihood and error functions for the two-class problem first:

$$p(\mathcal{D}|w, x) = \prod_{n=1}^{N} y(x^n; w)^{t^n} (1 - y(x^n; w))^{1-t^n} \tag{9.49}$$

$$E_D(\mathcal{D}|w, x) = -\sum_{n=1}^{N} \{t^n \ln y(x^n; w) + (1 - t^n) \ln(1 - y(x^n; w))\}. \tag{9.50}$$

Note that there is no β hyperparameter for this distribution. The corresponding output function is the logistic sigmoid (see (4.3)):

$$y = f(a) = \frac{1}{1 + \exp(-a)}, \tag{9.51}$$

where a denotes the activation of the output unit. It follows that the posterior distribution of the weights has the form

$$p(w|\mathcal{D}) = \frac{1}{Z_S} \exp(-E_D - \alpha E_W) = \frac{1}{Z_S} \exp(-S(w)). \tag{9.52}$$

As for the regression case, we approximate this distribution by a Gaussian with mean w_{MP}, the most probable weight vector found by optimisation of the total error function $S(w)$, and inverse covariance A, the Hessian matrix of $S(w)$ evaluated at w_{MP}. The hyperparameter α (or set of hyperparameters $\alpha_1, \ldots, \alpha_g$) can be learned from the training set using the evidence procedure in the same way as for the regression case omitting the re-estimation of β.

To make a prediction, we need to compute an integral over the posterior weight distribution. The probability that an input vector x belongs to class $\mathcal{C}_1$ is given by

$$P(C_1|x) = \int P(C_1|x, w)p(w|\mathcal{D}) \, dw \tag{9.53}$$

$$= \int y(x; w)p(w|\mathcal{D}) \, dw. \tag{9.54}$$

If we proceed as before and assume that the weight posterior is sharply peaked around w_{MP} there is still a problem because the output function $y(a)$ is not linear. This means that the prediction no longer equals the most probable output $y(x, w_{MP})$.

MacKay (1992b) assumes that a is locally a linear function of the weights. Its distribution is given by

$$p(a|x, \mathcal{D}) = \int p(a|x, w)p(w|\mathcal{D}) \, dw. \tag{9.55}$$

Making the same assumptions about the weight posterior as in Section 9.5.1, we obtain the same result but for a in the place of y; a has a Gaussian distribution with mean a_{MP} given by forward propagating x through the network with weights w_{MP} and variance

$$s^2(x) = g^T A^{-1} g, \tag{9.56}$$

where g is the gradient of a with respect to the weights w evaluated at w_{MP}. We can then rewrite (9.54) in the form

$$P(C_1|x, \mathcal{D}) = \int P(C_1)p(a|x, \mathcal{D}) \, da = \int f(a)p(a|x, \mathcal{D}) \, da. \tag{9.57}$$

Because $f(a)$ is not linear, this integral does not have an analytic solution, but MacKay (1992b) suggests the approximation

$$P(C_1|x, \mathcal{D}) \approx f(\kappa(s)a_{MP}), \tag{9.58}$$

where

$$\kappa(s) = \left(1 + \frac{\pi s^2}{8}\right)^{-1/2}. \tag{9.59}$$

What is the effect of marginalisation on the network output? The standard decision boundary to minimise the probability of misclassification is $P(C_1) = 0.5$. Considering (9.58), the network predicts 0.5 if and only if $a_{MP} = 0$. Hence for this decision boundary, the predictions made by the most probable output $y(x; w_{MP})$ and the marginalised predictions are the same. Equation (9.59) shows that $0 < \kappa < 1$ and hence

$$|f(\kappa(s)a_{MP})| \leq |f(a_{MP})| = |y(x; w_{MP})|, \tag{9.60}$$

where the inequality is strict for $a_{MP} \neq 0$. This means that the marginalised prediction always has a value closer to 0.5 than the most probable prediction (see Fig. 9.6 for an illustration of this effect). The interpretation is that the network predictions become less certain, and thiss effect increases as σ becomes larger in regions of low training data density.

Providing a reasonable approximation for the softmax output function is much harder, and is very rarely considered in the literature. Gibbs (1997) developed two variational schemes to provide upper and lower bounds on the relevant integral, but we have implemented one of his simpler and less computationally costly schemes. By an extension of the Mackay approach to logistic outputs, the moderated output for the jth class is given by

$$
\frac{\exp\left(\kappa(s^{(j)})a_{MP}^{(j)}\right)}{\sum_i \exp\left(\kappa(s^{(i)})a_{MP}^{(i)}\right)}. \tag{9.61}
$$

This approximation is based on the assumption that $\kappa(s^{(i)})$ is close to 1 for all i, which is only reasonable if the activations are all in the range $[-1, 1]$. We can expect the approximation to break down in regions where the unmoderated outputs are close to 0 or 1.

9.5.3 NETLAB Implementation

A generic function fevbayes plays a similar role to errbayes, gbayes and hbayes in making predictions. It computes a value extra, which represents the variance for linear outputs and the moderated prediction for logistic and softmax outputs.

```
1  function extra = fevbayes(net, y, a, x, t, x_test)
2
3  w = netpak(net);
4  g = netderiv(w, net, x_test);
5  hess = nethess(w, net, x, t);
6  invhess = inv(hess);
7
8  ntest = size(x_test, 1);
9  var = zeros(ntest, 1);
10 for idx = 1:1:net.nout,
11   for n = 1:1:ntest,
12     grad = squeeze(g(n,:,idx));
13     var(n,idx) = grad*invhess*grad';
14   end
15 end
16
17 switch net.outfn
18   case 'linear'
19     extra = ones(size(var))./net.beta + var;
20   case 'logistic'
21     kappa = 1./(sqrt(ones(size(var)) + (pi.*var)./8));
22     extra = 1./(1 + exp(-kappa.*a));
```

```
23   case 'softmax'
24     kappa = 1./(sqrt(ones(size(var)) + (pi.*var)./8));
25     temp = kappa.*a;
26     extra = exp(temp)./(sum(temp, 2)*ones(1, nout));
27   otherwise
28     error(['Unknown activation function ', net.outfn]);
29   end
```

The derivatives of the output activations g are computed in line 3, and the regularised Hessian A in line 4. These are combined to compute the covariance of the approximating Gaussian $g^T A^{-1} g$ in line 13. The variance error bar (9.48) is computed by line 19, the logistic moderated output (9.58) by lines 21–22, and the softmax moderated output (9.61) by lines 24–26.

This generic function is called by a network-specific evidence forward propagation function, such as mlpevfwd:

```
1   function [y, extra] = mlpevfwd(w, net, x, t, x_test)
2
3   net = mlpunpak(net, w);
4   [y, z, a] = mlpfwd(net, x_test);
5   extra = fevbayes(net, y, a, x, t, x_test);
```

The reason for the model-specific functions is that the list of return values from the standard forward propagation function does not contain the output activations in a consistent position. This is to improve the efficiency of the computation of model gradients and special purpose training algorithms.

9.6 Demonstrations of Evidence Procedure

9.6.1 The Evidence Procedure for Regression

Although the theory underlying the evidence procedure is quite complex, the application of the technique using NETLAB is not much more difficult than standard maximum likelihood training. This is shown by the demonstration program demev1 which applies an MLP to the noisy sine regression problem. To focus on the important aspects, only the parts of the script that are concerned with data generation, network initialisation, network training, and predictions are shown. In this program a single hyperparameter α is used in the prior for all the weights.

```
1   % Generate the matrix of inputs x and targets t.
2   ndata = 16;              % Number of data points.
3   noise = 0.1;             % Noise standard deviation
4   randn('state', 1729);
5   x = 0.25 + 0.15*randn(ndata, 1);
6   t = sin(2*pi*x) + noise*randn(size(x));
7
8   % Set up network parameters.
9   nin = 1;                 % Number of inputs.
10  nhidden = 3;             % Number of hidden units.
11  nout = 1;                % Number of outputs.
```

```
12  alpha = 0.01;            % Initial prior hyperparameter.
13  beta_init = 50.0;        % Initial noise hyperparameter.
14
15  % Create and initialise network weight vector.
16  net = mlp(nin, nhidden, nout, 'linear', alpha, beta_init);
17
18  % Set up vector of options for the optimiser.
19  nouter = 8;              % Number of outer loops.
20  ninner = 1;              % Number of inner loops.
21  options = zeros(1,18);   % Default options vector.
22  options(1) = 1;          % Display error values.
23  options(2) = 1.0e-7;     % Search precision of weights.
24  options(3) = 1.0e-7;     % Search precision of error.
25  options(14) = 500;       % Inner loop cycles.
26
27  % Train using scg, re-estimating alpha and beta.
28  for k = 1:nouter
29    net = netopt(net, options, x, t, 'scg');
30    [net, gamma] = evidence(net, x, t, ninner);
31    fprintf(1, '\nRe-estimation cycle %d:\n', k);
32    fprintf(1, '  alpha =  %8.5f\n', net.alpha);
33    fprintf(1, '  beta  =  %8.5f\n', net.beta);
34    fprintf(1, '  gamma =  %8.5f\n\n', gamma);
35    disp(' ')
36  end
37  fprintf(1, 'true beta: %f\n', 1/(noise*noise));
38
39  % Evaluate prediction and error bars.
40  [y, sig2] = mlpevfwd(net, x, t, plotvals);
41  sig = sqrt(sig2);
42
43  % Plot data, original function, and network prediction.
44  figure(h); hold on;
45  plot(plotvals, y, '-r')
46  xlabel('Input')
47  ylabel('Target')
48  plot(plotvals, y + sig, '-b');
49  plot(plotvals, y - sig, '-b');
50  legend('data', 'function', 'network', 'error bars');
```

Lines 1–6 generate a noisy sine training data set. Lines 8–13 define the network parameters: the new ones for the Bayesian procedure are alpha and beta_init. The MLP network is created in the usual way in line 16.

The next stage is to train the network. Lines 21–27 set up the parameters to do this. The variable nouter is used to control the number of weight optimisations performed and ninner is the number of evidence re-estimations after each weight optimisation. Note that the tolerance for the weight optimisation is set to a very low value (10^{-7}). This is because the Gaussian approximation to the weight posterior depends on being at a minimum of the error function. However, it is probably a more exact tolerance than is strictly necessary in practice. Lines 28–36 carry out the training. Line 29 optimises the weights with the Bayesian error function $S(\boldsymbol{w})$ computed by neterr, and line 30 re-estimates the hyperparameters using the evidence procedure. The remainder of the loop prints out the hyperparameter values, which helps to assess whether the procedure has converged. At the end of the process, the network data structure net contains weights that are set to $\boldsymbol{w}_{MP}$ (to be precise, a local minimum in the error surface) and hyperparameters α and β that are set to their optimal values. These can be monitored during training to assess convergence, as shown in Fig. 9.3.

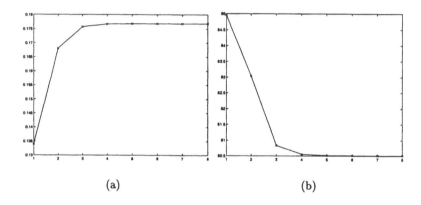

(a)   (b)

Fig. 9.3. Convergence of hyperparameters in evidence procedure. (a) α. (b) β.

The final stage is to make predictions with error bars. Lines 40–41 compute the mean prediction y and the standard deviation of the error bars sig using mlpevfwd following (9.48). Finally, line 45 plots the mean prediction and lines 48–49 plot the ± one standard deviation error bars from this prediction.

The results are shown in Fig. 9.4, which clearly illustrates the way the error bars grow much wider in regions that are distant from the training data. The converged values for the hyperparameters were $\alpha = 0.17685$, $\beta = 80.51202$ and $\gamma = 6.33676$. The true value of β is 100, so the evidence procedure is slightly overestimating the noise variance. The final value of the regularised error was 8, which is equal to half the number of data points, as predicted by theory.

9.6.2 The Evidence Procedure for Classification

Using NETLAB to apply the evidence procedure to classification problems is very similar to regression. In practice, it is better to use consistent priors, since the regularisation parameters for different weight groups can diverge

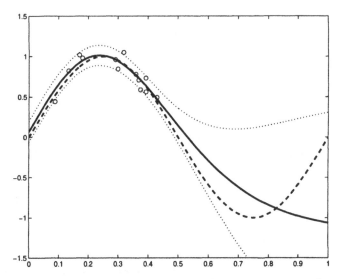

Fig. 9.4. Demonstration of evidence procedure for regression. Data (*circles*) generated from sine functions (*dashed line*). MLP mean prediction (*solid line*) with error bars at 2 standard deviations (*dotted lines*).

significantly, and a single regularisation parameter can give poor results. The following code fragment shows how this works in practice:

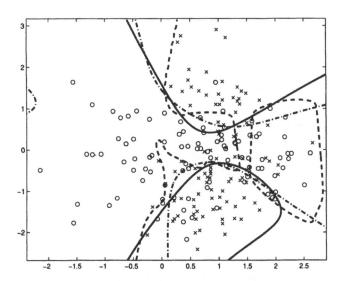

Fig. 9.5. Demonstration of evidence procedure for classification. Data drawn from two classes (*circles* and *crosses*) is classified by the optimal Bayes rule (*solid line*), MLP trained with evidence (*dash-dotted line*) and unregularised MLP (*dashed line*).

```
1  % Set up network parameters.
2  nin = 2;                    % Number of inputs.
3  nhidden = 8;                % Number of hidden units.
4  nout = 1;                   % Number of outputs.
5  aw1 = 0.01;
6  ab1 = 0.01;
7  aw2 = 0.01;
8  ab2 = 0.01;
9
10 % Create and initialise network weight vector.
11 prior = mlpprior(nin, nhidden, nout, aw1, ab1, aw2, ab2);
12 net = mlp(nin, nhidden, nout, 'logistic', prior);
13
14 % Set up vector of options for the optimiser.
15 nouter = 5;                 % Number of outer loops.
16 ninner = 2;                 % Number of innter loops.
17 options = foptions;         % Default options vector.
18 options(2) = 1.0e-5;        % Absolute precision for weights.
19 options(3) = 1.0e-5;        % Precision for objective function.
20 options(14) = 100;          % Number of training cycles in inner loop.
21
22 % Train using scaled conjugate gradients, re-estimating alpha.
23 for k = 1:nouter
24    net = netopt(net, options, data, target, 'scg');
25    [net, gamma] = evidence(net, data, target, ninner);
26    fprintf(1, '\nRe-estimation cycle %d:\n', k);
27    disp([' alpha = ', num2str(net.alpha')]);
28    % No beta term
29    fprintf(1, ' gamma = %8.5f\n\n', gamma);
30    disp(' ')
31 end
32
33 % Evaluate predictions.
34 [yg, ymodg] = mlpevfwd(net, data, target, [X(:) Y(:)]);
35 yg = reshape(yg(:,1),size(X));
36 ymodg = reshape(ymodg(:,1),size(X));
37
38 plot(data((label<=2),1),data(label<=2,2), ClassSymbol1, ...
39    'MarkerSize', PointSize)
40 axis([x0 x1 y0 y1]);
41 plot(data((label>2),1),data(label>2,2), ClassSymbol2, ...
42    'MarkerSize', PointSize)
43 % Bayesian MLP decision boundary
44 [cN, hN] = contour(xrange,yrange,y2g,[0.5 0.5],'--k');
```

In this example, the data is generated from a mixture of four Gaussians, with centres $(0, -0.1)$, $(1.5, 0)$, $(1, 1)$, and $(1, -1)$, which are assigned to two classes (the first two and last two centres respectively). The chosen covariance matrices ensure that there is a reasonable degree of class overlap. The results of using the evidence procedure are clear in Fig. 9.5. The predictions of the regularised network are very close to the optimal decision boundary computed using Bayes' rule on the known generating distribution, while the

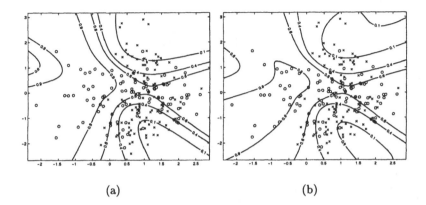

(a)   (b)

Fig. 9.6. Demonstration of moderated outputs. For the same data as Fig. 9.5, output contours of MLP trained using evidence procedure are shown. (a) Standard outputs. (b) Moderated outputs integrating over weight posterior.

unregularised network has an overly complex decision boundary characteristic of a model with too many parameters trained using maximum likelihood. The effect of 'output moderation' for the regularised network is demonstrated in Fig. 9.6, which shows that more of the space lies in the region where the network prediction lies in the range $(0.4, 0.6)$ and less in the extremes $(0, 0.1)$ and $(0.9, 1.0)$.

9.6.3 Automatic Relevance Determination

Using the evidence procedure with more complex priors is straightforward in NETLAB, since all the complexity is handled in the functions errbayes, gbayes and hbayes. To illustrate this, consider the demonstration program demard which uses an ARD prior to select relevant inputs for a regression problem.

```
1   % Generate the data set.
2   randn('state', 0);
3   rand('state', 0);
4   ndata = 100;
5   noise = 0.05;
6   x1 = rand(ndata, 1) + 0.002*randn(ndata, 1);
7   x2 = x1 + 0.02*randn(ndata, 1);
8   x3 = 0.5 + 0.2*randn(ndata, 1);
9   x = [x1, x2, x3];
10  t = sin(2*pi*x1) + noise*randn(ndata, 1);
11
12  % Set up network parameters.
13  nin = 3;                % Number of inputs.
14  nhidden = 2;            % Number of hidden units.
```

```
15   nout = 1;                    % Number of outputs.
16   aw1 = 0.01*ones(1, nin);     % First-layer ARD hyperparameters.
17   ab1 = 0.01;                  % Hyperparameter for b1.
18   aw2 = 0.01;                  % Hyperparameter for w2.
19   ab2 = 0.01;                  % Hyperparameter for b2.
20   beta = 50.0;                 % Initial beta.
21
22   % Create and initialise network.
23   prior = mlpprior(nin, nhidden, nout, aw1, ab1, aw2, ab2);
24   net = mlp(nin, nhidden, nout, 'linear', prior, beta);
25
26   % Set up vector of options for the optimiser.
27   nouter = 2;                  % Number of outer loops
28   ninner = 10;                 % Number of inner loops
29   options = zeros(1,18);
30   options(1) = 1;              % Display error values.
31   options(2) = 1.0e-7;
32   options(3) = 1.0e-7;
33   options(14) = 300;           % Inner loop cycles.
34
35   % Train using scg, re-estimating alpha and beta.
36   for k = 1:nouter
37     net = netopt(net, options, x, t, 'scg');
38     [net, gamma] = evidence(net, x, t, ninner);
39     fprintf(1, '\n\nRe-estimation cycle %d:\n', k);
40     fprintf(1, '  alpha = %8.5f\n', net.alpha);
41     fprintf(1, '  beta  = %8.5f\n', net.beta);
42     fprintf(1, '  gamma = %8.5f\n\n', gamma);
43     disp(' ');
44   end
45
46   % Plot the trained network prediction.
47   figure(h); hold on;
48   [y, z] = mlpfwd(net, plotvals*ones(1,3));
49   plot(plotvals, y, '-r', 'LineWidth', 2)
50   legend('data', 'function', 'network');
51
52   fprintf(1, '    alpha1: %8.5f\n', net.alpha(1));
53   fprintf(1, '    alpha2: %8.5f\n', net.alpha(2));
54   fprintf(1, '    alpha3: %8.5f\n', net.alpha(3));
```

Lines 1–10 create the dataset. This is based on the noisy sine wave dataset used in demev1 but has three input variables (lines 6–8):

- x1, which is the variable used to compute the target;
- x2, which is a noisy version of x1;
- x3, which is randomly sampled and independent of x1 and x2.

Lines 13–20 initialise the network parameters (including hyperparameters). The only change from demev1 is that there are separate initial hyperparameters for the prior for different groups of weights:

- aw1 is the hyperparameter for the input layer weights containing nin values, one for each input (in order to implement ARD);

- ab1 is the hyperparameter for the input layer biases;
- aw2 is the hyperparameter for the second-layer weights;
- ab2 is the hyperparameter for the second-layer biases.

Note that all the initial values are quite small, corresponding to a small amount of regularisation. It is good practice to start with relatively small α values so that the model is allowed sufficient flexibility to fit the data. Otherwise the model may end in a poor local minimum and remain essentially linear with a small value for β (corresponding to a large noise variance). The prior structure is created in line 23 with a call to mlpprior and used in the creation of the network in line 24.

The next step is to train the model. The parameters controlling the process are assigned values in lines 27–33. By way of a change from demev1, there are just two outer loops of weight optimisation and 10 inner loops of hyperparameter re-estimation. The training loop is in lines 36–44, and is very similar to that in demev1. Lines 47–50 plot the network prediction against the relevant variable x1, and can be seen to give a good fit to the underlying function. If required, error bars could be added just as in demev1.

Finally, the first three hyperparameters (that control the prior for each of the three input variables) are printed. Their values in this simulation are 0.17669, 29.34116 and 252090.81555 respectively. A small value for α_i corresponds to a large variance prior which allows weights of large magnitude. Such a variable (x1 in this case) is very relevant for predicting the output. Conversely, a large value for α_i corresponds to a small variance prior and constrains weights to small magnitudes. The variable x3 has a much larger value than the other two hyperparameters and is easy to identify as irrelevant. These conclusions are supported by the input layer weight matrix, which has the values

$$\begin{pmatrix} -3.17292 & 1.09373 \\ -0.19994 & 0.04644 \\ 0.00065 & -0.00028 \end{pmatrix} \tag{9.62}$$

where the ith row denotes the fan-in to the ith input unit.

9.7 Monte Carlo Methods

The basic operation in Bayesian inference is one of integration rather than optimisation. In the evidence procedure we have used approximations (for example, to the posterior weight distribution) and hyperparameter optimisation in order to perform the integrals. In this section we discuss Monte Carlo methods (see Chapter 8) in the context of prediction using neural networks.

Consider the distribution of output vectors as a specific example. The full predictive distribution, once we have observed the data set D, is given by integrating over the weight vector w

$$p(t|x, \mathcal{D}) = \int p(t|x, w)p(w|\mathcal{D}) \, dw, \tag{9.63}$$

where $p(w|\mathcal{D})$ represents posterior distribution of the weights. In the Monte Carlo approach we approximate integrals such as this by finite sums of the form

$$p(t|x, D) \simeq \frac{1}{N} \sum_{n=1}^{N} p(t|x, w_n), \tag{9.64}$$

where $\{w_n\}$ represents a sample of weight vectors generated from the distribution $p(w|D)$.

In the problems we are interested in, it is possible to evaluate $p(w|D)$ (up to an overall normalisation coefficient) relatively easily, while it is typically much more difficult to generate a sample $\{w_n\}$ from this distribution.

While the Metropolis–Hastings sampler has proven to be very useful in applications from many fields, its direct application to neural networks is at best limited as a result of the random walk nature of the trajectory through weight space. This causes progress to be slow, requiring large numbers of steps to give a reasonable representation of the posterior distribution. Increasing the step size does not solve the problem since this leads to an increase in the rejection rate. Instead we shall use the hybrid Monte Carlo algorithm, which largely avoids this problem.

One of the limitations of the Metropolis–Hastings algorithm is that it makes no use of gradient information. For neural networks, the technique of error back-propagation provides a computationally efficient algorithm for evaluating the derivatives of an error function with respect to the model parameters, and this makes them suitable models for hybrid Monte Carlo methods of sampling.

9.8 Demonstration of Hybrid Monte Carlo for MLPs

There are two demonstration programs for hybrid Monte Carlo sampling with MLPs. They show the effect of different HMC parameters on the resulting network predictions. Here we shall discuss demhmc3, which applies an MLP to the noisy sine regression problem.

```
1  % Generate the matrix of inputs x and targets t.
2  ndata = 20;              % Number of data points.
3  noise = 0.1;             % Noise standard deviation.
4  nin = 1;                 % Number of inputs.
5  nout = 1;                % Number of outputs.
6
7  seed = 42;               % Seed for random number generators.
8  randn('state', seed);
9  rand('state', seed);
```

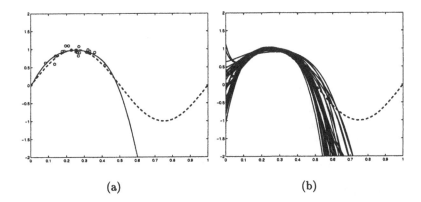

(a)   (b)

Fig. 9.7. Bayesian inference for a simple regression problem, with samples from the posterior distribution obtained using hybrid Monte Carlo. (a) Data (*circles*) and generating function (*dashed line*) with mean prediction (*solid line*). (b) Generating function (*dashed line*) and sampled predictions (*solid line*) from every 10th weight sample.

```
10
11  x = 0.25 + 0.1*randn(ndata, nin);
12  t = sin(2*pi*x) + noise*randn(size(x));
13
14  % Set up network parameters.
15  nhidden = 5;          % Number of hidden units.
16  alpha = 0.001;        % Coefficient of weight-decay prior.
17  beta = 100.0;         % Coefficient of data error.
18
19  % Initialise weights reasonably close to 0
20  net = mlp(nin, nhidden, nout, 'linear', alpha, beta);
21  net = mlpinit(net, 10);
22
23  % Set up vector of options for hybrid Monte Carlo.
24  nsamples = 300;           % Number of retained samples.
25
26  options = foptions;       % Default options vector.
27  options(1) = 1;           % Switch on diagnostics.
28  options(5) = 1;           % Use persistence
29  options(7) = 10;          % Number of steps in trajectory.
30  options(14) = nsamples;   % Number of HMC samples returned.
31  options(15) = 300;        % Burn-in
32  options(17) = 0.95;       % Alpha value in persistence
33  options(18) = 0.005;      % Step size.
34
35  w = mlppak(net);
36  % Initialise HMC
37  hmc('state', 42);
38  [samples, energies] = hmc('neterr', w, options, 'netgrad', ...
```

```
39                              net, x, t);
40  nplot = 300;
41  plotvals = [0 : 1/(nplot - 1) : 1]';
42  pred = zeros(size(plotvals));
43  fh1 = figure;
44  hold on
45  for k = 1:nsamples
46    w2 = samples(k,:);
47    net2 = mlpunpak(net, w2);
48    y = mlpfwd(net2, plotvals);
49    % Sum predictions
50    pred = pred + y;
51    h4 = plot(plotvals, y, '-r', 'LineWidth', 1);
52  end
53  pred = pred./nsamples;
54  % Plot data
55  h1 = plot(x, t, 'ob', 'LineWidth', 2, 'MarkerFaceColor', 'blue');
56  axis([0 1 -3 3])
57
58  % Plot function
59  [fx, fy] = fplot('sin(2*pi*x)', [0 1], '--g');
60  h2 = plot(fx, fy, '--g', 'LineWidth', 2);
61  set(gca, 'box', 'on');
62
63  % Plot averaged prediction
64  h3 = plot(plotvals, pred, '-c', 'LineWidth', 2);
```

Lines 15–17 set up the network parameters (compare demev1), while lines 20–21 create and initialise the network. The sampler parameters are initialised in lines 24–33. Each trajectory consists of 10 steps (options(7)) and the step size is 0.005 (options(18)); such short trajectories will still explore the weight space since persistence is being used. The retained samples and the burn in period both consist of 300 sets of weights. The sampling takes place in lines 35–39; netopt cannot be used since it assumes that the optimiser returns a single set of weights to unpack into the network data structure.

In lines 45–52 each set of sampled weights is placed in the network (line 47) and used to make a prediction (line 48). The average prediction is computed in line 53 (see Fig. 9.7 (a)). The spread of the predictions can be used to give error bars or plotted directly; Fig. 9.7 (b) shows how the predictions have much greater variance in regions outside the training set. The parameters of the sampling algorithm are quite well tuned for this problem: there are only 22 rejected steps in the burn in period and one more in the sample itself.

9.9 Worked Example: Improved Classification Approximation

Predictions made using the evidence approximation replaced the integral (9.54)

$$P(\mathcal{C}_1|x) = \int P(\mathcal{C}_1|x, w)p(w|\mathcal{D}) \, \mathrm{d}w \tag{9.65}$$

$$= \int y(x; w)p(w|\mathcal{D}) \, \mathrm{d}w \tag{9.66}$$

by the function (9.59)

$$\kappa(s) = \left(1 + \frac{\pi s^2}{8}\right)^{-1/2}. \tag{9.67}$$

The factor κ was chosen so that the approximation has the correct gain at $a_{MP} = 0$ as $s^2 \to \infty$. More recently, Williams and Barber (1998) have suggested an approximation to the integral replacing the logistic function $y(x; w)$ by a sum of five error functions (i.e. the cumulative distribution of a Gaussian). This has the advantage that the integral of the product of an error function and a Gaussian can be computed analytically.

```
1   function s = sigint(mu, var)
2
3   alpha = [-1.8961 -0.1193 -0.0691 1.0839]';
4   lambda = [0.41 0.4 0.37 0.44 0.39]';
5
6   l = lambda(2:length(lambda));
7   l0 = lambda(1);
8   v = erf(mu.*l./sqrt(1+2.*l.*l.*var));
9   v0 = erf(mu.*l0./sqrt(1+2.*l0.*l0.*var));
10
11  s = 0.5.*(1+ (v0 + alpha'*v)./(1+sum(alpha)));
```

This function returns the approximate integral of

$$\int \frac{1}{1 + \exp(-x)} N(x; \mu, \sigma^2) \, \mathrm{d}x. \tag{9.68}$$

The basis functions are $\mathrm{erf}(\lambda x)$ for the values of λ in line 4. These were chosen to interpolate the logistic function at $x = [0, 0.6, 2, 3.5, 4.5, \infty]$ giving rise to the coefficients α given in line 3. Some small adjustments are needed to account for the fact that the MATLAB function erf is

$$\mathrm{erf}(x) = \int_0^\infty \frac{1}{2\pi} \exp(-t^2) \, \mathrm{d}t, \tag{9.69}$$

instead of an integral with $-\infty$ as the lower bound.

We can compare the quality of this approximation with that given by the MATLAB function quad8, a high order quadrature method, applied over 10 standard deviations around μ. (The simpler function quad fails for numerical reasons.) On four test integrals with μ varying between 1 and 20 and σ^2 between 0.001 and 100, both methods agreed to within 3×10^{-4}, but sigint required 714 flops compared with 51065 for quad8. The Mackay approximation required 36 flops, but the error for $\mu = 20$ was 0.0165, confirming that sigint is likely to be more accurate for large activation values.

Exercises

9.1 (⋆ ⋆) Use the masking mechanism to write an optimisation algorithm for an MLP that alternately trains the input and output layer weights.

9.2 (⋆) Experiment with `demprior` to determine the effect of the hyperparameter controlling each group of weights. Start with those controlling the output weights and bias, since their effect is easier to see.

9.3 (⋆) Experiment with the effect of initialising α to a small value in the evidence procedure. Run the algorithm from several sets of initial weights and show that the network is more likely to end up in a local minimum than when it is initialised with small weights. Assess the effect on the mean prediction and the error bars.

9.4 (⋆ ⋆) Compare the quality and efficiency of training an MLP network using the evidence procedure with the same network trained using simple weight decay. Use cross-validation to select the weight decay parameter α.

9.5 (⋆) Complete the implementation of direct input-output connections for the MLP network that was started in Section 5.8 and Exercise 5.6 by extending `mlpprior` to allow for the new weights. You should extend the notion of a consistent prior to allow a weight group for the direct connections. Evaluate the model using the evidence procedure and HMC.

9.6 (⋆) Compare the quality of the generalisation of the ARD model in `demard` with a maximum likelihood fit to the same training data.

9.7 (⋆ ⋆) Write functions `glmevfwd` and `rbfevfwd` to perform forward propagation through GLM and RBF models using the evidence framework. Evaluate GLM and RBF models in a the evidence framework using nonlinear optimisation and compare the results with MLPs trained on the same datasets.

9.8 (⋆ ⋆) Using ARD as a model, develop a prior for the RBF model that groups the fan-out weights from each hidden unit together. Use this prior to determine the optimal complexity for an RBF network. Compare this technique with the dual basis function method discussed in Chapter 6 on the basis of generalisation performance and computational cost.

9.9 (⋆ ⋆) Apply rejection sampling to neural networks. Using Bayes' theorem, it can be shown that weight vectors can be generated from the posterior distribution $p(w|\mathcal{D})$ by sampling from the prior $p(w)$ and accepting them with probability given by $\max(1, \exp(-\beta E_D)$ (Bishop, 1995). Using a dataset of no more than 10 points and an MLP with one input and one output, implement and test this procedure. Iterate the algorithm until 10 samples have been generated. Comment on the efficiency of the method compared with hybrid Monte Carlo.

9.10 (⋆) Explore the evidence approximation and HMC in the context of large networks and small datasets. At what point does the evidence approximation break down and cause serious overfitting?

9.11 ($\star\star$) Apply the evidence procedure for a logistic MLP to a two-dimensional problem and generate plots of normal and moderated probabilistic outputs. Using a rejection option, evaluate whether moderated outputs help improve classification performance and test set likelihood.

9.12 ($\star\star$) Apply the evidence procedure for a softmax MLP and evaluate the quality of the approximation to the true posterior distribution by comparing the results with a sample generated using HMC.

9.13 ($\star$) Apply the convergence diagnostic tests of Section 8.5 to the results of the HMC demonstration programs demhmc2 and demhmc3 to assess whether the sampling algorithms have been run for long enough to reach the stationary distribution.

9.14 ($\star\star$) The HMC demonstration started from a randomly initialised network. It is perfectly legitimate to choose a better starting point by running a non-linear optimiser first to find a mode of the weight distribution. Implement this and compare the length of burn in period required to reach convergence.

9.15 ($\star\star$) Apply the Metropolis–Hastings algorithm to sampling from the posterior weight distribution. Compare a test set likelihood of the mean prediction and the rejection rate with HMC.

9.16 ($\star\star$) Apply HMC sampling to the MDN network. Use the same dataset as in demmdn but leave a gap in the input data in the range $(0.1, 0.25)$ to assess the effect on the network prediction of regions of low data density.

10. Gaussian Processes

Gaussian processes (GPs) are a relatively recent development in non-linear modelling (Williams, 1998), though they have a longer history in spatial statistics, where the technique is also known as 'kriging'. Gaussian processes are particularly suited to regression problems since in these circumstances we can perform the first level of Bayesian inference (computing the posterior distribution of the parameters) analytically. This is in contrast with neural network models where approximations (such as the evidence procedure; Section 9.4) or sampling (such as Markov Chain methods; Section 9.7) are used to evaluate the required integrals.

In this chapter we build up the theory of Gaussian processes in stages. We first start with a description of Bayesian generalised linear regression and show how this can be viewed as a Gaussian process predictor based on priors in function space rather than parameter space. We then go on to discuss the definition of suitable covariance functions and how their parameters can be learned from data. We conclude with some demonstrations of Gaussian processes in NETLAB, and show how they fit into the framework alongside other non-linear models.

Although Gaussian processes are a powerful method for regression, their application to classification applications is more problematic because the integrals which are exact with a Gaussian noise model are analytically intractable with a logistic or softmax output function. The worked example discusses one way of applying Gaussian processes to two-class problems using a variant of Laplace's method to approximate the relevant integrals.

All the functions discussed in this chapter are listed in Table 10.1.

10.1 Bayesian Regression

Suppose that we have a training dataset $\mathcal{D}$ with a one-dimensional target given by input-output pairs (x_1, t_1), (x_2, t_2), ..., (x_n, t_n) in the usual way. To motivate the introduction of Gaussian processes, we shall use generalised linear regression to model this data. In this model we carry out linear regression using a fixed set of M basis functions $\phi_1(x)$, ..., $\phi_M(x)$. The RBF with fixed (trained) basis functions is a special case of this model, as is linear regression (with all the basis functions being the identity). The model

Table 10.1. Functions in this chapter.

Gaussian Processes	
demgp	Demonstration of regression using a GP
demgpard	Demonstration of ARD with a GP
demprgp	Demonstration of sampling from GP priors
gp	Create GP
gpcovar	Compute covariance for GP
gpcovarf	Compute covariance function for GP
gpcovarp	Compute prior covariance for GP
gperr	Evaluate error function for GP
gpfwd	Forward propagation for GP
gpgrad	Evaluate error gradient for GP
gpinit	Initialise GP
gppak	Combine GP parameters into one vector
gpunpak	Separate GP hyperparameter vector into components

functional form is given by

$$y(x) = \sum_{j=1}^{M} w_j \phi_j(x), \tag{10.1}$$

or, in matrix form,

$$y(x) = \phi^T(x)w, \tag{10.2}$$

where w is the vector of weights. As in Chapter 9 we shall assume that there is a zero mean Gaussian prior on the weights and zero mean Gaussian noise on the outputs. In this framework it is possible to derive Bayesian predictions from two different viewpoints: weight space and function space.

10.1.1 Weight Space View

Suppose that the prior distribution of the weights has covariance Σ_w. The priors used in Chapter 9 were all diagonal matrices (i.e. there was no correlation in the weight prior) but we are allowing a more general covariance structure in this chapter. Assuming that the targets t_i are generated by Gaussian noise of variance σ_ν^2 added to the underlying function (so $\sigma_\nu^2 = 1/\beta$ from Chapter 9), the likelihood of w is

$$p(t_1, t_2, \ldots, t_N | w, x) = \frac{1}{(2\pi\sigma_\nu^2)^{N/2}} \prod_{n=1}^{N} \exp\left(-\frac{(t_n - y(x_n; w))^2}{2\sigma_\nu^2}\right). \tag{10.3}$$

The usual application of Bayes' theorem implies that the posterior distribution of the weights is given by

$$p(w|\mathcal{D}) = \frac{p(\mathcal{D}|w)p(w)}{p(\mathcal{D})}, \tag{10.4}$$

where the denominator is a normalisation constant $p(\mathcal{D}) = \int p(\mathcal{D}|w)p(w)\, dw$. However, since the prior and the likelihood are both Gaussian, their product is also Gaussian, and hence we don't need to compute (10.4) directly. It is simply necessary to compute the mean and covariance of the posterior distribution and the normalisation constant can be worked out from the standard formula for a Gaussian density. The mean of a Gaussian is the same as its mode, so we can find the mean of $p(w|\mathcal{D})$ by computing the most likely weights w_{MP} that minimise the negative log probability:

$$E = \frac{1}{2\sigma_\nu^2}\sum_{n=1}^{N}(t_n - \phi^T(x_n)w)^2 + \frac{1}{2}w^T\Sigma^{-1}w. \tag{10.5}$$

The covariance matrix is given by the inverse Hessian of this error function, a fact that we also used in the evidence approximation.

It is convenient to rewrite the problem in matrix form. Let Φ denote the $N \times M$ design matrix

$$\Phi = \begin{bmatrix} \phi_1(x_1) & \phi_2(x_1) & \cdots & \phi_M(x_1) \\ \phi_1(x_2) & \phi_2(x_2) & \cdots & \phi_M(x_2) \\ \vdots & \vdots & \vdots & \vdots \\ \phi_1(x_N) & \phi_2(x_N) & \cdots & \phi_M(x_N) \end{bmatrix} \tag{10.6}$$

$\beta = 1/\sigma_\nu^2$ and t denote the vector of targets. Then we can rewrite (10.5) as

$$E = \frac{\beta}{2}(t - \Phi w)^T(t - \Phi w) + \frac{1}{2}w^T\Sigma^{-1}w \tag{10.7}$$

$$= \frac{1}{2}w^T(\Sigma^{-1} + \beta\Phi^T\Phi)w - \beta w^T\Phi^T t + \frac{\beta}{2}t^T t. \tag{10.8}$$

This is a quadratic form in w, and has solution w_{MP} defined by

$$(\Sigma^{-1} + \beta\Phi^T\Phi)w_{MP} = \beta\Phi^T t, \tag{10.9}$$

which can be solved by calculating the pseudo-inverse of $A = \Sigma^{-1} + \beta\Phi^T\Phi$. So $w_{MP} = \beta A^{-1}\Phi^T t$ and the covariance matrix is A^{-1}.

Using this posterior weight distribution we can compute the predictive distribution $p(y|x^*, \mathcal{D})$ for a new input x^*. This will also be Gaussian, and has mean

$$y_{MP}(x^*; w_{MP}) = \phi^T(x^*)w_{MP} = \beta\phi^T(x^*)A^{-1}\Phi^T t, \tag{10.10}$$

and variance

$$\phi^T(x^*)A^{-1}\phi(x^*). \tag{10.11}$$

To compute the variance on the prediction of the target $t(x^*)$, we must add σ_ν^2 to this term to account for the noise added to the underlying function. In this way we can make predictions of the conditional mean and give error bars as well.

10.1.2 Function Space View

A *stochastic process* is a collection of random variables indexed by the input vector x. There are infinitely many random variables in the collection, though we will only ever observe finitely many of them at the training data points $x_1, \ldots, x_N$. We specify the process by defining the joint probability density functions of any *finite* subset $(Y(x_1), \ldots, Y(x_k))$ consistently. A *Gaussian process* is a stochastic process where every joint density function is Gaussian and is therefore defined completely by its mean and covariance. For simplicity, we will consider only Gaussian processes with zero mean. The covariance of $Y(x)$ and $Y(x')$ is usually defined by a function $C(x, x')$. If the covariance matrix is always diagonal, this means that $Y(x_1)$ is always uncorrelated with $Y(x_2)$ and so it is impossible to make any useful predictions at any input not contained in the training set. However, if the underlying function generating the data is smooth, it is reasonable to expect the covariance structure to contain off-diagonal elements.

In the function space view of Bayesian linear regression we consider the stochastic process generated by fixed basis functions with random weights. The value of the process at a point x is a random variable

$$Y(x) = \sum_{j=1}^{M} W_j \phi_j(x), \tag{10.12}$$

which is a linear combination of the M random variables W. Since W has a Gaussian distribution with zero mean and covariance Σ, it follows that Y is a Gaussian process with mean and covariance functions

$$E_W[Y(x)] = 0 \tag{10.13}$$

$$E_W[Y(x)Y'(x)] = \phi^T(x)\Sigma\phi(x). \tag{10.14}$$

The next question to address is how to make predictions with this model.

Recall that the training dataset consists of ordered pairs $(x_1, t_1), \ldots, (x_n, t_n)$. Now suppose that t_i is a sample from a random variable $T(x_i)$. To make a prediction T^* at a new input x^* we need to compute the conditional distribution

$$p(T^*|T_1, \ldots, T_N). \tag{10.15}$$

Since our model is a Gaussian process, this distribution is also Gaussian and is completely specified by its mean and variance. Fortunately, there are standard formulae for computing these values for a Gaussian distribution (von Mises, 1964). Let K denote the covariance matrix of the training data, k denote the $N \times 1$ covariance between the training data and T^* and k^* denote the variance of T^*. Then K_+, the $(N+1) \times (N+1)$ covariance matrix of $(T_1, T_2, \ldots, T_N, T^*)$, can be partitioned

$$K_+ = \begin{bmatrix} K & k \\ k^T & k^* \end{bmatrix}. \tag{10.16}$$

The predicted mean and covariance at x^* are given by

$$E[T^*] = k^T K^{-1} t \tag{10.17}$$

$$\text{var}[T^*] = k^* - k^T K^{-1} k. \tag{10.18}$$

With a little bit of linear algebra, it can be shown that (10.17) is equivalent to (10.10) and (10.18) is equivalent to (10.11).

So what have we gained from the function space view? For Bayesian linear regression, very little. In the weight space view we must invert an $M \times M$ matrix A while in the function space view we must invert an $N \times N$ matrix K. Since M, the number of basis functions, is usually significantly less than N, the number of data points in the training set, the weight space view is computationally more efficient. The advantage of the function space view is that it can be used for covariance functions for which the corresponding set of basis functions is infinite and hence impossible to analyse using the weight space view.

10.2 Theory of Gaussian Processes

The key insight that the function space view gives us is that we can define a covariance function for a Gaussian process directly without first defining basis functions and weights. If the prior is a general Gaussian process, then (10.17) shows that the prediction is a linear combination of the target values in the training set; the method is said to be a *linear smoother* (Hastie and Tibshirani, 1990); see also Section 6.6.

10.2.1 Model Definition

Assuming that a Gaussian process has zero mean, all that is required to define it is the covariance between any two points x and x'. The covariance $C(x, x')$

can be any function that will generate a non-negative definite covariance matrix for any ordered set of (input) vectors $(x_1, \ldots, x_n)$. It is non-trivial to define such functions, but several families can been found in the literature.

To simplify matters, unless there is prior knowledge to the contrary, it is usual to choose the covariance function to be *stationary*, i.e. such that the condition

$$C(x, x') = C(x - x'), \qquad (10.19)$$

holds. This means that the location of the points x and x' does not affect their covariance, just the vector joining them. An *isotropic* covariance is one that is a function only of the distance between points:

$$C(x, x') = C(\|x - x'\|). \qquad (10.20)$$

A Gaussian process can be viewed as Bayesian linear regression over a possibly infinite number of basis functions. A suitable set of basis functions is given by *eigenfunctions* of the covariance function. These correspond to eigenvectors in a function space. The function ϕ is said to be an eigenfunction of C with eigenvalue λ if it satisfies

$$\int C(x, x')\phi(x) \, dx = \lambda\phi(x'). \qquad (10.21)$$

For a general non-negative definite kernel C there are an infinite number of eigenfunctions $\phi_1, \phi_2, \ldots$ which are orthogonal and can be chosen to be normalised so that

$$\int \phi_i(x)\phi_j(x) \, dx = \delta_{ij}, \qquad (10.22)$$

where δ_{ij} is the Kronecker delta. Mercer's theorem (Wong, 1971) states that the covariance function can then be expressed as the weighted sum of its eigenfunctions:

$$C(x, x') = \sum_{i=1}^{\infty} \lambda_i \phi_i(x)\phi_i(x'). \qquad (10.23)$$

This is the infinite dimensional analogue of the expression of a positive definite matrix C as the product $U^T \Lambda U$ where U is the matrix of eigenvectors and Λ is the (diagonal) matrix of eigenvalues (see App. A). (Under certain technical conditions on C, the sum in (10.23) may be an integral.) If we choose these eigenfunctions as basis functions and make the prior over their weights be $\Lambda = \text{diag}(\lambda_1, \lambda_2, \ldots)$ then we obtain a Bayesian linear regression model.

Two different covariance functions $C(x^{(i)}, x^{(j)})$ are implemented in NETLAB. Both are stationary but non-isotropic. The full target covariance is given by $C(x^{(i)}, x^{(j)}) + \sigma_\nu^2 \delta_{ij}$, where σ_ν^2 is the variance of the target distribution.

Squared Exponential This covariance function is the exponential of a weighted squared distance between points in $\mathbb{R}^d$:

$$C(\boldsymbol{x}^{(i)}, \boldsymbol{x}^{(j)}) = v_0 \exp\left(-\frac{1}{2} \sum_{l=1}^{d} a_l (x_l^{(i)} - x_l^{(j)})^2\right) + b. \qquad (10.24)$$

The term b represents a bias that controls the vertical offset of the Gaussian process, while v_0 controls the vertical scale of the process. The squared exponential term captures the idea that vectors that are close in input space should give rise to highly correlated outputs. The a_l parameters allow a different distance measure for each dimension. If a_l is small then the lth input will be downweighted and have little effect on the input: this has a similar effect to Automatic Relevance Determination (see Chapter 9) except that there a large prior α corresponds to an unimportant input.

Note that all the parameters in this model must be positive, and so it is convenient to consider the parameter vector in log space:

$$\boldsymbol{\theta} = (\log v_0, \log b, \log a_1, \ldots, \log a_d, \log \sigma_\nu^2). \qquad (10.25)$$

Rational Quadratic The rational quadratic covariance is given by:

$$C(\boldsymbol{x}^{(i)}, \boldsymbol{x}^{(j)}) = v_0 \left(1 + \sum_{l=1}^{d} a_l (x_l^{(i)} - x_l^{(j)})^2\right)^{-\nu} + b. \qquad (10.26)$$

The parameters v_0, b, and $a_1, \ldots, a_l$ play the same role as in the squared exponential covariance function. The parameter ν controls the rate of decay of the covariance function: larger values of ν give a faster decay and hence a 'rougher' process.

One of the best ways of understanding the impact of the parameters on the type of process they generate is to sample functions from the prior defined by the covariance function. This is supported by the NETLAB function demprgp. It is provided with a user interface similar to that for demprior so that it is easy to change the values of the log hyperparameters using sliders. The following listing shows the part of the function concerned with sampling the prior and plotting the ten resulting Gaussian processes.

```
1  function demprgp(action)
2
3  % Much GUI code omitted
4
5  bias = get(biasslide, 'Value');
6  noise = get(noiseslide, 'Value');
7  inweights = get(inweightsslide, 'Value');
8  fpar = get(fparslide, 'Value');
9
10 xvals = (-1:0.01:1)';
```

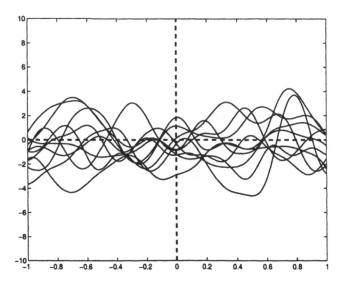

Fig. 10.1. Exploration of GP prior. Ten samples from GP with squared exponential covariance function (*solid lines*). The GP parameters (in log space) have the following values. Bias $\log b = 0$; scale $\log v_0 = 1$; weight $\log a_1 = 4$; noise $\log \sigma_\nu^2 = -11$.

```
11   nsample = 10;    % Number of samples from prior.
12   axis([-1 1 -10 10]);
13   hold on
14
15   net = gp(1, gptype);
16   net.bias = bias;
17   net.noise = noise;
18   net.inweights = inweights;
19   if strcmp(gptype, 'sqexp')
20     net.fpar = fpar;
21   else
22     fpar2 = get(findobj('Tag', 'fpar2slider'), 'Value');
23     net.fpar = [fpar fpar2];
24   end
25   cn = gpcovar(net, xvals);
26   cninv = inv(cn);
27   cnchol = chol(cn);
28   for n = 1:nsample
29     y = (cnchol') * randn(size(xvals));
30     plot(xvals, y, 'y');
31   end
```

Lines 1–4 extract values from the sliders. Line 10 creates a Gaussian process data structure, and its parameters are set in lines 11–19. (This will be clearer after reading Section 10.3.1.) Line 20 computes the covariance matrix K for the input data xvals using the covariance function (adding observation

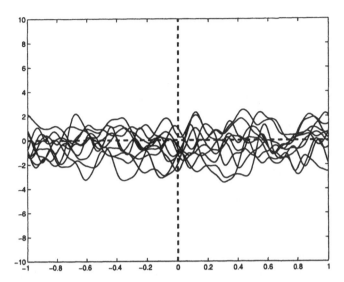

Fig. 10.2. Exploration of GP prior. Ten samples from GP with rational quadratic covariance function (*solid lines*). Bias $\log b = 0$; scale $\log v_0 = 0$; decay $\log \nu = 1$; weight $\log a_1 = 4$; noise $\log \sigma_\nu^2 = -11$.

noise), line 21 finds K^{-1} and line 22 finds a matrix L as the Cholesky decomposition of K^{-1}. Line 23 loops round each of the 10 sample functions to be generated, and line 24 creates a single function by drawing a sample from a normal distribution with mean 0 and covariance K. Figures 10.1 and 10.2 show the resulting function samples for the default parameters. Note how the squared exponential functions are smoother and have a slightly larger dynamic range.

10.2.2 Learning Hyperparameters

We have seen that once a covariance function has been fixed, it is easy to make predictions on new test points. However, it is unrealistic to assume that we know all the parameters of a covariance function *a priori*. An obvious approach is to adapt the parameters to model a training data set. This can be done by optimisation (in a maximum likelihood framework; compare with the evidence procedure for neural networks, which finds the most probable hyperparameters) or in a Bayesian approach, where a posterior distribution over the parameters is obtained. Note that the predictions are made in a Bayesian way (in effect, integrating over the infinite dimensional weight space) and we are now at the next level of inference determining hyperparameters. Because the integrals necessary for Bayesian prediction can be performed analytically, it is actually easier to understand how Gaussian processes work than the evidence procedure for neural networks, where several different approximations are needed to make the method tractable. Another advantage over neural networks is that the number of parameters is comparatively small; just $d + 2$ for the squared exponential covariance.

To use a non-linear optimiser to find the maximum likelihood values of the parameters we need to be able to calculate the dataset log likelihood and its derivatives. The log likelihood is given by

$$\mathcal{L} = -\frac{1}{2} \log \det \boldsymbol{K} - \frac{1}{2} \boldsymbol{t}^T \boldsymbol{K}^{-1} \boldsymbol{t} - \frac{N}{2} \log 2\pi. \tag{10.27}$$

The partial derivatives of $\mathcal{L}$ with respect to the hyperparameters can be expressed analytically using the equation

$$\frac{\partial \mathcal{L}}{\partial \theta_i} = -\frac{1}{2} \operatorname{tr} \left(\boldsymbol{K}^{-1} \frac{\partial \boldsymbol{K}}{\partial \theta_i} \right) + \frac{1}{2} \boldsymbol{t}^T \boldsymbol{K}^{-1} \frac{\partial \boldsymbol{K}}{\partial \theta_i} \boldsymbol{K}^{-1} \boldsymbol{t}. \tag{10.28}$$

Once these functions are computed, any of the optimisation functions in NETLAB may be used to find the hyperparameters.

Alternatively, using Bayes theorem, we can compute the density $p(\boldsymbol{\theta}|\mathcal{D})$. There are several different possibilities for a *hyperprior*, that is a prior distribution of the hyperparameters; for simplicity of implementation we use independent Gaussians with non-zero mean on the log parameters. To make a prediction for a new test point $\boldsymbol{x}^*$, we just average the usual predictive distribution over this density

$$p(y^*|\mathcal{D}) = \int p(y^*|\boldsymbol{\theta}, \mathcal{D}) p(\boldsymbol{\theta}|\mathcal{D}) \, d\boldsymbol{\theta}. \tag{10.29}$$

In general this integral cannot be computed analytically, but Monte Carlo methods can be used. As the gradient is easy to compute, hybrid Monte Carlo sampling is an effective way to proceed.

10.3 NETLAB Implementation

The NETLAB implementation of Gaussian processes has a similar form to other models. A data structure is used to hold all the main parameters of the model and forward propagation, error, and gradient functions are all provided. The two unusual features are:

- The training data is stored with the model in order to make predictions (because of (10.17) and (10.18)). The K-nearest-neighbour model knn is the only other NETLAB model with this property.
- The hyperprior distributions are Gaussian with a non-zero mean. This implies that they cannot be used with the NETLAB implementation of the evidence procedure which assumes a zero mean prior distribution over the parameters of interest. The hyperpriors are also defined using the variance instead of the inverse variance, α, used for neural networks.

10.3.1 Model Creation and Initialisation

The fields in the GP data structure are given in Table 10.2. The NETLAB

Table 10.2. Fields in GP data structure

Compulsory Fields	
type	string describing model type: always 'gp'
nin	number of inputs
nout	number of outputs: always 1
nwts	number of covariance function parameters
bias	logarithm of constant offset in covariance function
noise	logarithm of output noise variance
min_noise	minimum allowed output noise
inweights	logarithm of inverse length scale for each input
covarfn	string for covariance function: either 'sqexp' or 'ratquad'
fpar	vector of covariance function specific parameters
tr_in	training input data
tr_targets	training target data
Optional Fields	
pr_mean	Mean of hyperparameter prior
pr_var	Variance of hyperparameter prior
index	Index to hyperparameter groups

function gp creates a GP structure.

```
1   function net = gp(nin, covar_fn, prior)
2
3   net.type = 'gp';
4   net.nin = nin;
5   net.nout = 1;  % Only do single output GP
6
7   % Store log parameters
8   net.bias = 0;
9   net.min_noise = sqrt(eps);  % Prevent output noise collapsing
10  net.noise = 0;
11  net.inweights = zeros(1,nin);  % Input weights for cov. function
12
13  covarfns = {'sqexp', 'ratquad'};
14  if sum(strcmp(covar_fn, covarfns)) == 0
15    error('Undefined activation function. Exiting.');
16  else
```

```
17    net.covar_fn = covar_fn;
18  end
19
20  switch covar_fn
21    case 'sqexp'              % Squared exponential
22      net.fpar = zeros(1,1);  % One function specific parameter
23    case 'ratquad'            % Rational quadratic
24      net.fpar = zeros(1, 2); % Two function specific parameters
25    otherwise
26      error(['Unknown covariance function ', covar_fn]);
27  end
28  net.nwts = 2 + nin + length(net.fpar);
29
30  if nargin >= 3
31    if size(prior.pr_mean) == [1 1]
32      net.pr_mean = prior.pr_mean;
33      net.pr_var = prior.pr_var;
34    else
35      net.pr_mean = prior.pr_mean;
36      net.pr_var = prior.pr_var;
37      net.index = prior.index;
38    end
39  end
40
41  % Store training data, as needed for gpfwd
42  net.tr_in = [];
43  net.tr_targets = [];
```

Lines 8–11 initialise the common parameters for both covariance functions; the value of 0 for the log parameter corresponds to 1 for the actual parameter used. min_noise is added to the noise term σ_ν^2 when calculating the covariance to make sure that the noise variance never collapses to zero; this has been introduced to prevent singularities in the matrix inversions required for both training and prediction.

Lines 13–18 set the covariance function type for the model after checking against a list of allowed types and lines 20–27 set covariance function specific log parameters. Lines 30–39 initialise the hyperparameter prior. If the prior mean and variance are a scalar (lines 31–33) then the same mean and variance are used for all hyperparameters. Otherwise different priors may be used for different groups of hyperparameters (lines 34–37) with an index matrix used to determine group membership as for neural networks.

Lines 42–43 create the training data fields (inputs and targets) required for making predictions. These are empty matrices at this stage, but are set to their correct values in gpinit.

The purpose of the NETLAB function gpinit is to set the training data fields in the GP data structure (lines 15–16) and (optionally) to initialise the hyperparameters from a Gaussian distribution specified by the prior argument. This is done by sampling a vector from the prior and then calling gpunpak to put the parameters into the network data structure.

```
1  function net = gpinit(net, tr_in, tr_targets, prior)
2
3  if nargin >= 4
4    % Initialise weights at random
5    if size(prior.pr_mean) == [1 1]
6      w = randn(1, net.nwts).*sqrt(prior.pr_var) + ...
7        repmat(prior.pr_mean, 1, net.nwts);
8    else
9      sig = sqrt(prior.index*prior.pr_var);
10     w = sig'.*randn(1, net.nwts) + (prior.index*prior.pr_mean)';
11   end
12 end
13
14 net = gpunpak(net, w);
15 net.tr_in = tr_in;
16 net.tr_targets = tr_targets;
```

As with many other models in NETLAB, there are complementary functions to pack network parameters into a single vector (gppak) and unpack a vector into a GP data structure (gpunpak).

```
1  function hp = gppak(net)
2  hp = [net.bias, net.noise, net.inweights, net.fpar];
```

The parameter vector whose length depends on the covariance functions used (net.fpar) appears at the end of the packed vector hp. This makes the unpacking code marginally simpler:

```
1  function net = gpunpak(net, hp)
2
3  if net.nwts ~= length(hp)
4    error('Invalid weight vector length');
5  end
6
7  net.bias = hp(1);
8  net.noise = hp(2);
9
10 % Unpack input weights
11 mark1 = 2 + net.nin;
12 net.inweights = hp(3:mark1);
13
14 % Unpack function specific parameters
15 net.fpar = hp(mark1 + 1:size(hp, 2));
```

10.3.2 Making Predictions

Predictions for a new data point are made using the training data stored in the GP structure to compute the required covariance matrices. The prediction function gpfwd outputs both the mean and the variance of the predicted Gaussian distribution.

```
1  function [y, sigsq] = gpfwd(net, x, cninv)
2
3  if nargin == 2
```

```
4    % Inverse covariance matrix not supplied.
5    cninv = inv(gpcovar(net, net.tr_in));
6  end
7
8  ktest = gpcovarp(net, x, net.tr_in);
9  y = ktest*cninv*net.tr_targets;
10
11  if nargout >= 2
12    % Predict error bar
13    ndata = size(x, 1);
14    sigsq = (ones(ndata, 1) * gpcovarp(net, x(1,:), x(1,:))) ...
15      - sum((ktest*cninv).*ktest, 2);
16  end
```

Because the covariance matrix K^{-1} used in (10.17) and (10.18) depends only on the training data, it need only be computed once. To improve the efficiency of multiple calls to gpfwd, its inverse may be passed as an argument cninv. If there are only two arguments, then K^{-1} is computed using a call to gpcovar (lines 3–6). The vector k which represents the covariance between the prediction input, x, and the training data inputs, net.tr_in, is computed by a call to gpcovarp in line 8; this calculates the prior contribution to the covariance excluding the output noise model.

The mean prediction is made following (10.17) in line 9, and the conditional variance is computed according to (10.18) in lines 14–15. Figure 10.3.2 illustrates the relationship between the predicted mean and variance and the number of training data points.

It is convenient to divide the computation of the covariance matrices into three phases:

- gpcovar computes the full covariance matrix with entries $C(x_i, x_j) + \sigma_\nu^2 \delta_{ij}$.
- gpcovarp computes the prior covariance matrix with entries $C(x_i, x_j)$.
- gpcovarf computes the part of the covariance function that is input dependent, and omits the bias term b. Computing this separately is useful to improve the efficiency of the error gradient calculations (see gpgrad).

Thus gpcovar calls gpcovarp, which in turn calls gpcovarf. We start with the implementation of gpcovarf:

```
1  function covf = gpcovarf(net, x1, x2)
2
3  if size(x1, 2) ~= size(x2, 2)
4    error('Number of variables in x1 and x2 must be the same');
5  end
6
7  n1 = size(x1, 1);
8  n2 = size(x2, 1);
9  beta = diag(exp(net.inweights));
10
11  z = (x1.*x1)*beta*ones(net.nin, n2) - 2*x1*beta*x2' ...
12    + ones(n1, net.nin)*beta*(x2.*x2)';
13
```

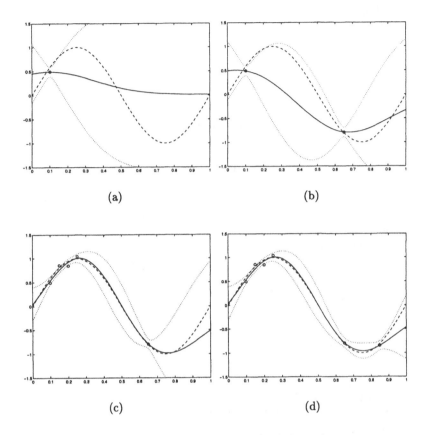

Fig. 10.3. Squared exponential Gaussian process prediction with fixed hyperparameters. Data (*circles*) generated from noisy sine function (*dashed line*). Mean prediction (*solid line*) and two standard deviation error bars (*dotted lines*) for training sets containing: (a) one point; (b) two points; (c) five points; (d) six points.

```
14   switch net.covar_fn
15     case 'sqexp'          % Squared exponential
16       covf = exp(net.fpar(1) - 0.5*z);
17     case 'ratquad'        % Rational quadratic
18       nu = exp(net.fpar(2));
19       covf = exp(net.fpar(1))*((ones(size(z)) + z).^(-nu));
20     otherwise
21       error(['Unknown covariance function ', net.covar_fn]);
22   end
```

This function computes the covariance matrix for two datasets x1 and x2. These must have the same number of columns (lines 3–5). Both covariance functions require a weighted sum of squares distance between each pair of points. Line 9 computes the weights $a_1, \ldots, a_d$ as the exponential of the inweights field. These are then used in lines 11–12 to compute

$$\sum_{l=1}^{d} a_l (x_l^{(1)} - x_l^{(2)})^2 \tag{10.30}$$

using an algorithm similar to that in dist2. Letting A denote the diagonal matrix $(a_1, \ldots, a_d)$ (the matrix beta in the implementation), (10.30) is equivalent to

$$A(x^{(1)})^2 - 2x^{(1)} A(x^{(2)})^T + A(x^{(2)})^2. \tag{10.31}$$

Line 16 computes the squared exponential covariance, remembering that net.fpar(1) is equal to $\log v_0$. Lines 18–19 compute the rational quadratic covariance, where in addition net.fpar(2) is equal to $\log \nu$.

The function gpcovarp adds the bias term to gpcovarf.

```
1  function [covp, covf] = gpcovarp(net, x1, x2)
2
3  covf = gpcovarf(net, x1, x2);
4  covp = covf + exp(net.bias);
```

Finally, gpcovar adds the output noise (line 12):

```
1  function [cov, covf] = gpcovar(net, x)
2
3  ndata = size(x, 1);
4  % Compute prior covariance
5  if nargout >= 2
6    [covp, covf] = gpcovarp(net, x, x);
7  else
8    covp = gpcovarp(net, x, x);
9  end
10
11 % Add output noise variance
12 cov = covp + (net.min_noise + exp(net.noise))*eye(ndata);
```

The function optionally returns the functional part of the prior covariance computed by gpcovarf in the variable covf.

10.3.3 Model Training

Whether maximum likelihood or hybrid Monte Carlo sampling is used to compute hyperparameters for a Gaussian process, it is still necessary to be able to compute the negative log likelihood (gperr) and its derivatives with respect to the hyperparameters (gpgrad). This is also integrated with the log of a non-zero mean Gaussian prior over the hyperparameters. Because this is not restricted to a zero mean prior, it cannot be calculated by the function errbayes.

The function gperr has the usual interface for a NETLAB error function.

```
1   function [e, edata, eprior] = gperr(net, x, t)
2
3   cn = gpcovar(net, x);
4   edata = 0.5*(sum(log(eig(cn))) + t'*inv(cn)*t);
5
6   % Evaluate the hyperprior contribution to the error.
7   % The hyperprior is Gaussian with mean pr_mean and variance
8   % pr_variance
9   if isfield(net, 'pr_mean')
10    w = gppak(net);
11    m = repmat(net.pr_mean, size(w));
12    if size(net.pr_mean) == [1 1]
13      eprior = 0.5*((w-m)*(w-m)');
14      e2 = eprior/net.pr_var;
15    else
16      wpr = repmat(w, size(net.pr_mean, 1), 1)';
17      eprior = 0.5*(((wpr - m').^2).*net.index);
18      e2 = (sum(e2, 1))*(1./net.pr_var);
19    end
20  else
21    e2 = 0;
22    eprior = 0;
23  end
24
25  e = edata + e2;
```

The data component of the error function is computed in lines 3–4 according to (10.27). The term $-N \log 2\pi / 2$ does not depend on the hyperparameters, so is dropped from the error function.

The component of the error function due to the hyperprior is computed in lines 9–20. If the prior is a single spherical Gaussian (lines 12–14) then we compute

$$e_2 = \frac{(w - \mu)^T (w - \mu)}{2\sigma^2},$$ (10.32)

which also ignores the normalising constant for this distribution. If there are multiple weight groups, then (10.32) is calculated for each group using the index matrix to decide group membership (16–18).

The gradient of gperr is computed using the function gpgrad.

```
1   function g = gpgrad(net, x, t)
2
3   % Evaluate derivatives with respect to each hyperparameter.
4   ndata = size(x, 1);
5   [cov, covf] = gpcovar(net, x);
6   cninv = inv(cov);
7   trcninv = trace(cninv);
8   cninvt = cninv*t;
9
10  % Function parameters
11  switch net.covar_fn
12    case 'sqexp'            % Squared exponential
```

```
13      gfpar = trace(cninv*covf) - cninvt'*covf*cninvt;
14    case 'ratquad'       % Rational quadratic
15      gfpar(1) = trace(cninv*covf) - cninvt'*covf*cninvt;
16      beta = diag(exp(net.inweights));
17      D2 = (x.*x)*beta*ones(net.nin, ndata) - 2*x*beta*x' ...
18         + ones(ndata, net.nin)*beta*(x.*x)';
19      E = ones(size(D2));
20      L = -exp(net.fpar(2))*covf.*log(E + D2); % d(cn)/d(nu)
21      gfpar(2) = trace(cninv*L) - cninvt'*L*cninvt;
22    otherwise
23      error(['Unknown covariance function ', net.covar_fn]);
24    end
25
26   % Bias derivative
27   fac = exp(net.bias)*ones(ndata);
28   gbias = trace(cninv*fac) - cninvt'*fac*cninvt;
29
30   % Noise derivative
31   gnoise = exp(net.noise)*(trcninv - cninvt'*cninvt);
32
33   % Input weight derivatives
34   if strcmp(net.covar_fn, 'ratquad')
35     F = (exp(net.fpar(2))*E)./(E + D2);
36   end
37
38   nparams = length(net.inweights);
39   for l = 1 : nparams
40     vect = x(:,l);
41     matx = (vect.*vect)*ones(1, ndata) ...
42          - 2.0*vect*vect' ...
43          + ones(ndata, 1)*(vect.*vect)';
44     switch net.covar_fn
45       case 'sqexp'          % Squared exponential
46         dmat = -0.5*exp(net.inweights(l))*covf.*matx;
47       case 'ratquad'        % Rational quadratic
48         dmat = - exp(net.inweights(l))*covf.*matx.*F;
49       otherwise
50         error(['Unknown covariance function ', net.covar_fn]);
51     end
52
53     gw1(l) = trace(cninv*dmat) - cninvt'*dmat*cninvt;
54   end
55
56   g1 = [gbias, gnoise, gw1, gfpar];
57   g1 = 0.5*g1;
58
59   % Evaluate the prior contribution to the gradient.
60   if isfield(net, 'pr_mean')
61     w = gppak(net);
62     m = repmat(net.pr_mean, size(w));
63     if size(net.pr_mean) == [1 1]
64       gprior = w - m;
65       g2 = gprior/net.pr_var;
```

```
66    else
67       ngroups = size(net.pr_mean, 1);
68       gprior = net.index'.*(ones(ngroups, 1)*w - m);
69       g2 = (1./net.pr_var)'*gprior;
70    end
71 else
72    gprior = 0;
73    g2 = 0;
74 end
75
76 g = g1 + g2;
```

The function is rather long since each group of hyperparameters requires a different form of gradient calculation. The key calculation for each hyperparameter is $\partial K/\partial\theta$, which can then be used in (10.28). (The 0.5 multiplier is left until the end of the function, for simplicity.) If θ denotes a hyperparameter, then the network data structure stores $\phi = \log\theta$, so by the chain rule

$$\frac{\partial K}{\partial\phi} = \frac{\partial K}{\partial\theta}\frac{d\theta}{d\phi} = \frac{\partial K}{\partial\theta}\theta. \tag{10.33}$$

Thus when we differentiate (10.24) and (10.26) with respect to a hyperparameter θ we must multiply the result by $\theta = \exp\phi$.

The first few lines compute the required covariance matrices. The variable cov is equal to K (line 5). We also make much use of covf since this is the part of the covariance that depends on the functional hyperparameters. The variable trcninv is equal to $\mathrm{tr}\,K^{-1}$ (line 7) and cninvt is equal to $K^{-1}t$ (line 8).

Let us write D for the weighted distance matrix with ijth entry

$$\sum_{l=1}^{d} a_l(x_l^{(i)} - x_l^{(j)})^2. \tag{10.34}$$

The first derivative we calculate is that of the squared exponential covariance with respect to v_0 (or rather, as always, $\log v_0$). Differentiating (10.24) with respect to v_0 gives $\exp(-D/2)$, and multiplying this by v_0 following (10.33) gives

$$\frac{\partial K^{-1}}{\partial\log(v_0)} = v_0\exp(-D/2), \tag{10.35}$$

which is simply the variable covf. Thus the derivative of $\mathcal{L}$ with respect to $\log(v_0)$ is given by combining (10.35) with (10.28) which yields line 13.

Line 15 computes the same derivative for the rational quadratic covariance. The variable D2 contains the weighted squared distances between each pair of input vectors (lines 17–18) and represents D. Then the covariance function is given by $v_0(1 + D)^{-\nu}$ and the derivative of this with respect to ν is

$$-v_0 \log\left[(1 + D)\right](1 + D)^{-\nu}. \tag{10.36}$$

This is computed and multiplied by ν, which equals `exp(net.fpar(2))`, to give the derivative with respect to $\log\nu$ in line 20. The required gradient is then calculated in line 21 using (10.28).

As the bias b is simply an additive term in both covariance functions, the required derivative is easy to work out,

$$\frac{\partial K}{\partial \log b} = b, \tag{10.37}$$

and this is calculated in lines 27–28. The noise derivative is similar, but only applies to the diagonal terms (line 31).

The input weight derivatives are more complicated, and it has not been possible to vectorise the program completely at this point and each weight is considered individually in the loop formed by lines 39–54. Line 35 computes an auxiliary matrix F

$$\frac{\nu}{\nu + D} \tag{10.38}$$

needed for the rational quadratic function.

The unweighted distance matrix `matx` computed in lines 41–43 has ijth entry equal to $(x_l^{(i)} - x_l^{(j)})^2$. The derivative of the squared exponential covariance function with respect to a_l is given by

$$-\frac{1}{2}v_0\left(x_l^{(i)} - x_l^{(j)}\right)^2 \exp\left(-\frac{1}{2}\sum_{l=1}^{d} a_l\left(x_l^{(i)} - x_l^{(j)}\right)^2\right) \tag{10.39}$$

which is computed in line 46 (after multiplication by a_l). The derivative of the rational quadratic covariance function with respect to a_l is given by

$$\frac{-\nu}{(1 + D)}v_0\frac{d\left(1 + \sum_{l=1}^{d} a_l\left(x_l^{(i)} - x_l^{(j)}\right)^2\right)^{-\nu}}{da_l}\left(1 + \sum_{l=1}^{d} a_l\left(x_l^{(i)} - x_l^{(j)}\right)^2\right)^{-\nu} \tag{10.40}$$

and this is computed in line 48 (after multiplication by a_l). The derivative $\partial K/\partial a_l$ is then combined with (10.28) in line 53. In lines 56–57 the gradient vector is put together from its components and multiplied by 0.5 to complete (10.28).

Lines 61–69 calculate the contribution to the gradient from the Gaussian prior over the hyperparameters. Since the log of a spherical Gaussian is a weighted squared deviation from the mean, the derivative is simply a weighted difference from the mean. This is computed in lines 64–65 for a single Gaussian prior, and for groups of hyperparameters in lines 67–69.

10.4 Demonstration Programs

Although it may take time to understand the theory behind Gaussian processes, applying them to regression problems is straightforward. There are two demonstration programs in NETLAB which use optimisation to determine the maximum likelihood hyperparameters.

10.4.1 Regression Demonstration

The program demgp shows how Gaussian processes can be applied to the noisy sine regression problem. The process can be divided into the same four stages as for the MLP (see demmlp1).

1. The training data is generated:

```
1  randn('state', 42);
2  x = [0.1 0.15 0.2 0.25  0.65 0.7 0.75 0.8 0.85 0.9]';
3  ndata = length(x);
4  t = sin(2*pi*x) + 0.05*randn(ndata, 1);
```

2. The Gaussian process model is created and initialised. The log hyperparameters are initialised by the function gpinit with zero mean and unit variance (line 8) so the initial values of the hyperparameters are in the region of $\exp(0) = 1$. The training inputs x and targets t are stored in the data structure net at the same time.

```
5  net = gp(1, 'sqexp');
6  prior.pr_mean = 0;
7  prior.pr_var = 1;
8  net = gpinit(net, x, t, prior);
```

3. The maximum likelihood hyperparameters are found using a non-linear optimisation function. This is done in the usual way by a call to netopt.

```
 9  options = foptions;
10  options(1) = 1;    % Display training error values
11  options(14) = 20;
12  [net, options] = netopt(net, options, x, t, 'scg');
```

At this point in demgp a second model with rational quadratic covariance is created and trained in a similar way.

4. The last step is to create some test data and make predictions.

```
13  xtest = linspace(0, 1, 50)';
14  cn = gpcovar(net, x);
15  cninv = inv(cn);
16  [ytest, sigsq] = gpfwd(net, xtest, cninv);
17  sig = sqrt(sigsq);
```

Note how the covariance matrix is precomputed by a call to gpcovar (line 15). This would increase computational efficiency if there were several calls to gpfwd (for example, if the test data only became available one

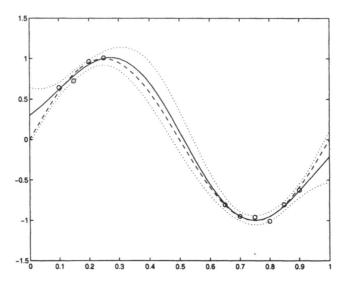

Fig. 10.4. Demonstration of GP regression. Data (*circles*) generated from sine function (*dashed line*). Squared exponential mean prediction (*solid line*) with error bars at 2 standard deviations (*dotted lines*).

point at a time). The matrix `sig` (line 17) contains the standard deviation of the predicted distribution at each point in `xtest`.

We can now plot the true function (line 21) and the predicted function with two standard deviation error bars (line 23).

```
18   fh1 = figure;
19   hold on
20   plot(x, t, 'ok');
21   fplot('sin(2*pi*x)', [0 1], '--m');
22   plot(xtest, ytest, '-k');
23   plot(xtest, ytest+(2*sig), '-b', xtest, ytest-(2*sig), '-b');
```

Figure 10.4 illustrates the results. As well as the usual rapid expansion of the error bars when the model is extrapolating (for inputs greater than 0.9 and less than 0.1), the width of the error bars increases in the range [0.25, 0.65] since the density of the training data is low in this region.

10.4.2 ARD Demonstration

Applying Automatic Relevance Determination to a Gaussian process is straightforward; when the hyperparameters are found by maximum likelihood, the input weights a_i can be read off directly from the GP data structure, as shown in demgpard.

```
1   randn('state', 42);
2   rand('state', 42);
```

```
3   ndata = 100;
4   x1 = rand(ndata, 1);
5   x2 = x1 + 0.05*randn(ndata, 1);
6   x3 = 0.5 + 0.5*randn(ndata, 1);
7   x = [x1, x2, x3];
8   t = sin(2*pi*x1) + 0.1*randn(ndata, 1);
9
10  net = gp(3, 'sqexp');
11  prior.pr_mean = 0;
12  prior.pr_var = 0.1;
13  net = gpinit(net, x, t, prior);
14
15  options = foptions;
16  options(1) = 1;
17  options(14) = 30;
18  [net, options] = netopt(net, options, x, t, 'scg');
19
20  rel = exp(net.inweights);
21
22  xt = linspace(0, 1, 50);
23  xtest = [xt', xt', xt'];
24
25  cn = gpcovar(net, x);
26  cninv = inv(cn);
27  [ytest, sigsq] = gpfwd(net, xtest, cninv);
28  sig = sqrt(sigsq);
29
30  figure(h); hold on;
31  plot(xt, ytest, '-k');
32  plot(xt, ytest+(2*sig), '-b', xt, ytest-(2*sig), '-b');
33  axis([0 1 -1.5 1.5]);
34  fplot('sin(2*pi*x)', [0 1], '--m');
```

The structure of this program is similar to that of demgp. First the data is generated (lines 1–8). The dataset is similar to that used in demard. There are three input variables: x_1, which the output depends on directly (it is a noisy sine function of x_1); x_2 which is a noisy version of x_1; and x_3, which is completely uncorrelated with the output.

In lines 10–13 the model is created and initialised. We have put a prior on the log hyperparameters with mean 0 and variance 0.1. This constrains the hyperparameters to be reasonably close to 1 unless there is strong evidence to the contrary from the data. The model is trained using 30 iterations of scaled conjugate gradient in lines 15–18. This can be compared with the 600 iterations (plus two batches of ten hyperparameter re-estimations) used in demard for an MLP on the same problem.

The input weights are computed in line 20 by taking the exponential of net.inweights. Their values are 9.8861, 0.022081 and 0.000088 respectively, showing that the GP has successfully determined the relative importance of each variable for its predictions.

Test inputs along the line $x_1 = x_2 = x_3$ are created in lines 22–23, and the Gaussian process predictions of the conditional mean and standard deviation are made in lines 25–28. The results (with error bars) are plotted in lines 30–34.

10.5 Worked Example: GPs for Classification

It is possible to apply the NETLAB Gaussian process model to classification problems as a discriminant function. However, as discussed in Section 4.1, it is preferable to estimate the class posterior probabilities $p(C_k|x)$, implying that the model outputs should be positive and sum to one. The outputs of a Gaussian process trained on data where the targets satisfy a 1-of-c encoding will not satisfy these constraints.

In this section we will consider only a two-class problem (for the more general case with more than two classes; see (Barber and Williams, 1997; Williams and Barber, 1998) and other references in (Williams, 1998). The answer to the problem of outputs that don't conform to the rules of probability is the same as for GLMs and MLPs; we apply a logistic transfer function to them, so the model output is $\pi(x) = \sigma(y(x))$. Of course, although the Gaussian process prior means that the activation $y(x)$ is Gaussian, the prior over $\pi(x)$ is definitely *not* Gaussian, so the integrals required for inference are no longer analytically tractable.

To be more concrete, making predictions for a test input x^* with a fixed set of hyperparameters θ, requires the integral

$$\hat{\pi}^* = \int \pi^* p(\pi^*|t, \theta) \, d\pi^*, \tag{10.41}$$

where $\pi^* = \pi(x^*)$. To find the posterior distribution of π^*, we use the distribution $p(y^*|t, \theta)$, defined by

$$p(y^*|t, \theta) = \int p(y^*, y|t, \theta) \, dy = \frac{1}{p(t|\theta)} \int p(y^*, y|\theta) p(t|y) \, dy \tag{10.42}$$

and then apply the appropriate Jacobian to transform the distribution. Because we are using a logistic sigmoid output function, the appropriate noise model (i.e. the conditional distribution of the targets given the outputs) is no longer Gaussian but Bernoulli

$$p(t|y) = \prod_{n=1}^{N} \pi_n^{t_n} (1 - \pi_n)^{t_n}, \tag{10.43}$$

which means that (10.42) is no longer analytically tractable. Faced with this problem, there are two ways to evaluate the integral: to use an analytically tractable approximation, or to use Monte Carlo methods. In this section we shall only consider the first approach (but see also Exercise 10.10).

There are several analytic approximations that can be used, but the obvious one to start with is Laplace's method (which we also used in the evidence procedure for MLPs; see Section 9.4.1). We approximate the function $p(y^*, y|t, \theta)$ by a Gaussian distribution centred on the mode of this function at $\tilde{y}$ with inverse covariance given by the Hessian $-\nabla\nabla \log p(y^*, \tilde{y}|t, \theta)$ so that inference is approximated by the usual equations with $\tilde{y}$ replacing t. The mode, which is unique, can be found using a variant of the IRLS algorithm (compare glmtrain).

Let $\Psi = \log P(t|y) + \log P(y)$ be the negative of the error function. Using $\log p(t_i|y_i) = t_i y_i - \log(1 + e^{y_i})$ we obtain

$$\Psi = t^T y - \sum_{i=1}^n \log(1 + e^{y_i}) - \frac{1}{2} y^T K^{-1} y - \frac{1}{2} \log |K| - \frac{n}{2} \log 2\pi, \quad (10.44)$$

where K denotes the prior covariance computed on the training dataset. As in IRLS we use a Newton–Raphson scheme

$$y^{\text{new}} = y - (\nabla\nabla\Psi)^{-1} \nabla\Psi, \quad (10.45)$$

to estimate y iteratively. Writing $W = \text{diag}(\pi_1(1 - \pi_1), \dots, \pi_n(1 - \pi_n))$, the weight matrix in IRLS (Section 4.5), we can calculate the required derivatives:

$$\nabla\Psi = (t - \pi) - K^{-1}y \quad (10.46)$$

$$\nabla\nabla\Psi = -K^{-1} - W. \quad (10.47)$$

After some algebra we obtain the following update equation for y:

$$y^{\text{new}} = K(I + WK)^{-1}(Wy + (t - \pi)). \quad (10.48)$$

Once the algorithm has converged to a solution $\tilde{y}$, the value of y^* is given by

$$y^* = k^T K^{-1} \tilde{y} = k^T (t - \tilde{\pi}), \quad (10.49)$$

using (10.46) and the fact that $\nabla\Psi = 0$ at a mode, so $K^{-1}\tilde{y} = t - \tilde{\pi}$. The variance $\text{var}(y^*)$ is given by $K_+(I_+ + W_+K_+)^{-1}$, where

$$K_+ = \begin{pmatrix} K & k \\ k^T & k^* \end{pmatrix} \qquad W_+ = \begin{pmatrix} W & 0 \\ 0 & 0 \end{pmatrix}. \quad (10.50)$$

These values can then be used to make moderated predictions as in Chapter 9. Note that this makes prediction a relatively slow process, since a large matrix ($N \times N$, where N is the number of training data points) must be inverted for each test point in order to calculate the prediction variance. If the decision boundary is 0.5, then the mean values are sufficient, since they are positive

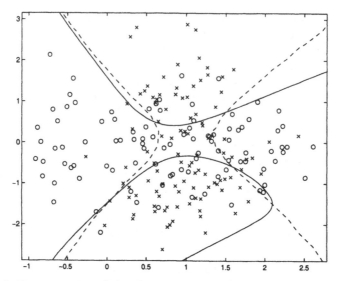

Fig. 10.5. Demonstration of classification Gaussian process using Laplace approximation. Data drawn from two classes (*circles* and *crosses*) is classified by the optimal Bayes rule (*solid line*) and a GP (*dashed line*) with hyperparameters set using the method of Exercise 10.8.

if and only if the moderated prediction is greater than 0.5. An example of its use can be seen in Fig. 10.5, which uses the same dataset as used for the demonstration of Bayesian classification with an MLP in Fig. 9.5.

This algorithm is implemented in two parts: gpcmode finds $\tilde{y}$; gpcfwd makes a prediction on a set of test points. Because it is an iterative algorithm, it is controlled with an options vector in which fields 1, 2, 3, and 14 have their usual interpretation.

```
1  function anew = gpcmode(net, options, cn)
2
3  if ~(isfield(net, 'tr_in') & isfield(net, 'tr_targets'))
4    error('Require training inputs and targets');
5  end
6
7  if nargin < 3
8    cn = gpcovarp(net, net.tr_in, net.tr_in);
9  end
10
11 % Now ready to find the mode
12 n = size(cn, 1);
13 anew = zeros(n, 1);
14 aold = zeros(n, 1);
15
16 if (options(14))
17   niters = options(14);
18 else
```

```
19    niters = 100;
20  end
21  ndata = size(net.tr_in, 1);
22
23  for iter = 1:niters
24    y = net.min_noise*anew + cn*anew;
25    temp1 = net.tr_targets.*y;
26    pi = 1./(1 + exp(-y));
27    w = pi.*(1-pi);
28    err = sum(temp1, 1) - sum(log(1+exp(y)), 1) - 0.5*anew'*y;
29    if options(1)
30       fprintf(1, 'Cycle: %4d  Error: %11.6f\n', iter, err);
31    end
32    gradPsi = net.tr_targets - pi - anew;
33    % Newton step.
34    M = eye(ndata) + muldiag(w, cn);
35    b = net.tr_targets - pi + w.*y;
36    [anew, cgflag, relres, cgiter] = ...
37      bicg(M, b, 1e-7, 100, [], [], aold);
38    if cgflag~=0
39      fprintf(1,'BICG Error. relres=%f, num. of iter.=%d\n', ...
40        relres, cgiter);
41      fprintf(1,'We just continue...\n');
42    end
43    % Check stopping condition
44    if (options(2) | options(3))
45      gg = sqrt(gradPsi'*gradPsi);
46      if options(1)
47          fprintf('Error gradient magnitude %8g\n', gg);
48      end
49      if (gg < options(2))
50        return;
51      end
52      if (sum(abs(anew-aold), 1) < options(3))
53        return;
54      end
55    end
56    aold= anew;
57  end
```

The parameter vector anew optimised and returned by the function is actually $K^{-1}\tilde{y}$, as this is more useful than $\tilde{y}$. The main loop starts at line 23. The current value of y is computed in line 24 as $K(K^{-1}y)$, with the addition of a small offset to prevent overflow and other floating point pathologies. The probability vector π is calculated in line 26, and the weight matrix W in line 27. Line 28 computes the y-dependent part of Ψ. The gradient (10.46) is computed in line 32 to help assess when the algorithm has converged.

The variable M contains the matrix $(I + WK)$ (line 34); muldiag is a utility function to compute the product of a full and diagonal matrix efficiently. Lines 35–37 compute the updated value of anew using the MATLAB biconjugate gradients algorithm to solve the linear equations. This has the advantage of being an iterative algorithm, so it can use aold (the value of anew on the previous iteration) as the starting point, making it more efficient than solving the equations from scratch each time round the loop.

The function gpcfwd uses gpcmode to make predictions. Unusually for a forward propagation function, it takes an options vector as an argument.

```
1   function [y, vary] = gpcfwd(net, options, x)
2
3   pvec = gpcmode(net, options);
4   kmat = gpcovarp(net, x, net.tr_in);
5   y = kmat*pvec;
6
7   if nargout > 1
8     ndata = size(x, 1);
9     ntrdata = size(net.tr_in, 1);
10    vary = zeros(ndata, 1);
11    K = gpcovarp(net, net.tr_in, net.tr_in);
12    % Compute pi_tilde
13    pi_tilde = net.tr_targets - pvec;
14    Wplus = diag([pi_tilde.*(1-pi_tilde); 0]);
15    % Preallocate array
16    Kplus = [K zeros(ntrdata, 1); zeros(1, ntrdata) 0];
17    kstar = K(1, 1);  % Assume stationary covariance
18    for n = 1:ndata
19      Kplus(1:ntrdata, ntrdata+1) = kmat(n, :)';
20      Kplus(ntrdata+1, :) = [kmat(n, :) kstar];
21      temp = Kplus*inv(eye(ndata)+Wplus* Kplus);
22      vary(n) = temp(ntrdata+1, ntrdata+1);
23    end
24  end
```

The mean predictions are obtained in line 5, using the output pvec of gpcmode, which is equal to $t - \tilde{\pi}$. To compute the variance of y^*, the matrices K_+ (lines 11, 16–17 and 19–20) and W_+ (line 14) are calculated.

Exercises

10.1 ($\star\star$) Implement Bayesian linear regression from the weight space viewpoint for linear and Gaussian basis functions.

10.2 ($\star\star$) Apply a Gaussian process to a simple regression problem and obtain the true Bayesian posterior distribution of the hyperparameters using HMC. Compare the accuracy of the predictions made by integrating over these parameters with that obtained simply predicting at the mode of the distribution (as in demgp).

10.3 ($\star\star\star$) Implement additional covariance function in the Gaussian process framework. The modified Bessel functions of orders $r = 1, 2, 3$ are given by the following equations:

$$C_1(x, x') = \exp\left(-\frac{\|x - x'\|_w}{\lambda}\right) \tag{10.51}$$

$$C_2(x, x') = \exp\left(-\frac{\|x - x'\|_w}{\lambda}\right)\left(1 + \frac{\|x - x'\|_w}{\lambda}\right) \tag{10.52}$$

$$C_3(x, x') = \exp\left(-\frac{\|x - x'\|_w}{\lambda}\right)\left(1 + \frac{\|x - x'\|_w}{\lambda}\right.$$
$$\left. + \frac{1}{3}\left(\frac{\|x - x'\|_w}{\lambda}\right)^3\right) \tag{10.53}$$

where $\| \cdot \|_w$ denotes the norm with each coordinate weighted as in the NETLAB implementation. The process of order r is $r - 1$ times mean-square differentiable, so C_1, which corresponds to the Ornstein–Uhlenbeck process, yields very 'rough' predictions, while C_2 and C_3 are smoother.

10.4 (⋆⋆⋆) The main obstacle to fast implementations of Gaussian processes is the need to compute the product of a matrix inverse K^{-1} and a vector y. Define the function

$$Q(x) = -x^T y + \frac{1}{2}x^T K x, \tag{10.54}$$

which is a quadratic form with Hessian $-K$ (Gibbs and Mackay, 1996). At the minimum of Q with respect to x, we have

$$\nabla Q_{\min} = y - K x_{\min} = 0 \tag{10.55}$$

and hence $x_{\min} = K^{-1}y$. We can therefore use any non-linear optimiser to minimise Q and thus compute $K^{-1}y$. Implement this approach using conjgrad and quasinew for some 'typical' covariance matrices K and assess the best choice of convergence criteria to trade off accuracy and efficiency.

10.5 (⋆⋆) Use the fast inverse matrix product algorithm from Exercise 10.4 in gpfwd, gperr and gpgrad and evaluate its effect on the accuracy and speed of training.

10.6 (⋆⋆) To compute error gradients, as well as computing a fast inverse matrix product, there is also a requirement to compute the trace of a matrix inverse. Let d be a random vector whose entries are drawn from a Gaussian with zero mean and unit variance. Then form

$$\tau = d^T K^{-1} \frac{\partial K}{\partial \theta} d. \tag{10.56}$$

The expected value of τ is

$$E[\tau] = \mathrm{tr}\left[K^{-1}\frac{\partial K}{\partial \theta}\right],\tag{10.57}$$

and hence we can compute the right-hand side by averaging τ over several different d vectors. As the size of K increases, the number of vectors required decreases (using the Central Limit Theorem).

Evaluate this method using typical covariance matrices K and the method of Exercise 10.4 applied to $d^T K^{-1}$ and determine the number of vectors d required for accurate results.

10.7 ($\star\star$) Extend your solution to Exercise 10.5 to use the fast trace calculation of Exercise 10.6. Evaluate the effect on accuracy and speed of training a Gaussian process.

10.8 ($\star$) Apply the logistic Gaussian process to a two-class prediction problem. A crude way to find a reasonable set of hyperparameters is to train a standard Gaussian process on the data as a discriminant with targets -1 and $+1$ (to ensure that the sigmoid of the classification GP is far from 0.5 at the training data points) and use the optimal hyperparameters from this model to make predictions with a logistic output using gpcfwd.

10.9 ($\star\star$) Continuing Exercise 10.8, apply the logistic GP to a two-dimensional problem and generate plots of normal and moderated probabilistic outputs. Using a rejection option, evaluate whether moderated outputs help improve classification performance and test set likelihood.

10.10 ($\star\star\star$) Implement a Monte Carlo Gaussian process approach to the two-class prediction problem in place of the Laplace approximation. Using metrop to integrate over the hyperparameters, which avoids the need to compute error derivatives, evaluate the accuracy and training time of the model compared with the Laplace approximation described in the text.

A. Linear Algebra and Matrices

Throughout the book, we have assumed that the reader is familiar with standard operations on matrices and vectors. This section gathers some results and techniques that may not be so familiar.

Linear Algebra

Although most of the time it is adequate to view vectors and matrices as n-tuples and $m \times n$ arrays of real values, there are a few occasions when a slightly more formal approach is needed.

We say that a set of vectors $B = \{v_1, \ldots, v_n\}$ is a *basis* of a vector space V if the following two conditions hold:

1. B *spans* V. This means that every vector $u \in V$ can be written as a linear combination of elements of B:

$$u = \sum_{i=1}^{n} \lambda_i v_i. \tag{A.1}$$

   for some choice of coefficients λ_i.

2. B is *linearly independent*. This means that if

$$\sum_{i=1}^{n} \alpha_i v_i = 0, \tag{A.2}$$

   then $\alpha_i = 0$ for $i = 1, \ldots, n$. This condition guarantees the uniqueness of the coefficients in (A.1).

Given a basis for V, we can represent each vector $u \in V$ by the n-tuple of coefficients in (A.1). The *standard basis* for $\mathbb{R}^n$ is the set of vectors e_i which are zero except for a 1 in the ith position. The *rank* of a matrix is the number of linearly indpendent columns.

There are two important spaces associated with an $m \times n$ matrix A. The range of A is the space spanned by its columns or, equivalently,

$$\operatorname{ran} A = \{y \in \mathbb{R}^m | y = Ax \quad \text{for some } x \in \mathbb{R}^n\}. \tag{A.3}$$

The rank of A is given by the dimension of its range. The null space (or *kernel*) of A is defined by

$$n(A) = \{x \in \mathbb{R}^n \mid Ax = 0\}. \tag{A.4}$$

An *inner product* is a map $(\cdot, \cdot)$ from pairs of vectors to the real numbers with the following properties:

1. Symmetric: $(u, v) = (v, u)$.
2. Bilinearity: $(u, v + \lambda w) = (u, v) + \lambda(u, w)$.
3. Positive definite: $(u, u) \geq 0$, with equality iff $u = 0$.

The usual dot product $(u, v) = u^T v$ is an inner product, but the equation

$$(u, v) = u^T A v, \tag{A.5}$$

defines an inner product for any positive definite symmetric matrix A.

A set of vectors $B = \{v_1, \ldots, v_n\}$ is said to be *orthogonal* with respect to an inner product if $(u, v) = \delta_{ij}$. The set is *orthonormal* if it is orthogonal and the norm of all the vectors is 1. Given an orthonormal set of vectors $\{v_1, \ldots, v_m\}$ it is always possible to extend it to an orthonormal basis $\{v_1, \ldots, v_n\}$ by a constructive technique known as the Gram-Schmidt process.

Eigensystems

An *eigenvector* of an $n \times n$ matrix A is defined by

$$Au_k = \lambda_k u_k. \tag{A.6}$$

Equations (A.6) for $k = 1, \ldots, n$ represent a set of coupled linear algebraic equations for the components u_{ki} of the eigenvectors, and can be written in matrix notation as

$$(A - D)U = 0, \tag{A.7}$$

where D is a diagonal matrix whose elements consist of the *eigenvalues* λ_k

$$D = \begin{pmatrix} \lambda_1 & & \\ & \ddots & \\ & & \lambda_W \end{pmatrix} \tag{A.8}$$

and U is a matrix whose columns consist of the eigenvectors u_k. The eigenvalues of a matrix can be found by solving the *characteristic equation*

$$|A - xI| = 0, \tag{A.9}$$

which is a polynomial of degree n. This shows that there are at most n eigenvalues, and up to n corresponding linearly independent eigenvectors. A general matrix A need not have a complete set of eigenvalues or eigenvectors.

A matrix is said to be *positive definite* if it has n positive eigenvalues (counting solutions to (A.9) of the form $(x - \lambda_i)^{m_i}$ m_i times).

Singular Value Decomposition

The singular value decomposition (SVD) of a matrix can be viewed as a generalisation of the eigensystem of a square matrix. An $m \times n$ matrix A can always be written in the form

$$A = U \Sigma V^T = \sum_{i=1}^{r} \sigma_i u_i v_i^T, \tag{A.10}$$

where r is the rank of A, U is an $m \times r$ matrix satisfying $U^T U = I_r$, V is an $n \times n$ orthogonal matrix, and Σ is a diagonal matrix of the *singular values* σ_i. The singular values are usually ranked in descending order.

   We can link the singular values with eigenvalues as follows. The matrix $A^T A$ is symmetric, so has n real eigenvalues λ_i; furthermore, it can be shown that they are non-negative. The singular value σ_i is simply the positive square root of λ_i. The geometric interpretation of the singular values of A is that they are the lengths of the semi-axes of the hyperellipsoid $E = \{Ax : \|x\|_2 = 1\}$.

Matrix Pseudo-inverse

Suppose that we have a set of linear equations defined by $Ax = b$, where A is an $m \times n$ matrix. When $m \neq n$, which is normally the case in data analysis, it is not possible to solve these equations by inverting A. The SVD enables us to:

1. find the exact solution with minimal norm, if there is one;
2. find the vector x with minimal norm that has the minimal residual $r = \|Ax - b\|$.

We form a matrix $\tilde{\Sigma}^{-1} = \text{diag}(\tau_i)$, where

$$\tau_i = \begin{cases} \frac{1}{\sigma_i} & \sigma_i \neq 0 \\ 0 & \sigma_i = 0. \end{cases} \tag{A.11}$$

Let

$$\bar{x} = V \tilde{\Sigma}^{-1} U^T b \tag{A.12}$$

(compare this with $A^{-1}b$). The matrix product $V \tilde{\Sigma}^{-1} U^T$ is the *pseudo-inverse* $A^{\dagger}$ of A. The solution is often made more robust by also setting τ_i to zero if the corresponding singular value is small compared to the largest singular value. A rough rule of thumb is that any singular value that is less than ϵ times the largest, where ϵ is the expected standard deviation of the noise in the data, should be set to zero in the pseudo-inverse (Golub and van Loan, 1996, Section 5.5).

Symmetric Matrices

In several chapters we need to consider the properties of real, symmetric matrices. Examples include Hessian matrices (whose elements are given by the second derivatives of an error function with respect to the network weights) and covariance matrices for Gaussian distributions. Symmetric matrices have the property that $A_{ij} = A_{ji}$, or equivalently $\mathbf{A}^\mathrm{T} = \mathbf{A}$ where $\mathbf{A}^\mathrm{T}$ denotes the transpose of $\mathbf{A}$.

The inverse of a symmetric matrix is also symmetric. To see this we start from the definition of the inverse given by $\mathbf{A}^{-1}\mathbf{A} = \mathbf{I}$ where $\mathbf{I}$ is the unit matrix, and then use the general result that, for any two matrices $\mathbf{A}$ and $\mathbf{B}$, we have $(\mathbf{AB})^\mathrm{T} = \mathbf{B}^\mathrm{T}\mathbf{A}^\mathrm{T}$. This gives $\mathbf{A}^\mathrm{T}(\mathbf{A}^{-1})^\mathrm{T} = \mathbf{I}$ which, together with the symmetry property $\mathbf{A}^\mathrm{T} = \mathbf{A}$, shows that $(\mathbf{A}^{-1})^\mathrm{T} = \mathbf{A}^{-1}$ as required.

An $n \times n$ real symmetric matrix always has n real eigenvalues and a set of n orthonormal eigenvectors. These properties hold for any real matrix A which satisfies $\mathbf{AA}^T = \mathbf{A}^T\mathbf{A}$. In particular, it is also true for *orthogonal* matrices, which satisfy $\mathbf{A}^{-1} = \mathbf{A}^T$.

A positive definite symmetric matrix A has a matrix 'square root' given by its Cholesky decomposition L which is a lower triangular matrix with the property that

$$A = LL^T. \tag{A.13}$$

Because L is lower triangular, it is possible to solve an equation of the form $y = Lx$ efficiently by forward substitution. Thus the Cholesky decomposition can be used to solve the linear equation

$$y = Ax = L(L^T x) \tag{A.14}$$

by backward substitution followed by forward substitution.

B. Algorithm Error Analysis

It is important to have a basic understanding of error analysis when implementing numerical algorithms since it is very easy to end up with grossly inaccurate results through not taking account of the differences between the exact arithmetic of a mathematical formula and the floating point arithmetic of its implementation on a computer. We shall briefly consider different sources of error (or approximation) and what effect they can have on our choice of algorithm and how the numerical details can best be implemented.

The two main sources of error are:

approximation error (also known, more commonly but less accurately, as 'truncation error'). This is caused by an algorithm that does not, even in principle, calculate the correct result. For example, instead of summing an infinite series

$$e = 1 + \frac{1}{1!} + \frac{1}{2!} + \cdots$$

in practice only a finite number of terms can be summed. A method that is exact in the limit when a step size is zero must be computed with a non-zero step size in practice; this is common when solving differential equations. An *iterative* algorithm, that computes a quantity exactly when an infinite number of iterations are used (such as finding the roots of a non-linear equation), only computes that quantity approximately when a finite number of iterations are used, as must be the case in practice.

rounding error is caused by the use of finite precision in arithmetic calculations. The inherent rounding (or *roundoff*) error involved in calculating a given quantity is known as the *conditioning* of a problem. The additional rounding error a particular numerical algorithm introduces is related to the *stability* of the algorithm.

The approximation error is determined by the choice of algorithm, while the roundoff error is also affected by the way in which an algorithm is implemented.

Floating Point Arithmetic and Roundoff Error

The starting point for error analysis is the floating point representation of numbers. If

$$x = a \times 2^b,$$

with $2^{-1} \leq |a| < 1$,

$$|a| = 0.\alpha_1 \ldots \alpha_t \alpha_{t+1} \ldots \qquad \text{where } \alpha_1 = 1,$$

then let

$$a' = \begin{cases} 0.\alpha_1 \ldots \alpha_t & \text{if } \alpha_{t+1} = 0 \\ 0.\alpha_1 \ldots \alpha_t + 2^{-t} & \text{if } \alpha_{t+1} = 1. \end{cases}$$

The rounding function $\mathrm{rd} : \mathbb{R} \to \mathbb{R}$ is defined by

$$\mathrm{rd}(x) := \mathrm{sgn}(x) \cdot a' \times 2^b.$$

The *machine precision* is given by eps $:= 2^{-t}$, and is the built-in variable eps in MATLAB. It is the smallest positive number that when added to 1 gives a result different from 1. Then

$$\mathrm{rd}(x) = x(1 + \epsilon), \tag{B.1}$$

where $|\epsilon| \leq \text{eps} = 2^{-t}$. *Roundoff error* is defined to be $|x - \mathrm{rd}(x)|$. The *relative error* is

$$\frac{|x - \mathrm{rd}(x)|}{|x|}$$

for $x \neq 0$. For our purposes, it is nearly always the relative error that is important. Any floating point operation introduces at least eps $= \epsilon_m$ in relative error.

Conditioning

It is important to be able to study the effects of roundoff error on numerical calculations. The most commonly used technique to study these effects is *differential error analysis*. In this approach we consider the effect of error propagation through a sequence of computations while disregarding second and higher order terms. This linearisation is valid if the relative errors are reasonably small.

The basic case is when $y = \phi(x)$ is a single function. We ask what are the effects of input errors on the output. Let $x \in D \subseteq \mathbb{R}^n$. Let $\phi : D \to \mathbb{R}^m$ be defined by

$$\phi(x) = \begin{bmatrix} \phi_1(x_1, \ldots, x_n) \\ \vdots \\ \phi_m(x_1, \ldots, x_n) \end{bmatrix}$$

and suppose that each ϕ_i has continuous first derivatives. Let $\tilde{x}$ denote an approximation to x (for example, induced by rounding error). Then we let $\Delta x_i := \tilde{x}_i - x_i$ and $\Delta x := \tilde{x} - x$ be the absolute error in x_i and x respectively. The relative error is

$$\epsilon_{x_i} := \frac{\Delta x_i}{x_i}$$

if $x_i \neq 0$.

The approximate result of the calculation is $\tilde{y} := \phi(\tilde{x})$. We expand this with a Taylor series; the $\doteq$ symbol denotes an approximation to first order, i.e. that ignores terms in $(\Delta x)^2$. For this to be valid, we are assuming that the absolute error is small in magnitude. Then

$$\Delta y_i := \tilde{y}_i - y_i = \phi_i(\tilde{x}) - \phi_i(x) \doteq \sum_{j=1}^{n} \frac{\partial \phi_i(x)}{\partial x_j} \Delta x_j$$

for $i = 1, \ldots, m$. So in matrix form

$$\Delta y \doteq [D\phi(x)]^T \Delta x.$$

If $y_i \neq 0$ for $i = 1, \ldots, m$ and $x_j \neq 0$ for $j = 1, \ldots, n$, so that the relative errors can be defined, then

$$\epsilon_{y_i} \doteq \sum_{j=1}^{n} \boxed{\frac{x_j}{\phi_i(x)} \frac{\partial \phi(x)}{\partial x_j}} \epsilon_{x_j}.$$

The boxed terms multiplying ϵ_{x_j} are the amplification factor for the relative error: they are known as *condition numbers*. If they all have small absolute values, then the problem (of computing ϕ) is *well-conditioned*, otherwise it is said to be *ill-conditioned*. This conditioning is inherent in the problem. **If a problem is ill-conditioned, then errors in the inputs will cause larger errors in the outputs, no matter what algorithm is used to calculate ϕ.**

For this calculation, there are a total of mn condition numbers, and this can be quite unwieldy to deal with. In special classes of problem, the definition of condition numbers is often simplified to make it easier to use them. For example in linear algebra, if a positive constant $c \in \mathbb{R}$ can be found such that

$$\frac{\|\phi(\tilde{x}) - \phi(x)\|}{\|\phi(x)\|} \leq c \frac{\|\tilde{x} - x\|}{\|x\|}$$

then we say that c is a condition number for ϕ. A suitable choice for c is the ratio of the largest to the smallest singular values, which is returned by the

MATLAB function cond. If a matrix A is ill-conditioned, then it is likely that solving the equations $Ax = b$ will give unreliable results.

Unfortunately, although floating point multiplication and division are well-conditioned, floating point addition and subtraction are not. When the quantities being added have nearly equal magnitudes but opposite signs, it is possible to lose most of the precision in the result. Thus algorithms must be inspected carefully, and rewritten if necessary to avoid this subtractive cancellation.

Most useful algorithms consist of a number of steps, and in these circumstances the rounding error may accumulate as the computation progresses. (The analysis is more complicated than we need here, but can be found in Stoer and Bulirsch (1983).) Any algorithm for computing y will have a bounded error $E_{r+1}y \leq |y|\text{eps}$ which occurs when the result of the algorithm is rounded. Similarly, when the input data is rounded (which will occur unless it is an exact machine number), a bounded error of the form $|\Delta^{(0)}(x)| \leq |x|\text{eps}$ will occur. So for any algorithm, we can expect an *inherent error* of magnitude

$$\Delta^{(0)}(y) := [|D\phi(x)| \cdot |x| + |y|]\,\text{eps},$$

where the first term is the magnification of the input error by the conditioning numbers. Roundoff errors in an algorithm are harmless if their contribution towards the total roundoff error is at most the same order of magnitude as $\Delta^{(0)}(y)$. If all roundoff errors are harmless, then we say that an algorithm is *numerically stable*.

References

Auer, P., M. Herbster, and M. K. Warmuth 1996. Exponentially many local minima for single neurons. In *Advances in Neural Information Processing Systems*, Volume 8, pp. 316–322.

Barber, D. and C. K. I. Williams 1997. Gaussian processes for Bayesian classification via hybrid Monte Carlo. In M. C. Mozer, M. I. Jordan, and T. Petsche (eds), *Advances in Neural Information Processing Systems*, Volume 9, pp. 390–396. MIT Press.

Baum, L. E. and T. Petrie 1966. Statistical inference for probabilistic functions of finite state Markov chains. *Ann. Math. Stats.* **37**, 1554–1563.

Baum, L. E. and G. R. Sell 1968. Growth functions for transformations on manifolds. *Pacific J. Math.* **27** (2), 211–227.

Becker, S. and Y. Le Cun 1989. Improving the convergence of back-propagation learning with second order methods. In D. Touretzky, G. E. Hinton, and T. J. Sejnowski (eds), *Proceedings of the 1988 Connectionist Models Summer School*, pp. 29–37. San Mateo, CA: Morgan Kaufmann.

Berger, J. O. 1985. *Statistical Decision Theory and Bayesian Analysis* (second edn.). New York: Springer-Verlag.

Bishop, C. M. 1994. Novelty detection and neural network validation. *IEE Proceedings: Vision, Image and Signal Processing* **141** (4), 217–222. Special issue on applications of neural networks.

Bishop, C. M. 1995. *Neural Networks for Pattern Recognition*. Oxford University Press.

Bishop, C. M., M. Svensén, and C. K. I. Williams 1996. GTM: The Generative Topographic Mapping. *Neural Computation* **10** (1), 215–235.

Bourlard, H. and Y. Kamp 1988. Auto-association by multilayer perceptrons and singular value decomposition. *Biological Cybernetics* **59**, 291–294.

Brent, R. P. 1973. *Algorithms for Minimization without Derivatives*. Englewood Cliffs, NJ: Prentice-Hall.

Brooks, S. P. 1998. Markov Chain Monte Carlo and its application. *The Statistician* **47**, 69–100.

Broomhead, D. S. and G. P. King 1986. Extracting qualitative dynamics from experimental data. *Physica D* **20**, 217–236.

Cover, T. M. and P. E. Hart 1967. Nearest neighbour pattern classification. *IEEE Transactions on Medical Imaging* **12**, 21–27.

Dempster, A. P., N. M. Laird, and D. B. Rubin 1977. Maximum likelihood from incomplete data via the EM algorithm. *Journal of the Royal Statistical Society, B* **39** (1), 1–38.

Duane, S., A. D. Kennedy, B. J. Pendleton, and D. Roweth 1987. Hybrid Monte Carlo. *Physics Letters B* **195** (2), 216–222.

Fahlman, S. E. 1988. Faster-learning variations on back-propagation: an empirical study. In D. Touretzky, G. E. Hinton, and T. J. Sejnowski (eds), *Proceedings of the 1988 Connectionist Models Summer School*, pp. 38–51. San Mateo, CA: Morgan Kaufmann.

Fletcher, R. 1987. *Practical Methods of Optimization* (second edn.). New York: John Wiley.

Gelman, A. 1996. Inference and monitoring convergence. In W. R. Gilks, S. Richardson, and D. J. Spiegelhalter (eds), *Markov Chain Monte Carlo in Practice*, pp. 131–143. London: Chapman and Hall.

Gelman, A. and D. Rubin 1992. Inference from iterative simulation using multiple sequences. *Statistical Science* **7**, 457–511.

Ghahramani, Z. and M. I. Jordan 1994a. Learning from incomplete data. Technical Report CBCL 108, Massachusetts Institute of Technology.

Ghahramani, Z. and M. I. Jordan 1994b. Supervised learning from incomplete data via an EM appproach. In J. D. Cowan, G. T. Tesauro, and J. Alspector (eds), *Advances in Neural Information Processing Systems*, Volume 6, pp. 120–127. San Mateo, CA: Morgan Kaufmann.

Gibbs, M. N. 1997. Bayesian Gaussian Processes for Regression and Classification. Ph.D. thesis, University of Cambridge.

Gibbs, M. N. and D. J. C. Mackay 1996. Efficient implementation of Gaussian Processes. Available from the web at URL http://wol.ra.phy.cam.ac.uk/mng10/GP/GP.html.

Golub, G. H. and C. F. van Loan 1996. *Matrix Computations*. Baltimore: Johns Hopkins University Press.

Grimmett, G. R. and D. R. Stirzaker 1992. *Probability and Random Processes* (second edn.). Oxford: Clarendon Press.

Hartman, E. J., J. D. Keeler, and J. M. Kowalski 1990. Layered neural networks with Gaussian hidden units as universal approximations. *Neural Computation* **2** (2), 210–215.

Hassibi, B. and D. G. Stork 1993. Second order derivatives for network pruning: optimal brain surgeon. In S. J. Hanson, J. D. Cowan, and C. L. Giles (eds), *Advances in Neural Information Processing Systems*, Volume 5, pp. 164–171. San Mateo, CA: Morgan Kaufmann.

Hastie, T. J. and R. J. Tibshirani 1990. *Generalized Additive Models*. London: Chapman & Hall.

Hastings, W. K. 1970. Monte Carlo sampling methods using Markov chains and their applications. *Biometrika* **57**, 97–109.

Hestenes, M. R. and E. Stiefel 1952. Methods of conjugate gradients for solving linear systems. *Journal of Research of the National Bureau of Standards* **49** (6), 409–436.

Hinton, G. E., P. Dayan, and M. Revow 1997. Modelling the manifolds of images of handwritten digits. *IEEE Transaction on Neural Networks* **8** (1), 65–74.

Hornik, K. 1991. Approximation capabilities of multilayer feedforward networks. *Neural Networks* **4** (2), 251–257.

Hornik, K., M. Stinchcombe, and H. White 1989. Multilayer feedforward networks are universal approximators. *Neural Networks* **2** (5), 359–366.

Horowitz, A. M. 1991. A generalized guided Monte Carlo algorithm. *Physics Letters B* **268**, 247–252.

Hughes, N. P. 1999. Artefactual Structure from Topographic Mappings. Master's thesis, Aston University, Birmingham, UK.

Jacobs, R. A., M. I. Jordan, S. J. Nowlan, and G. E. Hinton 1991. Adaptive mixtures of local experts. *Neural Computation* **3** (1), 79–87.

Jordan, M. I. 1998. *Learning and Inference in Graphical Models*. Dordrecht: Kluwer.

Khambatla, N. and T. K. Leen 1994. Fast non-linear dimension reduction. In J. D. Cowan, G. Tesauro, and J. Alspector (eds), *Advances in Neural Information Processing Systems*, Volume 6, pp. 152–159. Morgan Kaufmann.

Kincaid, D. and W. Cheney 1996. *Numerical Analysis* (second edn.). Brooks/Cole.

Klock, H. and J. M. Buhmann 1997. Mulitdimensional scaling by deterministic annealing. In M. Pelillo and E. R. Hancock (eds), *Energy Minimization Methods in Computer Vision and Pattern Recognition*, Lecture Notes in Computer Science, pp. 246–260. Springer.

Kohonen, T. 1982. Self-organized formation of topologically correct feature maps. *Biological Cybernetics* **43**, 59–69.

Le Cun, Y., J. S. Denker, and S. A. Solla 1990. Optimal brain damage. In D. S. Touretzky (ed), *Advances in Neural Information Processing Systems*, Volume 2, pp. 598–605. San Mateo, CA: Morgan Kaufmann.

Lowe, D. 1998. Characterising complexity by the degrees of freedom in a radial basis function network. *Neurocomputing* **19**, 199–209.

Lowe, D. and M. E. Tipping 1996. Feed-forward neural networks and topographic mappings for exploratory data analysis. *Neural Computing and Applications* **4**, 83–95.

MacKay, D. J. C. 1992a. Bayesian interpolation. *Neural Computation* **4** (3), 415–447.

MacKay, D. J. C. 1992b. The evidence framework applied to classification networks. *Neural Computation* **4** (5), 720–736.

MacKay, D. J. C. 1992c. A practical Bayesian framework for backpropagation networks. *Neural Computation* **4** (3), 448–472.

MacKay, D. J. C. 1994. Hyperparameters: optimise or integrate out? In G. Heidbreder (ed), *Maximum Entropy and Bayesian Methods, Santa Barbara 1993*. Dordrecht: Kluwer.

McLachlan, G. J. and K. E. Basford 1988. *Mixture Models: Inference and Applications to Clustering*. New York: Marcel Dekker.

Møller, M. 1993. A scaled conjugate gradient algorithm for fast supervised learning. *Neural Networks* **6** (4), 525–533.

Nabney, I. T. 1999. Efficient training of RBF networks for classification. In *International Conference on Artificial Neural Networks*, pp. 210–215. Edinburgh.

Neal, R. M. 1996. *Bayesian Learning for Neural Networks*. Number 118 in Lecture Notes in Statistics. New York: Springer-Verlag.

Neal, R. M. and G. E. Hinton 1993. A new view of the EM algorithm that justifies incremental and other variants. Technical Report CRG-TR-92-1, Department of Computer Science, University of Toronto, Canada. submitted to *Biometrica*.

Park, J. and I. W. Sandberg 1993. Approximation and radial basis function networks. *Neural Computation* **5** (2), 305–316.

Pearlmutter, B. A. 1994. Fast exact multiplication by the Hessian. *Neural Computation* **6** (1), 147–160.

Polak, E. 1971. *Computational Methods in Optimization: A Unified Approach*. New York: Academic Press.

Press, W. H., S. A. Teukolsky, W. T. Vetterling, and B. P. Flannery 1992. *Numerical Recipes in C: The Art of Scientific Computing* (second edn.). Cambridge University Press.

Rabiner, L. R. 1989. A tutorial on Hidden Markov Models and selected applications in speech recognition. *Proc. IEEE* **77** (2), 257–285.

Ripley, B. D. 1995. *Pattern Recognition and Neural Networks*. Cambridge: Cambridge University Press.

Rosenblatt, M. 1956. Remarks on some non-parametric estimates of a density function. *Ann. Math. Statist.* **27**, 832–837.

Sammon, J. W. 1969. A nonlinear mapping for data structure analysis. *IEEE Transactions on Computers* **18** (5), 401–409.

Shanno, D. F. 1978. Conjugate gradient methods with inexact searches. *Mathematics of Operations Research* **3** (3), 244–256.

Shapiro, J. S. 1969. *Smoothing and Approximation of Functions*. New York: Van Nostrand Reinhold.

Silverman, B. W. 1985. Some aspects of spline smoothing approach to nonparametric regression curve fitting. *J. Roy. Statist. Soc. B* **47**, 1–52.

Stinchecombe, M. and H. White 1989. Universal approximation using feedforward networks with non-sigmoid hidden layer activation functions. In *Proceedings of the International Joint Conference on Neural Networks*, Volume 1, pp. 613–618. San Diego: IEEE.

Stoer, J. and R. Bulirsch 1983. *Introduction to Numerical Analysis*. New York: Springer-Verlag.

Tarassenko, L. 1995. Novelty detection for the identification of masses in mamograms. In *Proceedings Fourth IEE International Conference on Artificial Neural Networks*, Volume 4, pp. 442–447. London: IEE.

Tarassenko, L. 1998. *A Guide to Neural Computing Applications*. London: Arnold.

Thodberg, H. H. 1993. Ace of Bayes: application of neural networks with pruning. Technical Report 1132E, The Danish Meat Research Institute, Maglegaardsvej 2, DK-4000 Roskilde, Denmark.

Thomas, A., D. J. Spiegelhalter, and W. R. Gilks 1992. BUGS: A program to perform Bayesian inference using Gibbs sampling. In J. M. Bernardo, J. O. Berger, A. P. Dawid, and A. F. M. Smith (eds), *Bayesian Statistics 4*, pp. 837–842. Oxford: Clarendon Press. Copyright MRC Biostatistics Unit, Robinson Way, Cambridge, UK.

Tipping, M. E. 1996. Topographic Mappings and Feed-Forward Neural Networks. Ph.D. thesis, Aston University, Birmingham, UK.

Tipping, M. E. and C. M. Bishop 1997. Mixtures of principal component analysers. In *Proceedings of the International Conference on Artificial Neural Networks*, Volume 440, pp. 13–18. IEE.

Tipping, M. E. and C. M. Bishop 1999. Probabilistic principal component analysis. *J. Roy. Statist. Soc. B* **61**, 611–622.

Tipping, M. E. and D. Lowe 1997. Shadow targets: A novel algorithm for topographic projections by radial basis functions. In *Proceedings of the International Conference on Artificial Neural Networks*, Volume 440, pp. 7–12. IEE.

von Mises, R. 1964. *Mathematical Theory of Probability and Statistics*. Academic Press.

Webb, A. 1999. *Statistical Pattern Recognition*. London: Arnold.

Williams, C. K. I. 1998. Prediction with Gaussian Processes: from linear regression to linear prediction and beyond. In M. I. Jordan (ed), *Learning and Inference in Graphical Models*, pp. 599–621. Dordrecht: Kluwer.

Williams, C. K. I. and D. Barber 1998. Bayesian classification with Gaussian Processes. *IEE Trans. Pattern Analysis and Machine Intelligence* **20** (12), 1342–1351.

Williams, C. K. I., C. Qazaz, C. M. Bishop, and H. Zhu 1995. On the relationship between Bayesian error bars and the input data density. In *Proceedings of the International Conference on Artificial Neural Networks*, Volume 409, pp. 160–165. IEE.

Wolpert, D. H. 1993. On the use of evidence in neural networks. In S. J. Hanson, J. D. Cowan, and C. L. Giles (eds), *Advances in Neural Information Processing Systems*, Volume 5, pp. 539–546. San Mateo, CA: Morgan Kaufmann.

Wong, E. 1971. *Stochastic Processes in Information and Dynamical Systems*. New York: McGraw-Hill.

Yamato, H. 1972. Some statistical properties of estimators of density and distribution functions. *Bull. Math. Stat.* **19**, 113–131.

Function Index

Subject Index

approximation error, 403

ARD, *see* automatic relevance determination

auto-associative network, 279

automatic relevance determination, 331, 366, 390

basis, 399

basis function
    dual, **214**
    Gaussian, **194**, 195, **199**, 205, 210
    $r^4 \log r$, **194**, 195, **199**, **206**, 210
    thin plate spline, **194**, 195, **199**, 205, 210

Bayesian decision rule, 110, 165, 166, 357

Bayesian inference
    evidence, **327**, 341
    generalised linear regression, 370, 372, 374
    hyperparameter, **330**, 331, 332, 334, 335, 342
    hyperprior, 343
    posterior, **327**, 371
    prior, **327**, 330, 334, 335, 370
    well-determined parameters, 345

Bernoulli distribution, **124**, 168, 392

between-class scatter matrix, 275

BFGS formula, 62, 76

binomial distribution, 135

Brent's algorithm, 44

canonical variates, 273

central differences, 35, 187

characteristic equation, 400

Cholesky decomposition, 88, 256, 288, 377, **402**

clustering algorithm, 101

condition numbers, 72, **405**

confusion matrix, **24**, 167

conjugate gradients, 37, **53**, 64, 75

constrained least squares, 143

correlation structure, 31

curse of dimensionality, 245, 284

curvature, 50, 51, 247, 329

data normalisation, 29, 217

decision boundary, 141, 142, 165, 352, 358

decision surface, *see* decision boundary

derivatives
    error gradient, 127, 157, 204, 268, 339, 378, 385
    Hessian, 129, 160, 188, 211, 340, 371, 402
    Jacobian, 209, 257
    output derivative, 128, 159, 208

DFP formula, **63**, 76

eigenvalue, 13, 228, 400, 401

eigenvector, 13, 53, 228, 400

EM algorithm
    factor analysis, 279
    Gaussian mixture model, 89
    GTM, 245, 254
    mixtures of PPCA, 238
    PPCA, 235, 278
    probabilistic graphical models, 90

error back-propagation, 156, 158, 179, 185, 205, 300, 362

error bar, 328, 351, 356

error function
    cross-entropy, **124**, 156
    entropy, **125**, 156
    Sammon stress metric, **264**, 281
    self-organising map, 243
    sum-of-squares, **124**, 156, 189, **201**

Lightning Source UK Ltd.
Milton Keynes UK
UKOW06f0903280515

252443UK00005B/30/P